New Orleans and the Creation of
Transatlantic Opera, 1819–1859

Opera Lab: Explorations in History, Technology, and Performance

A series edited by David J. Levin & Mary Ann Smart

ALSO PUBLISHED IN THE SERIES

Music in the Present Tense: Rossini's Italian Operas in Their Time
Emanuele Senici

Singing Sappho: Improvisation and Authority in Nineteenth-Century Italian Opera
Melina Esse

Networking Operatic Italy
Francesca Vella

"Don Giovanni" Captured: Performance, Media, Myth
Richard Will

CHARLOTTE BENTLEY

New Orleans AND THE CREATION OF *Transatlantic Opera*

1819–1859

The University of Chicago Press
CHICAGO & LONDON

The University of Chicago Press, Chicago 60637
The University of Chicago Press, Ltd., London

Published 2022
Printed in the United States of America

31 30 29 28 27 26 25 24 23 22   1 2 3 4 5

ISBN-13: 978-0-226-82308-9 (cloth)
ISBN-13: 978-0-226-82309-6 (e-book)
DOI: https://doi.org/10.7208/chicago/9780226823096.001.0001

This book has been supported by the AMS 75 PAYS Fund of the American Musicological Society, supported in part by the National Endowment for the Humanities and the Andrew W. Mellon Foundation.

Library of Congress Cataloging-in-Publication Data

Names: Bentley, Charlotte (Musicologist), author.
Title: New Orleans and the creation of transatlantic opera, 1819–1859 / Charlotte Bentley.
Other titles: Opera lab.
Description: Chicago ; London : The University of Chicago Press, 2022. | Series: Opera lab: explorations in history, technology, and performance | Includes bibliographical references and index.
Identifiers: LCCN 2022018125 | ISBN 9780226823089 (cloth) | ISBN 9780226823096 (ebook)
Subjects: LCSH: Opera—Louisiana—New Orleans—19th century. | Opera and transnationalism—Louisiana—New Orleans. | Music—Louisiana—New Orleans—French influences. | New Orleans (La.)—Civilization—Foreign influences. | New Orleans (La.)—Civilization—19th century. | BISAC: MUSIC / History & Criticism | HISTORY / United States / State & Local / South (AL, AR, FL, GA, KY, LA, MS, NC, SC, TN, VA, WV)
Classification: LCC ML1711.8.N25 B48 2022 | DDC 782.1/40976335—dc23/eng/20220427
LC record available at https://lccn.loc.gov/2022018125

♾ This paper meets the requirements of ANSI/NISO Z39.48-1992 (Permanence of Paper).

Contents

Abbreviations

HJA – Hogan Jazz Archive, Tulane University, New Orleans

HNOC – Williams Research Center, Historic New Orleans Collection, New Orleans

LARC – Louisiana Research Collection, Tulane University, New Orleans

LSM – Louisiana Historical Center, Louisiana State Museum, New Orleans

NONA – New Orleans Notarial Archives

NOPL – New Orleans Public Library

SCLSU – Special Collections, Louisiana State University, Baton Rouge, Louisiana

Introduction

This book is about nineteenth-century New Orleans and the people who made it a vital part of an emerging operatic world. Musicians and nonmusicians alike forged connections that led to the establishment of a transatlantic system of production and helped opera percolate into life beyond the theater. By focusing on a variety of individuals, their extended webs of human contacts, and the materials that they moved along with them, in this book I piece together what it took to bring opera to New Orleans and the ways in which the city's operatic life shaped contemporary perceptions of global interconnection.

Opera had been a part of the cultural life of New Orleans since the late eighteenth century, and also part of the city's bountiful mythology. Legend has it that the founding father of theater in the city was Louis Tabary, an early refugee from the Haitian Revolution, who arrived in the autumn of 1791, along with his troupe of actors.[1] Lacking a proper theater in which to give their performances, this plucky band are said to have performed wherever they could—in tents, in people's homes, even out on the street—until a theater was eventually built to house them. Attractive though this creation myth is, a question mark remains over its veracity; what is certain, however, is that Louis Alexandre Henry bought the deeds to a plot of land on St. Peter Street on June 4, 1791, and proceeded to build New Orleans's first theater, which opened late the following year.[2]

The date of the city's first opera performance has been lost to history, but operas had become fairly regular theatrical fare by 1796. In May that year, a local landowner, the Baron de Pontalba, wrote to his wife (away on a trip to Paris) that he had attended a performance of André Grétry's *Sylvain*, an opera that the couple had previously seen together at the theater.[3] From then on, operas were a constant presence in New Orleans, although the theaters at which they were performed were almost always in a precarious financial and legal position. Nonetheless, by 1808, the city had two theaters, one on St. Peter Street and another just three blocks away on St. Philip Street: quite a feat for a town of only 15,000 people. These theaters, combined with innumerable balls, pleasure gardens, parades, and visiting circuses, established New Orleans's reputation as a city of entertainment.[4]

The beginnings of this book's story, however, come a little later, when John Davis (like Tabary a Saint-Domingue refugee) opened his new theater in 1819. Located on Orleans Street in the middle of the French Quarter, only a stone's throw from the rear of St. Louis Cathedral, the new Francophone Théâtre d'Orléans sat at the geographical as much as the cultural heart of the city (see fig. I.1). This Théâtre d'Orléans was not the first venture of that name in the city (its two previous incarnations under different owners, like so many other buildings in nineteenth-century New Orleans, succumbed to flames), but it proved to be the most ambitious and by far the most enduring. The forty years between 1819 and 1859 were the Théâtre d'Orléans's "glory years," during which the theater administration recruited a troupe annually from Europe and poured huge sums of money into high-quality productions of a wide variety of theatrical genres, from *opéra-comique* to *grand opéra*, *vaudeville* to *drame*. It was the first, and for a long time the only, theater in North America to have a permanent, resident opera troupe.[5] So too did it play an important role in introducing French opera to other American cities, through the summer tours to New York, Boston, Philadelphia, and Baltimore that John Davis organized for the troupe between 1827 and 1832, and that his son Pierre continued in 1843 and 1845.[6]

The life of Davis's theater—the activities of its management, performers, and backstage personnel, as well as its audiences, critics, and other associates—underpins every chapter of this book and governs its chronological scope. It was not the only theater active in New Orleans in this period, although it was by far the longest lasting and the only one to produce opera regularly, and in various chapters I weave the activities of other theaters and social spaces in the city around its story. Particularly important are the theatrical activities of James Caldwell, an English-born impresario and actor, who went on to own theaters across the US South.[7] Caldwell made his mark on New Orleans's theatrical life from his arrival in the city in 1820, when he initially leased the Théâtre d'Orléans building on the French company's "off nights." Four years later, his company left the French theater to

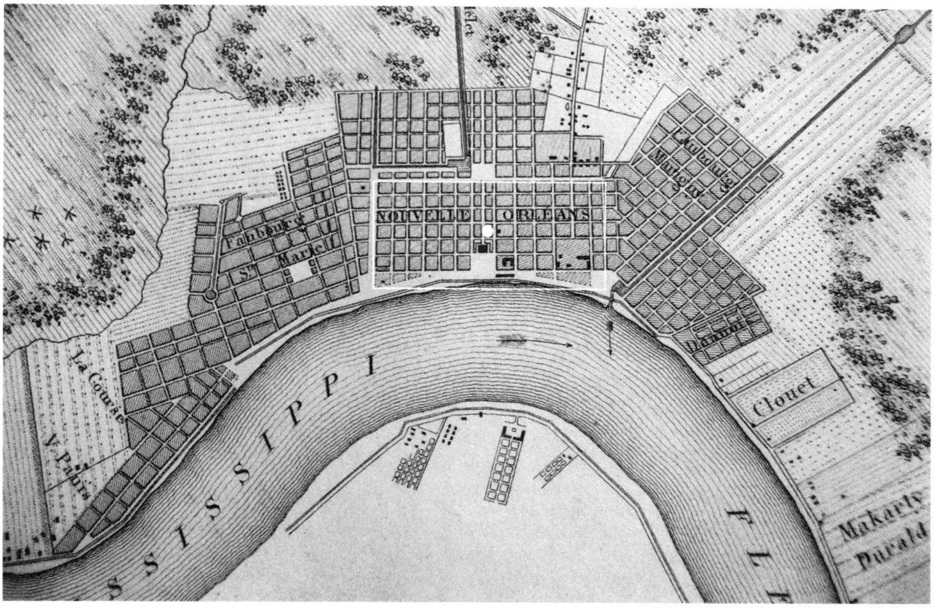

FIGURE I.1 Detail of map of New Orleans from Guillaume-Tell Poussin, *Travaux d'améliorations intérieures projetés ou exécutés par le gouvernement général des Etats-Unis d'Amérique de 1824 à 1831* (Paris, 1843), Bibliothèque nationale de France. GR FOL-PB. The rectangle shows the French Quarter, while the dot shows the position of the Théâtre d'Orléans.

move to his new American Theatre on Camp Street, and in November 1835 he opened the huge, 4,100-seat St. Charles Theatre only a couple of blocks away.[8] These theaters, both within a square mile of the Théâtre d'Orléans and both dabbling with opera performances alongside their regular spoken theatrical fare and variety entertainments, created significant challenges for the older Francophone theater. The connections and frictions between them, involving repertoires, audiences, and even personnel, are explored in the central chapters of this book.

Indeed, connection on a local level, but also on national and international ones, is fundamental to the story I wish to tell. Certain aspects of the city's operatic history—its repertoire and reception, in particular—have already been explored.[9] But the connections that were so integral to developing and sustaining its operatic life—connections that ultimately crossed national, linguistic, racial, and class boundaries—have received scant scholarly attention until now. Here, then, I set out to show how this interconnectedness is vital to a proper understanding not only of opera in New Orleans, but also of the emergence of international networks of opera and their significance for the nineteenth-century world.

Different kinds of connection emerge in different ways throughout the book, but all reveal the ways in which local cultural, sociopolitical, and even economic concerns in New Orleans were bound up with those of places far beyond the city. Some connections are purely practical, reflecting the movement of people and materials (such as scores, newspapers, and costumes) from place to place. Others, however, have a significant imaginative dimension, and they reveal how the act of engaging with opera—whether that be in the theater, or through reading about it, or dancing to or playing music adapted from operas—could facilitate identification with people and places near and far.[10] In other words, how imagining opera in all its forms could enable a sense of *being* in, of inhabiting, the nineteenth-century world, with all its messy colonial and postcolonial entanglements and manifold, competing claims to modernity.

The period covered by this study—1819 to 1859—was one of great change in New Orleans, during which the city's residents were repeatedly forced to reimagine their relationship with each other, with fellow Americans, and with Europe. In particular, the position of French speakers and their culture was altered enormously. Founded in 1718 as a French colonial town, New Orleans spent much of the second half of the eighteenth century under Spanish control, as a result of land concessions made in the Treaty of Paris in 1763, following France's defeat in the Seven Years' War.[11] The city's French-speaking population (a mixture of European-born immigrants, locally born people known as "Creoles," enslaved people, and free people of color) did not welcome their Spanish rulers, and they celebrated when Napoleon publicly reclaimed the lands in 1803 (he had, in fact, assumed control secretly in 1800).[12] Their joy was short lived, however, as later that year Napoleon sold the vast Louisiana Territory, and the port of New Orleans with it, to the fledgling United States of America under President Thomas Jefferson.[13] Louisiana gained its statehood just under a decade later, in 1812.

The French language still dominated public and private affairs in New Orleans at the time of the Louisiana Purchase. The Francophone population had, in fact, grown under Spanish rule (to the annoyance of the Spanish), as over 11,000 French-speaking refugees—black and white, enslaved and free—had arrived in New Orleans in the 1790s, fleeing the violence of the slave-led revolution on the island of Saint-Domingue (modern-day Haiti), which had been a French colony and Europe's major sugar producer.[14] They were joined between 1809 and 1810 by another wave of 9,000 Francophone refugees who, having initially settled in Cuba on their flight from Saint-Domingue, were forcibly expelled from the island (in response to the Napoleonic invasion of Spain in 1808) and made their way north.[15]

The question of what it meant to be French in early nineteenth-century New Orleans, then, was already complicated, with new French immigrants joining white Creoles, as well as free and enslaved black Francophones.[16] But after the Louisiana Purchase, the city's population—whether long-term residents of New Orleans or recent arrivals, from either Europe or Saint-Domingue—had to adjust to their new identity as *former* colonial subjects: before the Latin American independence movements of the 1810s and 1820s, they joined, along with the original thirteen states of the United States itself and Haiti, a select group of nations that had gained independence from colonial rule.

Joining the United States brought major demographic change to the city, as the first three decades of the nineteenth century saw a trickle of Anglo-American settlers from the northern states turn into a torrent, and by the 1830s French hegemony was severely threatened.[17] The ever-growing numbers of northern Anglophone settlers, combined with influxes of German and Irish immigrants, and the waves of people who inevitably passed through this port city, meant that the first half of the nineteenth century saw rapid and fundamental alterations to New Orleans's social structure.[18] Indeed, the city grew almost tenfold, from a population of 17,242 in 1810 to 168,675 in 1860, and between 1830 and 1860 it was in the top five largest cities in the United States (although it was only ever a fraction of the size of New York, the nation's largest urban center).[19] The French Quarter (the "Vieux Carré"), on the east bank of the Mississippi, soon came to be surrounded by an Anglophone "American Sector" to the southwest and the Faubourg Marigny (which was historically a highly mixed area in racial terms) to the northeast.[20] In 1840, the number of non-French speakers exceeded the number of French speakers (including slaves) for the first time. This was a period, then, in which the future looked very uncertain for the city's Francophones.

So, too, was this a period of shifting racial demographics and changing race relations. Enslaved people formed roughly 30 percent of the city's population in the years up to 1830,[21] and a significant proportion—some 23.8 percent by 1840—was made up of free people of color (called "gens de couleur libre" in French), among whom were artisans, clerks, and professionals of other sorts; a minority were slave-owning planters in their own right.[22] New Orleans's free people of color technically shared the same legal freedoms as the white population, but Paul F. Lachance has criticized a tendency he observes in earlier histories to characterize this group as "privileged," pointing out that they were privileged only in relation to enslaved people and were rarely able to achieve the levels of prosperity gained by wealthy white property owners.[23]

There was considerable linguistic diversity among the population of free and enslaved people of color in the early decades of the nineteenth century. Officially speaking, people enslaved and brought to New Orleans during the French colonial period (and their descendants) had learned to speak French, while those who were brought to the city after the abolition of the transatlantic slave trade in 1807 had most often been born and raised in the United States and had learned English.[24] In reality, people of color adapted these languages and created their own modes of expression: the Louisiana Creole language developed in the eighteenth century from the mixing of French with West African languages, and early varieties of African American English dialects appeared from the late seventeenth century.[25] These different linguistic backgrounds inflected their experiences in the city.

The early nineteenth century was also a period in which terminology for describing people's racial background proliferated, with labels such as "quadroon," "octoroon" and, more generally, "mulatto" being used to attempt to quantify and to explain different degrees of black and white ancestry.[26] Endeavors to taxonomize human beings in this way reflected a white, ruling-class desire to exert control over people whom they perceived to be different from themselves and, therefore, threatening to their social position.[27] In practice, however, the use of these terms was frequently imprecise, and became increasingly so as they inevitably accrued wider social and cultural meanings that helped cement not only racial (and racist) stereotypes, but also myths about the city of New Orleans. Clark has explored how the label "quadroon" gained a raft of exoticized, eroticized, and highly gendered associations, which were far from an accurate representation of historical reality, but which continue to this day to contribute to New Orleans's image as exceptional among American cities.[28]

Attitudes to race in New Orleans shifted across the first half of the nineteenth century. While Cécile Vidal argues that neither the bipartite model of race (black-white) discussed in studies of nineteenth-century North America, nor a tripartite model (black-mixed ancestry-white) based on social structures in the colonial Caribbean, really captures the understanding of race in French colonial New Orleans,[29] Amy R. Sumpter has argued that, in the years after 1830, New Orleans increasingly displayed a bipartite understanding of race, which reflected the city's increasing "Americanization."[30] Her assertion that the city's white population began to make less of a distinction between enslaved people and free people of color as the mid-century approached, treating them all as "Other" on account of their racial background, is borne out by the 1850 census for the city, which reveals a clear and consolidated division between majority black and majority white neighborhoods. Such unofficial segregation had been far less pronounced in earlier censuses; furthermore, as Emily Clark has discussed, people of color faced an increase in direct racism in the decade before the outbreak of the Civil War in 1861.[31] The period I am concerned with here, then, is one in which racial tensions grew in New Orleans, as they did across the rest of the South.

The theaters, and the Francophone Théâtre d'Orléans in particular, became a focus for press debates over Francophone identity and Louisiana's heritage, although questions of race were rarely foregrounded. Racial tensions were not absent from the theater, however, and racial conflict had a clearly identifiable impact on the composition of its audiences and the treatment of behind-the-scenes personnel at various specific moments in its history. As a space of social mixing, the theater and its activities provide a lens through which to view the city's shifting demographics and its attendant social frictions.

None of the city's theaters was a dedicated "opera house," and a building with that title did not exist until 1859, when the opening of a new French Opera House, the subject of the Epilogue, signaled the beginning of the Théâtre d'Orléans's decline. Nonetheless, the Théâtre d'Orléans produced far more operas and smaller musical theatrical works by the 1830s than it did spoken dramas, and it is worth taking a moment to explain a little more about my approach to opera in this book, particularly in light of earlier histories of musical and theatrical life in New Orleans by Henry Kmen, Jack Belsom, John Baron and, most recently, Juliane Braun.[32] Their insights have all formed important stepping-off points for my research, but here I take a considerably expanded approach to opera and the sources and methods through which I explore its history.

Staged and concert performances of opera inevitably form part of my considerations, as they represent the culmination—sometimes successful, sometimes less so—of extended processes of artistic and managerial labor that stretched across the Atlantic, as well as encapsulating so much of what opera was and is typically imagined to be. Kmen and Baron have already laid important groundwork in terms of piecing together details of the repertoire performed and relevant venues, as well as uncovering the names of many of the theaters' performers.[33] I build on this foundation by exploring the networks that extended far beyond New Orleans into which these performers and works fit. Belsom, meanwhile has looked closely at the reception of particular works performed at the Théâtre d'Orléans and, later, at the French Opera House.[34] While reception inevitably plays a role in this book, I am more concerned with opera's infusion into the life of the city in a broader sense: how opera left the stage behind and was adapted, refracted, and distilled into a potent imaginative force beyond the walls of the theater.

It is this suggestive "blurriness" of opera beyond the stage, its all-important slippage from text to performance to idea and back again, and the ways in which it was transformed into various material forms (libretti, sheet music, images of various kinds, and so on) that makes my considerations in this book distinct from, but complementary to, Braun's recent, sensitive consideration of spoken dramas written by people living or born in New Orleans in the nineteenth century.[35] She too considers various local, regional, and hemispheric identities, as they were formulated in the texts she examines, but ultimately my focus on opera as a shape-shifting art that permeated all manner of public and private spaces, inviting along the way a melding of the imagined and the real, furnishes a very different set of insights into the city and the nineteenth-century world.

The term "transatlantic opera" in the title of this book deserves a few words of explanation. The Atlantic, as both a physical and imaginative space, was of the utmost importance in nineteenth-century New Orleans. The ocean has also played a key role in the historiographical positioning of the city as part of a "circum-Atlantic" world (involving the circulation of goods and ideas between France, French North America, the French Caribbean, and French West Africa).[36] The term, as used by Joseph Roach, seeks to destabilize European-centered narratives of colonial history, and also avoid giving any single place unjustified historiographical weight. Given New Orleans's early connections with Saint-Domingue and Cuba, positioning the city in relation to Atlantic and Caribbean models provides an important means of understanding colonial New Orleans, and it is in this light that Juliane Braun has interpreted the beginnings of the city's theatrical life in the late eighteenth and very early nineteenth centuries.[37]

What these models do not do, however, is account for the changes in the city's networks and connections after the Louisiana Purchase, when increasing numbers of English speakers arrived in the city, and after the abolition of the international slave trade, when the direct connections with West Africa declined.[38] Given my focus on the period between 1819 and 1859, I have instead decided to emphasize trans- rather than circum-Atlantic connection, principally (but not exclusively) the bilateral relationships between New Orleans and France. Sometimes, connections that appear to be between New Orleans and France extend beyond them, to include other places within Louisiana and the United States, while others involve musicians who were born in Germany, Spain, or other European countries, and who came to New Orleans via France. I also explore more briefly expanded transatlantic networks involving London and New York, to take account of the activities of James Caldwell's American Theatre on Camp Street and, later, the relationship his St. Charles Theatre had with Italian touring troupes.

The Théâtre d'Orléans does not seem, however, to have maintained any formal connections with other colonial or former colonial Francophone theaters beyond Europe during this period. Francophone theaters were in operation in the Caribbean, on Guadeloupe and Martinique in particular, and a few of the Théâtre d'Orléans's performers undertook contracts there at various points in their careers, but I have not come across any institutional connections between these colonial theaters and New Orleans in the four decades explored in this book. Following the Haitian Revolution (the refugees from which contributed to the early theatrical life of New Orleans around the turn of the century), Francophone musical and theatrical life resumed on the island, but it had no evident links with either New Orleans or its former imperial center, France.[39] Similarly, while the Théâtre d'Orléans troupe visited Montréal during their tour in the summer of 1843, I have found no evidence of ongoing connections between its theatrical life and that of New Orleans.[40]

While the "transatlantic" is the spatial frame for this book, my broader historiographical approach draws on transnational history, mobility studies, and global microhistory. Transnational history has successfully destabilized the centrality of the nation-state as both the subject for analysis and the framework through which that analysis is conducted; in an opera studies context, Axel Körner and Paulo Kühl have questioned the "validity of national categories of analysis" that have for so long occupied scholarly focus for writing opera history, arguing instead for a transnational approach that looks at how opera's success and its significance were constantly reformulated beyond the nation.[41]

This is not, of course, to suggest that "the national" plays no role in transnational histories at large, but rather that its importance is reframed. Prasenjit Duara and many other historians have shown that the national need not be the endpoint of historical investigation, but rather can be seen as a relative and flexible concept shaped by networks of economic, cultural, and social processes that exist outside the constraints of national borders;[42] it is these networks and processes on which transnational histories focus. In keeping with this thinking, the notion of "transatlantic opera," as I envisage it, is not a distinct "type" of opera, replicating the national categories—French opera, Italian opera, and so on—which Körner and Kühl have sought to resist.

Rather, it is a framework through which to approach the connections that created and sustained New Orleans's musical life, and their ramifications on both sides of the Atlantic: it is a set of processes, involving the circulation of people, materials, and ideas.

To explore this circulation and the relational aspects of operatic life, I draw on mobility-focused approaches to opera. Katherine Preston's extensive work on touring opera companies in the United States highlights how, within the borders of a nation, an understanding of mobility—whether regularized into touring circuits or more ad hoc—is fundamental to creating a "joined-up" picture of operatic life that does not treat specific opera houses or places in isolation from their wider webs of connections.[43] On the other side of the Atlantic, Francesca Vella has shown how a networked approach to opera illuminates the construction of and shifting relationships between localisms, regionalisms, and internationalization in nineteenth-century Italy, in a way that mirrors many of my own approaches to New Orleans in this book.[44] While Vella draws on the work of mobility studies scholars, such as Stephen Greenblatt,[45] more influential for my own treatment of the entanglement of local, national, and inter- or transnational contexts has been the work of scholars in "global microhistory," who aim to illuminate global processes and structures through a microhistorical focus.[46] Certainly, the "global" has attracted increasing attention in opera studies in recent years. Jürgen Osterhammel's assertion that "opera underwent globalization early on," pointing to its movements beyond Europe with colonial endeavors, is a tantalizing prospect;[47] Benjamin Walton has argued convincingly for the emergence of a "potent fantasy" of "global opera" in the years around 1830, in which opera—in both its presence and absence—provided Europeans and non-Europeans alike with a means through which to imagine the wider world.[48]

The question of what a global history of opera might look like and whose version of the globe it reflects is still very much up for debate, but this book shares with Walton an interest in the ways opera facilitated for various groups of people—whether in New Orleans or Paris—a process of imagining themselves in relation to the wider world.[49] It does so by focusing in microhistorical detail on a single city, in order to draw out links—imaginative or otherwise—with other places, near and far. In this sense, it is in line with historian David Bell's call for a focus on "'small' spaces":

> Small spaces are not simply spaces that feel the impact of global forces. In some cases, they serve as profoundly intense, dynamic laboratories of change in their

> own right, and the processes of change that occur in them are much more than simple reactions to the global forces that impinge on them.[50]

This idea of "zooming in" in order to "zoom out," of putting New Orleans under the microscope in order to learn what it reflects of, and how it helped create, the nineteenth-century world, is fundamental to this book.

The agency of individuals underpins each of my chapters; the historical experiences of opera I have reconstructed (in so far as it is possible to do so) go beyond how people simply *felt* as they listened to or performed operatic works, extending to what practices or ideas associated with opera enabled them to *do* (and, by extension, to *be*). This is, nonetheless, not a story of "great" individuals, but rather an exploration of people who were in many respects unremarkable: the "workaday" singers and orchestral musicians, who never achieved celebrity; the people who were not musicians at all, but who ended up involved in the theater's business dealings; the audiences inside and outside the theater, who simultaneously associated opera with social activities of various kinds and made it an opportunity for imagined travel. Experience here, then, is not in the singular, and I provide a snapshot of these diverse experiences and the actions they enabled.

While human agency drives the narrative in many respects, it is balanced against explorations of the development and work of various institutions—the Théâtre d'Orléans and other theaters, the press in New Orleans and abroad, and the institutions of government in the city—whose power and influence was not fully attributable to specific individuals. Few studies on opera in the United States have adopted an institutional focus of this kind—there are no others covering the antebellum period, to my knowledge—for the very reason that in the case of many cities, theatrical or operatic enterprises were often so impermanent that they never really developed institutional status. Even in studies of New Orleans, the Théâtre d'Orléans has not typically been portrayed as having established systems or other institutional features. For John Baron and various others, the theater is simply one part of a much larger study of the musical life of the city.[51] Meanwhile, although the Théâtre d'Orléans forms a far more central part of Henry Kmen's work, his exclusively chronological approach, recounting various incidents relating to its management in various years alongside a more comprehensive account of its repertoire, means that the picture that emerges from his work seems to be one of the theater as a fragmented, somewhat ad hoc endeavor, or at least one that was wholly at the mercy of external circumstances.[52] As I will demonstrate, however, the theater's successful forty-year existence relied on a core of stable but flexible administrative practices.

My approach, then, has been to balance human inputs with the wider systems that enabled transatlantic operatic activity, and the distinctive identity the Théâtre d'Orléans developed through the combination of these factors. In this sense, it bears more resemblance to Mark Everist's approach to excavating individual contributions to the development of the Paris Odéon as an institution, than it does to Frederic Hemmings's *The Theatre Industry in Nineteenth-Century France*, which studies institutions in impressive detail, but positions individuals simply as users of an established system (as audiences, performers, and playwrights) rather than as having an active role in animating that system.[53] I want to focus on the ways in which agents engaged with institutions from both the inside and the outside, shaping them wherever they could and negotiating those issues that proved to be beyond their control.[54]

Uncovering human agency and institutional structures alike brought with it a specific set of historiographical challenges, and I think it is important to say something of my research process here. As I discovered early on, it was not difficult to accumulate a long list of names of European singers who worked in New Orleans. After all, the press in both New Orleans and Paris frequently mentioned performers, and the various surviving playbills from the time also list names. Uncovering the names of orchestral musicians and ballet dancers was more difficult, but with a bit of digging, the press—digitized and physical—eventually furnished a respectable number.

Getting beyond the names, however, was another matter. These performers were not the biggest stars of nineteenth-century operatic life, but people who worked contract to contract, rarely staying in one place for very long. They were not, on the whole, the type of performers of whom people wrote biographies. The rare examples of biographical vignettes that I have found were written by other musicians, who recalled their colleagues' life and work in later memoirs (such was the mid-nineteenth-century appetite for writing and reading memoirs). Female performers were particularly hard to trace since, in most cases, newspapers did not list their first names. The soprano Madame Bamberger, who was a prima donna at the Théâtre d'Orléans from 1838 to c. 1843, and whose husband was a cellist in the theater's orchestra, never had her first name mentioned in the New Orleans press, although her performances were discussed weekly in reviews published during her time in the city. In other cases, inconsistent orthography combined with performers' constant movement make them hard to trace. Some of the names I added to my list were not performers at all, but people whose lives were connected to the theater in other ways, through either their work or their social lives. Reviews and the other sources typically used by musicologists revealed little about them, but they nonetheless played an important part in operatic life.

Writing a history of operatic mobility that draws out human agency, then, meant taking on the challenges outlined above, and for me, this meant thinking more about the kinds of sources that might help me write such a history. At the very beginning of this project, back in 2014, I was struck by the fact that the press had been the dominant—sometimes exclusive—source for studying operatic life beyond Europe. That was certainly the case for existing accounts of musical life in nineteenth-century New Orleans, and a similar pattern emerged in other accounts of operatic life beyond Europe, such as Jean Fouchard's *Le Théâtre à Saint-Domingue* and his *Artistes et répertoire des scènes de Saint-Domingue*.[55]

I, too, began my research with the press, since one of the two major bilingual newspapers printed in New Orleans in the first half of the nineteenth century, *L'Abeille/The Bee* (1827–1923), is available online, as is the *Daily Picayune*, the city's first fully English-language newspaper (founded 1837).[56] So too have large numbers of newspapers published in Paris and regional France been digitized and made available on Gallica. On research visits to New Orleans and Paris, I supplemented my online reading of these digitized sources with physical newspapers, since the other New Orleans newspapers that proved most useful for my research—the bilingual *Courrier de la Louisiane/Louisiana Courier* (1807–1860) and the French-only *L'Impartial* (1839–1840)—were available only in hard copy, as were the numerous magazines and newsletters that flourished in the 1840s and 1850s.

The tendency to treat the press as the principal source for theater histories—particularly those that focus on places beyond Europe's major capitals—stems at least in part from a belief in the comprehensive coverage of newspapers, since many ran daily for periods of months or even years, containing regular adverts and theatrical news, and also from the practical convenience of being able to read through bound volumes of newspapers or scroll/keyword-search through their online counterparts. But, convenience aside, it struck me in the case of New Orleans that earlier scholars' focus on newspaper sources perhaps also reflected a deeper belief that few other traces of theater histories could have survived the ravages of the last 200 years.

They would not necessarily be wrong. There is no consolidated archive of any theater active in nineteenth-century New Orleans. Both the Théâtre d'Orléans and the first St. Charles Theatre succumbed to fire in the nineteenth century (in 1866 and 1842, respectively), and flames also claimed the Théâtre d'Orléans's successor, the French Opera House, in 1919, taking with them any records stored in these buildings. Nonetheless, in keeping with my ambitions to write an expanded, transnational history of opera in New Orleans, I wanted to treat the city's press not simply as a source of factual information about theatrical activities (or even as a source for reception history), but as a means through which to explore how the theatrical press functioned beyond Europe, and the roles that theatrical journalism could play both in the cultural life of a city like New Orleans and in creating a sense of global interconnection.[57]

I hope it does not seem too self-indulgent, then, to take a moment to reflect briefly on my research process, and how I sought other kinds of sources on both sides of the Atlantic. In New Orleans itself, I resolved to investigate the city's public records as, although they were not completely protected from the fires and floods that claimed the theaters and so many other buildings in nineteenth-century New Orleans, they were intended from the start to be preserved long term. I thought they might give me an insight into the position the theaters occupied in city life through the presence or absence of records relating to their activities. I did not expect that they would in fact furnish such an extensive or detailed insight into the running of an opera troupe. I turned first to the historical court documents held at the New Orleans Public Library, where the indexes for the city's various civil courts yielded results for cases brought by or against the theater's directors. These, some of which also included transcribed witness testimonies, revealed much about the way the theater operated as a business and how the inevitable disputes that arose between personnel and management were settled legally.

Emboldened by this successful foray into the city's public records collections, I decided to try the New Orleans Notarial Archives, to see if I could find anything else about the legal formalities of running a theater. The huge, chronological volumes of records kept by individual notaries in the city, who were called upon to witness contracts, loans, mortgages, and formal agreements of all sorts, proved challenging to search. There is no master index, making it very difficult to ascertain whether a volume was of use until I had called it up. What is more, it was common practice for individuals to use a variety of notaries, as the need arose, rather than staying with a single one, meaning that even if I had located one document of significance in a particular notary's records, there was no guarantee I would find another. While my search of these records was by no means exhaustive—that would be the work of a lifetime—I managed to identify several notaries whose services were used regularly by the Davises and others associated with the theater, and I focused my efforts on their volumes. The documents I found proved to be a vital source for understanding processes of transatlantic recruitment and the procurement of materials. The information I uncovered in them inspired further explorations across the Atlantic, and I spent time in Rouen and Le Havre, tracking down shipping registers and information about performers who had worked in or passed through those places.[58]

Digging in physical archives, however, was not on its own enough to develop this project. Throughout the research process, work in physical archives and online work with digitized sources went hand in hand. Sometimes the physical archival work came first, in others the digital (and sometimes in ways that initially inspired the sense of scholarly shame that Benjamin Walton has discussed so frankly in relation to the Googled historical quirk).[59] Nonetheless, traditional archival work and online work shaped each other so profoundly and to such an extent that any sense of "quirk shame" was replaced by a more reflective approach to digital sources and their relationship with physical archival research. From the start, I was under no illusion that Optical Character Recognition—often particularly unreliable on nineteenth-century documents with blurred or blotchy printing—could provide me with any real mastery over searchable sources: digital work has its own practices and its own ethics, but it strikes me that it works most successfully in historical research when treated as part of a continuous, reciprocal research process with physical sources and not viewed as either superior or inferior to "traditional" work with physical archives.[60]

Even with careful source work, the surviving evidence about operatic life in nineteenth-century New Orleans remains incomplete. The challenge, then, has been how to move between the available, sometimes limited, details and the bigger picture. It is an issue social historians have discussed extensively, and Miles Fairburn has pointed in particular to the problems that arise when generalizing from fragmentary sources if the historian fails to "demonstrate that the small number of cases making up the fragment have a reasonable likelihood of typifying the whole aggregate."[61] That is to say, it can be difficult to work out what is typical and what is exceptional from only fragmentary information.

The issue has been conceived of in different ways, but the two formulations most relevant for this study are Lara Putnam's "telling examples,"[62] and the term used by numerous microhistorians, the "exceptional normal," both of which have shaped the ways in which I have evaluated the available evidence and understood its role in the historical narrative.[63] Telling examples, to quote Glenda Goodman, who takes up Putnam's term in her 2015 essay about transatlantic music, are "individuals whose experiences and accomplishments belie expectations of what was possible, given their social status."[64] The exceptional normal, on the other hand, posits that it is not the mobility or the story of the individual figure that is exceptional, but rather the amount and variety of documentation still existing about that person's life. The people I focus on in this book sit squarely in neither category: many of them certainly defy expectations, but these are the expectations of modern readers about what was possible for people in the nineteenth century, not necessarily the expectations of people at the time; similarly, the amount of documentation available about these people has enabled me to piece together some of the details of their lives and careers, but the picture remains partial and, indeed, they were not the only people about whom I could have written this study.

Particularly important to mention here, while on the subject of incomplete evidence and how to read it, is the fact that while the archive for understanding operatic life in New Orleans in this period at large is far from comprehensive, sources relating specifically to people of color's involvement in operatic life are even less numerous. In spite of the official attempts to taxonomize people into racial "boxes" mentioned earlier, many sources I have uncovered from the first four decades of the nineteenth century make surprisingly little mention of people's race, especially if the people involved were free rather than enslaved. Ann Laura Stoler has extensively explored the epistemic preoccupations of colonial archives — the ways in which they curated who was allowed to know what, and how — and how the "inaccessibility" of such archives to the modern scholar comes not from infrastructural problems in the present day, but from a lack of familiarity with the ways in which colonial governments sought to record, order, and preserve different kinds of knowledge.[65] While the period explored in this book is not one of colonial rule in New Orleans, many of Stoler's points remain pertinent for dealing with early nineteenth-century archives in general. The difficulty of tracing people of color's contributions to operatic life, then, is due not only to the damage inflicted on the archive by time, but also by complex and sometimes contradictory nineteenth-century attitudes to recording their contributions and experiences.

Nonetheless, for much of its existence, the Théâtre d'Orléans was not an exclusively white space. Free people of color formed part of its audiences, and so too, for a considerable period, did enslaved people. The theater also employed some black backstage personnel, although, as Juliane Braun has pointed out, by the opening of the Théâtre d'Orléans, black performers had already experienced racist objections to their performance on the city's stages.[66] While various scholars have explored the contributions of people of color to life in New Orleans, examining the work of Francophone composers of color — Basile Barès, Edmond Dédé, and Samuel Snaër, among others—in the second half of the nineteenth century, there has been relatively little scholarship on people of color's involvement in theatrical life and even less about their involvement in opera.[67] Braun herself has recently contributed important early work in this area by looking at the role of black actors at New Orleans's earliest theaters—in particular the St. Philip Street Theatre—and their later involvement, as well of those of audience members, at the black-founded Théâtre Marigny (1837–1838) and the Théâtre de la Renaissance (founded 1840).[68] Neither of the latter institutions produced operas, however, and for that reason they have not formed a significant part of my study.

The picture that emerges from my discussions of the intersection of race and opera here is necessarily partial, but this book nonetheless participates in ongoing conversations about race in the antebellum city by exploring what it is possible to recover, even if in many cases information about people of color's involvement with opera is only available in refracted form, in the recorded perspectives of white people.[69] Furthermore, because of the white lenses through which black lives have been preserved, interpreting the sources that have survived brings its own challenges. Clark has already highlighted an important friction between white individuals' qualitative responses to race and their attempts to quantify it.[70] This friction between personal and systemic formulations, and the inconsistency with which individuals responded to issues of race, are important parts of understanding racial tensions in antebellum New Orleans; I have quoted nineteenth-century sources as they were written, in order to reflect that. I have nonetheless endeavored to render my translations of these French-language sources sensitively. In particular, the French term "nègre" (and its feminine counterpart "négresse"), which appears in the title of one of the novels discussed at length in chapter 5, was used frequently in the antebellum period to refer to black people, usually carrying the nuance of "slave." At the time, it was not considered any more or less offensive than the other terms discussed earlier, but its continued use in French expressions in recent years has been the subject of debate and criticism, because of its clear links with racism and slavery. The occasions on which it appears in this book are direct quotations, reflecting the attitudes and meanings of the nineteenth century.

Each of the five chapters provides a different take on the operatic life of New Orleans and the activities of the Théâtre d'Orléans in particular. Chapter 1 explores the challenges of financing and running a theater with transatlantic connections in the first half of the nineteenth century, from the perspectives of the theater's managers (John and Pierre Davis), its performers, and its audiences and critics. In it, I examine the methods the Davises used to raise the capital to keep the theater running, and how they recruited and paid performers from Europe; meanwhile, the performers themselves had certain expectations of the benefits of taking on a transatlantic contract, and I explore how these were sometimes met but at others horribly frustrated, as they faced issues concerning currency conversion and job stability that they had not expected. Finally, local audiences and the press in New Orleans had their own opinions on what performers and their artistic labor were worth and their own ways of expressing them. By focusing on these different perspectives, chapter 1 explores how the theater developed and sustained a transatlantic identity by investigating the interaction of individual human agencies with wider social and cultural systems on both sides of the Atlantic.

The second chapter focuses more specifically on the repertoire of the Théâtre d'Orléans, investigating the impact of French *grand opéra*'s arrival in New Orleans in the 1830s and arguing that the genre provided a focus for the negotiation of local, national, and international identities among opposing critical (and linguistic) factions within the city. Specifically, I explore the race to produce Meyerbeer's *Robert le diable* that took place between the Théâtre d'Orléans and James Caldwell's Anglophone American Theatre and, later, the reception of another *grand opéra* that found global popularity in the 1830s, *Les Huguenots.* I argue that these works invited the construction of imagined transatlantic communities of operatic spectatorship, by enabling operagoers to relate themselves to Parisian audiences. Accessing this privileged position afforded Francophone and Anglophone audiences alike the means to negotiate some of the local sociopolitical issues (particularly the shift away from French cultural hegemony in New Orleans in the period) that I have introduced above. Furthermore, I suggest, New Orleans audiences used *Robert* to position themselves at an international level, temporarily casting aside established cultural hierarchies (whether Creole/Anglo-American or European/North American) and colonial legacies.

While audiences are by no means absent from the discussion in chapters 1 and 2, chapter 3 places a much stronger focus on who was in the auditorium at the Théâtre d'Orléans and other theaters in the city at the time, exploring the race, economic status, and gender of theatergoers, and their behavior both as individuals and en masse. Drawing a distinction between the notion of the audience and that of a "public" for opera, I go on to examine how critics sought to create a public sphere in which operatic discourse could play out, positioning their self-envisaged role as twofold: shapers of taste and behavior (for both the theater administration and potential theatergoers) and ventriloquists for an imagined ideal public, for whom opera was both a cultural aspiration and an educational tool. The difference between the behavior of the imagined public and that of the theater's real-life audiences, of course, was sometimes stark: both had sets of specifically local and transatlantic elements in their perceptions of operagoing, but the way in which they chose to value each of them differed considerably.

Chapter 4 moves beyond a focus on experiencing opera in the theater, to explore the ways in which the people of nineteenth-century New Orleans were able to engage with opera through dance arrangements that could be performed in the ballroom or on the piano in the home and collectible bilingual opera libretti. These objects were both commercial souvenirs and repositories of highly personal memories: they belonged to a globalizing market for sheet music and operatic memorabilia, at the same time as they had a variety of specifically local contexts. I explore how these objects and their use fostered a sense of what I call "global intimacy" for consumers, which not only drew on identifiable transatlantic connections, but contributed to a broader kind of operatic globalization that was as much imaginative as it was traceable in terms of real-world connections.

Finally, chapter 5 turns the lens onto New Orleans and its operatic life from the outside, as it was seen by visitors to the city. The chapter focuses on the ways in which a Frenchman and an English-speaking visitor from New Hampshire immortalized the Théâtre d'Orléans and its activities in their novels and travel memoirs. In it, I argue that scenes featuring New Orleans's operatic life open up new perspectives on nineteenth-century perceptions of transatlantic travel and inter-cultural contact in the period, thus positioning opera not simply as a key part of New Orleans's identity for locals, but as a means of constructing the city for visitors and armchair tourists alike.

As the five chapters explore in their own ways, transatlantic connections developed flexibly across four decades. They were never fixed or rigid, although they were stable enough to create a sense of institutional identity for the Théâtre d'Orléans. Over time, individual links inevitably frayed, and some were renewed. Others were replaced in different ways or else abandoned entirely. The arrival and departure of individuals; the financial and administrative situation of the theater; the gradually changing position of French speakers in the commercial and cultural life of New Orleans beyond the theater; and social, political, cultural, and infrastructural developments in Europe and the wider United States all shaped the ways in which transatlantic connections were created, maintained, and understood.

1

"Un théâtre est une machine difficile à mouvoir"

Developing a Transatlantic Cultural Institution

In February 1843, *La Lorgnette*, a theatrical magazine in New Orleans, observed during the course of its musings on the activities of the Théâtre d'Orléans that "a theater is a difficult machine to power, and the cogs of which are many."[1] The characterization of the theater as machine is one that would undoubtedly have resonated with nineteenth-century readers, born in and of the industrial era. The image of the mechanical "cogs" translated the complexity of the organization and its structure into a familiar metaphor of mechanization, the likes of which they saw all around them, in the river- and oceangoing steamships moored down at the Mississippi dockside, in the six-mile-long Pontchartrain Railroad that connected the river to the lake north of the city from 1830, and in industries throughout New Orleans.

As with all nineteenth-century machines, however, the theater would have needed machinists: mechanization did not necessarily equate to automation. What I want to do in this chapter is think about what did "power" the theater—administratively, economically, and culturally—and what, or who, its "cogs" might have been. The picture of the running of the theater that I paint here is one of constant negotiation between the demands of the administration, performers, and public: my focus is largely on people as the driving force of the institution, but at the same time I am also interested in the factors that affected the theater's activities and its institutional identity that were beyond the control of individuals, emerging instead from wider economic, social, and cultural issues.

In this way, this chapter lays the groundwork for all those that follow, introducing the people and central questions that reappear in various ways throughout the rest of the book. It begins with an individual, John Davis, the man who founded the Théâtre d'Orléans and who guided it through its first seventeen years, weaving him into a larger story of the development of managerial and financial practices for the theater, which came to include his son, Pierre, a network of the Davises' friends and acquaintances and, at various times, a board of shareholders, and a performer-run Society of Artists. After that comes a focus on the performers employed by the theater, as a way not only to highlight a range of typical and exceptional career paths, but also to probe the limits of transatlantic operatic employment: the moments at which the performers' hopes and expectations of their mobile, international careers and the reality failed to align.

Many of my discussions here have, to borrow Tracy Davis's inviting description, an "economic flavor," in the sense that money inevitably underpinned all the theater's activities and those of its performers;[2] it was frequently a source of friction within the administrative structure, between performers and management and, importantly, between audiences and performers. While the Théâtre d'Orléans's administrative records have long since disappeared, it perhaps should not come as a surprise that the moments in the theater's operational history that are most recoverable are those in which financial problems and disagreements arose.[3] These were recorded, sometimes because disputes escalated to the level of court proceedings, sometimes because the wounded parties took their grievances to the press and, occasionally, because a letter or other piece of private correspondence tantalizingly preserves an individual's views about an issue. The economics of transatlantic theatrical management, then, could be messy, but this messiness reflected the complexities of sustaining connections across large distances, as well as the friction between local, national, and international systems of theatrical production and individuals' actions.

But money is only part of the story. Equally important are the cultural questions generated by the transatlantic operatic enterprise, both from the point of view of the present day looking back, and also for people at the time. Debates about how to value artistic labor (culturally as much as financially), varied attempts to understand the peripatetic careers of opera singers, and questions as to what extent the Théâtre d'Orléans was really a "French" theater beyond its commitment to performing in the French language emerge repeatedly in nineteenth-century sources, and I address them all to an extent in the course of this chapter.

Opera is less separable from the theater's activities at large here than it is in some other parts of this book. Performers and musicians engaged to work at the Théâtre d'Orléans inevitably found themselves at times performing in the whole mix of theatrical and musical genres the theater offered. Singers hired as principal operatic performers were sometimes called upon to fill in small parts in spoken dramas and variety performances, while lowly comic actors and principal tragédien(ne)s alike found themselves singing chorus parts and minor roles in operas as needed. These practices underscore the need to look at the running of the theater in holistic terms, rather than attempting to isolate opera, but since opera was by far the most resource-heavy of all the theatrical genres performed at the Théâtre d'Orléans and the one that generated the most heated debate, all the challenges and disputes discussed in this chapter were keenly heightened in relation to it.

GETTING THE THEATER OFF THE GROUND: DEVELOPING A SUSTAINABLE ADMINISTRATIVE STRUCTURE

Running a theater with a resident company whose members were recruited abroad brought with it a particular set of administrative and financial challenges and, perhaps unsurprisingly, the way in which these were addressed changed considerably across the forty years of the theater's existence. I want to begin by tracing some of those developments and exploring what they meant for the stability of the Théâtre d'Orléans, the people who were invested in it (financially as much as culturally) and, ultimately, the theater's local and transatlantic identities.[4]

The founding director of the Théâtre d'Orléans, John Davis, like many of the individuals whose stories are woven throughout this book, was an immigrant in New Orleans. Born in Paris in 1773 to Jean Davis and Anne Marie Davis,[5] he arrived in New Orleans in 1809 as a refugee from the slave-led revolution on the French-colonized island of Saint-Domingue (modern-day Haiti), which between 1791 and 1804 drove thousands of French sugar planters and enslaved people alike to flee overseas.[6] Like so many of the other Saint-Domingue refugees, he initially made his way to Santiago de Cuba, only for the Spanish colonial government to expel all French speakers from the island of Cuba in 1809, during the Peninsular War between France and Spain. Davis's arrival in New Orleans was accompanied by even more difficult personal circumstances: his wife, Marie Félicité Meunier, had recently died, leaving him with two infant children, Pierre (b. 1807) and Henri (birth date unknown). More tragedy followed when, on September 5, 1810, Henri also died.[7]

Davis resolved to make a life for himself and Pierre in New Orleans, but running a theater was far from his first idea about how to do so. Indeed, he was relatively unusual among American theater directors of the time in that he was not a performer himself. Instead, Davis was a businessman, with a portfolio of properties and investments around the city. It is not clear what he did in Saint-Domingue or Cuba (his name does not appear in connection with a theater in these places), but he must have brought some money with him to New Orleans, as he bought his first hotel—Tremoulet's, on the levee—in 1811, and over the next few years he acquired further hotels both in New Orleans and in the resort town of Mandeville, on the north shore of Lake Pontchartrain.[8]

Over the years, he diversified further, adding to his business empire with the Théâtre d'Orléans and its adjoining ballroom, cafés, and gambling saloon (fig. 1.1).[9] He created a central role for his facilities in the life of New Orleans, offering them as a venue for all manner of important civic meetings, as well as entertainments (Davis had a monopoly on gambling in the city for a number of years).[10] When the government house burned down in 1828, it was Davis's rooms that were chosen as the interim location for all government meetings.[11] While not all of his ideas came to fruition (indeed, his plan to demolish St. Louis Cathedral in order to make way for a larger theater was greeted with anything but universal acclaim), he gained a reputation for seeing almost anything as a business opportunity.[12]

Just such a business opportunity presented itself in the summer of 1816, when a fire destroyed the building of the old Théâtre d'Orléans, which had been struggling to attract audiences over the last couple of years. Davis saw potential in the site, and on November 14, 1816, he published a notice in a local newspaper, *L'Ami des lois*, informing the readers that he had "just purchased the remains [of the old Théâtre d'Orléans building] and the location at which it was situated."[13] He announced his plans to rebuild the theater in a more impressive style than before and to bring performers, decorations, and all other necessary materials from France, in order to maintain public interest. He intended, he said, to build a theater that would do "credit to a town of the second order in Europe," and he wanted to do it within the year.[14] What he needed now, he explained to the readers, was money. And he proposed a scheme to raise it.

The scheme he had in mind was a tontine, which, he pointed out, was a common system for raising capital in Europe and other parts of the United States but had not yet been used in New Orleans.[15] The premise of his system was that 467 shares would be sold at the price of $150 to raise capital of $70,050 (just over $1.3 million in today's money).[16] The people who bought into the tontine would each receive an equal dividend, and when a shareholder died, their share would be split among the surviving shareholders. When there were only ten surviving shareholders, they would own the building between them (and would be free to pass on their share to whomever

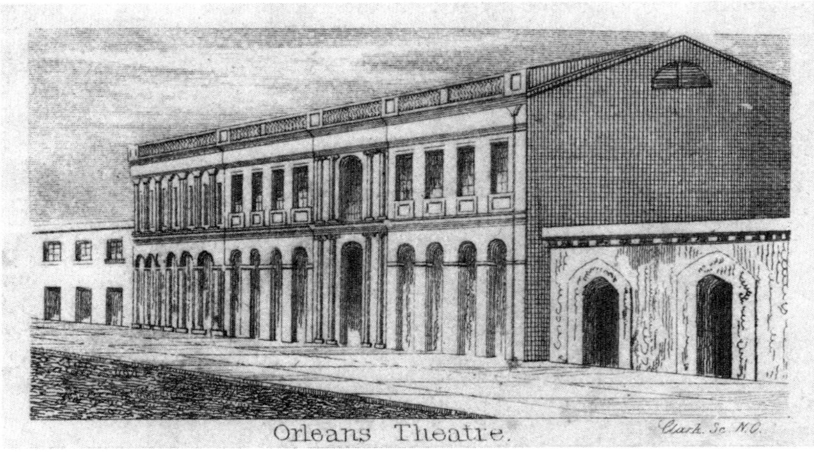

FIGURE 1.1 The Orleans Theatre (c. 1838), engraved by Clark. The Historic New Orleans Collection, Gift of Mr. and Mrs. Albert Louis Lieutaud, acc. no. 1957.73 i.

they chose upon their death). Davis would have control over the theater for the first five years, and after that the shareholders could rent it out, although Davis requested that they offer the lease to him first.[17]

Davis was right in saying that this was a common means of raising capital in Europe, and the building of numerous theaters was financed this way, not just in France, but also in Britain (and likely elsewhere too). But he was unable to stir up enough interest among New Orleans's wealthy investors. He ultimately failed to fill the tontine, which delayed the project, meaning that he did not manage to open the theater within a year (it finally opened at the end of November 1819, three years after he announced his plans).[18] In the absence of sufficient shareholders, Davis decided to finance the project independently.[19] To do so, he took out a number of personal loans. In 1819, he secured a loan of $15,000 from the city, and he also received several smaller "mortgages" formed by groups of individuals (many of them Davis's acquaintances, including some of his fellow former residents of Saint-Domingue).[20] Among them were a group of fourteen men who each gave $500 to provide $7,000 toward establishing the theater, and another smaller group of three also gave $500 each.[21] In return for their contributions to the theater fund, which Davis agreed he would begin to repay after a period of three years had elapsed, each of the men was to receive free entry to the theater's performances until such time as they had been reimbursed in full.[22] There were doubtless many more such mortgages and other loans, as Davis sought to fund the building of the theater and the recruiting of the first troupe in a piecemeal fashion. None of this stopped with the opening of the theater in late November 1819, and he continued to take on personal loans throughout the period in which he was in charge.

Although Davis had originally planned to make the Théâtre d'Orléans a theater that "would do credit to a town of the second order in Europe," in reality he ended up financing it in a way that did not really resemble French provincial practice. As Lauren Clay has put it, "when nineteenth-century [French] provincial theater companies faltered, municipal governments stepped in to support their opera and theater troupes with ever-larger cash subsidies, a financial dependence that only intensified over time"; Davis, however, could count on no such subsidy in New Orleans.[23] He took loans from the city council, but when he failed to pay them back, they took him to court, and he found himself embroiled very personally in the upkeep of the theater.

In the face of such expenses, Davis's finances fluctuated dramatically, and they were the subject of considerable gossip among his acquaintances: various letters from the time reveal speculations that he was on the verge of bankruptcy,[24] while others, only months later, suggest that he was earning vast sums.[25] He undoubtedly knew how to make money (and, indeed, to lose it again), but the financial stability of the Théâtre d'Orléans was extremely precarious during its early years; ticket sales alone were not enough to sustain the company, and the theater appears to have run frequently at a loss. Davis himself suggested as much when he wrote to the *Courrier de la Louisiane* in April 1835 in response to plans to open a second French theater in the city; he pointed out that it was difficult enough to sustain one theater financially, suggesting that opening another would mean the certain demise of both enterprises.[26]

Davis's precise motivations for fighting so hard to keep the theater open remain murky. As previously mentioned, he was neither a performer himself (unlike James Caldwell, his rival manager at New Orleans's American Theatre, which opened in 1824) nor, according to his stage manager, Jean Colson, was he even particularly interested in going to the theater.[27] So too must his business instincts have rebelled at the thought of preserving an enterprise that hemorrhaged money. But there are a number of plausible reasons why he might have gone to the lengths he did to keep it open. First, it played a role in drawing people to his other ventures that adjoined the theater building—the ballroom, the gambling house, the café—allowing them to generate additional revenue, which perhaps compensated in the longer term for the theater's losses. Such a mixing of business interests in and around the theater, in particular the combination of theater and gambling, was unusual in France and its colonies in this period (although it did, of course, develop at Monte

Carlo later in the nineteenth century), but many Italian theaters in the period relied heavily on the pairing of theater and gambling in order to make a profit.[28] In the United States, too, it was common for theater managers to have diverse business interests, in order to make their theaters profitable. James Caldwell, director of the Anglophone Camp Street and St. Charles Theatres in New Orleans, not only acted in productions given by his companies at various points but also founded the New Orleans Gas Light Company, the profits from which he used to build his St. Charles Theatre in 1835.[29]

Making theater one part of a larger business model meant a delicate balancing act for Davis, who had to ensure that the different elements of his entertainment complex on Orleans Street complemented and supported each other, rather than being in direct and destructive competition. When he leased the Orleans Coffee House to a man named Jackson Oliver in 1826, for instance, Davis promised in the contract that he would not undercut the sales of the enterprise by selling wines or liqueurs at any of his other bars adjoining the theater for less than 12.5 cents.[30] He also granted Oliver the privilege of supplying all the alcohol to the gaming tables in his casino. In return, Oliver would pay Davis $100 a month and promised to keep the Coffee House open until the close of the theater and ballroom every night. The individual parts of his entertainment complex on Orleans Street, then, existed in a delicate symbiosis.

Business aside, the maintenance of Francophone pride provided a cultural incentive for Davis to keep the theater running. In 1823, the Théâtre d'Orléans's stage managers (*régisseurs*), Auguste Douce and A. B. St. Estève, suggested as much, when they appealed for more public support in the local press, writing of "the attachment that all good Frenchmen carry in their hearts for the mother country," while the following year, supporters of the theater wrote in the local press of the Théâtre d'Orléans as "an establishment . . . from which we should for a long time draw an advantage in maintaining our tongue and our ways."[31] French cultural pride, moreover, was never very far from Francophone business interests in nineteenth-century New Orleans, and Douce and St. Estève acknowledged this link, pointing out "how useful an establishment like this is to civilization" and to all "who should vividly desire the prosperity of an establishment created for them, [and] to the commercial interests favored by the theater."[32] The Théâtre d'Orléans, therefore, came to play an important role in French speakers' conceptions of their cultural heritage in New Orleans, while also actively supporting Francophone economic activity in the city. This doubtless served as an imperative for Davis to maintain the theater, even if that meant sometimes running at a loss.

NEXT STEPS: PARTNERSHIP, INCORPORATION, AND CRISIS

While John guided the theater through its early years, his son was abroad. Aged twelve at the theater's opening, Pierre (nicknamed "Toto"), like so many other young men from reasonably wealthy French families in the city, spent most of his adolescence and early twenties in France.[33] There, he received what a *Historical Sketch Book and Guide to New Orleans* described in 1884 as "a classical education, acquired in one of the royal colleges."[34] Besides that, it suggested, "he had also gone through a complete course of musical studies, an artistic training which was of great service to him in the selection and formation of his opera companies in Europe."[35] In the early 1830s, his education complete, he moved back to Louisiana to work alongside John in running the theater, although there is no evidence that he took over any of his father's other business interests.

In 1834, John took the decision to make Pierre a legal partner in the running of the theater, giving father and son equal rights and equal shares of the profits. Pierre was to dedicate himself full-time to the theater, taking charge in all practical respects (recruitment and contracting, purchasing materials, etc.);[36] John, on the other hand, would be responsible in general for the finances of the theater. In the case of taxes, repairs, and so on, the pair would share the expenses between them. For the first two years they worked together but, when it came to the first renewal of the partnership in 1836, John decided to give up his share in the theater: at the age of sixty-three, he began to retire from his businesses, perhaps due to failing health, and he died three years later at his home in Mandeville, north of New Orleans.[37]

Instead of leaving Pierre to finance the theater alone, the Davises took the major decision to move away from the owner-impresario model, seeking shareholders and a board of financial directors for the theater. The Théâtre d'Orléans was incorporated for the first time on March 14, 1836, with Christoval Guillaume de Armas, one of a distinguished family of Creole notaries and businessmen in the city, as its first president.[38] Pierre remained the theatrical director. While John Davis had relied heavily upon his friends and associates for loans in order to keep the theater open in earlier years, the new Compagnie du Théâtre d'Orléans now formalized its financial dealings, through its reliance on its shareholders. On April 1, 1837, John Davis handed over his lease to the theater along with all its furnishings and equipment, as well as the adjoining ballroom complex, including all the equipment for the gambling saloon and other facilities to the Compagnie du Théâtre d'Orléans. In the final sale of the theater and all its properties, Davis profited to the sum of $275,000—a vast amount for the time, which would be equivalent to nearly $7.9 million today—from the enterprise that had consumed almost twenty years of his life and brought him close to bankruptcy at various points.[39] Meanwhile, the new financial model for the Théâtre d'Orléans relieved any single person from full personal responsibility for the theater, and instead made it a collective financial enterprise, which should have ensured greater financial stability and longevity.

Nonetheless, the theater's early years under Pierre's direction saw it regularly in dire financial straits: his ambitious programming (notably of large-scale French grand operas) and opulent sets cost the company dearly, leaving little room for maneuvering when it came to dips in the theater's incomings. One particularly difficult point came in February 1843, when the management gathered the performers together and announced that because receipts had been so low in the last few weeks, they were planning to end the theater season early, pay them the money they were owed for the rest of the month, and send them home to France with the final 50,000 francs ($10,000) remaining in the theater's coffers.[40] The performers, however, were not satisfied with this decision, and were determined to keep working. They formed themselves into the Society of Artists, electing five representatives from among their number, who were to liaise with the administration, and who quickly obtained permission from the theater administration to use the theater building and all its properties on a trial basis for the next few weeks. They wrote their own terms of engagement for the month of March: all would perform and receive a minimum of $40 at the end of the month, regardless of the roles they played.[41] If the box office receipts were great enough, the profits would be divided pro rata among the performers, according to their usual salaries. They agreed that they would review at the end of March: if things were going well, they would continue until May, and if they were not, the performers would take the management up on their offer of a return passage to Europe.[42] Through a combination of reducing ticket prices and offering lottery tickets for theater entry, they succeeded in maintaining their season through the end of April 1843, at which point they departed on a tour of the northern states.[43]

The debacle of February 1843 was not the Théâtre d'Orléans management's finest moment, and various local papers shared the opinion that Davis and the theater's board of shareholders had overreacted in ending the season when they did.[44] While the theatrical periodical *La Lorgnette* pointed out a number of specific things the management had done to contribute to the less-than-ideal financial situation, there was a larger context for this unusually catastrophic drop in the theater's finances. The financial crisis in the United States known as the Panic of 1837, which hit not long after John Davis retired and the Théâtre d'Orléans was incorporated, had severe and lasting consequences in New Orleans (and in the South in general), which persisted through 1843, meaning that in its first few years the Compagnie du Théâtre d'Orléans faced financial challenges over and above the normal difficulties of running a theater.[45] Writing in *La Lorgnette*, the magazine's critic-editor, Louis Placide Canonge, alluded to the current "public destitution" ("la misère publique") and the cuts individuals had been forced to make to their own spending in order to survive, leaving them unable to pay the same ticket prices as before the crisis.[46]

Compounding the theater's difficulties, Canonge suggested, was a problem specific to New Orleans. In 1836, the city had been divided into three municipalities; among many other administrative differences, each municipality printed its own money,[47] and, according to Canonge, the theater administration stopped accepting paper notes printed in two of the city's municipalities early in 1843: their value had recently depreciated because of the financial crisis, and the administration doubted the solvency of the specific banks that had issued them.[48] This, Canonge said, was the administration's biggest mistake, because people in possession of this currency (which is to say, most of the theater's patrons) stopped coming to the theater, since their paper money was no longer accepted there. In this case, local and national financial conditions, in combination with certain poor decisions made by the theater's management, caused a financial crisis for the theater. Fortunately, New Orleans's economy began to recover over the summer, and the Théâtre d'Orléans administration decided to take a chance on another season.

Financing the theater was never straightforward, however, and the rest of the 1840s proved bumpy for other reasons, principally disagreements between the individuals who owned the physical theater buildings (the Compagnie du Théâtre d'Orléans having sold them in 1848) and Pierre Davis, who continued to direct the company. In spite of such challenges, the theater stayed just about afloat, and Charles Boudousquié, who took over the direction of the theater from Pierre in 1853, managed to secure its future throughout the 1850s, until the company moved to the new French Opera House in 1859 (which I discuss in the Epilogue). Although the Théâtre d'Orléans moved over the years from a financial and administrative structure dependent on an individual to one that relied on a board of financial directors and shareholders, there was no single, reliable solution to the challenges of nineteenth-century theatrical management, especially in the absence of a significant municipal subsidy.

RECRUITMENT

By far the greatest single administrative challenge the theater faced in its regular business was the recruitment (and payment) of its performers, and this absorbed a great deal of its finances. Only a small part of the theater's recruitment took place locally in New Orleans, and that was generally for the orchestral rank and file, as well as backstage and front-of-house personnel.[49] In exceptional instances, recruitment for secondary personnel extended to the Northeast of the United States, such as when Louis Fiot, the Théâtre d'Orléans *régisseur* in the 1840s and early 1850s (whose series of bilingual opera libretti are discussed in chapter 4), engaged an American child dancer named Sarah Cohen from New York's Park Theatre in 1846.[50] Far more common for the recruitment of singers and principal orchestral musicians, however, was that someone from the theater administration or a representative appointed by them would make the journey to France to audition and contract performers.

The Théâtre d'Orléans administration usually sought to recruit its new troupe during the summer months. Although John Davis had attempted to keep the theater open year-round for the first couple of years, by 1824 he had decided to close over the summer, as audience numbers dwindled with the excessive heat and ever-present threat of yellow fever.[51] From then on, the theater season in New Orleans generally closed at the end of spring (usually late May or early June), providing an opportunity for the administration to turn its attention to recruitment.[52] The arrival of the new recruits several months later determined the start of the next season, but it was never possible to predict exactly when that would be. Although the new recruits left Europe in mid-September each year, the length of a transatlantic crossing could vary enormously. In some years, depending on the deal the Davises had been able to strike with a ship's captain, they departed from Le Havre (on the English Channel coast), while in others it was Nantes or even Bordeaux on the Atlantic coast, but the choice of port alone made little difference to the journey time at sea. Far more important was the weather, as, for much of the theater's existence, oceangoing ships were still reliant on wind and sail, meaning that it could take anywhere from six to ten weeks to make the journey from the French coast, across the Atlantic, through the Gulf of Mexico, and up the Mississippi to New Orleans. Overly still conditions could prove just as problematic as storms, and occasionally journeys could take even longer than ten weeks. Steam crossings of the Atlantic became possible in the 1840s (with passage at a much higher cost than on older sail-driven vessels), making journeys considerably shorter, but the theater continued its established pattern of opening the new season in the third week of November.

The Théâtre d'Orléans's recruitment process was personal and personalized. John Davis sometimes went to Europe himself, leaving New Orleans anywhere between late April and the beginning of June and arriving in Paris by the middle of summer. The trips were inevitably lengthy: in 1822, Davis left New Orleans in April,[53] and it was not until November 6 of that year that he returned to the city. He arrived on the *Cecilia* with twenty-five new recruits, having left Le Havre on September 16, and the *Courrier de la Louisiane* noted "with pleasure" that "M. Davis has obtained for us charming subjects for operas, comedies and vaudevilles, as well as a lovely troupe of dancers for ballets."[54]

From the early 1830s, Pierre took on recruitment responsibilities. The first recorded instance of his making the journey comes in the summer of 1832, when he would have been twenty-five years old.[55] His trip to Europe coincides with a year in which the Théâtre d'Orléans made a summer tour to the northeastern United States; Davis senior traveled with the existing troupe, while Pierre went to Europe. From then on, Pierre went more frequently to Paris than his father, and the partnership agreement made between father and son in 1834 detailed that Pierre's duties involved most of the practicalities, including recruiting and overseeing the day-to-day running of the theater. He spent the summer of that year in Europe and also that of 1836,[56] and he continued to make trips to Paris through his own period of directorship of the theater from 1837. Even after he formally handed over the direction of the theater to Charles Boudousquié in 1853, Davis continued to assist with recruiting performers in Paris, as the composer Giacomo Meyerbeer's appointment books attest in the summer of 1853 and the Parisian newspaper *Le Nouvelliste* noted in 1859.[57]

In the years when the Davises did not go themselves to Europe—it was, after all, a lengthy process that took them away both from the theater itself and from other business interests in New Orleans—they enlisted the services of other people to recruit performers on their behalf. Some of these appointed recruiters were based in New Orleans and were already employees of the Théâtre d'Orléans. Claude Bernard, the company's *régisseur*, was responsible for recruiting the troupe in the summer of 1840, as the *Revue et gazette musicale de Paris* reported that the troupe had left Le Havre for New Orleans under his direction on September 20 that year.[58] Eugène Prévost, the theater's Chef d'Orchestre, was charged with the task two years later in 1842. Both men were familiar with the intricacies of French operatic life and well placed to seek out and evaluate potential performers: Bernard had spent many years working in towns and cities around France, including a period in the 1820s as director of the Paris Odéon,[59] while Prévost, trained as a composer, had several of his operas performed at the Opéra-Comique in the 1830s and directed the theater orchestra at Le Havre before coming to New Orleans in 1838.[60] Meanwhile, the A. Elie who was responsible for recruiting the troupe in 1838 (and for recruiting both Claude Bernard and Eugène Prévost) was most likely Adolphe Elie, a violinist in the Théâtre d'Orléans orchestra, who gave violin lessons to the young Louis Moreau Gottschalk before the young prodigy left the city of his birth for Paris.[61]

Not all recruiters were in the regular employ of the Théâtre d'Orléans, however. In 1819 and 1824, John Davis granted power of attorney to a man named Jean-Baptiste Sel, living in New Orleans, to recruit performers on his behalf. In 1824 Sel traveled alone, but in 1819 he shared the responsibilities with Maurice Abat. Neither man was a professional musician: Sel was a painter, specializing in portraits and miniatures, while Abat, the son of a banker, was a businessman.[62] Although his motivations for doing so are irrecoverable, Davis nonetheless entrusted these two acquaintances with considerable responsibility for the theater and its performers. They were given free rein to recruit all "actors, dancers and singers or others whom [they] believe capable of fulfilling the aim of the theater," as well as making all the contractual arrangements with them.[63] Davis placed no financial limits on his recruiters, instructing them to pay whatever advances were necessary to secure the performers they had selected and promising to reimburse in full any costs the recruiter incurred on behalf of the theater.[64]

Appointing these men, neither of whom was professionally associated with the theater, to recruit the troupe appears at first glance to be a huge gamble for Davis: were they, as neither musicians nor members of the theater administration, really capable of judging a performer's suitability for the Théâtre d'Orléans? While there is no specific evidence of how Sel and Abat went about their recruiting once they arrived in Paris in 1819, evidence from other years suggests that the Théâtre d'Orléans recruiters did not operate entirely alone but relied on recommendations from well-connected musicians in Paris to locate suitable performers. Indeed, in July 1849, Pierre Davis made several visits to the composer Giacomo Meyerbeer while he was in Paris to discuss suitable performers for his operas, and Meyerbeer noted in his diary that he had "arranged for [Davis] to hear the singer Mme Moisson" following one such visit.[65] Moisson did not, in the end, go to New Orleans, but a few years later Meyerbeer played a similar role in helping Davis audition Anna Bertini, whom he duly contracted as the prima donna for the New Orleans troupe's 1853–1854 season.[66] The fact that Bertini had come on Meyerbeer's recommendation was in turn reported in the New Orleans press, which relished the opportunity to highlight a connection between their local theater and the celebrated composer of grand operas.[67]

While Meyerbeer was an exceptionally illustrious contact for the theater to have, the Théâtre d'Orléans recruiters relied more regularly on the advice of less well-remembered but nonetheless experienced theatrical recruiters in France, who would have helped mitigate any gaps in the knowledge or connections of the recruiter from New Orleans. One such man, linked repeatedly with the Théâtre d'Orléans and its recruitment over a number of years, was Gustave Collignon, who was born in Rennes in 1818 and trained at the Paris Conservatoire, where he won first prize for harmony and composition, as well as for his piano playing.[68] Collignon worked with the Théâtre d'Orléans from the early 1840s, helping Eugène Prévost recruit the troupe in the summer of 1842, and he was described in a theatrical periodical in New Orleans as a "theater broker" ("courtier des théâtres").[69]

The Davises were not alone, of course, in drawing on the assistance of theatrical agents to seek performers. Theater directors from across the French provinces and colonies (particularly in the Caribbean) looked to Paris to recruit new performers. As Frederic Hemmings has discussed, by the third decade of the nineteenth century, an older model of theatrical recruitment in which provincial theater directors would come up to Paris to sign contracts with new recruits in the Palais-Royal gardens had been replaced by "bureaux de correspondance dramatique" run by professional theatrical agents.[70] Provincial theater managers no longer had to travel to Paris to recruit troupes, but could write to these agencies and let them know of their requirements for the next season.[71] This would certainly have been the most straightforward and least time-consuming option for the Théâtre d'Orléans management, and it was a path that was common for the increasing number of French and Italian theater companies based outside Europe. Troupes for the Americas were frequently gathered in this way throughout the nineteenth century since, as John Rosselli has shown, Italian theatrical agents were willing not just to recruit performers, but to sell impresarios a whole "theatrical package," which included costumes and props as well.[72] French agencies would likely have offered similar deals.

Whether the Davises had any reason to distrust the packages offered by theatrical agencies, it is not possible to say, but they nonetheless avoided them in favor of using personal contacts (assisted as needed by theatrical agents) to recruit on their behalf. While Gustave Collignon initially fulfilled the agent role, working alongside the recruiters who had come from New

Orleans to Paris, his association with the Théâtre d'Orléans eventually became more personal: in September 1848, Collignon and his wife and child boarded the ship *L'Espirance* at Le Havre, along with the performers he had been involved in recruiting for the Théâtre d'Orléans, and traveled to New Orleans. He settled in the city for the rest of his life, becoming well known as a teacher and composer.[73]

The combination of recruiters sent from New Orleans and contacts in Paris allowed the Davises to establish a regular recruiting system and schedule for the Théâtre d'Orléans, in which singers were auditioned in July and August, before setting sail for New Orleans in mid-September. This pattern fit well with the Théâtre d'Orléans's seasonal summer closure, but it did not correspond with the long-established main season of theatrical recruitment in France. Indeed, in 1842, Louis Placide Canonge, a playwright and music lover in New Orleans, wrote an extended article for his theatrical periodical, *La Lorgnette,* in which he highlighted the disjunction between the French model of theatrical recruitment and that of the Théâtre d'Orléans. He suggested that the timing of the Théâtre d'Orléans's regular recruiting schedule did not work in its favor, saying that in order to find the best performers in France it was vital to be in Paris for the eight to ten days before Easter, which had historically been the period in which most theatrical recruitment for Paris and the provincial theaters had taken place.[74] Waiting until the height of summer to contract performers, he complained, meant that New Orleans was left with Europe's "dregs": performers who remained unemployed after the main recruiting period, or who could be lured away from their existing contracts.[75] He argued that the Davises put neither enough time nor money into securing the best troupes for the city, and he regarded Collignon as a swindler.[76]

There was perhaps some truth in Canonge's assertion that the Théâtre d'Orléans recruiters relied, at least on occasion, on being able to lure performers away from their existing contracts, as the singer and actress Béatrix Person recalled that she had been approached by the Théâtre d'Orléans recruiters after they had seen her onstage at Paris's Variétés theater, rather than because she had requested an audition.[77] But Canonge's insistence on the importance of recruiting in Paris in the days leading up to Easter was becoming increasingly outdated by 1842. The practice was gradually superseded through the 1830s and 1840s by the use of "bureaux de correspondance dramatique," meaning the Théâtre d'Orléans was far from alone by 1842 in not recruiting during this period.[78] Furthermore, taking a localized approach to seasons and, consequently, recruitment was common to many French provincial theaters of the time which, as Hemmings has shown, arranged their seasons in accordance with such factors as the climate, local parliament terms, and other needs of the theatergoing community.[79]

There was a considerable financial incentive for the theater administration to make the right decisions during the recruitment process as, even leaving aside the costs of paying performers' advances and salaries, the cost of transatlantic passage was substantial. In 1826, John Davis contracted a ship owner named A. P. Holdridge to bring his new recruits to New Orleans. Promising Holdridge at least fifteen passengers, Davis agreed to pay 550 francs (nearly $105) per performer for the voyage from Le Havre.[80] In today's money, his expenditure on fifteen passengers would have been roughly $42,000, and the cost was made all the more significant by the fact that he would have had to have had the same in reserve to pay their return passage to France at the end of their contracts.[81]

But, while the costs made it essential to make good initial decisions about which performers to contract, the recruitment pattern established by the Davises was not so rigid that recruiters from New Orleans were unable to make exceptional visits to Paris at other times of year (including the ten days before Easter), should there be a particular need for new performers, either because they had proved unsatisfactory, or because they had succumbed to illness. In early 1836, Pierre Davis had to do just that, as the quality of the performers had not been as high as expected, but it was nonetheless rare that he or another recruiter had to make a second trip to Europe because the original troupe had been found seriously lacking.[82] Recruitment, therefore, relied on the Davises' building networks of individuals to assist them and developing reliable processes for contracting performers that could be called upon year after year.

SINGERS AND THEIR CONTRACTS

The performers themselves, the fruits of the annual recruitment process, are the natural next step in this story: they were vital "cogs" in the wider theatrical machine, as they not only formed the public-facing front of the institution, appearing to audiences night after night, but the payment of their salaries placed large financial demands on the theater administration. The Théâtre d'Orléans's troupe was typically relatively large, comprising around fifteen men and ten women as soloists of various ranks in most years, along with additional chorus members and extras (referred to as "figurants"), two *régisseurs* (essentially stage managers, but who were involved to varying extents in both the artistic and administrative aspects of productions), a *chef d'orchestre*, and his assistant. Many orchestral principals were also recruited beyond the city, as were dancers (although the theater did not consistently employ a ballet troupe). They were joined on their arrival in New Orleans by additional local theater staff, such as machinists and lampists,[83] and supplementary orchestral players.

It is hard to make demographic generalizations about the people who undertook a transatlantic contract. They were a mixture of ages with varying degrees of experience, although the majority whose details can be recovered from shipping records were in their twenties and thirties; some traveled alone, while others brought with them their spouse, children, or other family members.[84] Some performers contracted to the Théâtre d'Orléans stayed in New Orleans only for the period for which they were first engaged, setting sail for France as soon as they could, while others renewed their contracts or returned to the city repeatedly over their careers. A few, like the *chef d'orchestre* Eugène Prévost and the soprano Julia Calvé, made New Orleans their home permanently, but they were the exceptions: on the whole, what characterized the Théâtre d'Orléans performers as a group, especially the singers, was that their careers involved a remarkable degree of mobility. Performers who stayed in one place for long periods of time were very much in the minority; for most, New Orleans was but one stop in an itinerant career.

Instead of attempting any kind of general survey, here I want to zoom in and use some of the theater's new recruits for the 1834–1835 season to give a snapshot of the Théâtre d'Orléans performers' many and varied career paths, both before and after their time in New Orleans, as in many ways they are representative of the careers of so many working musicians on the move. On November 15, 1834, the *Cecilia*, a three-masted ship, arrived at the New Orleans dockside, after a fifty-two-day transatlantic voyage from Nantes. On board were nineteen crew members and twenty-seven passengers, among whom, according to the preserved passenger list, were a doctor, a surgeon, several businessmen, and fourteen "actors": Pierre Davis and the new members of the Théâtre d'Orléans troupe.[85]

Unusually, in the autumn of 1834, few of the new recruits were singers: most of the vocal performers from the previous season were continuing. But among those who arrived was the new principal tenor, the twenty-eight-year-old Charles Heymann. Born in Frankfurt, Heymann was reported to have sung in Lyon and Amiens and a handful of other French regional theaters before his departure for New Orleans, but never in Paris.[86] Nonetheless, during the six years he stayed in New Orleans, his performances were important in sparking and shaping New Orleans audiences' love affair with French *grand opéra*: he sang the title role in Meyerbeer's *Robert le diable* at its New Orleans premiere in 1835, and Raoul in the composer's *Les Huguenots* in 1839 (both of which are discussed in chapter 2). Heymann returned to the French provinces in 1840, and he was engaged as a *ténor léger* in Dijon in 1842 and as premier *ténor* in Brest in 1843.[87] By 1845, he was singing in the much-lower-ranking provincial theater at Saint-Quentin.[88] What became of him after that, I have been unable to discover, but there is no evidence that he ever took on a contract in Paris, instead spending his whole career in the (northern) French provinces, with a six-year stint in New Orleans.

Two more of the incoming performers, Monsieur Clément and Madame Gertrude Bailly, traveled together with their six-year-old daughter. Bailly had trained as a singer at the conservatory in Lille, and he was applauded for his performances in *grand opéra* in New Orleans.[89] They were one of a number of families among the theater's performers in the late 1830s. Among their colleagues in the troupe were the husband and wife pair Adolphe and Minette Dunaud (accompanied by their twelve-year-old son),[90] and the soprano Mme Bamberger and her cellist husband.[91] While Bailly's daughter did not perform on stage, some other troupe members' children did: Aimée Prévost, the daughter of the *chef d'orchestre* Eugène Prévost, performed as part of the Théâtre d'Orléans troupe in 1854,[92] while the bass M. Douvry and his daughter appeared on stage together in 1845.[93]

Two of the passengers on the *Cecilia* listed as "actors"—Joseph Vallière and Charles Jobey—were orchestral musicians. Vallière, the Théâtre d'Orléans's new principal oboist for the 1834–1835 season, was born in Pamplona, Spain, on April 2, 1814,[94] and he trained at the Paris Conservatoire. He won second prize among the oboists in 1828 at the age of just fourteen and took first prize the following year.[95] I have been able to uncover nothing of his early professional life, before he boarded the *Cecilia* in 1834. His reception at concerts and in the opera orchestra in New Orleans was always glowing, but his career was sadly cut short: along with his colleague Bailly and another performer, he died of yellow fever during the summer of 1839.[96] Charles Jobey, meanwhile, was a fellow woodwind player—he was engaged as a bassoonist for the Théâtre d'Orléans—but he did not have the illustrious Paris Conservatoire training of Vallière. Born in Rouen in 1812 or 1813, he was only occasionally mentioned in press reports about the opera orchestra and concerts during his six years in New Orleans, and after his return to France he turned away from music as a full-time profession. He became a writer (I consider two of his stories at length in chapter 5) and a vigorous promoter of provincial journalism, editing newspapers in Rouen, Cognac, Rochefort, and various other towns.[97]

Jobey was far from alone in diversifying in this way: working musicians' careers were often not limited to a single path. Jules-Henri Brésil, who sang at the Théâtre d'Orléans in 1843–1844, also turned to writing, but in his case to writing libretti. He collaborated most notably with Adolphe d'Ennery on the libretti for Adolphe Adam's *Si j'étais roi* (1853) and Gounod's *Le Tribut de Zamora* (1881).[98] The tenor Archille Lecourt, meanwhile, moved from singing to theater direction after his eighteen-month stint in the Théâtre d'Orléans troupe. On his return to Paris in 1844, he initially accepted a contract at the Théâtre-Lyrique, before taking over the management of the Théâtre du Vaudeville from 1850.[99] For most others, their careers as performers were supplemented by activities as teachers and also as composers. Pierre-Jacques Chéret, who sang in New Orleans from 1819 to 1826, returned to Paris that year and made a career for himself as the composer of popular romances and short "dramatic scenes."[100]

These members of the troupe of 1834–1835, then, had a mixture of French provincial contracts, sometimes with engagements in Paris, but sometimes without: it was perfectly possible to sustain a career without a contract at a major Parisian theater. What the recruits of 1834 did not reflect, however, was the way in which many singers who took contracts at the Théâtre d'Orléans had careers that extended further afield to French theaters in neighboring European countries, or even elsewhere in the world. The soprano Uranie Cambier, for example, worked at the theaters in Brussels, Antwerp, and Liège before she went to New Orleans in 1855,[101] while Eugénie Geismar (another soprano) worked at The Hague before going to New Orleans in 1859, and at Ghent and Liège upon her return.[102] Meanwhile, some singers had experience at French colonial theaters in the Caribbean (the baritone Gustave Blès spent at least one season in Guadeloupe),[103] while the soprano Mademoiselle Fleury, who was part of the New Orleans troupe from 1822 to 1828, found herself singing in Mauritius and Calcutta with a touring French opera troupe in 1836.[104]

While the mobility of the performers' careers speaks for itself, the French press also played an important role in creating a public perception of transatlantic operatic performance. Newspapers inevitably picked up on the exceptional and most surprising examples of transatlantic careers, highlighting, among others, the case of the fourteen-year-old Béatrix Person, who tricked her mother into signing her contract to go to New Orleans (by covering "la Nouvelle" with her thumb, allowing her to assume that she was going to the French provincial town of Orléans for eighteen months), and the singer Pierre-Jacques Chéret, who was said to have stowed away on a ship from Le Havre to cross the Atlantic.[105] Theatrical gossip frequently exoticized or otherwise romanticized the picture of transatlantic theatrical engagements, but it also helped create the perception of "workaday" performers—not just big stars—as international artists.

The most illuminating example of this trend and the myths that could grow up around performers' movements is that of the eccentric tenor Théophile Rousseau-Lagrave, the son of a watchmaker from Château-Gontier, in northwest France, who experimented with painting and then with the monastic life before eventually turning to singing. He worked first in Rennes (1845), then Bordeaux (1849–1851), and at the Théâtre-Lyrique in Paris in the 1851–1852 season.[106] He returned to Bordeaux in 1853, before performing at the Paris Opéra in 1854. After a brief engagement there that was said "not to have left any great mark on the artistic world, or rather . . . was like a shooting star," he moved to New Orleans to sing with the Théâtre d'Orléans troupe between 1855 and 1858.[107]

But perhaps the most remarkable thing about Lagrave was the way that his death was reported in the French press. Indeed, he was afforded the dubious honor of the most complex demise imaginable: he was reported as having died in at least three different places at three different times. The Parisian paper *Le Ménestrel* felt obliged to quash rumors of his death in the summer of 1858, by saying the author knew that Lagrave was on his way to Paris from there, and preparing to sing at Le Havre and Rouen.[108] Although he had not died in 1858, the claim that he was coming to Paris was also untrue, as he was listed on playbills in New Orleans as late as December 1858. That same newspaper then published a statement in January 1861 to say that Lagrave's family had just heard the news of his death in New Orleans, "where his health had been unable to stand the climate" (despite his having lived there for five years already).[109] Other accounts suggest that he died in the middle of the Atlantic, drowned in a shipwreck on the way home to France.[110]

Myths of Lagrave's death were still emerging fifteen years later. One account from 1875, for example, stated that he had been found dead in 1860 by the gates of Milan.[111] This story resonates with that told by the singer-turned-writer Auguste Laget in his *Le Monde artiste* in 1883: he insists that Lagrave moved to Milan in the autumn of 1857, where he, "having barely settled in, threw himself to the study of the language and of Italian songs."[112] After his career as an Italian opera singer failed to take off, however, Laget reports that Lagrave sadly hanged himself a year or so later. While the dates of this story cannot possibly be correct, as he was still performing in New Orleans in December 1858, the details Laget provides about François-Marcel Junca (who had sung at the Théâtre d'Orléans at the same time as Lagrave) rushing to embrace his old friend's body and making the funeral arrangements give the sorry tale an air of plausibility.[113] Whatever the actual circumstances of his demise, the truth was probably less interesting than the layering up of myths around him. The fact that he was reported as dying at different times in so many different places is testament to the degree of travel that characterized his career: he was immortalized repeatedly as a peripatetic artist, with all the mystique that a roving career created. Indeed, the transatlantic operatic system relied as much on the discourses and perceptions of mobility that emerged around performers as on the practical facts of their movement.

A CONTRACT IN NEW ORLEANS

What, then, could a performer expect from a contract in New Orleans? An engagement of eighteen months was standard for most singers at the Théâtre d'Orléans once the theater had stabilized its patterns of seasons and recruitment in the mid-1820s. This meant that performers would spend two seasons and one summer break in New Orleans.[114] Since recruitment took place every year, some of the existing troupe would remain in the United States each summer to wait for the next season, while those who had completed their contracts would return to Europe, to be replaced by new recruits. When the management of the theater wanted to secure a first-class performer, however, they sometimes made shorter contracts, as in the case of the soprano Mademoiselle Cordier, who took a leave of absence ("congé") from her three-year contract at the Opéra-Comique in Paris to spend six months singing in New Orleans.[115] Shorter contracts, too, were sometimes used for non-singers, as in the case of Sarah Cohen, a young girl from New York, who was engaged by the Théâtre d'Orléans as a *danseuse* for "five to six months, at the discretion of the director, M. Davis," in 1846, during which time she was required to "dance in all the works that the administration decides to mount, in entr'actes, ballets, pantomimes" and also to play mime roles.[116]

The general terms of the theater's employment, which were standard for singers, orchestral musicians, and dancers, consisted of twenty-three clauses, and these can be found in full in the contract pro forma in the first appendix to this book.[117] They covered everything from the artists' general conduct (including the fines they would face for unprofessional behavior) and their rights in case of sickness, to the provision of costumes and materials, rehearsal and performance etiquette, and loyalty to the theater and its business. Even without the specific terms that were added to individual performers' contracts, the general terms of engagement give a detailed insight into the workings of this particular theater, as well as the nature of nineteenth-century theatrical employment more broadly. The clauses specifying the behavior of the orchestral musicians, for example, forbade them from climbing over the barrier between the orchestra area and the parterre to talk to friends during the intervals in performances. Others deal with the behavior of the domestic servant that performers were permitted to bring with them to the theater to help them dress.[118]

Furthermore, the general terms of engagement provide insight into the balance of power between employer and employee which, on the whole, was firmly skewed in favor of the theater management. There was nothing in the general terms and conditions that entitled a performer to leave of any kind (and I have not found any personalized, individual contracts that afforded performers any leave, either), meaning that they had to work anything up to five nights a week, for the months the theater was open. Nor were there any clauses about retirement benefits—something which employees at the Paris Opéra had been afforded after fifteen years of service until the 1830s—presumably because the usual contract length was only eighteen months: an operatic system built on short-term contracts gave the management no cause to think of their employees' futures.[119]

The three clauses relating to sickness, too, were in many respects directed more to the protection of the management against loss than to the benefit of the indisposed performer, as they dwell on all the ways in which a singer could attempt to cheat the management, by claiming themselves to be ill and then going out on "trips to the countryside," having "supper parties," or teaching "pupils in town."[120] If a doctor certified that a performer had faked an illness or was malingering, the management reserved the right to terminate their contract with immediate effect. The most the terms afforded the performer was immunity from being sacked for short-term illness (chronic illness, according to the final clause of the contract, was still a reason for the management to terminate a singer's contract), and in most other respects they offered little protection. Indeed, even if a doctor verified their illness, they were presumably still subject to other clauses in the contract that stated that they would be fined for causing a delay or other disruption to scheduled performances.

The contractual process at the Théâtre d'Orléans, therefore, was designed in large part to ensure that the performer agreed to do whatever the management required of them during the period of their engagement. In the case of the young dancer Sarah Cohen—still a child when she was employed by the Théâtre d'Orléans in 1846—there were no additional terms considering her status as a minor, and she was subject to exactly the same terms as her adult colleagues. This was not surprising at the time, as there were no child labor laws introduced in the United States until the twentieth century, but to a modern reader it appears quite shocking.[121] A child in Cohen's position needed the protection of a parent to ensure that her rights were upheld, and her father supervised her engagements and, when needed, took action to enforce her rights.[122] Béatrix Person, mentioned earlier in this chapter, who was engaged at the theater in 1838–1840, however, had no such protection, as she traveled alone, unchaperoned, at the age of fourteen. The recruiter for the Théâtre d'Orléans (violinist Adolphe Elie that year) did insist that her mother sign her contract, as she was still a child, but no one ensured that she was accompanied during her employment in New Orleans, and once she was in the United States she received no other special consideration for her status as a minor. Child labor was more of a "hot topic" in France in the 1830s than it was in the United States, with various groups campaigning for legislation to prevent children under the age of eight from working and to place restrictions on the number of hours children under the age of sixteen could work.[123] This legislation was passed in 1841, although how closely it was implemented during the 1840s and 1850s is not clear.

Although such power imbalances between management and performers are striking from a present-day perspective, at the time the performers who agreed to sign a contract to go to New Orleans presumably did not find its terms considerably worse than those they signed for other engagements both in France and elsewhere, or else they would likely not have signed it. Indeed, while they needed work, there were plenty of theaters in France, Europe, and the world beyond that needed performers, and New Orleans was far from their only choice: it was not a decision forced upon them, but a prospect that in many respects must have looked inviting.

In this light, it is worth reflecting on what singers who came to New Orleans were actually paid. Salaries were tailored to individuals, based on what they had managed to negotiate with the Théâtre d'Orléans's appointed recruiter before signing their contracts. As discussed above, in 1819 and 1824, Davis had given his recruiter, Jean-Baptiste Sel, complete liberty to negotiate salaries and advances with performers, based on what he felt they would be worth to the theater. In 1824, Sel engaged Boniface Henry Warnet and Edward Clozel, who signed their contracts within weeks of each other in Paris (September 9, 1824, and August 14, 1824, respectively). While Warnet was paid 1,000 francs upon signing his contract and 10,000 francs per annum, to be delivered in monthly installments, Edward Clozel was paid only 750 francs up front, with an annual salary of 6,000 francs to be paid in monthly installments. The difference between them was that Warnet was "one of the best performers," while Clozel was a lower-ranked performer.[124]

In 1840, performers' salaries had become higher still. Paul Coeuriot, a tenor of the second order, earned \$190 (950 francs) each month in the 1839–1840 season, while the theater's first-rank singers were paid an additional \$80 (420 francs) each month, giving them total earnings of 24,660 francs for a contract of eighteen months.[125] Some earned even more, at the management's discretion: the French press reported in July 1840 that Auguste Nourrit (the less well-known brother of the famous French tenor Adolphe Nourrit) had been engaged by the Théâtre d'Orléans for 35,000 francs for what appears to have been a single season of six months, making his monthly earnings roughly 5,833 francs.[126] To put into perspective just how impressive that salary was, if indeed it was accurately reported, Gilbert Duprez—the famous Parisian tenor whose arrival at the Opéra had displaced Adolphe Nourrit as Paris's top male star—earned 60,440 francs (combining his basic salary of 40,000 with additional benefits) for a whole year at the Paris Opéra in the 1844–1845 season.[127]

As in Europe, performers could supplement their basic salaries. I have found no mention of singers in New Orleans receiving "feux"—the additional, per-performance fees received by performers at the Paris Opéra and Opéra-Comique during this period—but benefit performances were written into performers' contracts.[128] Kimberly White has suggested that in Paris, benefit performances or concerts were only provided to lower-ranking performers if they had been "injured on the job and could no longer work," but in New Orleans even lower-ranking performers were contractually entitled to these lucrative events.[129] They often shared benefit performances, dividing the takings between them, but even half a benefit performance was a vital part of their engagement, providing a considerable supplement to their usual salary. Sarah Cohen, the aforementioned child dancer from New York employed by the Théâtre d'Orléans in 1846, was paid \$80 a month (which would have amounted to an annual salary of \$960, or 5,040 francs) but was additionally promised a fee of \$200 for half of a benefit performance, meaning that in a single evening she was able to earn two and a half times her normal monthly wage.[130]

The singers at the Théâtre d'Orléans were by no means badly paid compared with others in their position, as table 1.1 shows, although they earned nowhere near the massive sums commanded by the best-known Italian opera performers at home and abroad. In many cases, the wages they received in New Orleans would have been better than those which they would have been paid at most Parisian theaters. Indeed, among the musical theaters in Paris, salaries varied dramatically (as one would perhaps expect, given the large state subsidies given to the Opéra and Opéra-Comique in the early part of the nineteenth century). For a performer who was not able to secure

TABLE 1.1 Salaries paid to theatrical performers in Europe

ROLE/PERFORMER	LOCATION	MONTHLY SALARY	YEAR
Premier rôle[1]	Paris Odéon	FF 500	1829
Premier ténor[2]	Lyon	FF 416	1829
Premier ténor	Le Havre	FF 833	1840
Première chanteuse	Le Havre	FF 1,166	1840
Comédie/drame/ vaudeville performers	Le Havre	FF 416	1840
Premier rôle	Paris Opéra	FF 7,000/8,000	1840
Choriste	Paris Opéra	FF 45	1840
Remplacement[3] (understudy)	Paris Opéra	FF 600	1827
Giuditta Pasta[4]	Venice	FF 1,000 per performance	1833
Marietta Alboni[5]	Madrid	FF 2,660 per performance	1850

1. A proposed budget for the Paris Odéon in 1829 allocated 6,000 francs a year for a *premier rôle*, either male or female, who would play tragedies, dramas, and comedies, but only 5,000 if they could not play tragic roles. Anne Martin-Fugier, *Comédienne: de Mlle Mars à Sarah Bernhardt* (Paris: Seuil, 2001), 59.
2. In 1836, by contrast, the *premier ténor* at the same Grand Théâtre de Lyon received an annual salary of 30,000 francs for his services (2,500 francs a month), but this seems to have been an exceptional salary. See Martin-Fugier, *Comédienne*, 59–60. All of the information on French salaries in this table can be found in Martin-Fugier, *Comédienne*, 59–61.
3. Kimberly White lists the Remplacement's annual salary in 1827 as 7,200 francs in White, *Female Singers on the French Stage*, 62.
4. For information on the salaries paid to Italian opera singers, see John Rosselli, *The Opera Industry in Italy from Cimarosa to Verdi*, 58–65, and for information on Pasta, see 70. In 1827, Pasta was paid 57,500 francs plus a benefit performance for the April to July season in London. Rosselli, *The Opera Industry in Italy from Cimarosa to Verdi*, 64.
5. Rosselli, *The Opera Industry in Italy from Cimarosa to Verdi*, 65.

a *premier rôle* at the Paris Opéra (whether through age, through want of talent or training, or through lack of opportunity), the financial possibilities of a trip to New Orleans must have looked inviting. The fact that the abovementioned Edward Clozel could earn 500 francs a month as a low-ranking performer shows just how good the salaries in New Orleans were by comparison with similar positions in French theaters.

Moreover, to put the money at stake into perspective, all these salaries (with the exception of those of the poor *choristes* at the Opéra) were generally much larger than those earned by people in other skilled employment.

For example, a teacher in Paris could be expected to earn 1,800 francs a year by 1836,[131] and a professor could earn 4,000 francs a year in 1840.[132] A journeyman typically only earned three to five francs per day for between ten and twelve hours' work, while a workman could expect a maximum of one franc fifty cents for his labors.[133] Meanwhile, in Louisiana, 1840 saw the state attorney general earning $3,000 (15,750 francs) a year, and a plantation overseer could earn $425 (2,231 francs 25 cents) annually.[134] While it is hard to find enough salary detail across different professions in the same years to make an exhaustive comparison, from the details I have found, the wages earned by the Théâtre d'Orléans performers were high enough to place even second-rank performers into the highest wage brackets both in France and in the United States: the promise of such wages doubtless served as a considerable incentive for singers to make the move across the Atlantic.

PROBLEMS

Nonetheless, for some performers, a contract in New Orleans came with problems. On July 5, 1840, a letter appeared in the Parisian *Gazette des théâtres*: "Some more useful advice for artists who would like to go to New Orleans."[135] At length, it detailed the tribulations of ten performers who had undertaken a contract at the Théâtre d'Orléans, including several who had first arrived in the city on the *Cecilia* in November 1834. The performers bemoaned their treatment at the hands of the Théâtre d'Orléans management, noting everything from the ill effects of the local climate to unforeseen expenses, unpaid salaries, and rescinded passages back to France. They complained as follows:

> When they sign the contracts in Paris, the artists are showered with respect, with attention and care. They are promised the earth, but once in New Orleans all that changes, the direction shows its true colors, complaints are ridiculed and openly laughed at—and they find themselves stuck 2,000 leagues from France!!! . . . We have far too many colleagues who are in the most horrible position in New Orleans, on account of not having reflected enough . . . when they signed their contract in France; they are pariahs of the administration, which exploits their poverty . . . without a miracle, they will never see the soil of their homeland again.[136]

The complaints made by the signatories of this letter were far from unique: throughout the Théâtre d'Orléans's history, the principal source of dispute between the theater's performers and management, predictably enough, was money. In particular, the amount and timely payment of their salaries and the principal singers' responsibility for providing their own costumes, at their own expense, caused frequent complaints.

In order to prove their points about financial hardship, the ten artists who wrote to the *Gazette des théâtres* in 1840 listed the monthly expenditure of an individual performer "of the first rank," as shown in table 1.2. On top of these costs, they listed another $80 or 420 francs of "unforeseen expenses," which were presumably not monthly, but more irregular expenses, including clothing. The costs of such clothing, as given in the performers' letter, can be seen in table 1.3. The performers complained bitterly that in the face of such expenses, they were not being paid enough to live on.

TABLE 1.2 Monthly expenses of Théâtre d'Orléans performers

EXPENSE (PER MONTH)	COST IN DOLLARS	COST IN FRANCS
Lodging	$20	FF 104.80
Board	$25	FF 141
Personal laundry	$5	FF 26
Theater laundry	$5	FF 26
Domestic servant	$12	FF 67
Money spent for pleasure	$10	FF 53
Total	$77	FF 407.80

The letter supplies the costs in both dollars and francs.

TABLE 1.3 Costs of men's clothing, as stated in the performers' letter

ITEM	COST IN DOLLARS	COST IN FRANCS
1 Suit ("habit de ville")	$45	FF 236.25
1 Pair of trousers	$16	FF 84
1 Frock coat ("redingote")	$33	FF 183.75
1 Cotton shirt	$3	FF 15.75
1 Hat	$5	FF 26.25
1 Pair of boots	$8	FF 42
1 Waistcoat	$12	FF 63
1 Pair of gloves	$1	FF 5.25
1 Pair of socks	$0.50	FF 2.55
1 Regular cravat	$3	FF 15.75

The letter supplies the costs in both dollars and francs.

Given these figures alone, it is hard to see what exactly the performers who wrote to the *Gazette des théâtres* were complaining about. The second-rank tenor Paul Coeuriot's monthly salary of 950 francs (as stated in *L'Abeille*) would have been sufficient not only to cover his regular costs, but also to buy him a new suit each month, and yet he still signed the letter. The performers, however, went on to detail further expenses they incurred in sourcing suitable costumes:

> There was an artist who, in order to complete a costume for the role of a *voltigeur* [a light infantry soldier], spent $16 or 84 francs. The women are obliged to pay fees to their dressmaker and hairdresser—the least still costs 40 francs a month . . . Everything is at your expense, even the costumes for trouser roles; four years ago, when they put on [Fromental Halévy's] *L'Eclair*, the person who filled the role of Georges (being obliged to by the lack of tenors at that period) was forced to pay for the costumes from her own pocket.[137]

The example of the "*voltigeur*" is an important one here, as this was almost certainly a small role, rather than a principal part. Indeed, the general rules of the Théâtre d'Orléans made it clear that not only did the singers have to provide costumes when they played lead roles, but they also had to provide costumes when they were asked by the management to fill in minor or chorus roles out of convenience ("rôles de complaisance") or even roles *en travesti*.[138] These additional expenses could be quite considerable, as the performers pointed out in their letter to the *Gazette des théâtres*.

What added even further to at least some performers' costs for costumes was that they ordered them from Paris and had them shipped to New Orleans, as they continued to rely on their existing French networks to source their outfits. In 1842, Bernadet, a *basse-taille* (bass-baritone) in the Théâtre d'Orléans troupe, engaged the services of Jean-Louis Nonnon, costumier of the Paris Opéra, to whom he paid the significant sum of 666 francs for new costumes for his roles in New Orleans.[139] The desire to source costumes from Paris rather than locally was not necessarily an indication of snobbery on the part of the performers: newspapers from New Orleans at the time reveal that most upmarket shops selling clothing in the city in the early part of the nineteenth century imported their wares from Paris, so for the performers to do the same was not a snub to local resources, but a common and widely accepted way of procuring outfits.[140] Even beyond New Orleans, there are indications that it was not uncommon for theatrical performers to order costumes from Paris, as some French provincial theaters also made costume orders in Paris, at least for important and new productions. The Parisian

Tribune dramatique, for example, reported on a production of Halévy's *Les Mousquetaires de la Reine* in Amiens in December 1846, writing of "the luxury of costumes made by Nonnon of the Opéra."[141] Theaters and performers could turn to Paris for costumes when they wanted a production to carry an air of luxury or, indeed, as was the case with the *grand opéra* repertoire, when they needed costumes to reflect a particular historical period, rather than the contemporary outfits that most often suited for *opéra-comique*.[142]

The annoyance of the additional expense of costumes, however, reflects only a superficial level of conflict between performers and management over pay; at various points, they faced deeper issues. Indeed, in the 1840s, various performers felt they had been cheated by the theater administration. When he wrote to Nonnon about his costumes in 1842, the bass-baritone Bernadet complained openly:

> I am still here, my good Mr. Nonnon, for another month and a half. As soon as I leave this wretched place I will bring myself to Paris. . . . I was deceived by the directors, I have made a loss of eight percent, which is in fact 800 francs less than the engagement should have brought me, and that is without many other cases of filibustering that I have observed on the part of the direction.[143]

His complaints about the unfair loss of pay were shared by the artists in their letter to the *Gazette des théâtres* in 1840. First, they stated that they had only been paid for sixteen of the eighteen months of their contract, as the administration had failed to pay them for a couple of months over the summer. And second, they said that the administration would only pay them in promissory notes, not in cash (doubtless reflecting the theater's precarious financial situation in the early 1840s), and that in recent years, perhaps since the international financial crisis of 1837, banks had been reluctant to honor promissory notes.[144] As a result, in order to turn their monthly paychecks into cash, the artists had been obliged to pay an 8 to 10 percent fee each time.[145]

The disputes over salaries, as with the formation of the Society of Artists in 1843 discussed in the first part of this chapter, then, hint at wider economic issues of the time that extended far beyond the Théâtre d'Orléans and affected the burgeoning transatlantic theater industry at large. In particular, the performers' complaints in the *Gazette des théâtres* highlight not just the issue of turning promissory notes into cash in New Orleans, but of sending money back to France, whether that be to pay for costumes or support family and other dependents. The singers who signed their contracts in France (which is to say, almost all of them) signed documents in which their salary was listed in francs. Once in New Orleans, of course, they were paid not in francs but in dollars. This, the performers would have expected: a note on the theater's general terms, which all performers would have received in their contractual documents, stated clearly for their information that one dollar was the equivalent of 5.25 francs.[146] As the performers writing to the *Gazette des théâtres* discovered, however, when trying to send money across the Atlantic, correspondent banks in France might not have given precisely the same exchange rate as stated in the theater's terms (although it would have been close), and they would charge a further hefty fee to release the money to its intended recipient. The performers were therefore disappointed to discover that they did not have quite as much money as they expected, once such charges had been taken into account. While the performers' wages were good by both New Orleans and Parisian standards, the losses they incurred in converting promissory notes to cash and sending money abroad, as well as the various unforeseen expenses that arose, meant that what had seemed like a very good financial deal when they signed their contracts in Paris was no longer quite so good in practice. Such financial disappointments could serve as an uncomfortable reminder for performers that they were a long way from home.

THE STATUS OF ARTISTIC LABOR

Although some of the problems singers faced with their contracts and salaries were due to malpractice on the part of the management or issues with transatlantic movement and pay, an important component of the discontents was one of perception. That is to say, there was a disconnect between singers' perceptions of their own worth and managerial and public perceptions of the value of artistic labor. In the final part of this chapter, I explore how this disconnect generated considerable friction between performers and management and also, on occasion, between performers and the public.

The style in which the performers arrived in New Orleans gave them every reason to think they were to be treated as celebrities in the city. If the Parisian *Gazette des théâtres* is to be believed, the aforementioned new recruits of 1834, arriving on the *Cecilia,* had sustained themselves on lunches of twelve to fifteen dishes and dinners of in excess of twenty dishes over the fifty-two days of their voyage. In order to provide these impressive meals, there had been on board:

> A cow, 550 fowls, 2,000 eggs, twenty-four pigs and sheep, six calves, 300 crates of preserved products, peas, liver pâté, 150 cheeses, six barrels of fine wine, forty cases of Bordeaux wine and Champagne, twenty cases of liqueurs, 500 pounds of sugar, coffee, chocolate, etc.[147]

Every Thursday and Sunday evening, the article states, the dinner was followed by a ball. Such opulence must have felt unusual for many within the group, whose careers had involved little luxury up to this point, but one to which they hoped they would have the opportunity to become accustomed.

After their arrival in New Orleans, the way audiences treated key performers doubtless confirmed their sense of being stars. The men of the audience were known to lavish incredibly expensive gifts upon their most-beloved singers in ways that were reported internationally: the Parisian *Revue et Gazette musicale* reported in an article about the theater in New Orleans on July 1, 1855, that people threw diamonds "in the shape of a cross, in brooches, rings, in the most ravishing mounts" onto the stage for Mme Cambier after her performance in Fromental Halévy's grand opéra *Charles VI*.[148]

Principal performers—particularly the female singers—inspired passionate, partisan loyalties among the New Orleans public, but that public could also bring them back down to earth if their egos became overinflated. One particularly clear example of this is New Orleans's very own "diva war," which took place in the spring of 1841.[149] The Théâtre d'Orléans's two prima donnas that season were Mademoiselle Julia Calvé and Madame Bamberger. Calvé's fame was well established in New Orleans, as she had been singing at the Théâtre d'Orléans since 1837, while Bamberger had joined the troupe the following season and had been quietly gaining support. Fans of Calvé resented Bamberger as an interloper, while fans of Bamberger believed that Calvé's ego was overinflated. Not only did the two groups spar across the pages of the local press, but tensions came to a head physically in March 1841 when supporters of Madame Bamberger dared to throw bouquets to her following a performance in which Calvé had played the star role. Calvé threw her own bouquet to the floor and stormed from the stage in a fit of pique. Two nights later, at the next performance, the singers' supporters were ready to continue hostilities. Calvé, her composure restored, came to the front of the stage to seek forgiveness, explaining that she had not meant to insult the audience on her previous appearance. However, as the *Daily Picayune* reported, "either [her] apology was not humble enough or else the people in the house were determined not to forgive her, for a terrible din was kept up every time she attempted to sing during the evening, and not a note she uttered was heard."[150] The public did not allow her hubris to go unpunished.

The performers were right to believe that they and their art were generally highly appreciated in New Orleans, but underlying the disputes highlighted above were deeper questions about the social status and value of musical and theatrical artists in the city. When the ten performers sent their open letter of complaint to the Parisian press in 1840, it did not go unnoticed in New

Orleans: Parisian newspapers crossed the Atlantic on the ships that brought people and other goods, bringing news to the city between six and ten weeks after its publication in Paris. On September 16, 1840 (ten and a half weeks after the original letter appeared in the *Gazette des théâtres*), the New Orleans paper *L'Abeille* published a response to the performers' complaints.

Its author (who signed himself "G. A. M.") came to the defense of the Théâtre d'Orléans management, arguing that the performers (about many of whom he knew detailed personal information) were being deeply unfair in their complaints and suggesting that the signatories of the letter had an excessively elevated perception of their own importance. He stated that none of the singers who had complained were actually "of the first rank" as they had suggested, but instead were lesser performers who were trying to live a lifestyle ill suited to their means.[151] He was keen to point out that even lower-ranking singers were paid enough to live on, and took an unsympathetic tone with their complaints, saying that if they were struggling to pay their way, the men should stop "going to balls, gambling, and spending three-quarters of their time in restaurants and cafés," and the women should sacrifice some of their jewels and buy the latest dresses rather less frequently. These activities were what he claimed were causing their financial difficulties; the fact that audiences praised their work, the author argued, did not give performers the right to act above their station or their financial means.[152]

These performers, then, occupied a unique position within society in New Orleans. On the one hand, they were idolized and lavished with the most expensive of gifts, but on the other hand, they were simply providers of a particular kind of public service within the city: it would not be too great an exaggeration to suggest that access to theatrical performances in New Orleans in this period was almost seen as a citizen's right. In the course of his response to the performers' letter to the *Gazette des théâtres*, G. A. M. reduced them from their deified status to that of lowly workers, pointing out that they had a service to provide and that if they were not doing it satisfactorily, then they served little purpose. This precarious position offers a tantalizing glimpse of the bind of the nineteenth-century operatic performer: operatic labor was construed very differently from that provided by the many other skilled workers who crossed the Atlantic during this period, but at the same time the performers could not escape from reminders that they remained, in fact, dependent—and indeed disposable—employees of the theater.

When it came to resolving employment disputes, there were several available channels. The signatories of the letter in the *Gazette des théâtres* took an informal approach by writing to the Parisian press. While they claimed their aim in doing so was to save other performers from the trials and tribulations they had faced, they doubtless hoped that the potential for reputational damage caused by their words would shame the Théâtre d'Orléans management into improving conditions. As they all knew, the theater relied on being able to recruit performers in France, and if it no longer seemed like an attractive prospect to potential employees, it would find itself in big trouble. Besides their salary woes, the signatories of the letter sought to discourage potential recruits even further by emphasizing the dangerous climate of New Orleans, saying that five of their colleagues had died of yellow fever during their contracts (G. A. M.'s response in *L'Abeille*, however, was quick to argue that it was not yellow fever but sunstroke, caused by the Europeans' irresponsible behavior during the height of the summer heat, that had carried off the performers). What effect this strategy of appealing to the press had for the ten singers who added their names to the letter, I have not been able to discern, but it presumably did not end too badly for them: Paul Coeuriot, one of the signatories, sang again in the New Orleans troupe from 1844 to 1845.[153]

There were also more formal means of resolving disputes than writing to the press. On various occasions throughout the theater's existence, the administration appeared in court against performers in New Orleans. In 1826, John Davis took the performers Henry Warnet and Edward Clozel to court for breaching the terms of their contract by trying to leave their engagement before the end of their eighteen-month term.[154] Davis won the case, with the court finding that he had paid the performers fully and on time; he was awarded damages for the inconvenience caused by the performers' violations of their contracts. In another case, the father of Sarah Cohen, the previously mentioned child dancer, took Pierre Davis to court for breaking the conditions of his daughter's contract.[155] He sued him for $190 unpaid salary (two months' wages for her) and $250 damages. The court found that Davis had a right not to give Cohen performances, if he felt her dancing was not to the taste of the theater's audiences, but that he could not refuse to pay her: Cohen's father was awarded the $190 unpaid salary, but not the damages he had requested.[156]

While the fact that court proceedings exist at all reflects the way in which the employment of performers in New Orleans was a formalized process in which both employers and employees had rights, it was doubtless considerably easier for the Davises, as permanent residents of Louisiana and influential figures in city life, to take performers to court than it was for them—strangers in a foreign land—to undertake proceedings against their employers. Cohen and her father were American residents, based in New York before her engagement in New Orleans, but I have found no evidence of performers from Europe taking the theater management to court. This was not because they had no complaints, as the singers' letter to the *Gazette des théâtres* and Bernadet's note to Nonnon showed, but perhaps because it was harder or very expensive for them to access legal support. The Théâtre d'Orléans management, then, retained the upper hand in solving disputes with its performers.

To return to the analogy of the theatrical machine with which this chapter began: the Théâtre d'Orléans had its mechanical dimensions, in the form of the processes that regulated recruitment and other aspects of the administrative structure year after year. The people who have populated this chapter, however, were not simply the machine operators, but also its cogs, although they were all too human and unpredictable to be anything like mechanical components. Their interactions—the points at which they clicked or created friction—were shaped by individuals' actions and desires, but also by wider economic forces and social and cultural expectations.

The economic and cultural dimensions of transatlantic connection are not easily disentangled, as performers' concerns about wages quickly blurred with larger questions about how artists and their art should be valued. Behind these questions, too, lurked larger issues concerning the increasing mobility of the (operatic) world. Movement was on the one hand prized—indeed, fetishized—by the press and its readers, as people in New Orleans reveled in the fact that their troupe was recruited in Europe and readers on both sides of the Atlantic were treated to reports of performers whose incessant travels were stopped by death alone. But on the other hand, the specificities of place determined not only the practicalities of operatic production but also people's expectations of it.

The networks of transatlantic opera operated on a geographical level, connecting (and sometimes opposing) the city of New Orleans with provincial France, Paris, and many other places besides. But they also operated between people within a space, as the threads of relationships between individuals became bound together with interactions between professional groups—singers and managers, shipping agents and recruiters, and so on—in a less personal, but no less important sense. While geography gave the transatlantic networks their breadth, then, these varied human relationships gave them their body and substance. Combined, they made the Théâtre d'Orléans far more than an operatic machine.

2

Transatlantic Production and Transatlantic Reception

Positioning New Orleans through Grand Opéra

On July 4, 1849, the composer Giacomo Meyerbeer penned a short letter in Paris:

> I have asked the directors of the Opéra to permit you to come on stage at the Opéra during the performance today and the one on Friday (which will be the last of *Le Prophète*), in order to be able to examine more closely the décor, the stage machinery, etc.[1]

Written just over two months after the outstandingly successful (albeit much-delayed) premiere of *Le Prophète*, this message is a rarity in Meyerbeer's correspondence, one of barely a handful of surviving instances in which he requested a "laissez-passer" for anyone at the Paris Opéra in the whole duration of his career.[2] The honor would have allowed the recipient unparalleled insight into all the elements—human and mechanical—that brought his vast *grand opéra* to life. Any number of composers and critics would doubtless have leapt at such an opportunity, but the recipient was neither of those things: Meyerbeer's correspondent here was Pierre Davis, in Europe for the summer to recruit a new troupe. The pair met on several occasions in the late 1840s and early 1850s, with Meyerbeer arranging for Davis to purchase the scores for his latest operas, as well as occasionally assisting him with recruiting suitable prima donnas.

The letter from Meyerbeer to Davis demonstrates how the composer himself maintained an ongoing involvement in the dissemination of his *grands opéras* beyond Paris, and the surviving correspondence between Meyerbeer and his Parisian publisher, Louis Brandus, reveals that he sought to control that dissemination, by approving or denying the sale of his scores to opera companies in cities around the world.[3] More importantly for the purposes of this chapter, however, the letter from Meyerbeer hints at the lengths to which Davis went to research the look and sound of the original productions, before he then went on to import materials for the New Orleans productions from Paris.[4] As Jens Hesselager, Cormac Newark, and others have already observed, transferring *grands opéras* from the stage of the Paris Opéra to the (normally) smaller stage of a less well-known and well-funded theater was an extremely costly and technologically challenging process, which at times called the grandeur of *grand opéra* into question.[5] For Pierre Davis even to investigate the mechanics of producing *Le Prophète* at the Opéra, then, suggests impressively high aspirations for the Théâtre d'Orléans.

By 1849, the Théâtre d'Orléans administration already had considerable experience in staging *grand opéra*. From the theater's opening in 1819 and throughout the 1820s, its repertoire had been dominated by classic *opéras-comiques* from the late eighteenth century and turn of the nineteenth, with Grétry's *La Fausse Magie* (1775), François-Adrien Boieldieu's *Le Calife de Bagdad* (1800), and Étienne Méhul's *Une Folie* (1802) being among the most performed works.[6] John Davis attempted to add at least one work previously unheard in New Orleans each season of the 1820s; he introduced a handful of operas by Rossini (among them *Le Barbier de Séville* in 1822 and *La Pie voleuse* a few years later) and Mozart (*Don Giovanni*), as well as Weber's *Der Freischütz*, all in French translation.[7] Davis gradually added a few more modern *opéras-comiques* by composers such as Ferdinand Hérold and Daniel Auber, but the core repertoire remained surprisingly stable.

By the 1830s, however, audiences began to clamor for more: with two or three short comic works often programmed each night, and the troupe performing as many as five nights a week during a season, audiences inevitably became familiar with certain *opéras-comiques* to the point of exhaustion. The Davises therefore made a deliberate effort to introduce new, up-to-date works to the theater's repertoire on an annual basis; *grand opéra*, as a genre emerging in Europe during that decade, was well placed to meet audiences' demands for novelty in New Orleans.

The arrival of *grand opéra* in the 1830s marked a new and ambitious direction in the theater's programming, and from this decade on, audiences in New Orleans welcomed performances (frequently the American premieres) of many of the latest French *grands opéras* from across the Atlantic, as well as occasional local essays in the genre, such as Eugène Prévost's *Esmeralda* (1842) and the fifteen-year-old Ernest Guiraud's *Le Roi David* (1853).[8] By the mid-nineteenth century, there was nothing short of an insatiable appetite for *grand opéra* in New Orleans. In many cases, the Théâtre d'Orléans was able to produce works very quickly after their Parisian premieres: *Le Prophète,* for example, the work Pierre was granted permission to see from behind the scenes at the Paris Opéra, was performed in New Orleans on April 2, 1850, just under a year after its Parisian premiere. The city's love of *grand opéra* rivaled its popularity in many European capitals and lasted well into the twentieth century. By the time the New Orleans French Opera House, the theater that superseded the Théâtre d'Orléans, was consumed by flames in December 1919, Meyerbeer's *Les Huguenots* had been performed well over 200 times in the city; it was, appropriately enough, the last work heard there before the fire.[9]

Grand opéra's position in the life of New Orleans was by no means straightforward, however, especially in the first decade following its introduction. The genre became a focus for debates about contemporary cultural and political issues: the discourses that developed around it allowed people from different linguistic and cultural factions within the city to negotiate interconnected local, national, and international identities for themselves. At the same time, it served as an impetus toward significant developments both in opera criticism and in the structure and personnel of the troupe.

Underpinning this chapter, then, is a concern for the global afterlives of a genre that has been so closely linked both to the Paris Opéra and to French politics of the 1830s and 1840s in its historiography. While Hesselager and others have recently begun to explore *grand opéra* "on the move" in European contexts beyond Paris, here I want to go further, to explore the transatlantic processes that shaped *grand opéra*'s production and reception in New Orleans, and the lasting impact the genre had on musical and wider cultural life in the city.[10] By exploring the arrival of *grand opéra* in New Orleans—focusing in particular on the first productions of Meyerbeer's *Robert le diable* and *Les Huguenots*—it becomes possible to tease out concerns connected to issues of belonging: concerns that were both shaped by, and explored through, the reception of these works in the Francophone and Anglophone press in New Orleans.

THEATRICAL CRITICISM, CULTURAL RIVALRIES, AND THE OVERLOOKED *LA MUETTE*

Meyerbeer's *Robert le diable* was the second *grand opéra* to be heard in New Orleans. The first, Daniel Auber's *La Muette de Portici,* was first performed at the Théâtre d'Orléans on April 29, 1831—its American premiere—but it drew little comment in the city's press. At the time, New Orleans had two major newspapers, both bilingual, which published discrete French- and English-language sections.[11] The city's longest-standing newspaper, the *Courrier de la Louisiane/The Louisiana Courier* (to give the titles under which the French and English sections were published), did not even review the performance,[12] while *L'Abeille/The Bee* stretched to two short reviews in the French section. The first of these simply assessed the performance of the singers who, at this late stage in the theatrical season (it had started in mid-November 1830), were already very familiar to audiences.[13] The other review, meanwhile, consisted almost exclusively of superficial remarks about the "large musical conception" and referred vaguely to the "theatrical pomp and the decor," before concluding positively that "*La Muette* is one of the spectacles that one must see."[14] No critic commented further on the opera.

While such a brief response might seem surprising given the overheated critical excitement to be generated later over *grand opéra*, it is not necessarily out of keeping with the state of operatic criticism in New Orleans in the early 1830s, and it is worth taking a moment to outline briefly the history of the press in New Orleans during this period and the role of opera and theater criticism within it. Newspapers during the first half of the nineteenth century in New Orleans suffered from the same degree of impermanence as the city's early theaters. Many lasted only a few months before either the enterprise ran out of funds or the editor lost interest in the endeavor and moved on to other things.[15] With a population of just over 27,000 in 1820, of whom nearly a quarter were enslaved people, it is perhaps little surprise that many early newspapers in New Orleans were short lived:[16] although precise circulation numbers are not available for the first half of the nineteenth century, the reading public was not large, and the number of newly founded publications doubtless exceeded demand.[17]

Over the next two decades, however, New Orleans's population grew enormously, swelled both by English speakers moving from the northern states and by substantial waves of immigration from Germany and Ireland, alongside lower levels of ongoing immigration from France. The US Census recorded 46,082 residents in New Orleans in 1830; by 1840, this had swelled to 102,193.[18] These decades not only saw the number of newspapers published increase dramatically, but their content and outlook also changed significantly. The amount of news reporting increased, eventually overtaking their earlier role in transmitting official notices from the state and city governments. In the bilingual newspapers—*Le Courrier de la Louisiane* and *L'Abeille*—the English-language sections began to gain greater independence, no longer simply providing translations of the articles in the French section. The 1830s also saw the establishment of the first exclusively English-language newspapers, with the *True American* appearing in 1835 and *The Picayune* (shortly thereafter renamed the *Daily Picayune*) beginning publication in 1837, inspired by the "penny press" model that had emerged in New York earlier in the decade.[19]

The city's newspapers were the principal sites for the printing of operatic and musical criticism in this period, but most often this amounted to little more than notices about which works were to be performed, theatrical gossip, and assessments of the troupe's European performers. Scattered among this running commentary were frequent reminders to the people of New Orleans that they were very lucky to have a theater of such quality in their city.[20] No newspaper employed a specialist music critic for either its French- or English-language section in the 1820s, so they depended either upon the knowledge of the editor or upon articles submitted by readers for their theatrical news and reviews.[21] The lack of professional music critics, combined with the dominance of the Théâtre d'Orléans and its familiar repertoire in New Orleans's cultural life, meant that, for much of the decade, there was little incentive for Francophone reviewers to expand their critical vocabulary.

The opening of the English-born actor, impresario, and businessman James Caldwell's American Theatre on Camp Street in 1824 did little to inspire any increased critical fervor or rigor among the Francophone reviewers: they viewed the Anglophone theater's repertoire of abridged Shakespeare and light comic works (interspersed by musical performances from an orchestra that was by all accounts incomplete and of poor quality) as being of little interest to their Francophone readers. Instead, they continued to remind New Orleans's Creole and French residents to support the French theater.[22] The English-language sections of the papers, meanwhile, now had their own performers and theatrical gossip to discuss, and therefore paid even less attention to the activities of the French theater than they had done previously.

But it is nonetheless the case that Caldwell's American Theatre ultimately had an untold impact on musical criticism, and indeed on the success of *grand opéra* in the city, as became clear in 1835 with the premiere of Meyerbeer's *Robert le diable*. *Robert* was the second *grand opéra* to be heard in New Orleans, and the story of its arrival has since passed into the limited mythology surrounding opera in the city: Henry Kmen, Sarah Hibberd, and Catherine Jones have all discussed it to varying degrees.[23] In the weeks before the French theater's production of *Robert* in the spring of 1835, the city's Francophone press was shocked to discover that the opera was not only in rehearsal at the American Theatre, but the Anglo-Americans were going to beat the city's French speakers to the premiere of a new and important

French opera. *Robert* was performed in English at the American Theatre on Camp Street on March 30, 1835, finally reaching the stage of the Théâtre d'Orléans six weeks later, on May 12. The French, so most accounts conclude, were shaken by this challenge posed by the Americans to their cultural supremacy but took comfort in the fact that the Théâtre d'Orléans's production was of a higher quality.

The two productions existed as direct rivals for audiences, in a situation that mirrored the wider challenges facing New Orleans society at the time. The 1830s saw rapidly rising tensions between the city's Francophone and Anglophone populations, tensions that were raw in both the cultural and the commercial spheres. Following the Louisiana Purchase in 1803, New Orleans had seen ever increasing numbers of Anglophone settlers from the northern states move to the city; the 1830s saw a particular influx of these Anglo-Americans, whose arrival irreversibly altered the social and cultural makeup of the city, thus initiating the process of its integration and assimilation into the ever-growing United States.[24] This was a period in which the future of Francophone citizens and their leading roles in commerce and government became much less certain, and French linguistic and cultural hegemony in the city was significantly challenged.

Such fundamental tensions doubtless shaped the race to stage *Robert*, but it is their impact on the direction of operatic reception in New Orleans that will be my focus here. A detailed examination of the productions and their reviews reveals some of the intricate ways in which the *Robert le diable* incident allowed critics to explore new avenues of operatic meaning, shaping the future of *grand opéra* criticism in New Orleans and also opera's place within the city's cultural imagination more broadly. In turn, such an examination provides a way into understanding the nuances of cultural relations in New Orleans at the time.

RECONSTRUCTING THE PERFORMANCES

The only surviving evidence for the twin first productions of *Robert* in the city comes in the form of the reviews printed in the local press: any attempts to reconstruct what audiences actually saw onstage in 1835 is therefore inevitably filtered through the words of the critics. Nevertheless, in the case of *Robert* the number and length of the reviews, across both the English- and French-language sections of the press, mean that it is possible to piece together something of the two theaters' productions and the differences between them. Katherine Preston has already highlighted how important questions of adaptation were to the performance of opera in nineteenth-century

America, illustrating how alterations—both textual and musical, as well as more fundamental changes to the plot—were key to making English-language productions of operas attractive and, indeed, morally acceptable to a middle-class American public.[25] It is worth, therefore, excavating the details of the French- and English-language adaptations of *Robert* presented in New Orleans, in order to understand something not just of the differing linguistic contexts and performance traditions from which they came, but also of the way in which these twin productions were perceived in 1835.

There were key structural and musical differences between the two. Both the American Theatre and the Théâtre d'Orléans maintained Meyerbeer's five-act structure, but within that they made different alterations to the setting and also to the musical content. The reviews suggest that the American Theatre maintained the original locations for the first four acts, showing the Bay of Palermo in the opening act, then the palace, followed by the abbey and the palace again. The final scene of act 5, however, was set not inside the Cathedral of Palermo, as in the Parisian original, but concluded with a representation of Pandemonium itself: Bertram's fiery demise was given precedence over the potentially trite wedding scene for Robert and Isabelle.[26]

The reasons for this change of setting were hinted at in an article published in *The Bee* in advance of the American Theatre's premiere. The critic, who had not yet seen the work performed, suggested that the change had been made with the deliberate intention of increasing the visual spectacle of the opera's conclusion, saying:

> The drama, we understand, has been so worked as to give greater scope for the scene painter and mechanist than could be afforded by a merely literal translation from the original piece—A scene (the closing one we believe) embodying [the artist John] Martin's masterly picture of Pandemonium [1824], is spoken of by those who have seen it, as likely to prove one of the most splendid scenic effects ever witnessed within the walls of the theatre in this or any other country.[27]

So too did the French-language critics praise the American Theatre's attention to spectacle (just about the only part of the production about which they were not scathing), with one remarking that he could not "praise the artist responsible highly enough," and pointing to the interior of the palace in act 1 and the cloisters of the convent in act 3 as particularly exceptional.[28] The American Theatre had clearly invested a good deal of time and effort into the scenery: it had all been painted specially for the occasion, not locally, but by a Mr. Smith of Philadelphia (or so the critic for *The Bee* thought).[29] Nonetheless, the Francophone reviewer was disappointed that the props and other stage decorations did not measure up to the quality of the backdrops, pointing out that "the tombs, for example, are too straight, and the statue of Saint Rosalie could have been better drawn and painted."[30]

The Théâtre d'Orléans's *mise-en-scène* was reported to be more extensive than the American Theatre's overall but, unlike at that theater, it was not all new. An advert for the production suggested that the backdrop for the first act "representing the Lido, with the port of Palermo in view," was newly painted for the occasion by the theater's scenic artist, Louis-Dominique Grandjean Develle, as was the second tableau of the third act (showing the "galleries of the cloister of Saint Rosalie"), and also the backdrops for both scenes of the final act, one of which showed the entrance to Palermo cathedral, and the other the interior.[31] The other backdrops, showing "a room in the palace of the King of Sicily," "a somber landscape in the rocks of Saint Irene," "the bedroom of Princess Isabelle," and the stage curtain displaying a "hellish scene" for the occasion, were presumably served by stock scenery, since they were not listed among the new sets. While the French theater's décor was generally viewed as impressive, reviewers complained about the long breaks between acts as the stage was reset, stating that some of the intervals lasted as long as half an hour, in contravention of the city ordinances, which prescribed that they should last for a maximum of thirteen minutes.[32]

Press evidence, therefore, suggests that the Théâtre d'Orléans made no major structural changes to Meyerbeer's opera, but the American Theatre's alterations were likely more substantial, in keeping with its usual practice of adapting works heavily and combining them with other entertainments. Indeed, while the French theater presented *Robert* as a whole evening's entertainment (and with the extended breaks between scenes and acts, it would have been a lengthy evening), on at least one occasion the American Theatre's production was billed alongside a minstrel show performed by Thomas Dartmouth "Daddy" Rice, in which he played (in blackface) the character Jim Crow.[33]

This attitude applied equally to the theaters' respective approaches to the music of the opera. Both productions cut some of the music from the established Parisian version. Reviewers noted that the production at the American Theatre omitted Isabelle's Cavatine at the start of the second act, along with the duet for Robert and Isabelle in act 2, scene 3; meanwhile, the English-language reviewer for *The Bee* highlighted that the Théâtre d'Orléans's production omitted most of the "music of the princess [Isabelle] as performed at the American Theatre."[34] There are multiple possibilities as to what exactly the critic meant by this. Besides the Cavatine in act 2, scene 1 (which the critic stated had been cut from the American Theatre's performance), Isabelle has little by way of solo music in Meyerbeer's score that could have been noticeably cut or abridged: she sings briefly in act 2, scene 2 (after she has read Robert's note informing her of his impending arrival), and again in act 2, scene 6 (as an aside to bemoan Robert's absence), but nowhere else. Indeed, aside from the act 2 Cavatine, her most musically significant passage is the grand duet with Robert in act 4, scene 2. It is hard to imagine how the French theater might have cut Isabelle's music from this scene without impeding both the flow of the music at large and the plot, or why they might have done so.

"The music of the princess as performed at the American Theatre," however, was not necessarily Meyerbeer's music: it was common practice at Caldwell's theater to add other music (often popular songs, or favorites from other operas) to works, and this could be what the critic implies here.[35] Nonetheless, in the case of *Robert*, English-language reviewers generally implied that the American Theatre had, unusually, introduced relatively little external material into the opera, and that its rearranging consisted mainly of redistributing Meyerbeer's music between different characters in the opera. The performer playing Isabelle, then, was more likely singing music originally written for another character in the opera, and Isabelle's music may well have been redistributed among other characters in turn; one reviewer noted that although Mary Ann Wood was initially very pleasing in the role of Alice at the American Theatre,[36] "she afterwards represented the princess [Isabelle], and transferred most of the best music of Alice."[37] This kind of rearrangement took place fairly extensively in the American Theatre's production, with one reviewer pointing out, for instance, that the duet that was originally for Bertram and Raimbaud in act 3, scene 1, had been made a duet for Alice and Raimbaud instead.[38] This rearrangement of the music and text likely took place either to meet the practical needs of the American Theatre or at the specific request of leading singers, like Wood.

Of course, it is worth pointing out here that the performers and directors behind the American Theatre's production may well not have considered such textual liberties to be fundamental changes to the opera: after all, a necessary process of adaptation had already taken place in the translation of the French libretto into English for their performances. One review gives a glimpse of how exactly certain moments of the production compared to Scribe and Delavigne's libretto, as the critic provides the translation of certain sections as performed at the American Theatre, alongside the translations as performed at London's Covent Garden and Drury Lane.[39] As an example of this, table 2.1 shows the chorus from act 1, scene 7, as it appears in the French original, as it was rendered at the American Theatre, and as it was heard at Covent Garden and Drury Lane.

TABLE 2.1 Text for act 1, scene 7, as it appears in the French original and as sung at the American Theatre, Covent Garden, and Drury Lane

FRENCH ORIGINAL	AMERICAN THEATRE	COVENT GARDEN	DRURY LANE
O fortune, à ton caprice,	Gaily now our moments telling,	Fortune, queen of joys o'erflowing,	Fortune! Be not so capricious,
Viens, je livre mon destin;	Fortune lend thy pow'rful aid;	Hear, and all my vows command,	On her will still hangs our fate:
A mes désirs sois propice,	Pleasure ev'ry care controlling,	Come thy kindest smile bestowing	She may ever be propitious,
Et viens diriger ma main.	Brightly glitt'ring ne'er to fade.	And direct thy votary's hand!	And her favors on thee wait.
L'or est une chimère,	Gold is a profitless treasure,	What are heaps of treasure,	Gold is but a bubble,
Sachons nous en servir:	Not worth our anxious care;	If no inspiring bliss we share?	Unless it bliss can buy;
Le vrai bien sur la terre,	Wine and beauty give pleasure,	Here there's nought but pleasure,	What relief from trouble,
N'est-il pas le plaisir?	That with nought on earth can compare.	Worth a fleeting moment's care.	Is there but in joy?

English translations quoted in *The Bee*, May 16, 1835.

The American Theatre's translation, then, was even less literal than either of the London versions: it maintained neither the vocabulary nor the rhetorical structure of the original (since it dispensed with the question that ends the stanza), but it did preserve the rhyme scheme. From the collected examples provided in the review, the American Theatre's production does not appear to have drawn heavily on either the Covent Garden or the Drury Lane translations; it was an independent, original translation, not one derived from other successful English-language versions. In its poetic take on Scribe and Delavigne's libretto, it was also distinctively different from the French original. It was likely the reviewer's intention to stress this originality when he decided to go to the trouble of quoting from the various productions.

The two theaters' productions also differed in their use of orchestral resources and dancers, although the reviewers made clear that neither version was without its problems. The sheer number of orchestral musicians required to perform *Robert* was inevitably a challenge, and one scathing Francophone account of the American Theatre's production asked incredulously whether "an orchestra of fifteen or sixteen musicians is enough to execute an opera which, at the least, requires forty, and which furthermore should not have any gaps in the instrumentation for a skillful rendering."[40] At the Théâtre d'Orléans, meanwhile, one reviewer felt that "too often there appeared a deficiency of wind and bass instruments,"[41] although the theater, unlike the American Theatre, did boast a large church organ, which was called into service to good effect in the fifth act.[42]

The obligatory presence of a ballet in French *grand opéra* inevitably posed a challenge to theaters hoping to stage the opera beyond Paris, since few could rely on a ballet troupe of the size and level of training of the Paris Opéra's. Nonetheless, both the Théâtre d'Orléans and the American Theatre made efforts to provide a ballet for the third act, in which the ghostly nuns rise from their tombs. The Théâtre d'Orléans had first employed ballet dancers in 1822, when John Davis brought a small group of dancers back from France, but the history of onstage ballet dancing at the theater remains somewhat unclear: the theater played host to many visiting "dancing families" (as Kaye de Metz has called them) over the years, but it did not stage independent ballets with the same regularity as it did operas.[43] Similarly, the American Theatre played host to many of the same visiting dancers as the Théâtre d'Orléans, as they often took on engagements at both theaters for a few nights, as well as small numbers of "resident" dancers. These dancers were not, however, limited to what we would identify as ballet: alongside "pas de deux" and other recognizably balletic dances, they were regularly advertised as performing everything from jigs to polkas onstage.[44]

The need to provide a corps of dancers large enough and well trained enough to present the ballet of the nuns from *Robert* nonetheless strained both theaters' resources, and references to the theaters' dancers were frequently laced with sarcasm and outright ridicule. One Francophone reviewer mocked the American Theatre's decision to seat the ghostly nuns on "a kind of footstool," and suggested that it might be better to place those "parrot perches" in the niches around the back of the stage, or else disguise them so that they resembled sections of columns; he suggested none too kindly that, although the theater's production aspired to Parisian grandeur, the sight of fifty dancers dressed as holy women, squatting on footstools, would have had real Parisian audiences in fits of laughter.[45] So too was criticism leveled at the Francophone production: one reviewer expressed his disappointment that although the French theater had more dancers to represent the ghostly nuns, they were neither skilled ballerinas nor the slender beauties for whom he had hoped, and their dancing was more comical than sensuous.[46]

The productions, therefore, must have sounded and looked quite different, as the two theaters responded within the capacity of their resources to the demands of staging *grand opéra*. While it appears that the French theater stayed as close to the original Parisian version as was possible given material constraints, the American Theatre's production took greater liberties in textual, musical, and scenic terms, but those changes were less drastic than was typically the case at that theater. Flexibility was key to staging imported works, as the theaters strove to balance material and personnel needs with aesthetic decisions.

ROBERT LE DIABLE AND DEVELOPMENTS IN OPERATIC CRITICISM

The dual productions of *Robert le diable* in 1835 generated far more critical attention than any previous theatrical premieres in the city. Between the English- and French-language sections of *L'Abeille* and the *Courrier de la Louisiane*, one can count some twenty-one articles, many of which were lengthy. Only six of these appeared in the French-language sections of the papers: the rest were in English. The number of articles is remarkable, but so too is the fact that some of the English-language articles discussed the Théâtre d'Orléans's production in depth and vice versa. Furthermore, the large number of English-language reviews calls into question an impression conveyed in many of the later accounts of the productions that the French, intent on decrying the American performance of *Robert* and promoting their own production, generated much of the interest surrounding the affair.[47] It is the English reviews, not the French ones, that reveal the way critics used the work to help them make the first tentative movements away from the old school of dramatic criticism that had been prevalent in the city.

Significantly, in contrast to the early operatic criticism in New Orleans outlined above, in the English-language reviews of *Robert*, we can see the beginnings of what appears to be a work-centered, rather than a largely performer-centered, opera criticism.[48] Particularly significant in this respect is a pair of articles published in *The Bee* in advance of the work's first performance at the American Theatre.[49] These were not simply notices advertising or "puffing" the upcoming performance, but lengthy essays designed to introduce the reader to the opera and the historical events that formed the background to the story. The first to appear, on March 27, 1835, did not discuss the opera itself (although it promised it would be treated in a separate article very soon), but instead gave a detailed account of the historical figure of Robert, Duke of Normandy. The second article, from the next day, sketched out the opera's plot, and included quotations from the libretto of key choruses. In showing a concern for understanding the operatic text, rather than the way in which it was performed, these articles mark a departure from the familiar patterns of contemporary theatrical reporting in New Orleans. Their appearance in *The Bee* is particularly conspicuous in that they were printed on the front page, surrounded not by other articles on historical or artistic events but by reports on local legislative news and bills passed by the Louisiana Senate. These were, in other words, deemed worthy of a place alongside the city's "official" news.[50]

There are two distinct avenues to explore when considering how the English-language critics in New Orleans might have arrived at this new approach to *Robert*. The first relates to a set of specifically local issues, as *The Bee* had for several years been railing against the practice of "puffing" visiting star singers at the city's American Theatre, complaining that the "ov[er]-rehearsed eulogies" or outright scorn afforded to such performers was childish.[51] They called instead for a new style of theatrical criticism that was "unbought and impartial," and we can perhaps read their approach to *Robert* as an outgrowth of this debate: here was a work never before performed in the city that they could explore in ways distinct from their usual focus on performers.[52] This is not to say that the English-language critics drew a dichotomy between "event-based" and "work-based" composition (to use the somewhat loaded terms Carl Dahlhaus employed to describe audience expectations in the nineteenth century), but more simply that they saw this as an opportunity to connect the performance with the thing being performed.[53] Indeed, they felt that *Robert* could pave the way to a greater appreciation of music in the city, and went on to remark that the event was a reminder that there were "excellent opportunit[ies] for the organization of Philharmonic societies" in New Orleans.[54] Fundamentally, however, their approach avoided the two extremes of flattery and evisceration characteristic of reviews focused on star singers.

Beyond this, it is very likely that the Anglophone critics' newly angled concern for *Robert* was influenced by a set of debates about adapting the opera that had emerged in London when the work was first performed there in 1831–1832.[55] The circumstances surrounding these early productions of *Robert* in London provoked vocal outrage from Meyerbeer, lengthy copyright proceedings, and discussions in the press about fidelity when adapting works, as Christina Fuhrmann has shown.[56] While there is no concrete evidence in the New Orleans reviews that the critics knew the ins and outs of the situation in London, their assessments of *Robert* suggest that some familiarity with it was highly likely. Indeed, as explored above, the English-language critics discussed at length the version in which *Robert* reached New Orleans, quoting from its text and commenting on its rendering of Meyerbeer's music. To produce this version of the opera, the critic for the *Courier* proudly explained, Thomas Reynoldson, the Englishman who directed the production, had been able to procure a copy "of the original score as produced at Paris," on loan from Pierce Butler of Philadelphia.[57] With this statement, then, the reviewer validated the American Theatre's production as "authentic" by signaling its connection with Meyerbeer's original. By stressing the faithfulness of this production of *Robert* to the original, therefore, the English-language critics aimed to elevate it far above the level of the theater's usual offerings.

The reviewers claimed with particular pride that Reynoldson had not even rearranged Meyerbeer's score, as he had done when he produced a melodrama version of the work in New York,[58] but had "merely curtailed the parts of those instruments which he has not under command in his own orchestra."[59] In their eyes, then, this might have been Meyerbeer with holes, but it really was Meyerbeer. This was very much a relative concept (as we have seen, it appears there were in fact some changes to the score), but the fact remains that these reviewers made Meyerbeer's wishes much more prominent in the reception of *Robert* in New Orleans than those of any composer before him whose works had appeared on the city's stages.

The critics' discussions of fidelity, however, were perhaps less concerned with Meyerbeer as a composer and more with the geographical associations they made between him and the French capital. Indeed, the writer for the *Courier* stated that when *Robert* was "acted at the patent theaters of London, only the melody performed was original," but he took pains to point out that at the American Theatre in New Orleans, "the original music [was] . . . for the first time presented outside of Paris."[60] In such a light, the questions of authenticity extended beyond the composer and his score, revealing aspirations to the artistic status of Europe's great metropolitan cultural centers. Indeed, the reviewers pointed out that Reynoldson was well qualified to direct the American Theatre's production because he had "seen the work performed in Paris under the inspection of the composer" and had later performed in the opera himself at London's Covent Garden and King's Theatres.[61] He could therefore be relied upon to produce the work in New Orleans with faithfulness to the versions enjoyed in these cultural capitals.

The reviewers' phrasing suggests yet another nuance to their positioning of the American Theatre, one that appears to create an international hierarchy of cultural centers. That is to say, in their above formulation, fidelity to the Parisian production ranked above fidelity to the London ones, even though the American Theatre's performance bore more obvious similarities to those in London, given that it was in English and given Reynoldson's connections with the London productions.[62] While this turn to Paris might seem natural, since it was a French opera under discussion, London was the English-language reviewers' touchstone for theatrical excellence, and to compare a production favorably with London was usually considered exceptional praise indeed. Here, though, the reviewer proudly notes that the American Theatre had surpassed London in that all-important question of authenticity. Reynoldson, who was reported to have personally overseen every aspect of the production (not only was he translator, director, and editor, but he "taught the vocal corps and superintended the instrumental," as well as performing the role of Bertram), seems to have verged on cultural hubris: while Meyerbeer was known for meticulously presiding over the European productions of his own works, Reynoldson's fastidious attention to detail at the American Theatre almost "out-Meyerbeered" the composer himself.[63] For the Anglophone reviewers, the American Theatre's production was comparable only with Paris.

In drawing such a link, the review's significance was twofold: on the one hand, the critic posed a challenge to the local Francophone community, which had long-standing cultural ties to Paris. On the other, the review indicates that Anglo-Americans felt at home enough in New Orleans to imagine the city's international position as their own, even if the way in which they were able to do that was through *grand opéra*: a borrowing from French culture. Importantly, however, it was a piece of French culture newly arrived from France, rather than something well established among New Orleans's French and Creole communities. A battle over established cultural territory would have marked a purely local struggle, but the adoption of *Robert* (which was new to both the majority of the city's Francophone population and its Anglo-Americans) as the contested point reveals a new cultural confidence among the city's Anglo-American residents. In the discourse surrounding *Robert*, *grand opéra* became the representative of Anglo-American dreams of cosmopolitanism.

In the same moment, the Francophone citizens lapsed into near silence in the face of increasing challenges to their sense of national identity posed from both within and without. Of course, the American Theatre's production predictably rankled the French-language critics, resulting in an excoriating review in the *Courrier*.[64] But when it came to the French theater's production, the same critics had little to say,[65] with their comments tending toward nonspecific praise, such as "never has theatrical pomp been pushed to such a degree at this theater."[66] Nowhere did they attempt a comparison with the American Theatre.[67] Instead, they focused on growing internal divisions within the Francophone community, where plans were afoot for a new Francophone theater—a Théâtre Louisianais—in the city, which would promote the work of local composers and authors.[68] While these plans never came to fruition, their subtext was clear: the Théâtre d'Orléans was not doing enough to promote young and, more importantly—local—artists, instead focusing on recreating Parisian works.[69] A split was beginning to emerge between populations who located their Francophone identity back in France and those who located it in the Creole milieu of Louisiana. In such a moment of cultural confusion, the French theater's production of *Robert*, perhaps conveniently, slipped from the forefront of Francophone critical attention.

LES HUGUENOTS

If the English-language reviews of *Robert* in 1835 had driven the early critical fervor for *grand opéra* in New Orleans, by the time *Les Huguenots* received its first performance at the Théâtre d'Orléans on April 30, 1839, the situation was very different. French/Creole and Anglo-American tensions had developed in the four years since the race to stage *Robert*, and had been formalized in 1836 through the division of New Orleans into three distinct and semi-autonomous municipalities, each with its own council, taxes, schools, and other services, including the capacity to print its own money.[70] The municipalities were divided not only along linguistic but also (unofficially) along racial lines. The First Municipality, covering the French Quarter and the oldest parts of the city, was home predominantly to white Creoles and French immigrants, while the city's Anglo-American population occupied the Second Municipality to the south. The Third Municipality, covering the old Faubourg Marigny and other areas, was home to many Francophone free people of color, as well as growing populations of German and Irish immigrants. While this is, of course, a considerable oversimplification of New Orleans's demographics in this period, it is a useful illustration of the way in which large-scale social, economic, and cultural divisions between the different sections of society were solidifying.

The city's theatrical scene had also undergone some important changes. The American Theatre, located in the Second Municipality, had not continued its direct challenge to the Théâtre d'Orléans after *Robert*, but had returned to its usual repertoire of spoken drama and less ambitious musical works, as well as a variety of heavily rearranged operas given by visiting English-language companies. *Robert* might have been simply a publicity stunt on Caldwell's part, but his theater's lack of stability means that it is not possible to say for certain that he did not originally intend to create a more sustained rivalry with the French. The new English-language St. Charles Theatre, meanwhile, had opened on November 30, 1835 (also in the area that became the Second Municipality), again under the management of Caldwell, and each summer had played host to a visiting Italian opera company from Havana.[71] Their performances introduced audiences in the city to Italian opera in its original language and vastly expanded the repertoire known to the New Orleans theatergoing public. Up to this point, Italian repertoire in the city had been limited to a handful of works by Mozart and Rossini, performed either in French translation or arranged and translated for the English theaters.[72] The Théâtre d'Orléans's position in the life of the city as a whole was now even less certain: as the formation of the municipalities created more concrete cultural divisions, the appeal of internationally reputed Italian operas lured French/Creole theatergoers across municipal boundaries to the St. Charles.

Les Huguenots nonetheless received a lot of critical attention and drew full houses throughout the remainder of the 1838–1839 season. Although *Robert le diable* had also generated excitement, the situation this time was different. While the English-language critics had felt the need to build up to the first performance of *Robert* with information about its plot, libretto, and historical context, *Les Huguenots* clearly needed no introduction. The opera and its composer had entered the public consciousness of both Francophone and Anglophone residents well before its first performance in the city. Indeed, in December 1838, the recently founded English-language paper the *Daily Picayune* printed a fictional vignette entitled "Fireside Talk—No. IX." The story features a family, gathered in their sitting room one evening. The daughter plays a piece at the piano, about which she says the following:

> [It] floated in my brain for months—I heard it in my sleep—it was with me all day, like a divine presence. I tried to sing it, to touch the notes on the piano, but the moment I made an audible attempt, the fairy creation left me like a startled fawn. I was obliged to relinquish all attempts to embody it, and until this day, it has slept in my heart and memory, like a sacred trust. Tonight I find it among the collection of music sent me from Paris. It is from "Les Huguenots"—I prize it as I would a manuscript from Pompeii.[73]

Her mother, the author goes on to recount, kept "silence for a minute" following the performance, eventually breaking the reverie to point out that the opera would be performed "in fine style" at the French theater some months hence, and that they would soon have the "opportunity of luxuriating amid the beauties of the entire opera."[74]

Here, then, is an indication of the way in which *grand opéra* had entered the popular imagination in New Orleans by 1839.[75] While the family still looked forward to being able to see the opera at the theater, "the work" had achieved an identity outside of its onstage form. For the girl to prize the score (presumably either reduced for piano or arranged as drawing-room *morceaux*) as an object, and to describe the musical experience in such poetic terms, opens up a very different aesthetic avenue for the reception of *grand opéra* from any seen before in the city. Her description takes on an intensely Romantic quality, as she recalls the interiority of a musical experience for which she has heretofore been unable to find an external outlet. Since French opera in New Orleans had, at least in journalistic sources, almost always been discussed in terms of a theater-centered experience until this point (discussions of *Robert*'s plot and historical context can be understood to have been intended to enhance the reader's impending visit to the theater), such an interiorized approach was strikingly new.

The focus here on subjective experience rather than the details of a particular performance reflects, I suggest, a reconfiguration of the ways in which *grand opéra* was being imagined spatially and with regard to nationality among New Orleans's Anglophone reviewers. In fact, it reflects a paradox of national identity within the city more generally during this period: while the city's linguistic and, to an extent, racial divisions solidified in physical form through the separate municipalities, culturally speaking, the lines became blurred in many ways. The family in this story seems to be of French descent: the father is called Adolphe, while his wife is described simply as "La Madame." At first glance, then, this simply raises the question of why the *Daily Picayune*, an English-language newspaper, would print a story of Creole life. Was this some kind of nostalgic evocation of the French diaspora?

But the matter grows in complexity. The couple's children, both young adults, do not have French names: one is called Magnus, the other Boleyna, and, unlike their parents, they do not litter their speech with French phrases. In fact, on the one occasion that Magnus uses a French word, he immediately follows it with "as mother calls it," thus distancing himself from the French language of his parents. Furthermore, Boleyna's score might have come to her from Paris, but she tells her father that she first heard the music of *Les Huguenots* on the family's visit to Hoboken, New Jersey, the previous summer. Far from this being a story of a Creole family clinging desperately to the culture of the "old country," then, this is *grand opéra* representing the crossing of geographical and cultural boundaries and also, potentially, temporal ones. Indeed, a sense of timelessness and spacelessness is evoked by her valorizing the score through a comparison with the classical world, by way of Pompeii. In this light, the paper's evocation of this apparently Creole family perhaps has more to do with their status as a cultural elite within New Orleans than with any specific questions of nationality.[76]

When it came to talking about the Théâtre d'Orléans's production of *Les Huguenots, The Bee* printed an anticipatory article on the day of its premiere, which pointed out that the theater's management had sought to ensure that this was the most lavish production possible (the cost, he claimed, amounted to "upwards of $12,000," a phenomenal sum for the time).[77] Describing the success that the opera had achieved in Paris, the author declared that he expected it to achieve similar acclaim in New Orleans. And with that, the English-language press said no more about the work. Such a dearth of English-language critical reporting perhaps affirms not a lack of interest in *grand opéra* on the part of the Anglo-Americans, but rather the elite cultural status the English-language press fashioned for the genre: wealthy Anglo-American families in the city made sure that they and their children spoke French as well as English, marking them out as part of the highest class of society (perhaps by virtue of the fact that it was the language of Paris, or perhaps because it was increasingly becoming a minority language in New Orleans).[78] Thus they were able to read French-language theatrical reports anyway. In this way, the English-language press positioned *grand opéra* above the arena of local tensions, on a cultural plane accessible to supranational elites.

The French-language critics, on the other hand, perhaps mindful of their lack of interest in *Robert* four years earlier, published numerous articles about *Les Huguenots. L'Abeille* included several full reviews of the opera, along with related correspondence from readers. Also in contrast with the reception of *Robert,* this news was not (for the most part) positioned between legal and commercial reports. Instead, particularly lengthy reviews were sometimes set apart in a dedicated arts feuilleton.[79] This partly reflects the perceived importance of *Les Huguenots,* but also that *L'Abeille* had, in 1839, employed a dedicated music critic for the first time, and was keen to advertise that fact through the creation of a feuilleton, which presented separate operatic reviews.[80] All of this provided the Francophone reviewers space to influence how the genre articulated local, national, and international identity.

They did not always do this in ways that would appear most obvious to a modern reader, however. There were numerous resonances between the dramas that unfolded at the theaters in this moment and the situation in which the New Orleans Francophones found themselves. For one thing, the fact that the plot of *Les Huguenots* revolves around a struggle between opposing Catholic and Protestant factions might have provided critics with ample points of comparison with the current local situation, even if the Catholic Francophone community saw themselves as the oppressed rather than the oppressors. What is more, in the same week as the *Les Huguenots* premiere, the Théâtre d'Orléans also premiered a local spoken drama by the playwright Auguste Lussan called *Les Martyrs de la Louisiane* about the attempts of the eighteenth-century French citizens of New Orleans to resist occupation (albeit, in this instance, occupation by the Spanish).[81] To be sure, reviews of *Les Martyrs de la Louisiane* included references to "the mother country" and appealed to the Francophone residents' feelings of resentment toward another culture's intrusion into their own. The critics did not, however, draw explicit connections between the Francophone population and the Catholics in *Les Huguenots*: not a single review analyzed the plot of the opera.[82] Instead, discussions of the "local" took place through examination of the performers and the work's scenery and spectacle, focusing in particular on the work of the scene painter, Develle. That Develle's contribution to the production was perceived as being central was evident even before the opera's first performance. In fact, advertisements for the work in the press gave little indication of its musical contents, but listed the locations in which the acts were set, having informed the readers that all of the scenes had been painted by Develle specifically for the occasion.[83]

Develle's work was so integral to the impression of the whole that in one performance he was called onto the stage during the second act of the opera to take multiple bows, as the audience was overawed with his backdrop depicting the garden at the Château de Chenonceau.[84] An article in *L'Abeille* even claimed that his backdrops for the work were veritable *chefs d'œuvre* and reminded the people of New Orleans just how fortunate they were to have such a master among them.[85] Not only had the theater imported large amounts of key material, but it also had the resources locally to implement and indeed add to them. The city's Francophone critics were proud of this achievement: justly so, given the fact that productions of *grands opéras* in many European cities and towns frequently lacked the resources to create a sense of spectacle.[86] Develle, then, became a figure through whom the press could express their pride at the quality of New Orleans's production of *Les Huguenots* and, moreover, mark the success of the work as specifically French within the city.

While the critics focused on the local dimensions of the production, they also used *Les Huguenots* as a way of transcending the local in their discussions, much as the Anglophone critics had done in the reception of *Robert le diable*. They did this particularly through their detailed discussion of Meyerbeer's music, which in and of itself revealed a significant development in their critical practices: while Meyerbeer's score had been a source for discussions of fidelity in the reception of *Robert* in 1835, nowhere had the critics attempted to provide much by way of musical analysis. In contrast, the reviews of *Les Huguenots* dwelt at great length on the score and the role that Meyerbeer and his "prodigious talent" had played in the work, placing his importance above that of Scribe and his libretto.[87] Certainly, Meyerbeer as composer was perceived to be fundamental to the opera's identity as a work, with his music contributing the vast majority of the opera's artistic worth.

Although the critics were keen to focus on the music, many of the reviewers expressed difficulty in judging the score satisfactorily, on account of both its size and its complexity.[88] It was only after repeated hearings, they claimed, that the work could be fully understood, and the critic for *L'Abeille* noted with pleasure that at the final performance of the season the work was performed to "a serious, attentive public . . . brought together by an understanding of the creations of genius."[89] Such work-oriented remarks do not, of course, reveal very much about the critics' personal experiences of *Les Huguenots*. What is most striking about them is less their surface description than their rhetorical construction, and specifically their similarity to the opera's initial Parisian reception three years earlier. We only need to glance at Berlioz's comments that "several attentive listenings are required in order to understand such a score completely" to begin to see where these similarities might lie.[90]

While the new analytical bent of the reviews could well have been partly to do with the fact that the recently employed music critic for *L'Abeille* had greater technical expertise than his predecessors, there is also a sense in which the critics in New Orleans deliberately and self-consciously emulated both the details and the attitudes of the Parisian reception in their own printed assessments of the work.[91] In so doing, they tapped into a vein of international critical rhetoric: a trend had developed in Paris (and was taken up in other European capitals) for reviewers to describe operas that they felt would enter a newly developing repertoire of "great" works in such terms of musical uncertainty, thus signaling them to be worthy of repeated listenings and canonical longevity.[92] By couching their responses to *Les Huguenots* in such international operatic discourse, then, the New Orleans critics asserted through their very language that New Orleans was at once capable of mounting productions of international repute and of understanding them within the sophisticated critical frameworks developing in Europe. As with the Anglo-American reviewers' responses to *Robert*, in the Francophone reception of *Les Huguenots, grand opéra* once again became a means of projecting international ambitions, but now for a very different subgroup within society.

The question of what exactly this self-conscious evocation of international critical rhetoric might have meant to the Francophone critics of New Orleans is not, however, as straightforward as it might initially seem. And nor was it as straightforward as the Anglo-Americans' self-positioning had been in relation to *Robert*. Indeed, the "international" sphere of music criticism to which they alluded in their reviews was, after all, French, and it is clear that reviewers felt somewhat uncertain as to quite what the "old country" and its musical output meant for them. A review of *Les Huguenots* in *L'Abeille* and the impassioned response it provoked from a reader illustrate this particularly well.[93] The review begins boldly with the well-known quotation from Rousseau that "the French will never have music,"[94] going on to justify the claim by stating "that is to say an indigenous music, national, absolutely its own," since French composers, "from Lully to Meyerbeer, have always followed in the wake of the great composers of Italy and Germany."[95] For the reviewer, even music accepted as French (and he gives Rameau's works as an example here) is not as purely French as it might seem.

This opinion is refuted strongly in the letter from the reader, however, who argues that "things that were written in France and on French libretti are French": "the tree," he points out, "might be exotic, but the fruit is indigenous."[96] Lest such an argument not be satisfactory, he also turns to the writings of Madame de Staël, reminding his readers that if "genius has no sex," nor does it have a "patrie." For him, musical genius is in its very essence cosmopolitan, but such cosmopolitanism can bear national fruit.[97] The letter writer, then, saw the line between the national and the cosmopolitan as permeable: the national could become cosmopolitan in the hands of a genius and, importantly, the cosmopolitan could become national through the same process.

Questions over Meyerbeer's nationality and what that meant for *grand opéra* had abounded in the initial Parisian reception of *Les Huguenots*, but the letter writer's conclusions here open up the possibility of a particularly suggestive position for *grand opéra* in New Orleans. Both the French-language and English-language press in the city read *Les Huguenots* in relation to ideas of cosmopolitanism, but with significant differences. For the Anglophone author of the story in the *Daily Picayune*, the cosmopolitanism exemplified by *grand opéra* was an ambition of cultural elites: the preserve of people able to appreciate it within an emerging "highbrow" cultural sphere, which transcended time, place and, above all, nation. Meanwhile, for the French-language press, cosmopolitanism remained firmly tied to the idea of nation, as mediated through their local experience of Anglophone-Francophone tensions. In their eyes, *grand opéra* could be read as both cosmopolitan (meaning its prestige exceeded boundaries, both local and national) and specifically French. By relating to *grand opéra*'s cosmopolitanism through a deeper sense of heritage, the Francophone community sought not only to confirm their entry into an international cultural sphere (as the Anglo-Americans had done with *Robert*), but to maintain local "ownership" over the material on account of their French descent.

GRAND OPÉRA'S LEGACY IN NEW ORLEANS

Grand opéra had varied legacies in nineteenth-century New Orleans. While it served as a focus for the exploration of Francophone-Anglophone tensions at a particular moment in New Orleans's history in the late 1830s, its impact on the local press culture of opera was equally profound. Operatic criticism in the city's bilingual newspapers expanded rapidly in an attempt to come to terms with the significance reviewers read into these new works. The result was a move toward a work-based criticism, at least for initial productions of new operas, although few were as extensively discussed in the mainstream press as *Robert* and *Les Huguenots*.

The years following the introduction of *grand opéra* to the city saw the emergence of a slew of arts journals and music periodicals, in which works could be discussed at greater length than in the newspapers, and in a vocabulary suited to a readership of dedicated amateurs. Publications such as *Le Franc Parleur* and *La Créole: Gazette des salons, des arts et des modes* emerged in the 1830s, before *La Lorgnette* and *La Revue louisianaise* were founded in the 1840s, and *La Loge de l'opéra* and others in the 1850s.[98] The effect was most profound in the Francophone sphere: with the exception of the short-lived bilingual *La Loge de l'opéra/The Opera Box*, which was produced in 1856 and 1857, there do not seem to have been any English-language music periodicals produced in New Orleans before the Civil War.[99] While many of the new publications lasted only a few months, they reveal an engagement with opera that grew out of the style of criticism developed in *L'Abeille* and *Le Courrier de la Louisiane* in response to *grand opéra*. As this more specialist reception culture grew, the city's principal newspapers continued to print theatrical news, but relieved themselves to an extent of any major critical duties, instead providing mainly advertisements and short articles about theatrical matters more generally. *Grand opéra*, therefore, contributed to the emergence of new avenues for opera criticism and public engagement with opera in New Orleans, some of which will be discussed in greater detail in chapter 3.

The arrival of *grand opéra* also had a lasting impact on the Théâtre d'Orléans on a practical level, fundamentally altering the composition of its troupe. Unlike in provincial France, where theaters sometimes employed separate troupes for spoken drama and *opéra-comique*, throughout its history the Théâtre d'Orléans had a single, multipurpose troupe. Until the 1830s, its singers were engaged in line with the role "types" required for *opéra-comique*, whereby character and vocal types aligned. A female singer engaged as a "Mère Dugazon," for instance, would be a mezzo-soprano or occasionally a soprano who would play the role of a mother and would not be expected to display elaborate vocal flexibility; a man engaged as a "Trial" would be a tenor who specialized in playing servants and other low-class characters, and his voice would most likely have a nasal, thin tone.[100] From the late 1830s, however, singers were employed specifically for *grand opéra* ("première chanteuse de grand opéra," "premier ténor de grand opéra," etc.) for the first time.[101] In so doing, the theater administration placed less emphasis on the character types a performer might play and more on their vocal qualities, in particular the power of their delivery for both male and female singers.

Grand opéra's significance in New Orleans, then, extended far beyond the boundaries of the city, to entangled levels of national and international import. The genre seems to have played a significant role in helping reshape the ways in which people in New Orleans produced and, even more importantly, thought about opera, as well as how they were able to project those ideas. By positioning New Orleans's operatic life both internationally and in an American context, as well as seeing it as something that was local and individual, the critics used *grand opéra* as a means through which they could simultaneously assert their city's position as a cultural leader and also play out anxieties from close to home about the future of Francophone cultural influence. Meanwhile, the material and other practical consequences of *grand opéra*'s international dissemination—the challenges and successes of production at theaters of a very different kind from the Paris Opéra—resulted in both the solidification of the Théâtre d'Orléans's existing transatlantic links and the formation of new ones. Through *grand opéra*, New Orleans confirmed its place in the ever-expanding operatic world of the nineteenth century.

3

Audiences and Publics

Opera in the Sociocultural Fabric of New Orleans

> Whatever taste it may have for the performing arts, the portion of the population that sustains the Théâtre d'Orléans is barely numerous enough to cover the extraordinary expenses caused by travel and the remoteness of the place where we find ourselves recruiting. It is easy to understand when one considers that the audience is always the same; anyone who has observed those around them at a performance with a keen eye is pretty much certain to find those same neighbors at the next performance.[1]

When John and Pierre Davis wrote to *L'Abeille* on April 17, 1835, their words were tinged with irritation and pleading: for a couple of weeks, there had been notices in the press concerning plans for a second French theater in the city, and they felt that such an enterprise would do untold damage to the business of the Théâtre d'Orléans. They appealed to the city's Francophone population, via the press, to support the existing theater, rather than creating further competition. While the Davises were surely right that another Francophone theater would pose a significant challenge to the Théâtre d'Orléans (and I will return to the proposed new theater later in this chapter), their claims about the Théâtre d'Orléans's audience and its composition invite further investigation. Emphasizing that the audience was only just large enough to sustain the existing theater was surely a tactic any theater director would have adopted when faced with potential competition; presenting the audience as "always the same" could be read either as an acknowledgment of that audience's loyalty or as a complaint that it was hard to draw new patrons.

Working out who exactly was in the audience for the theater's performances is not an easy task: no records of ticket sales survive for the Théâtre d'Orléans or any other of New Orleans's theaters, nor are there any subscriber lists or requests for subscription such as those that Steven Huebner, James Johnson, and Eleanor Cloutier have fruitfully made use of in their studies of opera audiences in Paris in the first half of the nineteenth century.[2] Occasional preserved diaries and letters make mention of operagoing, but few provide much detail about either the people with whom the author attended the opera or what their responses to the experiences were.[3] Nonetheless, the very elusiveness of concrete records of the audience, both en masse and as individuals, as Carlotta Sorba has argued, has made audiences a subject of fascination for media historians.[4] For my purposes, knowing who was in the theater is key to understanding how they responded to opera and how opera was valued in society in nineteenth-century New Orleans.

The terms "audience" and "public" are frequently used interchangeably in general parlance and musicological scholarship alike, both to speak of the people who were in the theater and their responses to opera as a kind of "collective spectator" (to borrow Sorba's term).[5] Here, however, I want to tease the two terms apart and suggest that interpreting them as being not completely synonymous can help cast opera's social position in nineteenth-century New Orleans in quite different lights. In doing so, I draw on ideas explored in sociological and public relations scholarship, which have brought considerable nuance to the concept of publics. Following Robert Wakefield and Devin Knighton, in this chapter I take as my guiding principle that idea that audiences are formed as a consequence of individuals' interactive responses to a specific stimulus (whether that be a performance, another event, or even an advertisement) and, in the context of nineteenth-century theatrical performance, their co-presence in time and space.[6] Publics, meanwhile, again following Wakefield and Knighton's definition, self-organize independently of a specific stimulus event and coalesce around an issue.[7] In John Dewey's influential formulation of the role of publics in political process, that issue was always something that negatively affected the individuals who went on to form a public.[8] For my purposes, however, publics for opera and theater could be not just sparked by dissatisfaction but deliberately cultivated to encourage further development of something the constituent members viewed as being fundamentally positive.

This chapter unravels what each of the terms "audience" and "public" might mean for understanding both how the social makeup of New Orleans shaped its engagement with opera and the inverse: how opera served as a stimulus for the specific social dynamics of New Orleans. While chapter 2 began this work, with its focus on tensions between Francophone and Anglophone critics and residents more broadly, this chapter moves beyond linguistic divisions in its approach to the relationship between opera and the social makeup of the city. The first half casts light on the audiences themselves, building up a picture of who was in the opera house and how they behaved, before the second half considers various formulations of both "the public" and the role a public sphere for opera could or should play in nineteenth-century New Orleans.

The idea of a public sphere, of course, has long been discussed. Habermas saw the public sphere as a necessary requirement in a democracy, mediating between state and society, and which relied on individuals participating not for their own private interests, but for those of the general populace.[9] In the nineteenth century as today, publics inevitably relied on media of various kinds to help constitute them and hold them together, and a public is, therefore, to an extent an abstraction, which involves real individuals, but is not limited conceptually to specific, identifiable individuals: it is a kind of imagined community in which, as Michael Warner has argued, individuals only participate in so far as they pay attention to the issue or subject at its heart.[10] If their attention wanes, they cease to participate in that imagined community.

New Orleans in the first half of the century was ripe for the development of a discursive public sphere for opera, because of its thriving—indeed, hyperactive—press. As explored in chapter 2, the city's newspapers had long included advertisements for and reviews of performances, which initially tended more toward a focus on performers than works, but which became more interested in the latter in the wake of grand opera's arrival in the city. In the 1840s a variety of new magazines and papers were founded that paid more focused attention to the theatrical and broader artistic life of the city.[11] While the public sphere in which these publications engaged, and which they helped create, was highly local in certain respects, it was in other senses transatlantic. That is to say, it was developed through reference to a range of connections that extended far beyond the boundaries of the city.

By nuancing the respective pictures of audience and public in New Orleans in the first half of the nineteenth century, then, I demonstrate that the "public" as it was formulated in the local press differed quite considerably from the actual historical makeup of the Théâtre d'Orléans and other theaters' audiences in New Orleans during this period. The friction between abstracted—sometimes idealized—conceptions of the public and the reality of audience composition and behavior in turn reveals much about the social positioning of opera in New Orleans at this time. So too does this friction lay bare the aspirations that emerged through and were attached to the city's operatic life, in particular questions of democracy and elitism, and specific nuances attributed to operatic culture of different national origins in the local press.

UNDERSTANDING THE AUDIENCE

The Davises' letter to *L'Abeille* in 1835 said nothing about the internal diversity of the theater's audiences, and yet from a modern perspective—and, indeed, for foreign visitors to the city during the first half of the nineteenth century—this was one of the most striking things about a visit to the theater in New Orleans. The physical layout of the Théâtre d'Orléans is a good place to begin an exploration of its audience demographics, as different areas of the auditorium were reserved for specific groups of patrons. Older theaters in the city had traditionally comprised two tiers, of which white patrons occupied the first, and free people of color the second.[12] Davis's Théâtre d'Orléans, however, had three, allowing it to accommodate larger numbers of people. The first tier was reserved for white families, including children (occasional advertisements for tickets suggest that children were admitted at half price).[13] Initially, the second was for women (who could attend alone or accompanied by a slave or domestic servant), and the third for free people of color, who, Juliane Braun notes, were furious to discover that they would not be allowed to occupy the second tier in the new theater, as they had done in earlier ones.[14] Single men, meanwhile, stood or sat on benches in the area directly in front of the stage (known variously as the pit, orchestra, and parquet) and under the first tier of boxes (the parterre).

Not long after the theater's opening, however, John Davis developed plans to reallocate areas of the auditorium. He observed that the second tier of the theater, which he had originally designated as an area for white women, was rarely full, and he wanted to allow free people of color to sit there instead, claiming that the third tier did not have sufficient capacity for them. Davis planned to allow enslaved people to sit in the third tier, so long as they had their enslavers' permission. This might have meant that the slaveholder themselves would be watching the performance from a box in a lower tier, and the enslaved person had accompanied them to the theater, but it is notable that even if this were the case, the setup allowed the enslaved person to sit and watch the performance from their own seat, not standing behind their master or outside their box, where they might have been called upon to carry out other services during the performance.

Upon hearing of Davis's planned changes, the town corporation intervened and forbade him from implementing them, insisting that if he found any free people of color sitting in the second tier, he should inform the police and have them removed.[15] Davis was enraged that this ruling would limit his finances, and he took the corporation of New Orleans to court in 1820, claiming that their restrictions had lost him $15,000 of business and explaining pointedly that if the city's white women patronized his theater more enthusiastically and consistently then the issue would not have arisen.[16] While Davis ultimately failed to recoup from the mayor the $15,000 he believed he was owed, free people of color were permitted to occupy the second tier from the following season, and enslaved people were allowed to use the third.

While Davis viewed allowing free and enslaved people of color to attend the theater as a good business prospect, they did not always feel welcome there in practice. In 1837, various events challenged the position of free people of color in the second tier. Renovations to the theater that year improved and enlarged the boxes, which were then made available to families, meaning that the individual free people of color who had previously sat there felt unwelcome. In another incident from the same year, albeit one reported many years later, a group of white men apparently prevented free people of color from occupying their usual seats in the second tier, supposedly because the daughters of the white men objected to the elegance and luxurious dress of the free women of color; Juliane Braun has explored how the insult and the renovations to the second-tier boxes prompted a temporary large-scale exodus of free people of color from the Théâtre d'Orléans.[17] While the Théâtre d'Orléans managed to regain their patronage, at least to an extent, and it continued to advertise dedicated seats for them into the 1850s,[18] the break from the theater in 1837 led a group of free people of color to found their own theater, the Théâtre Marigny, which was superseded eighteen months later by the Théâtre de la Renaissance.[19] While the Théâtre de la Renaissance had an orchestra, neither theater performed operas, and therefore it never posed direct competition to the Théâtre d'Orléans in that respect.

Nonetheless, the Théâtre d'Orléans was not alone among the city's theaters in the first half of the nineteenth century in opening its doors to a racially diverse audience. Caldwell's American Theatre on Camp Street and his St. Charles Theatre both sold tickets for free and enslaved people of color.[20] As at the Théâtre d'Orléans, segregation was the norm, at least in official terms, with black and white patrons having different areas of the theaters' auditoriums designated for their use. In practice, however, the theaters may well not have enforced such separation particularly strictly. Indeed, as Juliane Braun has observed in the case of the Théâtre Marigny and the Théâtre de la Renaissance, both of which initially permitted mixed patrons but changed their admission policies to permit people of color only, it was almost impossible to implement such rules fully, since "phenotype as a distinguishing feature was unreliable."[21] Blunt legal or administrative divisions between black and white, therefore, did not map in a meaningful way onto the complexity of everyday experiences and perceptions of race in nineteenth-century New Orleans.

Another layer of complexity to the theater's racial demographics develops from the fact that the people who paid for their place in the audience of the Théâtre d'Orléans were not the only people who were exposed to opera within the walls of the theater. Numerous individuals heard and caught glimpses of productions from spaces other than the auditorium, as they worked in the corridors, foyers, loges, and on the doors during performances and rehearsal periods. Some sold refreshments and newspapers, others worked backstage, either helping maintain the theater and its buildings or as stagehands and in other jobs assisting productions. In the 1820s—the only decade for which I have been able to find any documentary evidence about behind-the-scenes personnel—the theater employed a free man of color, Ange Jean-Baptiste Nicolas Oddo, as its concierge at the stage door (about whom, more below)[22] and another, Louis Pepite, as a stage designer.[23] Pepite and his colleague Jean Baptiste Fogliardi, a white immigrant of Italian descent, worked for the theater for a number of years, but while Fogliardi received considerable acclaim for his work, Pepite's name was rarely mentioned in the same press reports that lauded his white colleague.

Numerous enslaved people worked in the theater, too, alongside white personnel, although their names and their specific contributions are almost entirely unrecorded. Louis Neel, a white lampist employed by the theater in 1823, recalled working alongside an enslaved man named Jean Pierre,[24] and various other individuals working in the backstage area were referred to in records simply as "un nègre" or "une négresse," without their names being given.[25] While the absence of personal information about these individuals in archival records is in some respects a barrier to understanding their engagement with the theater's performances of opera, Marisa Fuentes has argued that we should perhaps not be afraid to imagine or at least to engage in conjecture about the roles and experiences of enslaved people, suggesting that we must not "let our desires for empirical substantiation remand these fleeting lives back into oblivion."[26] In this light, it becomes an important historiographical exercise in itself to imagine Oddo hearing snatches of rehearsals as the sounds drifted down from the auditorium to his loge or Jean Pierre catching glimpses of the performance on stage as he hurried about his duties trimming the wicks on candles and oil lamps. All these under-documented individuals contributed to keeping the theater running, and all surely heard bits of opera (and in some cases more) while they worked. While their responses to these experiences are lost, they are nonetheless an important part of the picture of the people who contributed to an extended operatic establishment and the experiences it created.

THE ECONOMIC STATUS OF THE AUDIENCE

Intersecting with the racial and gender composition of the theater's audiences are questions of financial status. In the absence of details about individuals provided by subscriber lists or sales records, ticket prices provide a starting point for exploring the economic positioning of opera and its audiences in nineteenth-century New Orleans. The ticket prices of the Théâtre d'Orléans's early days perhaps reflect more about Davis's inexperience in theatrical administration than they do of the economic situation of the patrons themselves. Initially, they fluctuated frequently, as Davis struggled to set them at a level that ensured attractiveness to audiences as well as generating profits for the theater. At the theater's opening in November 1819, tickets were priced at $1.50 for most areas of the auditorium and $1 for the parterre and gallery areas.[27] A subscription, guaranteeing access on Thursdays and Sundays throughout the season (i.e., roughly 104 performances, since the theater was initially open all year round), cost $100 for the higher-priced sections and $70 for the cheaper ones.[28] By the following year, he had lowered the price of admission substantially: he stated that the most expensive tickets were 80 cents, those in the second tier were priced at 60 cents, and those in the pit/parquet and parterre areas cost 50 cents.[29] He also lowered the price of a subscription that year to $80 for reserved seats in the most expensive areas, $60 for unreserved seats, and $50 for free people of color. At times, he was prepared to drop the prices even further, as needed: in March 1824, faced with poor receipts as audiences were temporarily lured away by the novelty of Caldwell's American Theatre, which had opened three months earlier, Davis solicited new subscribers for a mere $30 to see the theater through until the arrival of the start of the next season in the fall.[30]

Still, throughout the theater's lifetime, complaints appeared in the press that its ticket prices were too high to attract a full house. During the financial crisis in the early 1840s (as discussed in chapter 1), which resulted in Pierre Davis briefly ceding his direction to the performer-organized Society of Artists, the theatrical magazine *La Lorgnette* urged the administration to lower the cost of admission.[31] In a series of articles, the magazine pointed out that the population of New Orleans was suffering the aftereffects of the nationwide financial crash of 1837, and the author of one such article suggested that reducing tickets by 40 or 50 cents across the board would make a huge difference to the theater's receipts; in response, the Society of Artists reduced all the $1.50 tickets to $1 and the $1 tickets in the parterre to 65 cents in February 1843.[32] Even this smaller reduction at a time of financial difficulty across the city proved enough to draw audiences back to the theater: the Society of Artists made it to the end of April (after which they left on a tour of the northern states), and the theater's regular administration took over again before the reopening in the fall.

While there were frequent, small changes to ticket prices, across the lifespan of the Théâtre d'Orléans they remained remarkably stable, and there was no sustained rise in cost. Indeed, in November 1859, only a month before the opening of the new, dedicated French Opera House, tickets at the Théâtre d'Orléans were almost exactly the same price as they had been originally advertised when the theater opened in November 1819, costing $1.50 for the most expensive seats. There were now more cheaper seats, however, with tickets in the pit/parquet having been reduced to $1 and those in the gallery to 50 cents.[33]

In absolute terms, it is hard to work out who among the population of New Orleans would have been able to afford a seat in the theater and how regularly. Katherine Preston has suggested that an admission charge of 50 cents—the price of a gallery ticket—would have been within reach of working-class theatergoers in New York.[34] There is little reason to assume that it would have been beyond the means of similar groups in New Orleans, but even so, it may not have been a fee that they would have been able to pay multiple times a week. More instructive for understanding the kind of patrons the Théâtre d'Orléans might have attracted, then, is a brief comparison with how its ticket prices related to those of other theaters in New Orleans and elsewhere in the United States.

When Caldwell's St. Charles Theatre (fig. 3.1) opened at the end of November 1835, tickets for seats in the boxes cost $1.50, those in the amphitheater and pit $1, and those in the gallery 50 cents.[35] Free people of color and enslaved people (who, as at the Théâtre d'Orléans, were allowed to attend only with a written note of permission from their masters) could enter for $1 and 50 cents, respectively.[36] These prices were identical to those charged at the Théâtre d'Orléans during 1834–1835.[37] Meanwhile, the American Theatre on Camp Street charged $1 for tickets in the parquet during the 1839 season, but seats in the boxes were, unusually, less expensive, costing 75 cents each.[38] On balance, then, the Théâtre d'Orléans's tickets were roughly on a par with those charged by the American and St. Charles Theatres for their regular performances.

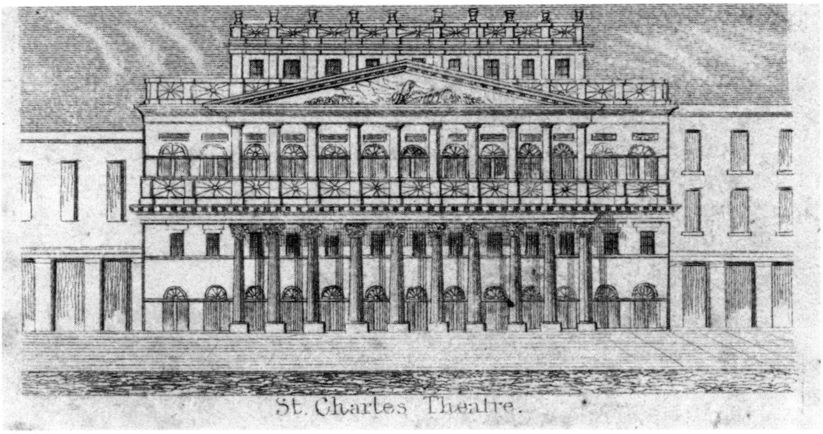

FIGURE 3.1 St. Charles Theatre (c. 1838), engraved by Clark. The Historic New Orleans Collection, Gift of Mr. and Mrs. Albert Louis Lieutaud, acc. no. 1957.73 iii.

Performances by visiting companies and stars, however, were frequently priced much higher. When Fanny Elssler performed at the St. Charles Theatre in 1841, the admission fee was $5.[39] Tickets for Jenny Lind's visit to the same theater ten years later were likewise set at $5 for all areas of the auditorium besides the gallery, where they were $1.[40] Meanwhile, when Max Maretzek and his visiting Italian opera company gave performances in April 1852, tickets in the boxes were set at $2.60, those in the parterre at $1.50, the second tier at $1, and the gallery at 50 cents.[41] Compared with the price of entry to the regular troupe's performances at the Théâtre d'Orléans, then, these visitors' performances were extremely costly and exclusive, and they relied on the exceptional, one-off nature of the visits to persuade audiences to part with their money.

A brief comparison of the theaters' regular prices with those of other entertainments in the city is also a useful way of positioning the social and economic status of opera in New Orleans at the time. An evening at the opera at the Théâtre d'Orléans cost much the same as a one-off visit to an art exhibition or a diorama in the city: in the cheaper seats, an evening at the theater cost less than visiting the "Love in All Shapes" exhibition at the Gallery at Plough's Museum ($1) in April 1839 or Hanington's Grand Dioramas ($1, children half price) in May the same year.[42] However, such entertainments were much more expensive than attending a performance by a visiting ventriloquist at the St. Charles Theatre in 1847 (25 cents or 50 cents, depending on the seats),[43] a night at the Olympic Circus in 1849 (25 cents or 50 cents),[44] or a minstrel show at Dan Rice's Amphitheater (25 cents or 50 cents).[45] These entertainments, of course, relied on bringing in very large audiences and incurring minimal production costs in order to make a profit; producing opera, and relying on imported materials and performers, as the Davises pointed out in the letter to *L'Abeille* with which I began this chapter, was an extremely costly enterprise, and these costs were inevitably reflected in the ticket prices.

Nonetheless, the stability of the ticket prices and their comparability with other nonoperatic performances at the American Theatre and the St. Charles suggests that there was no deliberate positioning of opera as an exclusively elite entertainment at the Théâtre d'Orléans. The theater did not increase its regular prices when it staged operas (indeed, its regular prices were based on its staging of operas), unlike some theaters elsewhere in the United States that performed opera less frequently. Indeed, Katherine Preston has highlighted how, in 1825, New York's Park Theatre doubled its usual admission prices when Manuel García visited, charging $2 for a seat in a box and $1 for a seat in the pit;[46] meanwhile, in 1835, boxes to watch the Rivafinoli troupe's performances in New York were not available on general sale, but were allocated by lot to wealthy shareholders, and seats in the rest of the house were raised considerably from their usual prices.[47] With a plentiful supply of opera, the Théâtre d'Orléans did not need to raise its prices to stimulate interest or compensate for unusual costs.

The picture that emerges from these figures, then, is that opera was not positioned either by necessity or by deliberate design as something that was out of reach of all but the wealthiest patrons at the Théâtre d'Orléans. Sociologically speaking, the theater was a much more complex and potentially democratic space than we might assume, in the sense that it was occupied simultaneously by various different social, economic, and racial groups, who were able to interact, at least in passing, in its foyers, staircases, and corridors, if not in the theoretically more segregated space of the auditorium.

AUDIENCE BEHAVIOR

While the above paints a picture of audience demographics and the social and economic status afforded to opera, I now want to consider briefly how those individual groups acted collectively as an audience in the theater. A mixture of internal decisions by the theater's management and factors external to the theater constantly shaped who was in the building on any given evening. While the Davises emphasized the consistency of the audience in their complaint to *L'Abeille*, in reality—at least on the small scale—the audience at the Théâtre d'Orléans was far from a fixed entity. Its composition changed depending on the night of the week, the month of the year, what was being performed, and by whom. Seasonal factors affected attendance, as the winter months—especially January and February—saw members of the planter class come into the city from their properties farther upriver and avail themselves of the entertainments and social opportunities available in the city, before returning to their plantations or traveling on to Europe in the spring.[48] On a night-by-night basis, the weather strongly affected audience numbers: even aside from the heat and disease that led John Davis to close the theater over the summer months from 1824, during the rest of the year heavy rain could turn roads and sidewalks into seas of mud, and a sudden cold snap (snow was not unknown) could keep people at home.

Indeed, the inconsistency of audience attendance was a constant strain for the Théâtre d'Orléans's administration. It was often easy to determine in advance which nights would be exceptionally popular, but it was not always straightforward to predict which would be a complete flop, owing both to the abovementioned climatic factors and also to competition from other local theaters and entertainments. On December 11, 1842, the playwright and theater critic Louis Placide Canonge highlighted one case of exceptionally and unexpectedly poor attendance in the theatrical magazine *La Lorgnette*.[49] He reported with horror that there were only nine people in the audience (in an auditorium with a capacity of 1,800) for the performance he attended at the Théâtre d'Orléans three days earlier, during a very cold week. The first tier, he observed, contained just one person: a single woman, who "regarded the empty benches with a feeling of terror."[50] Three evenings later, he noted with relief, the audience swelled to fifty, and by the following week, the auditorium was full for the premiere of *Guillaume Tell* (a work from which various acts had been presented in previous seasons, but which had not been given in its entirety before).[51] It was not the case, then, that audiences placed such value on the theater or opera that they would turn out at all costs, and the Davises resorted at various times over the years to begging in the local press for people to support the French theater.

Once in the theater, audiences' behavior could be quite shocking by modern standards. James Johnson and Katharine Ellis, among others, have highlighted how early nineteenth-century audiences were frequently noisy and mobile, moving around the theater, socializing, and sometimes vocally expressing their responses to what was happening on stage, and the Théâtre d'Orléans was no exception to this.[52] Silent listening within the opera house was far from the norm, judging by the frequent reports of tumultuous applause and sometimes furious hisses and whistles from a full crowd.[53] When

Canonge recalled the disastrous night in December 1842 on which only nine people attended the evening's performance, he wrote candidly of how those who were present continued their own conversations loudly across the auditorium, in total disregard of the performance taking place in front of them. So disheartening was the experience for the performers that they began to chat among themselves onstage and to call out to people in the wings, planning social events and ordering drinks.[54]

The recoverable traces of audience behavior suggest that while the theater was a special social space in many respects, shared by people from all different parts of society, it was not necessarily "sacralized," to use Lawrence Levine's term: it did not inspire reverential or unusually restrained collective behavior from its audiences.[55] Indeed, audiences responded in highly physical ways to the performances, showering their favorite performers with flowers, brooches, and other gifts.[56] Those who were less well liked were often pelted with peanuts and pistachios, to the point that theaters felt the need to ban their consumption on the premises.[57] Pickpocketing and other kinds of antisocial behavior also took place in the theater on occasion,[58] despite the presence of police officers.[59] Although the pit/parterre, as in Europe, was generally perceived as being the most volatile area of the theater, poor behavior affected even the most expensive seats. In 1853, Canonge himself was involved in a fight with a writer named Charles Testut in the corridors behind the first tier of boxes, after Canonge accused Testut of penning a critical review of a play recently performed at the Théâtre d'Orléans.[60] Testut was left bleeding and dizzy after Canonge apparently (or so Testut recalled) hit him on the head with a lead ball.

There were occasional instances of serious violence behind the scenes at the Théâtre d'Orléans, too. On February 23, 1823, the previously mentioned Ange Jean-Baptiste Nicolas Oddo, concierge of the Théâtre d'Orléans and a free man of color, was attacked by Henry Beebe, a New York–born mason and painter.[61] At about half past six that evening, Oddo had been sitting by the fire in his room at the back entrance to the Théâtre d'Orléans with a member of the theater orchestra and one of the theater's two policemen, when he heard the door open, and Beebe entered. Oddo went out to meet the new arrival and refused him admittance to the theater, stating that he had received instructions not to allow anyone in. Beebe protested and, after a brief argument, withdrew a dagger that he had concealed within his cane, and stabbed Oddo in the leg, wounding him slightly. Although Beebe was then dragged from the building by Thomas Raffo, the theater policeman, he quickly pushed his way back in, flung himself on Oddo, and stabbed him in the chest. The dagger just missed his heart and punctured a lung. Oddo died from his wounds some twelve days later, having had the unusual opportunity of recording his own murder testimony against Beebe.[62]

This incident took place in the context of a period in which the Théâtre d'Orléans building played host to both John Davis's Francophone company and James Caldwell's Anglophone company. Caldwell arrived in New Orleans in 1820, with a small troupe of performers, but it was not until 1824 that he opened the American Theatre on Camp Street. Davis, always on the lookout for a business opportunity, agreed to rent the Théâtre d'Orléans to him on a long-term basis for the evenings when the French company was not using it, from the fall of 1820. Under this arrangement, Davis's company would perform on Tuesdays, Thursdays, and Sundays, while Caldwell's troupe took the other evenings of the week.

Witness reports of the attack on Oddo reveal persistent underlying tensions between Anglophone and Francophone companies that, on this occasion, erupted into violence within the corridors of the theater: Beebe had been invited to the Théâtre d'Orléans by Caldwell's stage manager, Richard Russell, even though the invitation went against an agreement between Davis and Caldwell that no visitors should enter the theater building at that time. Witnesses for Caldwell's company accused Oddo of causing trouble for the Anglophone staff, with Caldwell himself describing the murdered concierge as "frequently insolent," while many of the French company's staff staunchly defended Oddo's character and conduct, stating that he was only carrying out his instructions.[63] The linguistic rivalries explored in chapter 2, then, did not exist simply on the level of discourse, but could have serious personal consequences for individuals.

But on the whole, examples of extreme violence within the walls of any of the city's theaters were exceptional. Henry Kmen notes that behavior among the Théâtre d'Orléans's audiences was generally viewed as being more respectable than at the city's Anglophone theaters, where audiences, particularly in the pit, sometimes brawled their way through performances and occasionally ripped apart their seats.[64] In reality, however, both the assertions of civility in the Théâtre d'Orléans and of disorder at the Anglophone theaters were likely frequently exaggerated in the city's Francophone press, which delighted in presenting the Anglophone population of New Orleans as less refined than the French.

Tensions over theatrical matters (such as Canonge's personal assault on Testut) could sometimes bubble over, and minor annoyances could escalate very quickly (as in Beebe's assault on Oddo), but the city's theaters were not unusual in this—violent assaults and organized duels were part of life in nineteenth-century New Orleans—and there are far fewer records of such events occurring within the walls of the theater than in the world beyond. Audience disruptiveness tended more toward noisiness than aggression. While there is little sense that the theater inspired any kind of markedly or self-consciously "elite" behaviors from its patrons in the first half of the nineteenth century, nor is there evidence to suggest that theatergoers, whatever their gender, race, or class, perceived the auditorium or the wider theater buildings as generally hostile or threatening spaces.

FROM AUDIENCE TO PUBLIC: THE CREATION OF A PUBLIC SPHERE FOR OPERA

In the moment of being in the theater during an operatic performance, audiences tended to *react* to what was being performed in front of them and the social situations in which they found themselves within the theater, rather than *reflecting* on them. While audiences' immediate and sometimes visceral reactions were powerful in themselves in shaping performers' careers and the theater administrations' programming decisions, the cultivation of a discursive public sphere for opera in print developed a more nuanced and goal-directed means of shaping the Théâtre d'Orléans's theatrical practice. The second half of this chapter examines some of the ways in which that public sphere was formulated, exploring the ways in which print allowed for the discussion and potentially the resolution of issues concerned with opera and operagoing. A public sphere for opera, then, involved not only reporting on operatic events, but also treating operatic production and operagoing as social practices that required constant cultivation and improvement from an engaged public.

New Orleans's press expansion in the years around 1840 not only presented various images of a public for opera in the city, but it helped foster the development of a rhetorical public sphere. I want to turn first of all to two short-lived but influential publications that emerged in New Orleans in the years on either side of 1840: *L'Impartial* (October 1839 to April 1840) and *La Lorgnette* (December 1841 to April 1843). Both made deliberate efforts to make their readers feel like an engaged, theatergoing public, and they focused extensively on the activities of the Théâtre d'Orléans. *La Lorgnette* was devoted almost exclusively to opera and theater, while *L'Impartial* looked more like the city's newspapers, but carried longer articles exploring issues rather than simply recounting news, and it devoted far more attention to the city's theaters than the main newspapers. The aforementioned Louis Placide Canonge, playwright, journalist and, later, theater director, forms an important link between these two publications. He was a regular contributor of articles on music and the theater to *L'Impartial,* and his time working for the paper allowed him to develop many of the ideas about journalism and its purposes that he later went on to display in *La Lorgnette,* for which he served as editor and chief writer.

Neither *L'Impartial* nor *La Lorgnette* had an exclusively musical focus nor provided detailed analyses of scores, although both engaged in work-based criticism to an extent, carefully considering the background, plot, and musical highlights of works that were new to stages in New Orleans. More important for my purposes here, however, was that both of them devoted considerable space to issues concerning both the aesthetic and social aspects of engaging with opera in New Orleans. In particular, these publications explicitly cultivated a sense of dialogue and debate between theater administration, performers, the press, and their readers.

Both accepted letters and contributions from readers (as did a number of New Orleans's newspapers at the time), but their role in fostering a public sphere for opera was not confined to providing a forum for debates in print, and instead sought deliberately to provoke conversations and changes in behavior in the world beyond. Indeed, "provoke" is the key word here: far from simply providing an opportunity and space for readers to comment on opera, the intended purpose of both publications was to galvanize readers (whether they were patrons of the city's theaters, part of the theater management, performers, or writers for the press) to act to improve the operatic life of the city. The strategies they adopted to do so frequently relied on inspiring anger and/or laughter among readers, often through the printing of satire and gossip. Besides any sense of public or journalistic duty to educate or improve, in their articles there is also a strong sense that the writers—especially Canonge—simply enjoyed being provocative.

A series of articles published in *L'Impartial* in 1839 give an insight into the process by which the paper explored the relationship between the press, the theater administration, and audiences, seeking to promote debate and, ultimately, change. On November 14, 1839, the paper, which had commenced publication only two weeks earlier, printed two striking and unusual notices. Under the title "Théâtre d'Orléans: Relâche" appeared a small image of a skull, and the following text:

> Ladies and gentlemen,
>
> Your presence is requested at the procession, service and burial of the Théâtre d'Orléans, deceased on the 12th at 5 to 10 in the evening, after a short illness. The cortege will leave from the mortuary where the corpse is displayed, Orleans Street, between Bourbon and Royal.

The march is arranged thus: the head of the convoy will be led by the ex-orchestra of the poor deceased, and funeral marches will be played. The extras and stooges (etc.) will follow. The tam tam and the Jingling Johnny will be the chief mourners. The ex-*régisseur* is tasked with attaching the funeral crepes and the ex-lampist with the distribution of little candles. The autopsy of the cadaver proved to the assembled crowd that the above mentioned died of consumption. Sensitive hearts, pray to God for the repose of his soul!!! Requiescat in pace! . . . Amen.

N.B. The editors of the journals of this town must pronounce funeral orations on the grave of the deceased, and our stenographer is able to transmit them to the public. In our next numbers, we will make sure to make known the vices and virtues, if any, of the deceased, as well as the causes and the symptoms which gave rise to and accompanied this cruel but inevitable catastrophe.

The master of ceremonies, Grisbourdon.[65]

This, then, was a satirical piece: a death notice for the Théâtre d'Orléans, which personified the theater, detailing an absurd funeral service for it. The implication was that the theater was struggling and that, even if it was not quite dead, it was having to suspend public performances temporarily, as indicated by the word "relâche" in the article's heading. The image of the funeral procession, leaving from "the mortuary" (the site of the theater on Orleans Street), under the direction of musicians, the former *régisseur,* and the former lampist, struck a deliberately humorous tone that could hardly have failed to amuse readers.

The deeper purpose of the article, however, only becomes evident when it is read alongside another article that was published directly below it in *L'Impartial.* The second article was an obituary ("Article nécrologique"), invoking an individual's more personal response to receiving the imagined news of the theater's demise.

Yesterday, on returning home, I found on my table a letter to my address. I broke the seal. Alas! Such was my grief! It was a burial notice, and of which burial: of the illustrious and thrifty Théâtre d'Orléans! The poor unfortunate. It had succumbed last night at 5 to 10, to an attack of sudden insufficiency.

After having struggled for three days against death . . . and feeling his end approaching, he rallied all his forces and had his heirs summoned. They arrived silently, and when they were close enough to hear: "My children," the Théâtre d'Orléans whispered to them, ". . . I have two or three little bits of advice to give to you, and which my impending death will no doubt compel you to follow, if you wish to prosper! First: you should never undertake the performance of any local work, considering that for 8 sous a piece, you can procure in Paris—and by the thousands—dramas, vaudevilles, and others. And then (and this is especially important), never have any trade or any contact with feuilletonistes! The feuilletoniste is a vampire: he sucked out the last drop of my blood! Alas! Alas! It is a journal that you must pursue with your hatred and your bans on entrance, until the extinction of natural warmth and of your lamps; for that is what killed me, and it will kill you all."

He was going to say more, when death came to cut off his breath! He fell into the eternal slumber, having [in life] made so many others on this earth drop off! He leaves an inconsolable family and numerous blunders to repair!

And we, the poor feuilletoniste, we, against whom he vomited all his anger, we pity him, however, and we miss him! But we take courage and we cry with the gospel: "The good Lord gave the Théâtre d'Orléans! The good Lord has taken away the Théâtre d'Orléans! Blessed be the name of the Lord!"[66]

The first and most obvious thing to observe from the two is that their author (or potentially authors, given the fact that they were signed with different pseudonyms) is critical of the theater administration. In the final lines of the first article, marked "N.B.," the author writes pointedly that the journalist's role at the funeral of the personified theater will be to explicate its "virtues, *if any*," implying that there were in fact not many. In the second article, the criticism becomes even more obvious, speaking of the theater's "blunders," which its descendants will be left to repair.

Particularly keen among the author's criticisms is what he characterizes as being a highly dysfunctional relationship between the theater administration and journalists. Indeed, the words of the theater on its deathbed suggest that the theater administration viewed the journalist to be a monster or vampiric parasite, draining its lifeblood. And yet the author of the second article responds in a benevolent vein, taking the moral high ground by saying that even though the administration has been so cruel to him in his role as a journalist, he will miss the departed theater. In the first article, too, the journalist vows to be present at the personified theater's graveside, "[pronouncing] funeral orations on the grave of the deceased," which the stenographer will communicate to the reading public. Doing so is described as the journalist's obligation ("doit"), and the impression here, then, is that journalists had a duty to provide a channel between events and the public: directly and truthfully communicating news to their readers. The relationship between the administration and the journalist, then, is characterized as a difficult one, but the articles present the journalist as taking the moral high ground and seeking to communicate transparently with the public.

JOURNALISTS, ADMINISTRATION, AND READERS

These articles did not appear out of nowhere. The 1839–1840 season, during which they were written, had not begun well for the Théâtre d'Orléans, as indeed these satirical articles suggested. In the summer of 1839, the theater lost three of its performers swiftly and unexpectedly—Vallière, the lead oboist; Bailly, the principal bass; and Fay, another singer—to yellow fever.[67] The administration struggled to find replacements quickly, as the new troupe had already left on a ship from Le Havre by the time the deaths were announced. These difficulties doubtless made Pierre Davis and his administration particularly sensitive to criticisms, such as they apparently perceived in *L'Impartial*'s satirical death notices; at a time when they desperately needed to maintain audiences, they appear to have viewed press reports as trying to undermine the theater.

As a result, the theater administration denied journalists free entrance to performances, in the hope of curtailing their criticisms.[68] This was not a one-off occurrence, as a few years later, in January 1842, Canonge reported (with a degree of pride) that the sale of *La Lorgnette* had been banned in and outside the Théâtre d'Orléans because the theater administration objected to his criticisms of their management practices, and he bemoaned having his free admission to the theater taken away once again.[69] All of this demonstrates, then, that the relationship between journalists and the theater administration was not a distant one, taking place in print only, but had tangible real-world ramifications.

Indeed, there is evidence that the theater administration and individual performers responded to press criticisms by, at least on occasion, changing things about theatrical practice and specific performances. On January 8, 1843, for example, *La Lorgnette* suggested that a number of the major chorus scenes in *Les Huguenots* required improvement and made suggestions about intonation and stage movement; over the next few issues, the magazine went on to comment favorably on how the direction had put these suggestions into practice.[70] In terms of individual performers, too, magazines like *La Lorgnette* sought to exert influence, such as when on February 3, 1842, an article criticized the soprano Julia Calvé's costume, suggesting that she wore her gray dress so frequently (presumably across several different roles) that it looked tired and drew attention for the wrong reasons, before an article just under three weeks later complimented her for wearing a new gown.[71]

On other occasions, however, performers and administration alike did not take kindly to press advice (particularly when it came from an identifiable individual). Some took offense at the criticisms leveled at them and their work, and they revoked their subscriptions to particular magazines, as was the case with the theater's *régisseur* M. Bernard, who was frequently referred to as "Bernard, ex-subscriber to *La Lorgnette*."[72] More dramatically still, early in 1842 Canonge reported (with a certain degree of pride) that he had been punched in the nose in the street by a performer named Clément, after *La Lorgnette* published articles that were critical of his stage presence.[73] These publications, therefore, formed a kind of feedback loop between journalists, performers, and management, which was sometimes able to drive changes in practice.

The theater's administration and the articles' authors had different interpretations of the rationale for writing such pieces and what they achieved, however. The fact that the theater management saw fit to suspend journalists' free entry to the theater and to block the sale of certain publications within its walls suggests that the theater management perceived a kind of directly causal relationship between press reports and its falling receipts. Several days after the satirical death notices for the theater were printed in *L'Impartial*, however, Canonge published an article under his own name, in which he attempted to offer something by way of an explanation for the earlier articles (although he did not go so far as to disclose whether or not he had written them himself).[74] He suggested that the theater administration had entirely misinterpreted their point, saying they had not intended to attack or destroy the work of the theater, which, after all, was where "Creoles and French . . . can still proudly see our mother tongue dominating: to kill it would be to kill ourselves."[75] He insisted that the theater's efforts to produce French-language opera had his full support, but that the administration had lessons to learn.

An article published a few days earlier in *L'Impartial* provided a clearer rationale for why exactly the paper had taken the approach it did and what exactly those lessons might be. In it, the author claimed that the purpose of the death notices had been to show the theater administration that the public, in buying its tickets to attend the theater, had effectively bought the right to pass judgment on the performances and that the theater administration should not be trying to prevent it from doing so.[76] As consumers, the article suggested, local theatergoers should be able to express their opinions on the theater freely; this was a point Canonge reiterated strongly in *La Lorgnette* just over two years later when he pointed out that if he had to pay $24 a month to enter the theater (free passes for journalists having been suspended once again), he had bought the right to express himself freely.[77] In this instance, then, Canonge seemed to position himself as a conduit for the voice of the people, suggesting that journalism was not a one-way endeavor, bringing news of theatrical matters to general readers, but might also bring their views to the theater management.

Indeed, instead of suggesting that there should only be interaction between journalists and the theater administration, *L'Impartial* and *La Lorgnette* attempted to create the conditions for their readers to also debate key issues and effect change in theatrical practice. Both publications' frequent use of pseudonyms played a part in this. While writing under pseudonyms was extremely common in the nineteenth-century press the world over, it created a number of perceived problems at the time, and not just in New Orleans.[78] Journalistic anonymity was much debated, with advocators claiming that it led to a unity of editorial position within a publication and helped foreground ideas rather than the personality of the individual journalist; detractors, however, suggested that anonymity was cowardly and allowed journalists to avoid taking responsibility for the impact their words had.

Although writing under a pseudonym undoubtedly created a protective veil for individual journalists to a certain extent, I suggest that it also played a role in engaging readers to debate and discuss articles and issues, thereby contributing to the formation of a public sphere. Indeed, the use of pseudonyms seems to have become something of a game, and a deliberately maddening one at that. While *La Lorgnette* and *L'Impartial* both used initials as pseudonyms, some of the names attached to the theatrical articles in *L'Impartial* were more outlandish: "Grisbourdon," "Un Hibou de ses amis," "Un quidam," and "a young man of no consequence" ("un jeune homme sans conséquence"), among others. Such comical and bizarre pseudonyms became a topic of discussion for readers in and of themselves, as an article printed in *L'Impartial* on November 17, 1839, observed, playfully describing a group of readers sitting together to discuss who might have written the two death notices in the issue of three days earlier:

> –If it were M. T. . . . they say. –But no, someone else replies, it isn't M. T. . . . He never goes to the theater. –Maybe it is M. M., thought a third. –It could be, they reply. –Was he at the theater that day? –No. –It's definitely not M. M. . . . –Ha! I've got it, he was clever; why wouldn't it be M. G.? We attributed to him the other day an article on the Physiology of the Toilette, signed X. Y. Z., and the damnable factum on the theater carries the same initials. –Irrefutable! No objection to that. Let's vote on it! And on that strong proof, it was unanimously decided that it was M. G. Nonetheless, someone changed his mind and remarked that the initials could well be a means employed by the editors to throw off the curious.[79]

In this way, writing the theatrical articles under pseudonyms was designed to provoke an active engagement among readers with both the theater and the press. Thus, various rhetorical strategies and techniques cultivated a sense of a discursive public sphere that took place both in print and in the world beyond.

FROM THE LOCAL TO THE TRANSATLANTIC

While *L'Impartial* and *La Lorgnette*'s attempts to create an operatic public were intensely local in certain respects, in both, local aspects of a public sphere—in which many of the participants knew or had a connection to others within it—operated in tandem, and sometimes in conflict, with transatlantic references and links. Indeed, attempts to shape theatrical practice and bring local citizens into debates cultivating the theatrical life of the city were set alongside a more abstract, aspirational approach to opera's role in the social and cultural life of New Orleans.

The idea of a distinct public for opera was frequently evoked when the press—either Francophone or Anglophone—wished, in a typically self-aggrandizing fashion, to praise the city and its residents as culturally superior to those elsewhere. To give but one of many examples of this, in December 1838 a group of New Orleans residents floated plans to found a permanent Italian opera company in the city, capitalizing on the acclaim afforded to three visiting Italian troupes whom actor-impresario James Caldwell had brought to his St. Charles Theatre in the previous two years.[80] The local English-language *Daily Picayune* praised the endeavor, remarking:

> The city of New Orleans is with us, both in an appreciation of the troupe under consideration, and in a love for Italian operas in the abstract. To the praise of our citizens it can be said that they form the *first community in this country* [italics my own] who have supported them, from a taste at once musical and deeply refined.[81]

Appreciating opera "from a taste at once musical and deeply refined" rather than for the purpose of gaining social status, the author implied, set the residents of New Orleans apart from those of other major cities in the United States. Not only were they able to appreciate performances of Italian operas, given by visiting troupes, but they were able to appreciate it "in the abstract," in the absence of regular performances.[82] The reasons for this, the author went on to suggest, were obvious:

> We need not go into a consideration of the causes of this—they are known to every child. We are a Southern people—our city is the central point for all nations, and the proportion of those who come here, with a taste for sweet sounds,

> is to those who "have no music in their souls," as ten to three—voilà tout. The Frenchman, the German, the Neapolitan and the Spaniard, form two thirds of our population, and the two last named nations, would, in the person of the lowest labourer, give their last dollar to the characters of their native airs.[83]

Here, the author links European (but not Anglophone) heritage with musical taste. And, furthermore, he reveals distinctly Rousseauian thinking, linking musicality both with speakers of Romance languages (particularly Italian) and with southernness. His characterization of the love for opera shown by the people of New Orleans extends beyond national pride or allegiance to one's country of origin to a more fundamental kind of musicality.

Such a characterization, then, suggests the author believed that an appreciation of opera and, by extension, music was inherited, innate, and linked to certain national backgrounds. Taking this position served the author for the *Daily Picayune* well as a means of justifying the cultural superiority he posited for New Orleans over other American cities. But, in comparison with many other accounts from the time, such as those already discussed in relation to *L'Impartial* and *La Lorgnette*, this characterization of the city's public for opera is not just abstract, but surprisingly limited: it implies that it was somehow "readymade," based on cultural or linguistic heritage, rather than something that needed to be actively cultivated.[84]

While this is undoubtedly a very different understanding of what a public could or should be from those explored above, it is nonetheless revealing in the way that the formulation of a public sphere for opera in New Orleans in this period inevitably transcended local particularities, reflecting a range of links and perceptions that extended beyond the boundaries of the city. Indeed, in the second of *L'Impartial*'s two satirical death notices for the Théâtre d'Orléans, the author suggests that a key reason for the personified theater's imagined demise was the management's overreliance on imported works. Indeed, the author complained that the theater administration was reluctant to produce anything locally written, suggesting that they relied exclusively on cheap Parisian "dramas, vaudevilles and others."

L'Impartial was not alone in expressing a fear that giving precedence to transatlantic connections and creativity over local ones was stifling local culture. In 1835, plans were floated to set up a Théâtre Louisianais, as I mentioned briefly in chapter 2, in order to allow the works of the "citizens of this country" to take precedence over foreign works.[85] An article about the plans for this theater published in *L'Abeille* stated confidently that "in giving local young people the means to create works conforming to their own tastes, we will see a host of works of genius bursting forth, which, without this [theater], would remain buried in the dust of storerooms, or in the dusty paperwork of notaries or lawyers."[86] Only the works of local citizens, they suggested, could truly satisfy the needs of local audiences. In both these characterizations, the Théâtre d'Orléans and its activities are seen as failing to foster local operatic composition.

The question of who or what counted as "local" was a particularly fraught one in the United States in this period, and not just in relation to opera.[87] Numerous articles from the time (in New Orleans's press as well as papers from much further afield) discussed the merits of fostering the talents of people born on American soil, while others decried their existing efforts as lacking in anything distinctively American. At the same time, the Théâtre d'Orléans performed operas by Pierre-Jacques Chéret, Eugène Prévost, Gregorio Curto, and various others whose names as composers would have been largely unfamiliar in Europe, but who were well known to theatergoers in New Orleans, as they all spent time living and working in the city as employees of the Théâtre d'Orléans.[88] But to some, they would not have counted as "local," since they were born across the Atlantic. These debates were not easily resolved anywhere in the United States, as Katherine Preston has shown in her discussions of Jeannette Thurber's efforts and frustrations in developing her National Conservatory of Music and American Opera Company several decades later, in the 1880s.[89]

While such issues were seen as important in intellectual circles, complaints about the programming of European works at the Théâtre d'Orléans were largely confined to debates in the press, and there were no obvious displays of discontent among theatergoers. The same familiar European works continued to draw audiences, and new works written by "local" composers often only had short runs at the Théâtre d'Orléans before disappearing from the stage. A desire to switch the balance between local and imported works presented on stage, then, seems to have been more of a critical construct than a significant matter of importance to the wider population of operagoers in the city. Audience preoccupations and those of the critics who concerned themselves with the formulation of an ideal operatic public could sometimes diverge quite strikingly.

Even so, many of the same critics who decried the lack of attention paid to local composers and writers also devoted considerable time and effort to cultivating discussions about opera that extended across the Atlantic. Canonge, a proud Creole born in New Orleans, for instance, was frequently aggrieved that his own plays and vaudevilles had failed to receive the attention he wished for them in his home city, but as editor of *La Lorgnette* he established a dedicated Parisian correspondent for the magazine for its final few months in 1843.[90] Most of this correspondence was in the form of open letters, which discussed theatrical goings-on in Paris, or short biographical accounts of singers and their activities. The correspondent signed all his letters "Théop. G. . . . ," suggesting that he may have been Théophile Gautier, who went on to establish himself as one of Paris's most celebrated theater, ballet, and music critics.[91] In 1843, Gautier was the theater critic for the Parisian newspaper *La Presse*, a post he had held since 1837, and it is unlikely that he would have been a well-known name for readers in New Orleans, while still in the very early stages of his career.[92]

La Lorgnette, however, did not need its Parisian correspondent to be a well-known figure. What mattered instead was the exclusivity of the correspondent's reports to the magazine, and it regularly printed comments that all the reports received from the correspondent were unpublished elsewhere ("Toutes ces esquisses sont inédites").[93] The purpose of this, then, was to create a sense that the opera-focused press in New Orleans was an independent equal of Paris and did not need to rely on reprinting secondhand news. Moreover, by stressing that the reports had not been published anywhere else, the magazine hinted to its readers that by reading them they might be privy to information that might not even have been widely known to Parisians. As such, the creation of a transatlantic link in *La Lorgnette* was designed to empower readers to think about opera beyond the confines of the local, by allowing them to feel connected—via a channel of reporting unique to them—to the operatic sphere in Paris. This was not perhaps an invitation to participate in the same kind of intensely engaged ways that the same publications advocated in relation to the local scene, but it functioned as a way of conceiving of and bringing together a more abstract public, the members of which wished to be aware of debates and issues taking place elsewhere (either in the critical sphere or in geographically distant places).

L'Impartial and *La Lorgnette*, then, were short-lived publications, but they are significant to the history of opera in New Orleans in the sense that they both cultivated discussions of an ideal operatic public and sought to create an active public sphere for opera. They were far from the only publications to participate in these processes, but their intense focus on the Théâtre d'Orléans and their connection through the figure of Canonge makes them a particularly illuminating case study. In particular, they illustrate how the notion of a public was formulated not simply through a local frame of reference but also through the evocation of a range of transatlantic connections. While audiences for opera in the theater produced an intensely local set of social relationships, the public sphere—which transcended these local particularities—inevitably reflected a range of links and perceptions that extended further afield.

Teasing apart audiences from publics, therefore, provides a way into understanding some of the manifold factors that affected how people could and did engage with opera, inside the opera house and beyond, and how print journalism attempted to mediate that engagement. The difficulty in approaching both audiences and publics lies in the anonymity that often blankets them: in the absence of records of specific individuals, studying audiences means sketching out groups of individuals and their collective behavior, while in the case of publics, journalists' pseudonyms in many cases obscure individuals' identities, and we have only their words as a record of changing behaviors. All of this can create an uncomfortable sense of distance from the real people that comprised these groups.

That notwithstanding, both give an indication of the social and cultural values afforded to opera in nineteenth-century New Orleans in a broader sense. The Théâtre d'Orléans was theoretically a space open to all (even if in reality changing attitudes to race and the cost of tickets posed a challenge to that openness) and, on a rhetorical level, opera was not positioned as something socially elite and exclusive. What emerges from an exploration of audiences and publics as separate but related entities, then, is that neither received opera passively. At their most engaged, audiences responded vocally to the performances of works and participated wholeheartedly in the social possibilities offered to them in the theater that were not so easily accessible elsewhere in city life. The impetus to create a public sphere for opera, meanwhile, emerged from twin roots. Some critics felt that New Orleans already had (on account of its European-descended population) an ideal public, who would always love opera and whose existence elevated New Orleans to cultural heights not yet reached by any other American city. Others, more realistically, realized that a public engagement with opera needed to be constantly cultivated rather than simply stated, not so much to promote opera as an aesthetic ideal (although that sense was present too, to an extent) as to foster a particular set of social and cultural relationships in city life. While the Théâtre d'Orléans was run as a private enterprise, not as a state- or municipality-controlled institution, the attempts to develop a public sphere for opera in which debate between management, press, readers, and theatergoers could take place suggest efforts to make opera an integral part of society in which everyone had a stake and about which everyone could have their say. More than simply reflecting the societal makeup of New Orleans, therefore, attending and discussing the opera actively helped weave the city's intricate sociocultural fabric.

4

Opera's Material Culture and the Creation of Global Intimacy

> I wonder how many old ladies start to go through an unused hall closet . . . and find a treasure, long since buried under piles of trash, mourned for, and, as in the case of many departed things, at length given up for lost—then forgotten. In just such a dark closet, from beneath a pile of old magazines (what they were kept and stored for goodness knows) and crazy bits of bric-a-brac . . . I found two bruised music books.[1]

Born in Kentucky, Eliza Ripley moved to New Orleans at the age of three.[2] As the daughter of a wealthy Anglo-American family, Ripley's reminiscences of her youth in the 1840s and 1850s tell of trips to the opera, evenings spent dancing with friends in ballrooms and private homes, and her efforts, at her father's insistence, to learn both the French language and the piano: in other words, the typical activities of a reasonably wealthy young woman in New Orleans at the time. But what is most interesting about the quotation from her memoirs given above is its unusual emphasis on material possessions—musical albums that were once prized, but long since forgotten—and the questions it prompts about what a focus on such physical objects might contribute to an understanding of transatlantic operatic life. Indeed, among the pieces Ripley rediscovered from flipping through the two dusty volumes—from the 1840s and 1850s, respectively—would have been piano adaptations of opera excerpts: at one point in her narrative, she recalls her youthful performances of a transcription of the overture to *La Dame Blanche* (performances she describes, with tongue firmly in cheek, as "masterpieces").[3]

Having explored in the previous chapter how opera's role in the social life of nineteenth-century New Orleans extended beyond the walls of the theater, here I want to take a step further and explore what Peter Mondelli has called the "material sociability" of opera: the ways in which opera's social roles in the city were shaped—and strengthened—by a variety of technologies and media besides the press in the second half of the 1840s and the 1850s.[4] It is no coincidence that the decades with which I am concerned here are those from which Ripley's rediscovered music books dated. In fact, they are a natural setting for a discussion of opera and material culture, not just in New Orleans, but across the United States and Europe. In the 1830s, large-scale printing and the lithograph (which had been invented in 1796) became commercially viable, creating flourishing markets for mass-produced literature and images throughout the 1840s and 1850s; the technique of chromolithography (which enabled the printing of multiple color images with relative ease) was patented in 1837, and became widespread a few years later.[5] In New Orleans itself, the 1840s saw a huge increase in the number of magazines and technical periodicals (mostly short lived), among other printed items, produced for sale.[6] This was also the decade in which music publishing became established there, with William T. Mayo, A. E. Blackmar, and Louis Grunewald all setting up firms on Canal Street.[7] Before that point, little music was published in the city, even if it had been written there, and music shops frequently forged deals with northern publishers to have their names added as secondary imprints to sheet music printed elsewhere.[8] By the second half of the 1850s, however, substantial quantities of sheet music were being published in the city.

At the same time as local and national production infrastructures improved dramatically, these decades also saw greatly increased and accelerated international circulation not just for printed items, but for goods of all sorts. Oceangoing steamships cut journey times across the Atlantic dramatically in the 1840s,[9] and New Orleans, which had already prized imported European products in earlier decades, became absolutely saturated with them. Music shops frequently advertised the receipt of a new shipment of music or instruments from Europe in the local press, alongside the countless other businesses advertising imported furniture, fashions, and luxuries of all sorts. Plenty also came from elsewhere in the United States: principally New York, Philadelphia, and other northern cities. The glut of imported goods generated less dispute in New Orleans than the issue of imported operatic works explored in chapter 3, perhaps because, in this increasingly globalized commercial sphere, American-produced goods were also being exported to other parts of the world. While a reliance on imported culture implied to its critics that New Orleans and the United States had never fully broken free of their European colonial roots, there was no doubt by the mid-nineteenth century that America was able to hold its own in networks of trade and commerce that extended beyond its borders.

Opera's material culture during these years, however, highlighted how the commercial and the cultural spheres could easily overlap. Sheet music excerpts, transcriptions and arrangements, and printed libretti; cartoons, sketches, and lithographed images (photographic images were to come later) were all products designed specifically to be bought and consumed, but they also reflected different ways of engaging with and understanding opera. In what follows, I argue that locally produced aspects of this material culture in New Orleans reveal varied and self-conscious attempts to capitalize on the internationalization of operatic circulation (in performance, as well as in material forms), and that, in so doing, they created new social and cultural roles for opera both within and beyond the opera house.

The materials on which this chapter is based are principally of two sorts: popular sheet music for solo piano and a series of opera libretti, both published in the late 1840s and early 1850s. These are but fragments of a corpus of opera-based products available in nineteenth-century New Orleans, but they are nonetheless remarkable for having survived into the present day in the number that they have (albeit scattered through archives across Louisiana). More remarkable still is the fact that their authors are traceable, meaning that some of the specific circumstances of their creation, dissemination, and use can be reconstructed to a greater degree than those of many other, similar items.

The author of the sheet music on which I will focus, Herman Edward Lehmann, arrived in New Orleans from Germany in the 1830s. He became a brass player in the orchestra of the Théâtre d'Orléans (he played the French horn, trumpet, and cornet) and led a dance orchestra in the Orleans Ballroom, which neighbored the theater.[10] But alongside these roles, he also composed and published a variety of short pieces and arrangements of operatic melodies for piano. Copies of more than thirty of his works, including eleven opera-based pieces, survive, either loose or bound into handsome volumes assembled for and by wealthy young women in the city, like those Eliza Ripley rediscovered in her closet.[11] The libretti to which I will then turn, meanwhile, were designed by Louis Fiot. He was a French speaker and "régisseur de la scene" ("stage manager") at the Théâtre d'Orléans, and he published his series of thirty bilingual (French-English) libretti between the mid-1840s and the mid-1850s.[12]

How exactly to approach this specific selection of items? James Q. Davies has speculated in relation to musical annuals of the 1830s that there is "no doubt that these period pieces . . . invite a certain style of hermeneutic engagement, one mindful of local interests and contexts," but he notes equally that information about such contexts is often far from forthcoming; ultimately, he adopts what he calls a "spacious approach," exploring what commercially produced albums of sheet music more broadly might have meant in the context of practices of gift-giving and consumerism of the time, as well as contemporary expectations of femininity.[13] Here, I want to acknowledge the usefulness of Davies's "spacious approach" while also excavating the historical particularities around the specific items I consider as far as is possible (and it can indeed be possible, as Candace Bailey has demonstrated in her work on musical binders' volumes),[14] in order to tackle the ways in which a developing local and localized material culture was nonetheless bound up with patterns of circulation and identification that extended beyond the city.

Both Lehmann's sheet music and Fiot's libretti were commercial souvenirs of a sort: they were designed to be bought and kept and, as I will show, they were each commemorative in their own ways. Alexander Rehding has convincingly positioned the rise of the musical souvenir as the diminutive commercial counterpart to the development of ideas about music's monumentality in this period, suggesting that "the souvenir miniaturizes and domesticates the monument, and mass-produces it in unlimited quantities; in short, the souvenir commodifies commemoration."[15] Lehmann's sheet music and Fiot's libretti both reflect something of this commodification: they turned opera into something that could be purchased, "possessed" and, importantly, taken into the home.[16] They nonetheless suggest quite different memorial roles for operatic souvenirs, projecting different attitudes to the local adaptation and international standardization of operatic repertoire, to the public and private contexts in which opera functioned in New Orleans's social life, and to the "afterlives" of operatic events and operatic works.

MUSICAL SOUVENIRS BETWEEN THE LOCAL AND THE GLOBAL

Eliza Ripley's music books, like the volumes compiled by many other young women in the city, would have contained a mixture of music published in New Orleans and elsewhere, including pieces by Lehmann. At first glance, there appears to be little to differentiate his works from the glut of imported popular sheet music by which they were surrounded both in these young women's volumes and on the shelves of New Orleans's music stores. Many of his original compositions—short, technically undemanding pieces for solo piano—take the names of flowers from across the globe ("Jasmine," "Lilas Blanc," "Le Lys," "Hortensia," etc.), and his eleven surviving opera arrangements are based on just six works, all of which were popular sources for transcription and arrangement across the Atlantic: Auber's *La Sirène*, Meyerbeer's *L'Etoile du nord* (three arrangements), Grisar's *Les Amours du diable* (three arrangements), Adam's *Si j'étais roi*, Maillart's *Gastibelza*, and Verdi's *Il trovatore* (two arrangements).[17]

Like so much popular sheet music of the period, his works were exclusively in dance forms, mainly waltzes, schottisches, polkas, and quadrilles, which were immensely popular in urban social life across Europe and the Americas, as well as in colonial cities further afield. Such dances, as Derek B. Scott has shown, cast off their original national or class associations in the international market and became part of an aspirational, cosmopolitan, middle-class musical culture.[18] His opera arrangements, too, saw the operas' music transformed into these dance forms, which, as Mark Everist and Maribeth Clark have both demonstrated, was a common way of repurposing opera for performance in the world beyond the theater in the decades around 1850.[19] Lehmann's pieces were not only surrounded on the music shop shelves by international imports, but in terms of genre, they were part of a globally circulating popular repertoire.

On closer inspection, however, Lehmann's pieces were intensely and specifically local, while still retaining their global outlook. His music certainly had a largely local circulation, with the exception of a select few pieces (none of which were opera arrangements) that he chose to republish in New York in the 1850s, and he self-published most of his pieces from his address at 194 St. Anne Street in the French Quarter, rather than engaging in the larger publisher networks maintained by Mayo, Blackmar, and others.[20] The markers and purposes of locality in Lehmann's music are a good place to start for gaining an understanding of how the interplay of the local and the global (and, in some cases, the specifically transatlantic) drove the development of opera's material culture in New Orleans and, in turn, fostered specifically local ways of engaging with imported opera.

The two most obvious strategies of local identification in these pieces involve linking the sheet music with specific events and people. In the case of the opera arrangements, several were closely linked to the specific context of the operas' New Orleans premieres. Lehmann's arrangements of *Si j'étais roi*, *Les Amours du diable*, and *Les Filles de marbre* were all published in the same year as their source works' first performances in the city.[21] For his pieces based on Meyerbeer's *L'Etoile du nord*, the timeline was even shorter: the opera was first performed at the Théâtre d'Orléans on March 5, 1855, just over a year after its Parisian premiere in February 1854, to great enthusiasm, and it was given six times in two weeks.[22] Only just over a month later, on

April 17, *The Bee* (the English-language section of *L'Abeille*) carried a notice thanking Lehmann for having published his "brilliant and beautiful polka on a theme from *The Star of the North*." Two other arrangements based on the same opera appeared soon after, capitalizing on the initial enthusiasm surrounding *L'Etoile du nord* in the city.[23] This correspondence between the premiere of the stage work and the release of Lehmann's arrangements stood in contrast to the order of arrival of an opera in many cities beyond Europe (including New Orleans itself, in some cases), where opera potpourris, vocal scores, and other excerpted or arranged forms circulated long before the operas were ever staged there.

Nonetheless, the linking of specific pieces and local events was a feature common to Lehmann's work even beyond his opera arrangements. The cover of his "Pelican Polka," for instance, states explicitly that the work was "executed for the first time in 1853 at the Grand Ball given at the Pelican Club."[24] Around the edges of the title page, surrounded by curlicues, are the names of the fifteen members of this exclusive sports club, and it is likely that they were responsible for commissioning the work.[25] There are other instances, too, of works being commissioned from Lehmann to mark events of significance in New Orleans. His "General Henry Clay's March," which was performed in its original version "for fifty brass instruments" in a Grand Concert on November 7, 1844, was commissioned specially by a group of subscribers for performance during the period of the presidential election that year, in which Clay was the Whig Party candidate.[26]

Even if they were not linked to a specific event, almost all of Lehmann's pieces preserved an important degree of local rootedness through their dedications to specific people. Eliza Ripley fondly recalled in her memoirs the practice of dedicating musical works to "people of note"—often young women—within New Orleans society. She mentions Lehmann directly, saying:

> A belle of the '50s was Miss Estelle Tricou. Lehman [*sic*] . . . wrote "Souvenir de Paris" in her honor. Miss Estelle was bright and sparkling and beautiful, so was much in evidence . . . Lehman [*sic*] dedicated his "Clochettes Polka Mazourka," a fine, inspiring bit of dance music it was, too, to Mme Odile Ferrier . . .[27]

Such dedications were a crucial part of the marketing strategy for this music. Although Matthew Head has written of the "redundancy" of bland dedications to "the fair sex" at large, given that women were the chief consumers of popular sheet music regardless of such dedications, Lehmann's dedications to specific local women suggests a much more targeted attempt to appeal to consumers in New Orleans.[28] The high social status of these young women was particularly significant.[29] Lehmann's "Le Lilas Blanc" polka, for example, was dedicated to Mlle Heloise Cenas, the daughter of a socially influential notary, and others, too, were dedicated to the daughters of important, wealthy families in the city.[30] Such works were sometimes commissioned as a personalized musical gift for their dedicatee—a process Eliza Ripley referred to as "getting it done"—from a suitor, but whatever the exact circumstances of their composition, the composer stood to profit by linking his latest pieces to the most fashionable families and young women of the day.[31]

Although Lehmann's original compositions were all dedicated to young women, some of his opera arrangements were dedicated instead to musicians, which offered additional marketing opportunities. The arrangement of *L'Etoile du nord* that Lehmann published in April 1855 employed a double-pronged appeal to both locality and "of-the-moment" significance: not only was it published rapidly after the opera's New Orleans premiere, but it was dedicated to Louis Moreau Gottschalk, one of the city's most famous musical sons, who was giving concerts there during a tour in the spring of 1855.[32] Besides linking the arrangement with Gottschalk's name, Lehmann's piece reveals an attempt to embed the dedicatee in its musical substance, by reflecting his virtuoso pianism. Its fluid triplet passages beneath extended melodic lines played in the upper register in the right hand (fig. 4.1) allude to Gottschalk's performances of opera fantasias, making this one of the most technically challenging of Lehmann's pieces, while never exceeding the capacities of a reasonably accomplished amateur pianist. As such, it is a pianistic counterpart to the sheet music souvenirs of the castrato Velluti that Sarah Fuchs has argued were a way for amateur performers to feel as if they were acquiring his performance practice.[33] It is unlikely that Lehmann intended Gottschalk to play the piece himself but, given that Gottschalk was so well known for his own pianistic extemporizations on operas, Lehmann surely sought to capitalize on his visit to the city by providing a piece in a similar vein that amateur performers could manage for themselves.

Marketing these musical souvenirs relied just as much on their visual aspects as on their musical and textual content, and many of Lehmann's compositions have intricately designed, lithographed covers created by people working in New Orleans. A copy of one of the opera arrangements, a polka on Adolphe Adam's *Si j'étais roi* published in 1856, even has its cover lithograph in color, adding a touch of luxury to the item and emphasizing its

FIGURE 4.1 Second page of "*L'Etoile du nord*, grande polka" by H. E. Lehmann, dedicated to Louis Moreau Gottschalk (New Orleans: H. E. Lehmann, 1855). Maxwell Sheet Music Collection, Box 420, Folder 29, Hogan Jazz Archive, Tulane University, New Orleans, LA.

modernity.[34] Not all, of course, had such lavish designs—the pieces printed in the mid-1840s tend to be less complex in their lithography than those produced a decade or more later—but those that do were clearly designed to stand out from plainer pieces on the market.

Although it is not one of the pieces with the flashiest covers, Lehmann's polka-mazurka arrangement of Albert Grisar's comic opera *Les Amours du diable* reveals how embedding a dedicatee visually in the sheet music created an important sense of both locality and transatlantic connection. The piece was one of a set of three arrangements of *Les Amours du diable* that Lehmann produced in 1856 and early 1857. Although almost completely forgotten today, the opera was very popular in the 1850s. Premiered at the Théâtre Lyrique in Paris in 1853, it had immediate success at its first performances in New Orleans in 1856, and Lehmann's arrangements were produced over the following months.[35]

The cover image for the polka-mazurka, drawn by an artist in New Orleans named Tolti, is a contrast to the images for the other two arrangements in the set, which were drawn by a different artist and which feature characters and scenes from the opera. It foregrounds instead a specific performer, the soprano Pauline Colson, to whom Lehmann dedicated the work.[36] Colson had appeared in the New Orleans premiere of the opera in 1856, and the illustration is a simple portrait of her in the role of the demon Urielle (fig. 4.2); the music consists of many of the most prominent melodies she sang in the opera, simplified and written out for piano. The decision to focus on Colson was a significant one in that she had in fact sung the role not only at the work's New Orleans premiere but also at its Parisian one in 1853.[37] Although this is not mentioned specifically in the sheet music, I suggest that Tolti's image would have made the link clear to consumers. Indeed, his portrait, with its clean lines and lack of intricate shading, bore a close resemblance to a Parisian engraving by Alexandre Collette of Colson in the role that was available as a print in Paris from 1853 (fig. 4.3). In the two images, Colson wears an almost identical costume: a dark dress with a pattern of stars, with a feathered headdress, and she carries a small dagger.

While Tolti's lithograph of Colson in the role on the one hand likely highlighted a simple fact of theatrical reality—that she wore the same costume in the two productions because she was required to provide her own dress—it would also have highlighted an important sense of transatlantic connection for those looking at the sheet music.[38] The fact that Colson had created the role of Urielle in Paris was well known in New Orleans: being able to link the premieres of a work in Paris and New Orleans, to place New Orleans's

FIGURE 4.2 Cover of H. E. Lehmann's "Polka Mazurka" on Grisar's *Les Amours du diable* (New Orleans: H. E. Lehmann, 1856), showing Pauline Colson in the role of the demon, Urielle. M1 .M86 LARA Box 1, Item 17, Louisiana and Lower Mississippi Valley Collections, LSU Libraries, Baton Rouge, LA.

FIGURE 4.3 Pauline Colson in the role of the demon Urielle in Grisar's *Les Amours du diable*. Alexandre Colette, Paris, 1853. Bibliothèque nationale de France.

production alongside that of a major operatic center, was a source of local pride.

Opera lovers in New Orleans might even have been familiar with Parisian images like Collette's, as portraits of singers in costume circulated widely and rapidly across the Atlantic, alongside newspapers, journals, and other printed materials like the sheet music itself. Indeed, it was common for publications in New Orleans—musical and nonmusical—to reprint images from elsewhere (be that Europe or the northeastern United States) or to produce images that were closely inspired by them. In 1843, Louis Placide Canonge's theatrical magazine, *La Lorgnette*, introduced as a trial the inclusion of full-page lithographs, which Canonge explained were "the exact reproduction of those from [the Parisian satirical newspapers] the *Charivari* and the *Corsaire*," made by "a young man of this town."[39] Alongside them, Canonge intended to include "images of local interest, especially if our politicians lend themselves to caricature: which happens unfortunately altogether too commonly."[40] In the end, it seems that only one image on a specifically local theme was ever printed (a sketch of the Bayou St. John, just to the north of the city, rather than a political caricature),[41] but Canonge's aim to include a mixture of Parisian and local images in a similar style nonetheless suggested that knowledge of a shared iconographic language between New Orleans and Paris was important.

The polka-mazurka arrangement of *Les Amours du diable*, then, shows how dedications and cover imagery combined to make these opera arrangements attractive products in New Orleans's sheet music market. Lehmann's pieces were literal souvenirs in the sense that they commemorated specific people and events in the life of the city, through their dedications and their relationships with the musical components and the cover imagery. Furthermore, considering these aspects in combination shows how a sense of counterpoint between local contexts and ones that were either specifically transatlantic (i.e., the links with Paris) or more generally cosmopolitan (i.e., the internationalized generic context in which such dance-form pieces were rooted) was also key to the commercial viability of these products.

THE INTIMACY OF OPERA ARRANGEMENTS

The notion of commemoration, as discussed above, was key to the status of Lehmann's sheet music as a saleable souvenir, but there is a more complex sense in which these items captured the intricacies of social relations of the time. For the elderly Eliza Ripley, the process of flipping through her rediscovered music books proved to be a particularly poignant experience:

> I am not half through, but I am weary of looking over these old music books. So many memories cluster about every page—memories of lovely dances with delightful partners. . . . Memories of sweet girls, now old and faded, or, better than that, listening to the "Music of the Spheres." Memories of painstaking professors whose pencil marks are all that is left to bring forcibly to mind their patient personality.[42]

The link between the music and memory she evokes is both strong and varied: memories of people, events, and places crowd her mind as she looks at pieces by Maurice Strakosch, William Vincent Wallace, and Lehmann himself, among many others. Some of her reminiscences are prompted by physical marks on the pages in front of her—the pencil additions of piano teachers from her youth—but others are more loosely inspired, reminding her of her school friends, dances she had been to, and people who had been admired in New Orleans during her youth. Her memories are deeply personal, but the kinds of social relationships she remembers, and the places through which they were mediated, were woven into the fabric of Lehmann's opera arrangements for his customers, even at the moment of their publication.

Indeed, the commercial aspects of these works were frequently entangled with more profound social meanings for popular sheet music and more complex contemporary ways of understanding opera; digging further into the ways in which the musical and social aspects of these works entwine reveals much about how people in New Orleans continued to engage with opera beyond the auditorium of the theater in the 1840s and 1850s and how opera shaped sociability in the city. In this, Lehmann's sheet music serves as what Thomas Christensen has referred to in his work on four-hand piano transcriptions of symphonic repertoire as a "historical frame of musical reception." More than simply historical, moreover, it is musical reception that is inextricable from wider social practice.[43]

In aesthetic terms, Lehmann's arrangements raise perhaps even more questions than the transcriptions Christensen discusses. Not only did his pieces transform music that was written for full orchestra and voices into something that fit under the two hands of an amateur pianist, but they condensed several hours of dramatic performance into often only six or seven pages of piano music.[44] In most respects, Lehmann's pieces simplified opera, by reducing the original orchestral textures into a straightforward melody and accompaniment, by reharmonizing, and by homogenizing meters and rhythms to fit with those of the dance forms in which they were recast. They also stripped away the text and, unlike many instrumental opera fantasias of the day, there was rarely a clear narrative goal behind the manipulation and reordering of themes.[45]

However, I want to suggest here that such changes amount not to a simplifying or "cheapening" of opera for purely commercial purposes, but that they were part of a process of transforming imported opera into something deeply intimate, by blurring the geographies of its performance and creating intricate links between different facets of social life in the city. Christensen has written of the way in which transcriptions for domestic use "destabilized" the relationship between genres and specific performance spaces, thereby inviting music intended for public performance into the private spaces of the home.[46] Lehmann's pieces operated in a similar way, with the musical content and the sheet music itself linking the theater, the ballroom, and the home. In so doing, his pieces position opera at the heart of social connectivity in New Orleans in the 1840s and 1850s.

The sheet music Lehmann produced is in many ways far removed from the theater and its staged operatic works, given the absence of voice, text, and orchestra, but he nonetheless deliberately preserved certain kinds of connection with the staged operas in his sheet music. He made a point of labeling each melody or even rhythmic figure he took from Meyerbeer, not by reference to particular acts or arias, but with reference to the action happening onstage when the music was heard. Passages in the "grande valse" are labeled "the madness and sorrow of Catherine," "the departure of Catherine," and "the song of farewell," to give but a few examples.[47] In other instances, the connection takes the form of a focus on a particular character and their music: Lehmann wrote a whole arrangement based around the music of Azucena in *Il trovatore*.[48] There are even on occasion explicit links back to the original orchestration, such as at the start of his "grande schottische," "Le Camp Russe de *L'Etoile du Nord*," where he labels a rhythmic figure "drum" ("tambour") and a rising arpeggio figure "cornets."[49] The material form of the sheet music, then, bears out a connection to the stage work and its musical and dramatic performance within the theater, even as it reduces the orchestral texture for the two hands of the piano, and prioritizes adherence to dance meters over musical complexity.

But there is a more important frame of reference than the theater itself for understanding Lehmann's opera arrangements. Many of his works started life as music for the ballroom, played by an ensemble of musicians, before he later rearranged them as piano pieces for publication. His polka on Adam's *Si j'étais roi* was danced at a ball at the Masonic Hall in the first week of February 1857, and a columnist in the newly started (but short-lived) bilingual magazine *La Loge de l'Opéra/The Opera Box* noted that it was one of the highlights of the evening.[50] Indeed, in New Orleans, as in urban centers across the world, favorite opera melodies inevitably found their way into the ballroom. The city's theaters could double as ballrooms, and the pit of the Théâtre d'Orléans was sometimes covered over to create one big space for large dances, with the music often directed by Lehmann himself.[51] Even within the context of staged performances, the lines between opera and the ballroom could be deliberately blurred, such as when a group of masked revelers were apparently invited onstage at the Théâtre d'Orléans to dance "a grand polka and galop" during the masked ball finale to Auber's *Gustave III*, as part of the city's Mardi Gras festivities in 1852.[52]

The sheet music that Lehmann published of his arrangements, however, was not necessarily a direct transcription for piano of the music performed at balls, and it bears out its connections with the ballroom in interesting ways. Several of the pieces include separate passages specifically marked "introduction pour danse" and "introduction de salon" or, simply, "introduction." The dance introductions were generally very short—just a few bars setting up the prevailing meter and rhythm—which prepared the dancers to begin. The "introductions de salon," on the other hand, were generally musically more complex. Lehmann's waltz on Meyerbeer's *L'Etoile du nord*, for instance, begins with a full-page salon introduction (simply marked "introduction") (fig. 4.4).[53] It opens with the pianissimo motif—a low sustained note over a rumbling bass, marked $\frac{4}{4}$, maestoso—that begins Meyerbeer's opera. This then turns into the solemn "marche sacrée" from the act 2 finale, before Lehmann brings the introduction to a close with a climax followed by a fade to silence. Such a passage, of course, would have been far from suited to the ballroom, or even a smaller-scale dance in a private home. Among the inevitable chatter or other noise of a ball or party, the beginning of the work would have been entirely lost, not to mention the fact that the expectant dancers would have been left standing still for the better part of a minute throughout the $\frac{4}{4}$, maestoso section, completely unprepared for the lively waltz to follow. This salon introduction, then, was not to serve the needs of dancers, but instead effectively distills the dramatic trajectory into an intimate form, suitable for domestic performance. For those who did want to dance, there follows a brief "introduction obligée" at which one could start in the case of a ball, skipping the longer introduction entirely (fig. 4.5). In this case, the fanfare-like figures of the $\frac{3}{4}$ allegro "introduction obligée" would prepare the dancers for the waltz to follow.

When writing this music, then, Lehmann was clearly aware that his music could and would have multiple uses in nineteenth-century New Orleans, as both an accompaniment to dancing (either in a public ballroom or at

FIGURE 4.4 Introduction to "La Couronne impériale de *L'Etoile du nord*, grande valse" by H. E. Lehmann (New Orleans: H. E. Lehmann, 1855). "Music Collection of New Orleans Imprints," M1 .M86 LARA, Box 5, Item 15, Louisiana and Lower Mississippi Valley Collections, LSU Libraries, Baton Rouge, LA.

FIGURE 4.5 "Introduction obligée" to "La Couronne impériale de *L'Etoile du nord*, grande valse" by H. E. Lehmann (New Orleans: H. E. Lehmann, 1855). "Music Collection of New Orleans Imprints," M1 .M86 LARA, Box 5, Item 15, Louisiana and Lower Mississippi Valley Collections, LSU Libraries, Baton Rouge, LA.

a private gathering) and for playing in the home without dancers, for the amusement of the performer and/or a small group of listeners. In the case of the waltz on *L'Etoile du nord*, the "introduction de salon" and the "introduction pour danse" were not necessarily mutually exclusive but led from one to the other naturally. That is to say, while most dance introductions for waltzes would set up the $\frac{3}{4}$ meter through the introduction of a crotchet pulse in the left hand, here the bar-long, fanfare-like gestures that comprise the "introduction pour danse" help smooth the transition between the longer introduction and the waltzes that form the main body of the piece, and also create continuity between the sections.

The contemporary consumers of this sheet music hold the key to understanding the triangulation between the theater, the ballroom, and the home. While a wide variety of people would have heard Lehmann's arrangements in the theater and ballroom, the people who played this music in the home would almost exclusively have been young women; the various spaces allowed young women the opportunity to behave and interact with others in different ways. There were ballrooms and balls catering to all classes and sectors of the population in nineteenth-century New Orleans. While, as contemporary visitors to the city frequently remarked, certain ballrooms had a reputation for sudden and precipitous descents into violence and others for sexual debauchery,[54] the city's private subscription balls attracted the elites of New Orleans society, and the most feted belles of the day were to be found there, to be admired by all.[55] The attendees at these balls were commented on (with their names disguised in subtle and sometimes not so subtle ways) in the local press, as was everything from the décor of the ballroom to the food served.[56] For those who could not afford entrance to these most elite events (which could cost up to $30 for entry to a series of eight dances), printed reports allowed them to imagine what an evening in lofty company must have been like.[57]

Families taking their daughters and other female relatives to balls—whether the most exclusive or their more affordable counterparts—knew that they would inevitably be admired, both as representatives of respectable families and as potential brides. There were, of course, large numbers of social rules surrounding the behavior of both men and women at balls, and etiquette governed how men and women could relate to each other after being introduced at such an event. Guides published in other parts of America that found their way to New Orleans provide a hint of some of these rules of interaction: one, originally published in New York in 1844, pointed out that if a couple introduced for the first time at a public ball were to meet again in the street on another occasion, decorum dictated that they could not assume any acquaintance, their ballroom introduction not serving as a suitable introduction in the "real world."[58] Even those who had met at private gatherings should be wary: gentlemen "should allow recognition to proceed from the lady, and only to be returned, not presumed."[59] The ballroom in many respects, then, seems to have been a "special" space, operating a little outside the rules of normal existence, with ballroom introductions and interactions being distinct from those in the outside world. It was only after a "real world" introduction that a young man could hope to begin the process of courting a young woman, which would involve visiting her at the family home.

These home visits were, at least in Creole families, often formal and highly supervised: Creole families tended to be highly conscious of a need to preserve their high social status and *francophonie* when assessing potential mates for their children.[60] The earliest stages of courtship involved a suitor coming to visit a young woman in the family parlor, where other female relatives would be present.[61] Depending on the attitude of the particular family, these visits could be relatively private or highly formal. By contrast, in spite of its size and public nature, the ballroom could allow for a greater sense of intimacy. All the fashionable dances of the period—the waltz, the polka, the quadrille, and the schottische—were partnered dances, which offered the potential for a degree of physical contact between the sexes that was not permissible in other social spaces. The ballroom became a kind of surrogate for the private spaces of the home, by providing a socially sanctioned opportunity for intimacy that was generally not possible within the context of closely supervised parlor visits. In this way, the ballroom came to serve as the whole city's living room, and lines between public and private were blurred.

What, then, does all this mean for understanding Lehmann's opera arrangements? In the context of a parlor visit, a young lady might be called upon to play the piano to entertain her suitor. A musical education was as much a part of reasonably well-off young women's upbringing in New Orleans as it was in the rest of the antebellum South,[62] and Lehmann's works were perfect for a young woman to perform in social settings, as decorum required that she not display "unseemly" virtuosity.[63] His pieces made moderate technical demands of the performer—far removed from those required to perform opera fantasias and other showpieces by Liszt, Thalberg, William Vincent Wallace, and others whose works were also available in the city—making them suitable for performance to any visiting company.[64]

As she played (perhaps to her male visitor, perhaps to a gathering or, more often, alone), the woman performing this music in the home was encouraged to remember a set of specific social situations, local events, places, and people (including, perhaps, closer physical proximity to her suitor than was permitted in the context of a domestic visit). The piano sheet music, therefore, facilitated an imaginative link (perhaps in addition to or perhaps, for those who were not part of the highest social elites, instead of a memorial one) between the parlor and the ballroom. If the ballroom blurred the lines between the supposedly public place and the semiprivate nature of the interactions that took place there, these pieces of sheet music blurred the distinction between the privacy of the domestic parlor and the world beyond.

This blurring created a sense of intimacy, of closeness and introspection, in which opera had a particular role to play. Indeed, the performance of operatic arrangements in the ballroom evoked perceptions of intimacy and introspection from dancers. In January 1839, one male ballgoer was moved to write to the *Daily Picayune*:

> I think, however, that more hearts were in danger last night than on the former evenings. The ball was not entirely so gay; there was a subdued tone about it which made one turn more to his partner and look more into himself. There was depth to the sentiment that all felt. We had gold instead of tinsel. The music was fine beyond compare. The most delicious morceaux from *L'Ambassadrice*, *Le Domino Noir*, and other fine operas, rendered dancing a matter of feeling. You felt that such sounds were only meant to accompany the "poetry of motion."[65]

While other kinds of music might simply have produced enjoyment, this report suggests that operatic music in the ballroom moved the dancers in more fundamental ways. Such descriptions are, perhaps, at odds with the resistance in critical circles to opera-based quadrilles that Maribeth Clark has discussed in relation to 1830s Paris, resistance that was based on the belief that such quadrilles "transformed the potentially sublime into the banal; those who enjoyed them avoided the transcendent."[66] In the Parisian context, she argues that the quadrille threatened music's emerging position as high art, because the immense public enthusiasm for dancing took attention away from the "truly great" (i.e., sonatas and symphonies, but also the "operas of Mozart, Weber, and Meyerbeer" from which quadrilles were frequently adapted).[67] Behind such claims are ideas of high and popular music not only in terms of repertoire, but also in terms of listening practices. Paris in the 1830s, as James Johnson has argued, saw the emergence of silent, attentive listening, and this is the period in which, so conventional narratives go, the ear gained primacy as the arbiter of musical experience.[68]

In reality, the linearity of any shift from inattentive to attentive listening would have been far from smooth, and in the North American context in the late 1840s and early 1850s, any sense of opera as "high art" was yet to emerge, as Katherine Preston and Lawrence Levine have argued.[69] Dancing opera in New Orleans, therefore, not only preserved a longer-established model of operagoing as a social event, but also presented a model of musical experience that was not determined by the listening ear alone; when dancing an opera quadrille, musical experience was not necessarily cerebral or interpretative, but rather something that, as the ballgoer suggested in his letter to the *Daily Picayune*, was felt in and enacted by the body. Opera linked the physical movement of dancing with a deeper, introspective emotional response. Lehmann's sheet music, meanwhile, positioned both the embodied experience of operatic works through dance and the auditory experience of listening to dance music drawn from opera as complementary. While these pieces did not integrate the two entirely—there is still a physical separation between the sections for dance and salon performance in the sheet music—the process of sitting at the piano and navigating these different sections enabled the performer at home to reconcile the two approaches imaginatively.

Imagination, again, is key to the sense of intimacy created by these pieces and, by extension, to the social significance of this sheet music in 1840s and 1850s New Orleans. As Lisa Lowe has recently put it, paraphrasing the work of Lauren Berlant, intimacy is socially and culturally constructed: it is "the affective medium for . . . the subject's felt sense of individual belonging in liberal society; fantasy, sentiment, and desire in literature and popular culture produce the contours of intimacy that mediate the individual's inhabiting of everyday life in social relations."[70] Lehmann's sheet music opera arrangements, then, did not just reflect, but helped facilitate particular ways of being in the social life of the period.

I do not mean to suggest that readings of intimacy in and through these pieces are in any way in conflict with the commercial aspects explored above. Intimacy could be commodified, as Eleanor Cloutier has demonstrated in her discussion of the emerging celebrity culture around the soprano Giulia Grisi in 1830s London.[71] There, she argues, people could "possess" different versions of the singer, as created through press reports and gossip, as well as pieces of sheet music that purported to reflect arias "as sung by" Grisi. In this light, it is fitting to return to the lithograph discussed above of Pauline Colson on the cover of Lehmann's polka-mazurka arrangement of Grisar's *Les amours du diable*, which similarly allowed those who purchased the sheet music to "possess" Colson. But the intimacy of that possession operated alongside the knowledge of Colson's transatlantic connection, of her Parisian as well as her New Orleans performances in the opera. That knowledge might, paradoxically, have enhanced rather than inhibited the intimacy of possession: Lowe stresses how intimacy in her definition relied not simply on physical proximity or the interiority of the individual, but was propagated, fostered, and regulated through colonial and commercial networks across continents.[72]

These works, then, perhaps went some way toward creating a sense of "global intimacy" for the consumer. The way in which Lehmann's sheet music preserved simultaneously local and international, public and private connections would have again facilitated a set of imaginative experiences for the female performer of this music in her parlor in New Orleans. Aside from the knowledge that the performers who had created operatic roles in New Orleans had also done so across the Atlantic in Paris, the specifically local nature of her memories or imaginings of particular events and people in New Orleans would have been played off constantly against an awareness that she was part of a larger, international community of other young women playing a widely popular genre of commercially available sheet music. The city and the world beyond—sometimes formulated specifically in terms of Parisian connections and sometimes in a far less geographically specific sense—were therefore likely to be juxtaposed in the performer's mind as she played the music. What Lehmann's sheet music did was use the already permeable boundaries between public and private, between the theater, the ballroom, and the private parlor, to foster a sense of "inhabiting" (to borrow Lowe's term) the social relations of everyday life and, along the way, to create a sense of that everyday life as being something shared by people beyond New Orleans. His works, then, contribute to a cosmopolitan, bourgeois fantasy of connection, enabled by opera.

CANONIZING OPERA: FIOT'S LIBRETTI

Like Lehmann's sheet music, Louis Fiot's thirty libretti—released between the mid-1840s and mid-1850s, while he was stage manager at the Théâtre d'Orléans—are operatic souvenirs of a kind. Although their souvenir status relies on some of the same commercial and commemorative strategies as Lehmann's pieces, they offer additional avenues for understanding opera's material culture in nineteenth-century New Orleans. In contrast to the sheet music, they reveal less about the intricacies and intimacies of social life in the city and more about a changing aesthetic identity for opera within the opera house, in light of a growing consciousness of the internationalization of operatic performance and material culture.

Fiot grandly entitled his series "Chef-d'oeuvres [*sic*] of the French Opera."[73] The libretti, however, were not especially grand in themselves: they were simply small pamphlets with bright paper covers, available in green, red, and yellow among other colors (see fig. 4.6).[74] They had obvious commercial intentions, as the insides of the colorful jackets were covered in adverts for sheet music, music teachers, and other nonmusical products and services. But they appear to mark a key turning point in the material history of opera in New Orleans, as they are the earliest surviving examples of anything akin to an opera program in the city.[75] From the period before 1845, there are only very occasional surviving examples of playbills, which were printed on long, thin strips of fragile newsprint paper, and contained nothing more than the bare essentials for advertising a performance.[76]

Unlike earlier playbills, Fiot's editions stand out as items that were not purely functional. On the one hand, they were notionally designed for use within the theater, allowing their owners to follow along with the onstage action, but audiences in New Orleans had managed perfectly well without locally produced libretti before this point. While Fiot's editions never attained the level of luxury (thick, card-like paper with elaborate borders and numerous lithographed images) of the commemorative programs that were printed in New Orleans for Jenny Lind's concerts in the city in 1851 (see fig. 4.7),[77] they were nonetheless designed to be kept and even collected.[78]

Indeed, Fiot's own comments in the preface to his 1853 edition for Mozart's *Don Giovanni* (under the title *Don Juan*) reveal that he wanted consumers to treat the series as a whole:

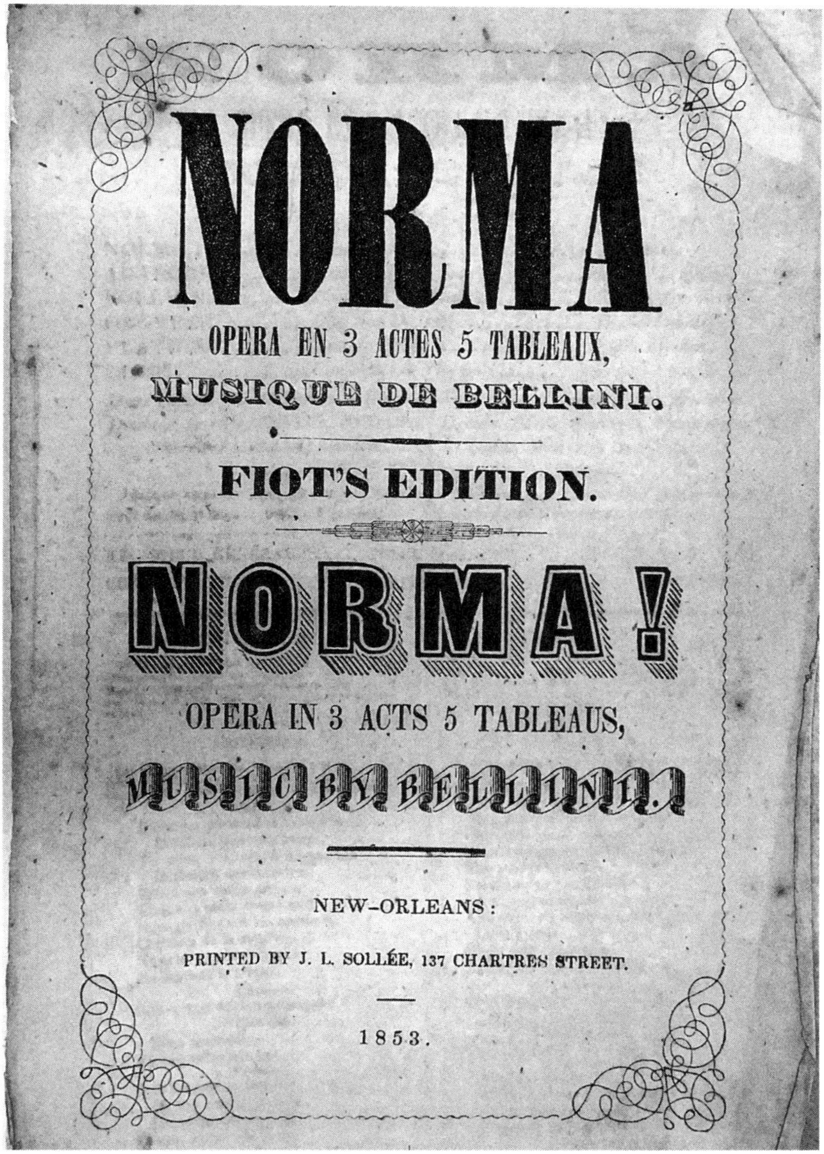

FIGURE 4.6 Cover of Fiot's edition of Bellini's *Norma*, New Orleans, 1853. Albert Voss Collection, Manuscripts Collection 856, Series 1, Box 1, Folder 2, Louisiana Research Collection, Tulane University, New Orleans, LA.

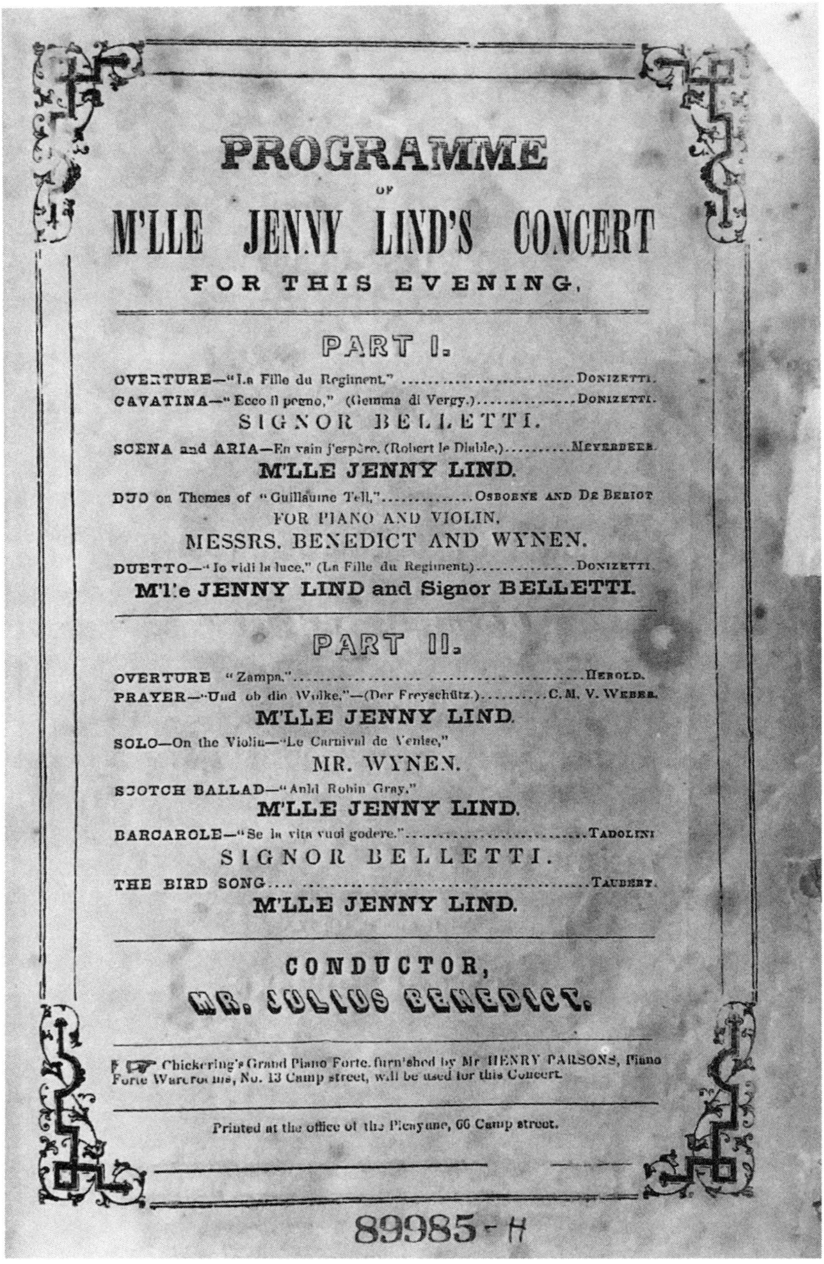

PROGRAMME

OF

M'LLE JENNY LIND'S CONCERT

FOR THIS EVENING.

PART I.

OVERTURE—"La Fille du Regiment," .... DONIZETTI.

CAVATINA—"Ecco il pegno," (Gemma di Vergy.) .... DONIZETTI.

SIGNOR BELLETTI.

SCENA and ARIA—En vain j'espère. (Robert le Diable.) .... MEYERBEER.

M'LLE JENNY LIND.

DUO on Themes of "Guillaume Tell," .... OSBORNE AND DE BERIOT

FOR PIANO AND VIOLIN.

MESSRS. BENEDICT AND WYNEN.

DUETTO—"Io vidi la luce," (La Fille du Regiment.) .... DONIZETTI.

M'lle JENNY LIND and Signor BELLETTI.

PART II.

OVERTURE "Zampa," .... HEROLD.

PRAYER—"Und ob die Wolke,"—(Der Freyschütz.) .... C. M. V. WEBER.

M'LLE JENNY LIND.

SOLO—On the Violin—"Le Carnival de Venise,"

MR. WYNEN.

SCOTCH BALLAD—"Auld Robin Gray,"

M'LLE JENNY LIND.

BARCAROLE—"Se la vita vuoi godere." .... TADOLINI

SIGNOR BELLETTI.

THE BIRD SONG .... TAUBERT.

M'LLE JENNY LIND.

CONDUCTOR,

MR. JULIUS BENEDICT.

☞ Chickering's Grand Piano Forte, furn'shed by Mr HENRY PARSONS, Piano Forte Warerooms, No. 13 Camp street, will be used for this Concert.

Printed at the office of the Picayune, 66 Camp street.

89985-H

FIGURE 4.7 Title page of program for one of Jenny Lind's concerts in New Orleans, 1851. 976.31 (780.73) S136p, Louisiana Research Collection, Tulane University, New Orleans, LA.

> The editor begs leave to inform the public that he will continue this publication, uniform with the pieces already issued, in order that the different pamphlets may be bound together in volumes. . . . Encouraged by the liberal patronage extended by the public to his publication, the Editor will spare no pains or expense, to deserve the continuation of their favour. Henceforth, each piece, whatever its size or title may be, will be sold at 25 cents. The complete series, bound in two volumes, and containing 30 pieces, $5.00. A discount of 20 percent will be allowed to booksellers and agents, by applying to the General Depot, at Mr. PAYA & Co, 56 Chartres Street.[79]

Offering a reduction of $2.50 on the price of buying the libretti individually, Fiot encouraged his customers to invest in a full set. Even if they did not purchase the complete, ready-bound collection for $5, surviving copies show that some had their own personal selections of Fiot's libretti bound together in a hardback book, in much the same way as amateur pianists, like Eliza Ripley, bound sheet music they owned into personalized volumes.[80]

The information in the libretti was evidently included with posterity in mind, and they all displayed a keen awareness of both the local and wider history of the work they presented. Most provided the date of the work's first performance in New Orleans, and many others listed the names of the New Orleans cast for performances in the season during which Fiot's edition of the libretto was published. In the case of many of the later works in the series, this was the cast of the opera's New Orleans premiere, and occasionally, as figure 4.8 shows, the commemoration extended to a lithographed portrait of a key performer.

Many of Fiot's libretti also included details of the work's Parisian premiere, and sometimes even the Parisian cast, which was printed in addition to the New Orleans performers' names. In certain cases, this served to highlight singers who had appeared in both Parisian and New Orleans productions. The 1856 libretto for Adolphe Adam's *Si j'étais roi*, for instance, listed the casts not one on top of the other as was often the case, but side by side, as shown in figure 4.9. It would surely have immediately struck local readers that Pauline Colson had premiered the role of Nemea both in Paris and in New Orleans; they would also have recognized that François-Marcel Junca, although he did not reprise his role as Kadoor for the New Orleans premiere, was a current member of the Théâtre d'Orléans troupe, and some would likely have remembered that Neveu, who played the role of Zizel in early Parisian performances, had been part of the New Orleans troupe from 1836 to 1840.[81]

FIGURE 4.8 Sketch of Anna Widemann in the role of Arsace from Fiot's edition of *Semiramis* (New Orleans: printed by J. L. Sollée, Chartres Street, 1852), The Historic New Orleans Collection, acc.no. 80-68-L.1.

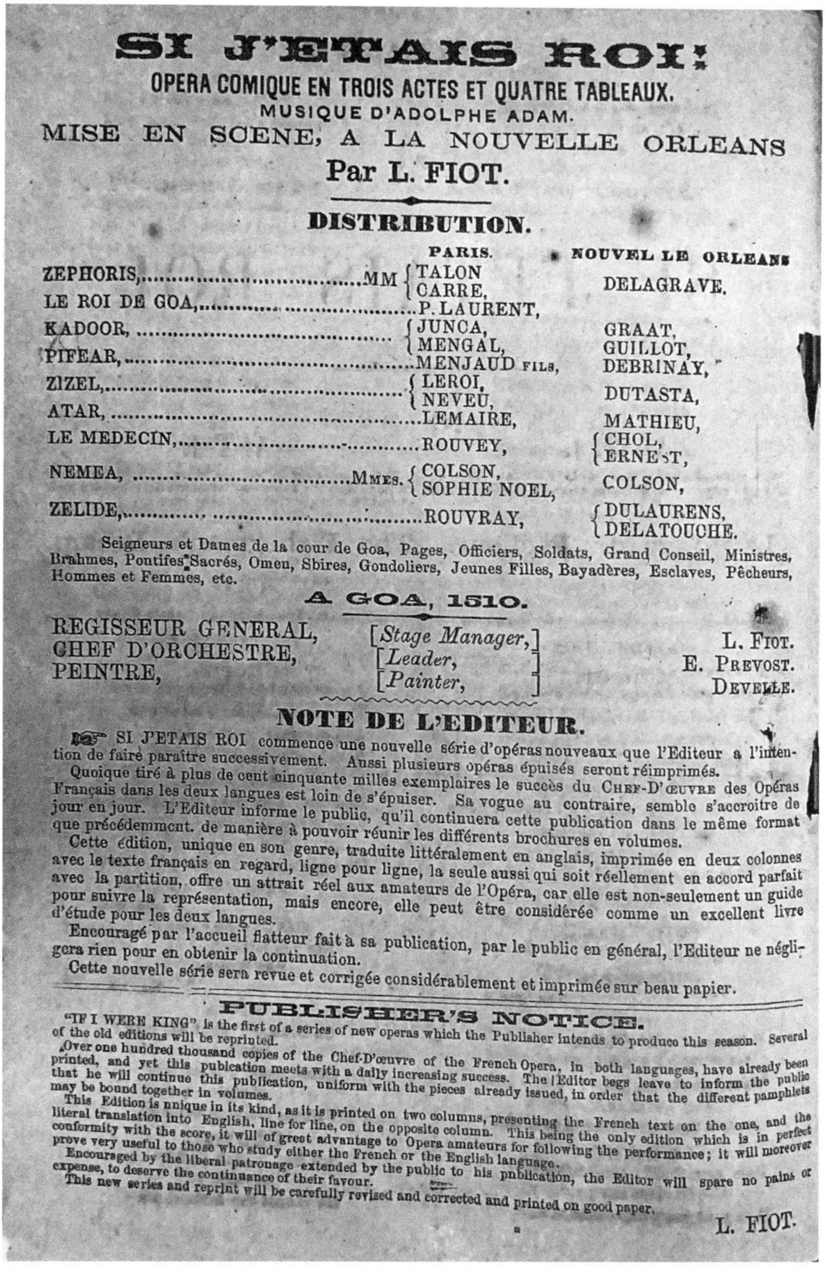

SI J'ETAIS ROI!

OPERA COMIQUE EN TROIS ACTES ET QUATRE TABLEAUX.

MUSIQUE D'ADOLPHE ADAM.

MISE EN SCENE, A LA NOUVELLE ORLEANS

Par L. FIOT.

DISTRIBUTION.

	PARIS.	NOUVELLE ORLEANS
ZEPHORIS,	MM { TALON, CARRE,	DELAGRAVE.
LE ROI DE GOA,	P. LAURENT,	
KADOOR,	{ JUNCA, MENGAL,	GRAAT,
PIFEAR,	MENJAUD FILS,	GUILLOT, DEBRINAY,
ZIZEL,	{ LEROI, NEVEU,	DUTASTA,
ATAR,	LEMAIRE,	MATHIEU,
LE MEDECIN,	ROUVEY,	{ CHOL, ERNEST,
NEMEA,	MMES. { COLSON, SOPHIE NOEL,	COLSON,
ZELIDE,	ROUVRAY,	{ DULAURENS, DELATOUCHE.

Seigneurs et Dames de la cour de Goa, Pages, Officiers, Soldats, Grand Conseil, Ministres, Brahmes, Pontifes Sacrés, Omeu, Sbires, Gondoliers, Jeunes Filles, Bayadères, Esclaves, Pêcheurs, Hommes et Femmes, etc.

A GOA, 1510.

REGISSEUR GENERAL,	[*Stage Manager*,]	L. FIOT.
CHEF D'ORCHESTRE,	[*Leader*,]	E. PREVOST.
PEINTRE,	[*Painter*,]	DEVELLE.

NOTE DE L'EDITEUR.

☞ SI J'ETAIS ROI commence une nouvelle série d'opéras nouveaux que l'Editeur a l'intention de faire paraître successivement. Aussi plusieurs opéras épuisés seront réimprimés.

Quoique tiré à plus de cent cinquante milles exemplaires le succès du CHEF-D'ŒUVRE des Opéras Français dans les deux langues est loin de s'épuiser. Sa vogue au contraire, semble s'accroitre de jour en jour. L'Editeur informe le public, qu'il continuera cette publication dans le même format que précédemment. de manière à pouvoir réunir les différents brochures en volumes.

Cette édition, unique en son genre, traduite littéralement en anglais, imprimée en deux colonnes avec le texte français en regard, ligne pour ligne, la seule aussi qui soit réellement en accord parfait avec la partition, offre un attrait réel aux amateurs de l'Opéra, car elle est non-seulement un guide pour suivre la représentation, mais encore, elle peut être considérée comme un excellent livre d'étude pour les deux langues.

Encouragé par l'accueil flatteur fait à sa publication, par le public en général, l'Editeur ne négligera rien pour en obtenir la continuation.

Cette nouvelle série sera revue et corrigée considérablement et imprimée sur beau papier.

PUBLISHER'S NOTICE.

"IF I WERE KING" is the first of a series of new operas which the Publisher intends to produce this season. Several of the old editions will be reprinted.

Over one hundred thousand copies of the Chef-D'œuvre of the French Opera, in both languages, have already been printed, and yet this publication meets with a daily increasing success. The Editor begs leave to inform the public that he will continue this publication, uniform with the pieces already issued, in order that the different pamphlets may be bound together in volumes.

This Edition is unique in its kind, as it is printed on two columns, presenting the French text on the one, and the literal translation into English, line for line, on the opposite column. This being the only edition which is in perfect conformity with the score, it will of great advantage to Opera amateurs for following the performance; it will moreover prove very useful to those who study either the French or the English language.

Encouraged by the liberal patronage extended by the public to his publication, the Editor will spare no pains or expense, to deserve the continuance of their favour.

This new series and reprint will be carefully revised and corrected and printed on good paper.

L. FIOT.

FIGURE 4.9 Cast list inside Fiot's edition of *Si j'étais roi*, New Orleans, 1856. Albert Voss Collection, Manuscripts Collection 856, Series 1, Box 1, Folder 1, Louisiana Research Collection, Tulane University, New Orleans, LA.

There are two important points to note from all of this: first, that the libretti sought to position the New Orleans premiere alongside its Parisian equivalent (placing the two in a kind of historical continuum) and encouraged the reader to draw connections between them. In certain cases, the memorial link was made even more explicit by the inclusion of a review of the Parisian premiere, such as the page-long review of Verdi's *Jérusalem* from *La France musicale* that Fiot reprinted in his edition of the work's libretto. In these cases, the implication was that the New Orleans performances should be read in light not of local criticism of the work, but of the reception of its Parisian premiere.[82] Second, printing the cast lists served both to fix the libretto and the work to a particular moment in time and then to elevate that moment to timelessness. While the names of the New Orleans cast might have been current at the time of the libretto's production, it would not have been long before the list of performers no longer served as a helpful guide to performances at hand. Instead, the libretto became a monument to a past cast, to be remembered nostalgically alongside the great performers of the Parisian premiere.

Here, then, as with Lehmann's compositions, there is a sense that opera's material culture in New Orleans—ephemeral though it might appear from the papery fragility of its products and its attempts to capture occasions with "of the moment" relevance—was undergirded by a desire to preserve, to memorialize, and indeed to insert New Orleans into a larger, transatlantic operatic history. While, for Lehmann, this involved a turn to opera's diffusion in social life—to the ways in which operas could be broken down, transformed, and repackaged beyond the stage—Fiot's libretti resonate more with contemporary trends toward consolidating and stabilizing the notion of the operatic "work."

The repertoire Fiot selected perhaps holds the key to understanding both his aims for the series and the significance of the editions in this respect. The first eight works he chose for publication were *grands opéras* (for a full list of Fiot's libretti, see table 4.1),[83] and among them, unsurprisingly in light of the debates around the works discussed in chapter 2, were *Robert le diable* and *Les Huguenots,* as well as the initially overlooked *La Muette.* There are no examples of the late eighteenth-century and early nineteenth-century *opéras-comiques* that had formed the mainstay of the theater's repertoire from its opening until the 1830s, but nor were all the works modern (indeed, Mozart's *Don Giovanni,* under the title *Don Juan,* was one of Fiot's selections). Instead, there is a sense that the operas he selected were in some way "great works," worthy not only of the title "*chefs d'œuvre,*" but of immortalization.

TABLE 4.1 Fiot's libretti

NUMBER	FRENCH TITLE	ENGLISH TITLE (AS LISTED IN LIBRETTO)	WORDS BY	MUSIC BY
1	*Les Huguenots*	*The Huguenots*	E. Scribe	Meyerbeer
2	*La Juive*	*The Jewess*	E. Scribe	Halévy
3	*Robert le Diable**	*Robert the Devil*	E. Scribe	Meyerbeer
4	*La Favorite*	*The King's Mistress*	Gust. Vaëz	Donizetti
5	*Guillaume Tell*	*William Tell*	De Jouy	Rossini
6	*La Muette de Portici*	*The Dumb Girl of Portici*	E. Scribe	Auber
7	*La Reine de Chypre*	*The Queen of Cyprus*	De St. George	Halévy
8	*Les Martyrs*	*The Martyrs*	Scribe	Donizetti
9	*Anne de Boulen*	*Anna Bolena*	Castil Blaze	Donizetti
10	*Les Mousquetaires de la Reine*	*The Queen's Musketeers*	De St. George	Halévy
11	*Charles VI*	*Charles VI*	C. Delavigne	Halévy
12	*Lucie de Lammermoor**	*Lucia di Lammermoor*	D. Vaëz	Donizetti
13	*Lucrèce de Borge**	*Lucretia Borgia*	E. Monnier	Donizetti
14	*Norma**	*Norma*	E. Monnier	Donizetti
15	*Othello**	*Othello*	Royer and Vaez	Rossini
16	*Ne touchez pas à la reine**	*Hands Off the Queen*	Scribe and Vaez	Boisselot
17	*Puritains*	*I Puritani*	E. Monnier	Bellini
18	*L'éclair**	*Lightning*	De St George	Halévy
19	*Le Somnambule**	*The Somnambula*	E. Monnier	Bellini
20	*Haydée**	*Haydee*	E. Scribe	Auber
21	*Jerusalem**	*Jerusalem*	A. Roger, G. Vaez	Verdi

TABLE 4.1 *continued*

NUMBER	FRENCH TITLE	ENGLISH TITLE (AS LISTED IN LIBRETTO)	WORDS BY	MUSIC BY
22	*Le Prophète**	*The Prophet*	E. Scrib	Meyerbeer
23	*Le Caïd**	*The Caid*	T. Sauvage	A. Thomas
24	*Les deux Foscari**	*The Two Foscari*	The brothers Scudier	Verdi
25	*Sémiramis**	*Semiramis*	[?]	Rossini
26	*Don Juan**	*Don Juan*	E. Deschamps, C. Blaze	Mozart
27	*Moise**	*Moses*	[Etienne de Jouy]	Rossini
28	*Marguerite d'Anjou**	*Marguerite d'Anjou*	[T. Sauvage]	Meyerbeer
29	*L'Etoile du nord**	*The Star of the North*	Scribe	Meyerbeer
30	*Si j'étais roi**	*If I Were King*	Dennery and Brésil	Adolphe Adam

The information given here in square brackets was not provided on the printed libretti, but I have supplied it in keeping with the information in the rest of the table. Asterisks next to an opera's French title indicate that I have located a copy of that libretto. Errors and misspellings are Fiot's.

Fiot's selections, then, suggest important parallels with the shift from performer-centered to work-centered music criticism in the wake of *grand opéra*'s introduction to New Orleans discussed in chapter 2. His general preface to the edition states:

> This Edition is unique in its kind, as it is printed on two columns, presenting the French text on one, and the literal translation into English, line for line, on the opposite column. *This being the only edition which is in perfect conformity with the score,* it will be of great advantage to Opera amateurs for following the performance.[84]

While stressing the uniqueness of the edition was, of course, a convenient sales tactic, the fact that Fiot emphasized that it was "in perfect conformity with the score" suggests a system of values behind the publications that placed the music above all other elements. The libretto's role, as Fiot positioned it, was to help people better follow the music, and his, he claimed, would do so perfectly. To what extent anyone actually used these libretti in the theater is long forgotten, but the desire to stress the conformity of libretto and score places a clear emphasis on the operatic work as text.

Indeed, Fiot's libretti hint at an increased standardization of operatic performance in this period, at least in theory. In contrast to libretti produced for opera productions in other places in the world, such as those Vera Wolkowicz has examined in her discussions of Bellini's *Norma* in Buenos Aires,[85] Fiot's libretti bear no traces of local adaptations, nor of cuts or alterations to the structure of the works.[86] Even in the case of *Robert le diable*, at the premiere of which at both the French and American theaters in 1835 various cuts and alterations were made, Fiot's libretto is almost completely identical to the version used in Paris following the initial changes made after the work's premiere. Whether or not Fiot's vision always corresponded with actual theatrical practice—and indeed, it ignored all the other places besides the theater through which canons of opera could be formed, such as in the ballroom, or in excerpts or arrangements played in the home—his intention that his editions should correspond exactly to onstage performances places particular importance on a stable, fixed version of the operatic text.[87]

It would perhaps not be too much of a stretch to suggest that Fiot's editions were closely involved with self-conscious processes of canon formation in New Orleans. Not only did they reflect changes in critical discourse in the city, but they also played a role in driving these processes by creating a collection of the "greatest" works that could be bought and returned to repeatedly.[88] The establishment of *grand opéra* in New Orleans as a regularly performed repertoire, the new, work-based criticism that grew along with it, and the emergence of cheap print technologies entwined to create an environment in which Fiot could enact a simultaneous materializing and monumentalizing of works.

Much, but not all, of the repertoire included within Fiot's series was French. In contrast to earlier periods in which the operatic repertoire known in any form in New Orleans had been almost exclusively French, by the 1840s and early 1850s, when Fiot published his editions, the Théâtre d'Orléans's repertoire included a growing number of Italian works in French translation, ranging from Rossini, through Donizetti and Bellini, to Verdi, following on from the initial fervor for Italian opera created by Caldwell's visiting Italian troupes from Havana between 1836 and 1842.[89] Even Mozart eventually made it into the series, a fact that is particularly surprising, given that earlier in the century audiences at the Théâtre d'Orléans had expressed dislike for all of the Mozart works the management had attempted to produce.[90] Fiot's publication of the libretto is not necessarily an indication that public taste had changed (although he surely would not have chosen to sell a libretto for an opera of which no performances were given), but rather that the work was now seen as being "great" and worthy of immortalization in this manner.[91]

As Karen Ahlquist and Benjamin Walton's chapters (on New York and the Río de la Plata, respectively) in the recent *Oxford Handbook to the Operatic Canon* highlight, performance statistics can be a poor measure of canonicity.[92] Indeed, Fiot's selections for his series were not simply based on what was most performed among the Théâtre d'Orléans's repertoire in the 1840s and 1850s: although the grand operas and two- and three-act comic operas that his libretti preserve were regularly programmed, the theater gave vaudevilles and short, one-act comic operas on a nightly basis. These, of course, were not reflected among Fiot's choice of "chefs d'œuvre." Instead, Fiot's putative canon, as framed in his libretti, represents a rather self-conscious attempt to capture something of the local operatic reality, at the same time as it imagines an international—cosmopolitan—canon with significance beyond the city of New Orleans.

Tracing the influence of Fiot's libretti on how his customers and the operagoing public at large thought of opera is more difficult than drawing conclusions about how his libretti presented opera. Demand for the libretti was high enough for Fiot to produce several editions, as he revealed in his preface to the libretto for *Don Juan*:

> One hundred thousand copies of the Chef-d'oeuvre [*sic*] of the French Opera, in both languages, have already been printed, and yet, this publication meets with a daily increasing success. Several exhausted editions have been corrected, revised and republished.[93]

The idea that 100,000 copies of these libretti had been sold between c. 1847 and 1853 is remarkable, especially since the total population of New Orleans in 1850 was only 116,375.[94] But in spite of their obvious specifically local features (such as the cast lists discussed above), these libretti had a wider sphere of influence. They were sold in New York as well as in New Orleans: libretti printed in 1848 listed the address of the "New York Depot" as "Mr. Corbyn's Dramatic Agency Office, 4 Barclay Street," while by 1850 the retailer was given as "Douglas, 11 Spruce Street."[95]

The fact that the libretti were sold in New York perhaps casts a different light on both the inclusion of local details and the standardization of the operatic text in Fiot's editions. The Théâtre d'Orléans troupe had visited New York on its tours of the Northeast from the late 1820s, introducing audiences in the city to various French operas for the first time. The latest of these tours were in 1843 and 1845, respectively, and audiences in New York may well still have remembered some of the performers' names by 1848, when Fiot's libretti went on sale there. Léon Fleury, Mme Fleury-Jolly, and Mme Lecourt, among others, had performed in New York on the company's tour three years earlier, and their presence in cast lists in Fiot's libretti may well have jogged consumers' memories, even if the specific works in which they were listed, like Bellini's *La Somnambule*, were not those that they had performed to audiences in the city during the tours.[96]

The sale of Fiot's libretti in New York, then, might have been a means of continuing in material form (and with an expanded international repertoire) the work begun by the Théâtre d'Orléans troupe on its tours, of introducing the cities of the Eastern Seaboard to opera in French. If the libretti were to serve as cultural ambassadors in the Northeast, shaping the operatic tastes of consumers there, then Fiot would likely have wanted to make sure that the canon of works he advocated bore the distinctive marks of New Orleans (which included, in the case of the Italian works, the "local" stamp of the French language). That is to say, he might have been promoting a developing international operatic canon, but he was keen to reveal the influence of New Orleans as a leader in operatic taste, from which the people of New York could learn.

Again, it is impossible to trace the precise impact Fiot's libretti had (or, indeed, failed to have) in New York, but it is nonetheless tempting to speculate that they may have had some influence on American operatic culture at the mid-century. While opera had its origins in Europe as an elite art, in the United States, there was little sense of a cultural hierarchy until well into the second half of the nineteenth century, as Katherine Preston, Joseph Mussulman, Lawrence Levine, and others have shown.[97] Opera was often treated as a kind of "variety entertainment," to be rearranged at will. Fiot's editions, at least in theory, promoted a new sense of operas as "works," less easily rearranged or interrupted. As such, we can perhaps tentatively read them, and their sale in the Northeast in particular, as foreshadowing the repositioning of foreign-language opera from a popular entertainment to an aesthetically elevated, elevating and, by extension, elite art in the United States in the second half of the century.[98] While the rise of opera as high art in America has typically been tied to Italian- and German-language works, Fiot's libretti provide a hint of the influence French-language materials and operas might also have had on this process, albeit perhaps to a less obvious extent.

Fiot's libretti laid the way for other series of libretti in New Orleans, such as those published by Jean Schweitzer later in the 1850s, and thus they led to the continued development of a material culture for opera.[99] None, however, attempted to strike quite the delicate balance between functionality and commemoration, the local and the international, work and performer that Fiot managed to achieve in all of his libretti in various ways. While printed libretti were notionally intended to enhance operagoers' experience in the theater, Fiot's editions served both as a collectible commodity that entwined the operatic histories of New Orleans and Paris, and also as a means of shaping operatic taste, within the city of New Orleans and beyond its limits.

Fiot and Lehmann would certainly have known each other, at the very least as acquaintances and colleagues: they were both employed at the Théâtre d'Orléans in the 1840s and 1850s. Their libretti and sheet music reflect some of the ways in which people who worked at the theater could diversify their earnings. For Lehmann, in particular, his sheet music was part of what we might today call a "portfolio career," something many of the other musicians who populate this book also had to greater or lesser extents. That is not to say that they could not survive on the pay they were offered by the Théâtre d'Orléans—both, after all, chose to spend at least a decade in the theater's employ—but rather that producing these items benefited them as much as it did their consumers.

As Fiot's libretti and Lehmann's sheet music show, not all operatic souvenirs were alike: though they shared both commercial aims and a commemorative dimension, they reflected quite different social and cultural roles for opera. For Lehmann, opera in adapted forms was a catalyst for social intimacy, while for Fiot, opera could be mobilized as a tool of cultural self-confidence. Both, nonetheless, were deeply locally rooted but also looked outward, beyond the city, and relied on perceptions of opera as international and, indeed, of opera's material culture as international for their appeal to customers.

These items, then, even though they were locally produced in New Orleans, by people connected to the Théâtre d'Orléans, have something to say about operatic globalization. Indeed, while so many of the things I have discussed in the rest of this book are specifically about transatlantic connection, these elements of material culture are suggestive of something beyond direct links between New Orleans and Paris (although those still remained important). They were not designed to appeal simply to French-speaking consumers in New Orleans: Lehmann's pieces had a range of Anglo-American and Francophone dedicatees, and he himself, as a German immigrant, did not fit neatly into the Francophone-Anglophone dichotomy explored in chapter 2. Fiot's libretti, too, were in many respects designed to appeal to

Anglophone consumers as much as French speakers: they emphasized the bilingual element, and the title of the series—"chef-d'oeuvres"—was an anglicization of the French "chefs-d'œuvre." Their English translations were not always idiomatic—one English-speaking owner of some surviving libretti annotated them with exclamation marks and question marks at moments where the English text was particularly wayward—but they nonetheless show attempts to reach an Anglophone audience both in New Orleans and in New York.[100]

While the transatlantic frame remains important for understanding these operatic objects, it is also distinctly "leaky." They imply a frame of reference that extended beyond the specific relationship with Parisian operatic productions, based on imagined sets of consumers and emerging canons of "great" works. Operatic productions within the Théâtre d'Orléans continued to rely mainly on transatlantic connections for their performers and materials but, beyond the theater, opera's material culture combined those transatlantic elements with specifically local significance and reference to a more generalized cosmopolitan connection. In this, they perhaps hint toward the globalized operatic world that was to emerge in the second half of the nineteenth century.

5

Reimagining New Orleans in Operatic Travelogues

> "Let us go to the theatre!" said the doctor . . . From the cemetery to the theatre! And of a Sabbath evening, too! Both the time and the contrast are equally characteristic of the city I describe. So true it is, that the manners and opinions of a people are best studied in the most common and every-day acts of life.[1]

The author of these words, Edward H. Durell, was not alone among visitors to New Orleans in the 1830s, either in finding himself drawn to the Théâtre d'Orléans or in describing the theater as a window onto the character of the city. From the Duke of Saxe-Weimar-Eisenach, who visited in 1825, to Eliza Potter, a black hairdresser from New York working in the South during the early 1850s, numerous and varied individuals committed to paper their opinions about New Orleans.[2] Collectively, these writers created a set of "must-sees" or "must-dos" for a visit to the city—part of a process Derek Gregory has called the "scripting" of the travel experience—and the theater became one such site: the Théâtre d'Orléans proved fascinating to Anglophone and Francophone visitors alike.[3]

Most recollections of visits to the theater were brief, giving only a mention of the work performed and a note on the quality of the performers and, frequently, a quick description of the theater itself and the people encountered there. A few, however, placed a rather more extended focus on the theater, and on operatic performance in particular, and in this chapter I want to focus on three of these: the travel memoir written by the aforementioned Durell (*New Orleans as I Found It*) and two works—a short story and a novel—by a Frenchman, Charles Jobey.[4]

Jobey has already appeared in this book in various guises: he was born in Rouen in 1812 or 1813, but spent the six years between 1834 and 1840 as a bassoonist in the orchestra of the Théâtre d'Orléans. After his return to France, he turned to writing, publishing fiction and nonfiction books, contributing to Parisian periodicals—*Le Monde illustré, Journal pour tous* and *La Semaine des familles,* among others—and promoting provincial journalism.[5] His novel *L'Amour d'un nègre* and the short story variously published as "Le lac Cathahoula" and "Souvenirs de la Louisiane" drew heavily on his experiences in Louisiana.

Edward Henry Durell, meanwhile, was an American, born in 1810 in Portsmouth, New Hampshire. He read law at Harvard, becoming fluent in German, French, and Spanish, and then went into legal practice. The visit to New Orleans in 1835–1836 that he later recorded in *New Orleans as I Found It* was his first, and lasted only a few days, but inspired him to relocate permanently to the city.[6] By the time he published *New Orleans as I Found It* in 1845, he had been living in New Orleans for several years.

Although they differed in their cultural and linguistic backgrounds, as well as their reasons for being in New Orleans, Jobey and Durell's accounts of their travels are in many ways complementary. Neither was a fleeting visitor—a "tourist," in the pejorative sense the word came to acquire—and they spent years living and, indeed, working in New Orleans. Both, however, wrote for audiences beyond the city: Durell chose to publish his account with a company in New York, and Jobey's works were published in Paris in the handful of years around 1860 ("Le lac Cathahoula"/"Souvenirs de la Louisiane" was also serialized in Louisiana, but I will discuss the differences in that version later).

While the previous three chapters of this book were concerned with how people in New Orleans looked out to the world beyond, this final chapter flips the lens, reading the city through the eyes of visitors from both sides of the Atlantic. As I argue throughout this chapter, the extended focus on the theater, opera, and music in Jobey and Durell's accounts served as a way for them to explore the nature of transatlantic and even global interconnections in the period. The operatic activities of the Théâtre d'Orléans formed the starting point for the authors' cultural self-reflection and their shaping of the city's image for people internationally. Transatlantic operatic connection was far from unidirectional, especially in its imaginative dimensions: news and stories about operatic activity in New Orleans spread back across the Atlantic, helping shape perceptions not just of New Orleans, but also of French culture and its place in the world.

Travel writing allowed musicians to engage in varied sociopolitical debates throughout the nineteenth century, as Virginia Whealton has recently demonstrated in her work on travelogues (musical as well as in prose) by composers and virtuoso pianists, who explored themes of nationalism, democracy, and imperialism in their writings.[7] The texts I consider in this chapter similarly engage in debates of their time, touching on issues of race, the relationship between New Orleans and its former imperial center, and the friction of cultural encounter in an increasingly connected world. Travel writing's potential as a source for opera history specifically has also been examined: Benjamin Walton has explored how opera became a discourse through which an array of European travelers—Charles Darwin, Victor Jacquemont, and Emily Eden, among others—were able to describe and express their reactions to the novel places and people they encountered.[8] Building on Walton's work, I want to go further in this chapter, to suggest that not only did opera serve as a descriptive resource for travelers, but that writing about opera allowed the authors to make sense of their real-life travels and to create an imaginary travel experience for their readers.

The notion of an "imaginary" travel experience is particularly important here, given that Jobey and Durell's texts are not simple guidebooks, but sit on the cusp between documentary travel memoir and fiction.[9] Durell's text is a highly esoteric, at times surreal, mixture of fantastical stories and factual description. Jobey's texts, meanwhile, owe much to the exotic fiction that became so popular in nineteenth-century France, and they share with works like Chateaubriand's *Atala* (1801), *René* (1802), and *Les Natchez* (1826) an authorial insistence on true-to-life detail in the context of a wider fictional narrative.[10] Jobey described his works as "*romans*," although he asserted solemnly that his work "contains true descriptions" of America and that the details "are of the greatest exactitude."[11] In the preface to a collection of his short stories, published in Paris in 1861, he noted:

> We have always thought it indispensable to have traveled in order to talk of distant lands, to write on the habits and customs of the people who inhabit them. We were wrong, we now recognize, as every day we see people who have never gone beyond the boundaries of Paris writing very amusing stories in which the scenes take place four thousand leagues from here.[12]

While he conceded that a bit of invention could prove the key to success in the booming travel literature market of the mid-nineteenth century, his focus on the accuracy of his descriptions and his own experiences in Louisiana suggests that he hoped such details would set his stories apart from the swathes of exotic stories by those who relied on imagination alone.

Such an admission about travel writing's play between fact and fiction resonates with Tim Youngs's claim that travel literature is essentially "hybrid," relying on the permeability of stylistic and generic boundaries for its impact.[13] Other scholars have similarly argued that travel writing operates in spaces of transculturation,[14] or spaces "in-between," to borrow Homi Bhabha's term.[15] The slippage between the factual and the fictional, the location focused and the character focused, the real and the literary in Jobey's texts, therefore, becomes crucial to understanding opera's role as more than a piquant background detail.

In the wake of Mary Louise Pratt's seminal *Imperial Eyes*, travel writing's relationship with empire has been well explored, and it has been seen in many circles as another method by which Europeans constructed and controlled the rest of the world.[16] Opera's history, like that of travel writing, was entwined with empire: the earliest opera performances beyond Europe were in places colonized by Europeans, and the building of a theater or opera house in these places was often linked to European ideas of "civilization" in contemporary discourses, as Rogério Budasz, Walton, and others have discussed.[17] In practice, however, music and opera's status as a marker of such "civilization" was far less stable, and music's limitations in processes of cultural encounter are something that both Vanessa Agnew and Ruth Rosenberg have explored.[18] In my readings of Jobey and Durell's texts in this chapter, opera is not just a way of "translating" a "foreign" or "exotic" experience for readers, but an idiom shared—albeit with differing inflections—by the population of New Orleans and the visiting authors. I ultimately argue that these texts turn to opera and musical performance to bypass a focus on nation and empire (in the case of Durell) and to evoke moments of cultural encounter that undermine Europeans' certainty of their own superiority (in the case of Jobey). A focus on opera in these texts, then, offers an insight into the subtleties of cultural interaction between France and its former colony, and between Europe and the independent United States in the mid-nineteenth century.

INSIDE AND OUTSIDE THE THEATER: OPERA AND THE EXOTIC IN *L'AMOUR D'UN NÈGRE*

Jobey's novel *L'Amour d'un nègre* was published in Paris in 1860. In fact, it was published twice that year: once with A. Varigault, and again as part of the Collection Michel Lévy—a series of inexpensive books whose cover color indicated their price—which emerged as part of the great boom in book publishing in the middle decades of the nineteenth century.[19] As a green-covered paperback, *L'Amour d'un nègre* cost only a single franc (much less than the twenty-two francs that most novels had cost early in the century),[20] and it was advertised in the Lévy brothers' catalog alongside works by such well-known authors as Dumas and Flaubert, as well as French translations of works by Charles Dickens and Harriet Beecher Stowe. Although there is no surviving information about how many copies were actually sold, its price and small format would have made it accessible to a range of Parisian readers.

The novel follows a young Parisian named Charles Roger, who goes to New Orleans in 1834 to settle his late father's estate; it tells the story of a disastrous love affair, which results in Roger's transformation from an eligible bachelor and wealthy heir to a hunted and broken man.[21] As Jobey sketches out Roger's new surroundings, the theater emerges as a recurring if initially apparently minor figure, and later, at the very heart of the novel, there is a lengthy scene set in the Théâtre d'Orléans.[22] It is here, during a performance of Auber's one-act *opéra-comique, Le Concert à la cour,* that Roger's fortunes take a sudden and dramatic turn for the worse.

Roger has gone to the theater at the instigation of his capricious new fiancée, Camillia. She wants him to report back on the evening's events: Mademoiselle Dupuis, a young soprano, and Madame Saint-Clair, the established prima donna, have been vying for position for weeks, and earning passionate partisans within the Théâtre d'Orléans audience; that night is expected to be the moment of reckoning. At the theater, Roger finds that the assembled throng is loudly discussing the matter, and disagreements are already breaking out. Not long after the start of the performance, Dupuis is drowned out by a barrage of whistles from her opponents, while a man clambers onto a bench in the parterre, shouting, "Mademoiselle Dupuis! The role of Adèle is not yours, and we will not let you play it!"[23] The ensuing melee is nothing if not operatic:

> At these words a tempest bursts forth, everyone is on their feet, in the orchestra, the parterre, in the boxes; they exchange insults, threats. The actress, cause of all this noise, takes the opportunity to faint on the stage. The disorder is at its height, personal provocations are exchanged: blows, bellows, fists rain down on all sides. A dagger is drawn, and in an instant twenty, fifty, one hundred, two hundred daggers, knives, dart-sticks, pistols, shine in the room.[24]

The rioting mob spills out into the street, where two people are killed, many injured, and dozens more arrange duels to settle personal scores. As Roger and his companions go to leave their box, they are confronted by a young man named Simpson, Roger's bitter rival for Camillia's love. In the midst of the chaos, Simpson challenges Roger to a duel with pistols. When they meet the following day, Roger kills Simpson and is forced to flee New Orleans, destined to many months of wandering the United States and longing to be reunited with his beloved Camillia.

What to make of such an overly dramatic scene, and of opera's role within it? At first, it might seem as if, in his avowed quest for authentic detail, Jobey were drawing upon a memory of a real event: "diva wars," as discussed in chapter 1, were commonplace in New Orleans as they were the world over, when supporters of one slighted leading lady would vie with those of her rival. The divas in question here—Mme St-Clair and Mlle Dupuis—were real-life contemporaries of Jobey's at the Théâtre d'Orléans.[25] There is little, however, to support the notion that any theatrical quarrels escalated beyond scuffles in the parterre.

Contextualizing Jobey's scene within long-standing literary traditions, on the other hand, opens up a very different set of interpretative possibilities. The *soirée à l'Opéra* was an oft-employed device in eighteenth- and nineteenth-century Parisian novels, to the extent that Cormac Newark has observed that the novels of Balzac's *La Comédie humaine* "at times seem mainly populated by characters who like nothing better than discussing productions at the Opéra and its back-stage ins and outs."[26] Newspapers and magazines in New Orleans, too, were full of short stories and serialized works of fiction about operagoing. Jobey's evening at the opera in *L'Amour d'un nègre*, then, had an established literary precedent and a well-developed generic context on both sides of the Atlantic.

But Jobey's scene does more than simply capitalize on a literary vogue. As Newark has argued, opera became part of the frame of reference for French novels of the period because operagoing formed a regular part of the social experience of their bourgeois and aristocratic readership: the opera house came to function as a microcosm of society at large.[27] That society, of course, was almost exclusively Parisian, with occasional provincial detours, such as the evening at the opera house in Rouen that becomes the catalyst for Emma Bovary's second bout of adultery in Flaubert's *Madame Bovary* (1854). Jobey's microcosm of society, however, is explicitly not Parisian, nor from the French provinces, nor even from Europe. Instead, his *soirée à l'Opéra* attempts to provide the French reader with a distillation of a society some 5,000 miles away.

Sure enough, throughout most of the book, Jobey paints an image of New Orleans as exotic, and as intriguingly (sometimes dangerously) unfamiliar. Roger's bumbling Parisian uncle, Monsieur Potard, accompanies him for the first part of the novel, and it is through his eyes that Jobey introduces his reader to the unfamiliar world of New Orleans. A man of creature comforts, Potard is unable to cope with the climate, and he is horrified when confronted with the local cuisine. In the few chapters before his return to France, he serves as a comic foil to his infinitely more open-minded and likeable young nephew, as Jobey draws on long-standing tradition to satirize the small-mindedness of the European traveler abroad.[28] Although Roger, by contrast, embraces the unfamiliarity of New Orleans, he still finds himself marveling at the exotic. Since articles about New Orleans in Parisian journals of the period focused on everything from the dangerous wildlife to the appearance of local women to unfamiliar burial customs, developing the sense of peril found as early as L'Abbé Prévost's *Manon Lescaut* (1731), such a response from Jobey's protagonist is perhaps unsurprising.[29]

But Jobey's use of the theater within the novel complicates the picture. Indeed, in contrast with the more straightforwardly foreign outside world, he presents the experience of operagoing to his Parisian readers, at least initially, as entirely recognizable: Roger is listening to an *opéra-comique* by Auber, the performers' egos are as inflated and fragile as those of any Parisian prima donna, and they have the same power to inspire partisan support. Even the audience reminds Roger of what he has left behind in France. Arriving at the theater early, he observes the rapidly filling auditorium: the Louisiana belles (and, of course, men of social status) in the first tier, the second tier occupied by free people of color, and the third tier filled with slaves.[30] The parterre (though not mentioned by Roger) would have been filled with less affluent white men; it is here that the unrest breaks out.

Although the social makeup differed strongly from Parisian custom, as Roger watches the slaves, in "white dresses, yellow or red tignons" and eating their pecans, figs, and oranges, all he can think of is how like the "titis of the [Parisian] boulevards" they are, up there in New Orleans's equivalent of the *paradis*.[31] While such a description might be read as a quasi-satirical comment on the colorful social composition of Parisian theater audiences, Roger is in no way cynical. Indeed, the initial experience of operagoing in New Orleans turns out to be oddly familiar, even uncannily Parisian. For one brief moment before the performance begins and chaos breaks out, the distance between New Orleans and Paris is reduced to almost nothing, as Roger sits in the theater and thinks of home.

In these terms, it is tempting to read Jobey's Théâtre d'Orléans as offering a utopian bastion of French culture, uniting New Orleans's disparate social factions—black and white, Francophone and Anglophone—in their shared desire for opera, even as they occupy distinct areas of the theater. Indeed, Roger is there because Camillia's slave told her it would be a night of great importance. In Jobey's account, all sections of society are equally keen to patronize the theater. The parterre and orchestra areas are so full that the audience overflows into the corridors, and the first tier is filled three deep; meanwhile, the second tier is completely full with "only half of those who presented themselves at the box office," while in the third tier, enslaved people are "packed in like sardines."[32] Not only are all strata of society present in the theater, but they are actively participating in the debates, and loud conversations about the forthcoming performance "take place in all parts of the auditorium."[33] The theater is therefore characterized as a space with rules slightly different from those in the outside world: a place where everyone from Creole elites to slaves can openly express an opinion on the performers in the troupe.

The theater also achieves a special geographical status in Jobey's novel, as it serves as a familiar point of orientation for the European abroad. It functions within the novel as a kind of North Star, the guiding light by which Jobey helps the visiting Roger and his Parisian readers alike to navigate in the city. On several occasions, for example, meetings between characters take place in a restaurant that is described as being "opposite the French theater," with this location providing a counterbalance to the unfamiliar food Roger and his uncle find the restaurant serves.[34] The geographical prominence of the theater at the heart of the French Quarter gives it a significance for the European visitor as much as for the locals.

But if in some respects the Théâtre d'Orléans appears to be a reassuring symbol of unity and civilization in an otherwise exotic locale, Roger is soon confronted with the fact that image and reality diverge, and opera is simultaneously a catalyst for social disintegration. The scene at the opera elaborates on and intensifies many aspects of New Orleans's unfamiliar and divided urban politics, sketched out in the earlier part of the novel. In particular, it is concerned with mounting tensions between French and English speakers in the city during this period: the scene sees the culmination of the love rivalry between Roger (a Frenchman) and Simpson (whose name reveals him to be Anglo-American), leading ultimately to the duel and Simpson's death. The theater was a particularly fitting setting for Jobey to have chosen for this moment of confrontation between the Frenchman and the Anglo-American, given the highly charged theatrical rivalries I explored in chapter 2.

But even if the events at the opera in Jobey's novel go some way toward undermining its image of cosmopolitan civilization, and the multitude of knives, daggers, and dart sticks appear to verge on savagery, in many ways the riot precipitated by the performance might have struck Parisian readers as familiar. On the one hand, the episode is simply a typical piece of novelistic drama, and on the other it hints at well-known (but not necessarily any less fictional) stories of incidents both on and off the operatic stage. Descriptions of the scene's theatrical violence would surely have brought to mind the onstage revolutions of *grand opéra*, while the audience fracas might have recalled the fabled riot at a performance of Auber's *La Muette de Portici* in Brussels in 1830.[35] After all, it is another Auber opera that is being performed in *L'Amour d'un nègre*. Whether in Europe or New Orleans, then, opera's civilized image is shadowed by the potential for violence.

Jobey, therefore, uses the scene at the opera to facilitate a very particular kind of literary tourism for his readers. In his hands a familiar novelistic device, operatic performance, becomes the means through which an "exotic" society at large is translated and reduced into a recognizable form. But the result is not a straightforward domestication of the exotic. Instead, while the world outside the theater remains largely Other, the opera becomes a way of presenting Parisian readers, like the Parisian protagonist Roger, with an uncanny experience, as they are forced to recognize themselves in that Other.

This experience is not necessarily a comfortable one, as the ending of the novel emphasizes. Indeed, the scene at the opera sets in motion a chain of events that ultimately shake Roger's belief in the civilization and even the humanity of his French-descended Creole counterparts in New Orleans. When he eventually returns to the city after his exile and attempts to find his beloved Camillia, he is greeted with the terrible news that she has killed her slave Lisimon (a man whom she abuses horrifically throughout the novel) and his mother in the most appalling way. The reason for such violence was that Camillia had just given birth to Lisimon's child; unable to cope with the reputational damage that public knowledge of her affair with an enslaved man would bring, she has killed Lisimon and left her baby on the sidewalk to die.[36]

By the time Roger arrives, she has fled to Europe, and abolitionists from the North have stirred up a riot among New Orleans's black population in response to her crimes. Roger reunites with Cora—Camillia's slave, whom Jobey characterizes as being far more cultured and perceptive than her white mistress, and whose interest in opera had resulted in Roger's fateful evening at the theater—while she and her mother are fleeing from the mob ransacking Camillia's house. Roger exclaims that Camillia's behavior should be a mark of national shame for the United States ("Quelle honte pour un pays!"); Cora points out in reply that perhaps the greater shame is that Camillia has been able to avoid facing any consequences of her actions by fleeing to France.[37] Roger, his ideals about love and hopes for his future in the United States shattered, decides to leave for Mexico with Cora and her mother.

The ending of Jobey's novel, then, espouses clear abolitionist sentiments in its condemnation of Camillia's treatment of both her slaves and her own baby and its assertion that such behavior was not simply a shame on an individual, but on the nation as a whole. Nonetheless, the specifics of the way in which Jobey expresses this set his story apart from many other novels about the United States by French authors in this period. Philippe Roger has argued that French writers of the nineteenth century (and beyond) regularly showed considerable anti-Americanism in their characterizations of Anglo-Americans, often positioning their treatment of enslaved people as reprehensible.[38] In Jobey's novel, however, it is not the Anglo-Americans who bear the brunt of the author's censure, but the Creoles—people of French descent—whom Jobey positions as decadent and degenerate. The ending of the novel, therefore, holds up a mirror to the French reader, and France itself is positioned as complicit in Camillia's crime: her escape across the Atlantic means she will never have to face the consequences of her actions.

"LE LAC CATHAHOULA"

The other work by Jobey that I want to address is the short story "Le lac Cathahoula"/"Souvenirs de la Louisiane," which resonates with some of the themes explored in *L'Amour d'un nègre*, but which grants opera and music an even more extensive role. The story had a more complex publication history than *L'Amour d'un nègre*, and it was the only one of Jobey's stories (as far as I have been able to discern) to be published on both sides of the Atlantic. Between 1856 and 1861, it appeared in four subtly different versions: it was serialized as "Souvenirs de la Louisiane" in the *Journal pour tous* (Paris, 1856), *La Loge de l'Opéra* (New Orleans, 1856–1857), and *Le Villageois* (a newspaper published in the small town of Marksville, Louisiana, some 150 miles from New Orleans, in 1857–1858).[39] In 1861, it was republished in Paris under the title "Le lac Cathahoula," as part of a collection of Jobey's short stories entitled *L'Amour d'une blanche*. While *L'Amour d'un nègre* was intended solely for a European French audience, then, "Souvenirs de la Louisiane"/"Le lac Cathahoula" was also available to readers in Louisiana.

"Souvenirs de la Louisiane"/"Le lac Cathahoula" opens with a mysterious nocturnal gathering: it is an August night in the late 1830s, and a group of travelers waits on the main square of the small town of St. Martinville, just over 100 miles to the northwest of New Orleans. They are about to embark on a trip to Catahoula Lake,[40] eleven miles away through thick forest, for a few days of hunting, fishing, and exploring the wilderness. The story follows their progress, documenting encounters with bears, wild bulls, and alligators in the densely wooded landscape. Their safe passage through this unfamiliar terrain is ensured by their knowledgeable guide (a freed slave named Jean-Louis), his servant (an old French sailor named Lucien), an enslaved man named Harris, and a local landowner and slaveholder (Zénon Judice), all of whom accompany them. But these travelers are neither intrepid explorers nor run-of-the-mill tourists: they are instead performers from the Théâtre d'Orléans, who have ventured into the depths of rural Louisiana on a summer tour.

The tale has a first-person narrator, whom we might assume to be Jobey himself: certainly, the other characters—Paul Coeuriot, Félix Miolan, Joseph Vallière, MM. Welsh, Bailly, Heymann, Dunaud, and Mmes Dunaud and Person—were real people, contracted to the theater at the same time as Jobey, and the narrator lists "yours truly" ("votre serviteur") among the performers.[41] The action almost certainly had a basis in reality, as, alongside the theater's ambitious northern tours in the summers of 1828–1832, 1843, and 1845, in many other years performers would arrange smaller, informal tours of the towns of rural Louisiana, in an effort to make a little extra money during the closure of the theater back in New Orleans.

Opera makes its appearance during a series of unexpected musical performances at the story's conclusion. The performers and their companions finish a meal and sit down beside the lakeside to enjoy the sunset (a scene illustrated in the *Journal pour tous* on March 22, 1856 [fig. 5.1]). Harris, the enslaved man traveling with the group, serenades the assembled company. Seeing the praise afforded to Harris, the aging French sailor, Lucien, offers to sing, and horrifies his audience with a bawdy, chauvinist sailors' song. As they recover from this assault on their ears, silence falls among the company, and Jobey describes the plentiful, unfamiliar sounds of the natural world around them. Eventually, one performer dares to "mix his voice with this grand symphony of nature," and Vallière, the theater's oboist, serenades them with the "air du sommeil" from Auber's *La Muette de Portici*.[42]

Finally, as the sun sinks behind the treetops, the troupe comes together to sing the prayer from the third act of the same opera:

> And the vaults of the virgin forest resounded, for the first and likely for the last time, with this beautiful prayer from *La Muette*, of which the singing, so simple, so broad, begins with a pianissimo, resembling a breath of a breeze, and finishes with an energetic fermata, the echo of which returned to us like distant thunder.[43]

FIGURE 5.1 Illustration showing sunset over Lake Catahoula in "Souvenirs de la Louisiane," *Journal pour tous* (Paris), March 22, 1856. Bibliothèque nationale de France.

As the sounds die away, the singers turn to see Harris, Lucien, and Jean-Louis on their knees in the sand at the lake's edge, moved to prayer by the performance. The episode takes on a special poignancy, as it turns out to have been an unwitting swansong for some of them: in a brief final paragraph, we learn that the following day the group set off back to St. Martinville, where three of them, Vallière included, died from yellow fever.[44]

This extended scene by the lakeside, then, takes the form of a series of sonic encounters in the wilderness, not only between different groups of people, but between man, music, and nature. While Bernard McGrane has suggested that "to travel is to see—travel is essentially a way of seeing, a mode of seeing; it is grounded in the eye, in our visual capacity,"[45] Jobey's story relies on sounds—musical and of the natural world—to evoke the unfamiliar environment, but also to explore the experience of being in that environment. The focus on an aural understanding of the world is something that has been well explored in sound studies, and also something that Alessandra Jones has recently touched on in her discussions of silence in Austrian-occupied Venice in the early 1850s and its importance for understanding Verdi's *Rigoletto*.[46] A focus on the relationship (and, indeed, incongruities) between aural and visual presentations of the world can indeed shed much light on the role opera plays in Jobey's travel narrative: accepting the invitation to listen to the travel experience in "Souvenirs de la

Louisiane"/"Le lac Cathahoula" leads to different readings of the story than a visual focus alone suggests.

The first thing Jobey's sonic focus does is destabilize some of the power structures that might otherwise be taken for granted. At first, opera's role appears to replicate existing narratives about its role within processes of colonialism: indeed, the progression Jobey creates from Harris's solo song to the collected troupe's climactic performance presents opera as an art that, if not directly civilizing, at least has far more emotional power than any of the other sounds—musical or natural—heard. Its impact on the story's three nonoperatic "Others" (the freed slave, the slave, and the lower-class white man who fall to their knees during the performance) is, needless to say in this context, especially profound.[47] As Roy Bridges, among many other authors, has suggested, "travel writing became increasingly identified with the interests and preoccupations of those in European societies who wished to bring the non-European world into a position where it could be influenced, exploited or, in some cases, directly controlled."[48] At first, it seems as if Jobey, a European performer, is using opera to assert similar ideas. Focusing more closely on the individual performances, rather than simply assessing the visual markers of those performances' effect (the kneeling audience, for instance), however, allows for a more complex reading of the cultural encounters that Jobey explores in the short story, and an understanding of the differing nuances audiences on both sides of the Atlantic might have taken from it. In particular, it is worth dwelling on the first of the performances, the song sung by Harris, which precedes opera's entrance into the story, to examine how Jobey uses musical performance to characterize the enslaved man.

Harris sings his song at the request of Madame Dunaud, one of the European singers in the party; before he does so, his master, Zénon Judice, who is also traveling with the group, explains the subject of the song for the Europeans: the previous winter, Judge Préval of New Orleans had decided to give a ball for enslaved people in the city. He charged a dollar each, to cover the costs of the musicians and refreshments, and a large crowd arrived, dressed in finery borrowed from their white masters. Partway through the evening, however, the white people realized their clothes and slaves were missing (and that their money had been similarly "borrowed" to pay the entrance fee), and the jailer arrived to shut down the party. Préval was fined $100 and vowed never to give another ball without a permit.

Jobey presents the song as an improvisation, since Judice calls Harris to sing and "show the honorable company your talents as an improvisor."[49] Harris's performance and his fluency in improvising—he sings "without pause or hesitation"—impress the gathered European performers deeply.

His apparent skill as a quasi-troubadour figure shows an impressive degree of sophistication, but at the same time, Harris remains intriguing in his Otherness.[50] The Europeans praise his quick poetic mind, but the spontaneity of his song's conception positions it not so much akin to art song (or, indeed, opera) as part of an unfamiliar folk tradition. Indeed, this moment of musical and poetic outpouring from a slave in the wilderness nods to but also refigures earlier tropes of colonial encounter, such as Chateaubriand's reminiscences of seeing Native Americans dancing to a version of Madeleine Friquet or de Tocqueville's surprise meeting with a Native American who could sing French airs.[51] It appears, then, that Harris, the singing slave who improvises so naturally, takes on the role of what Jennifer Yee has called the "bon nègre": a kind of black, enslaved counterpart to the familiar figuring of the Native American "noble savage" in this forest backdrop,[52] whose idealized talent stands in stark contrast to his curtailed personal freedom.[53]

The song that Harris sings, however, was a real song, and its full text can be found in appendix 2. Moreover, it would have been familiar to both black and white residents of New Orleans: its status as an improvisation is more complicated than Jobey suggests (although his readers in France would not have known). William H. Coleman transcribed its text in his *Historical Sketchbook and Guide to New Orleans and Environs* of 1885, as did George Washington Cable in the illustrated *The Century Magazine* in February 1886, and it was also printed in the *Daily Picayune* of March 4, 1900.[54] The text of the song was highly consistent between these versions, but these authors' descriptions of the music to which it was sung vary considerably. Cable notated a fragment as he heard it sung by a street vendor in New Orleans in G major and upbeat $\frac{6}{8}$ time, but the unnamed author of the article in the *Daily Picayune* from 1900 called it "a sort of crooning, dirge-like thing that defies placing on paper."[55] Jobey's own use of the song in "Souvenirs de la Louisiane"/"Le lac Cathahoula" makes no mention of the musical specifics of Harris's performance, and focuses instead on his skill as a poetic improvisor: this serves to underline the importance of *music* to the later operatic performances in contrast with Harris's song.

The linguistic specifics of the song doubtless formed a considerable part of its appeal for Jobey and his readers, as when Harris sings, it is not in French but in Louisiana Creole: a language that developed in Louisiana in the eighteenth century through contact between French speakers and speakers of a variety of African languages.[56] It was predominantly, although not exclusively, spoken by Louisiana's African-descended residents (both free and enslaved). The language would have been alien to Jobey's Parisian readers, although it would likely have been rather more familiar to many of his

Louisiana readers, as even if they did not speak it themselves, they would have heard people using it.[57]

The use of Louisiana Creole in the story certainly adds local color on a superficial level, but it also helps bring depth to the portrayal of Harris and his interactions with the white, European performers. Indeed, although Harris's song was not of Jobey's invention, his rendering of it in "Souvenirs de la Louisiane" appears to be the earliest written record of the song: in fact, the *Anthologie de poésie louisianaise du XIX siècle* suggests in passing that Jobey's version in *Le Villageois* was one of the earliest instances of any author—Louisianian or European—attempting to transcribe Louisiana Creole, which was even by the first half of the nineteenth century thought of as a low-status language.[58] By the time the story appeared in *Le Villageois* in November 1857, it had already been published in Paris (1856) and New Orleans (1856).

The use of Louisiana Creole in the story is also important for the characterization of Harris, whose words are almost always written in the language (only occasionally are they translated into French and followed by a note that he spoke in the Creole language). On the one hand, this serves to underline his difference from the French-speaking Europeans and his wealthy white master, Zénon Judice, but on the other, Jobey's decision to transcribe Harris's words in Louisiana Creole allows him to speak with his own voice and in his own tongue throughout the story, thereby granting him a measure of agency as a character.[59]

Indeed, within Jobey's text, Harris has a degree of freedom of expression that appears to go beyond the simple characterization of "bon nègre." The song he sings, for instance, was understood in nineteenth-century Louisiana as being critical of white authority.[60] Judge Préval's paternalistic assumptions that he will be able to bring enslaved people and free white people together in harmony at his dance (stanza 6: "blanc et pi noir / yé dansé bamboula," "white and black / they danced the bamboula")—for his own financial gain, no less—are punctured first by the arrival of the jailer and then again by the fine he receives.[61] The song highlights the polarized treatment of wealthy white people and enslaved people, contrasting Préval's wounded pride and lighter wallet with the harsh physical punishments given to the black dancers, who were sent to jail and whipped (stanza 9 reads: "Yé méné yé tous, / Dans la calabous; / Lendemain matin, / Yé fouetté yé bien," "They led them all / to the jail; / The next morning, / they whipped them well"). The final two stanzas underscore the satire by focusing entirely on Préval's hurt feelings with no concern for the dancers' lasting injuries (stanza 17: "Povć mouché Préval," "poor Mister Préval").

Of course, the freedom of expression Harris has in singing this song exists only within a carefully controlled framework: Zénon Judice, his white master, cuts off the applause, telling the Europeans not to praise slaves too highly, in a way that mirrors the curtailing of the ball in the song Harris performs. Jobey himself was clearly critical of the fact that slavery remained an institution in the United States well after its abolition in Europe (although these abolitionist sympathies did not prevent him from using essentialist descriptions of Harris "and others of his race").[62] At times, he condemns slavery outright in the story, exclaiming: "May the shame of this monstrosity fall upon the Christians of the nineteenth century."[63] This line, and a few other similar comments, however, appear only in the two Parisian versions of the story and are absent from the ones published in Louisiana.

It is not possible to tell whether Jobey himself decided to remove them, or whether his editors made the decision on his behalf, but their absence from the Louisiana publications reveals just how sensitive a subject the future of slavery had become in the state by the late 1850s; in January 1861, Louisiana seceded from the United States and joined the Confederate States in an attempt to prevent the abolition of slavery. When Jobey republished his story as "Le lac Cathahoula" in Paris later that year, he added a footnote referencing the outbreak of the Civil War directly, remarking that "today, brothers are fighting among themselves; tomorrow, perhaps, the rebelling slaves will slaughter their masters."[64] Jobey's characterization of Harris and the Europeans' interactions with him is, therefore, more nuanced than it initially seems. While the text preserves some of the essentialized stereotypes of a non-white, non-European "Other," Jobey's portrayal of Harris throughout the scene in which he sings reveals how a desire to create an attractive "local color" for his "armchair tourist" readers could be entwined with a deeper reflection on racial and social division in the world of the time.

THE WILDERNESS

The wilderness setting of the tale—in which the social codes of the city (of which Harris sings) are stripped away, and the white Europeans are removed from their usual environment—essentially enables Harris's performance: it is the wilderness that has brought the Europeans together with him, and they have relied on his knowledge and strength to keep them safe on their journey. The rural setting also plays an integral part in the reader's understanding of the role opera plays in the story. Paul Smethurst has pointed out that in the late eighteenth century and first half of the nineteenth, the way in which people conceived of the natural world was radically reoriented: human dependency on nature was seen as diminishing (and science started to replace it as the object of wonder), and the "natural world itself was becoming increasingly dependent on human agency."[65] Travel writing, of course, came to reflect these changing attitudes, revealing ways in which authors newly constructed an image of nature. As Smethurst argues, for all its heterogeneity, travel writing broadly "disseminates an ideology of global vision and power in searching for order and structure in the natural world," just as it has been seen to do in human societies.[66]

Initially, Jobey's whole operatic episode in the wilderness seems set up to emphasize difference: between the supposedly improvised, "natural" characteristics of Harris's song and the sophisticated, prescribed operatic excerpt, between human music and the sounds of the natural world and, of course, between opera's accustomed urban location and the wilderness. But on closer inspection, the narrative becomes less clear cut, as these differences themselves seemingly enable operatic performance to reach a state of perfection. When Vallière plays Auber, for example, Jobey remarks:

> Vallière had chosen his moment well to make the majority of us, who heard him every day at the theater, feel emotions that had been unknown to us until that moment.—It is not in concert halls, theaters, in the light of chandeliers, nor in front of ladies done up in lace and diamonds that we must hear the oboe; it is at the calm and red hour of twilight, beside a lake, in the shadow of the woods, amidst the peaceful retreats of nature.[67]

When music and nature meet, music gains its full emotional power, and in true Romantic style, the sublimity of the landscape reflects the sublimity of the art performed, thus intensifying the experience of listening. The experience reaches its zenith when the troupe comes together to perform, with the "natural" sound of the human voices in harmony surpassing even the impact of Vallière's solitary oboe upon the three kneeling figures. In this communal musical performance in the wilderness, we might even read opera as being momentarily refigured as a kind of folk music.

Even the performers' "natural" harmony with the landscape, of course, could be read in terms of operatic power relations, with Europeans positioning opera against the magnificent environmental backdrop in order to bring the non-Europeans to their knees. But the natural world is more than simply a backdrop here, or something that can be tamed at will by humankind: instead, it is a character in its own right, an active participant in the story, which adds its varied voices—from the "rustling of the foliage," the "plaintive note of the mockingbird," and the "softened voice of the ocelot" to the "sonorous cries of the caimans, tormented with amorous ardor"—to the exchange.[68]

The natural world makes its presence felt here in a way that complicates opera's relationship with its already unusual surroundings. It is not opera that has the final say in this encounter, but nature. When the troupe sings together, the physical features of the landscape resonate in response to them: the "virgin forest resounded" to their voices. In Jobey's description, this response is unique to operatic performance, and there is no suggestion of such interaction in the case of Harris's or Lucien's songs. Furthermore, the sounds of opera are not only echoed back, but are adapted by the landscape, taking on qualities of the natural world as they resemble first the breath of a breeze and then distant thunder. The landscape, then, has the last word, as it returns the final notes of the troupe's performance in more sublime form. Opera, a product of the urban environment, can stun other human beings into silence, but cannot silence the natural world.[69]

In "Le lac Cathahoula," Jobey complicates the narrative of operatic colonialism by refiguring the geographical setting—from the inside (of the opera house) to the outside, from the urban to the rural—and, therefore, the balance of power between the cultural product and its surroundings. The tale is not so much of opera's power to tame or to civilize in ostensibly exotic environments, but rather about how opera has been absorbed and altered by those environments: its echoes return to the European performers with an air that is slightly disquieting, like the distant thunder simulated in Jobey's description. Rather than proclaiming French cultural domination in a quasi-imperial manner, "Le lac Cathahoula" hints at the process of letting French culture go, to be assimilated into an environment that makes it its own.

In this way, the episode reveals much about French (and, indeed, more broadly European) perspectives on the United States up to the mid-nineteenth century, perspectives that are conflicting in many respects. On the one hand, it fits with ubiquitous European narratives from the period that positioned the United States as a land without culture, while hinting at the role the Théâtre d'Orléans troupe played in remedying that lack (especially through its large-scale summer tours of the Northeast). The operatic performance in "Souvenirs de la Louisiane"/"Le lac Cathahoula" could then be seen as a wry comment on the troupe's role as missionaries in the cultural wilderness.

But at the same time, the wilderness is not portrayed as something that must be tamed, but something that actually enhances opera's impact, acting as a sounding board for the troupe's performance: in this way, the scene presents a European fantasy of the Americas, of the kind that had been epitomized in the work of Chateaubriand.[70] In its focus on the natural world, "Souvenirs de la Louisiane"/"Le lac Cathahoula" presents a dream of European travelers' interactions with an untamed landscape that is fascinating, sublime and, as the operatic performance goes to show, responsive to their influence all at the same time.[71] The American wilderness seems placed to fulfill the desire for "authentic" experience that was common to so much travel writing, even if, in a period of rapid urbanization for the United States (and, indeed, when the nation was on the brink of Civil War, as it was when Jobey's story was finally published in Paris), it was already a utopian dream. But if the United States remained a screen onto which Europeans could project their fantasies, the role of opera in this story at least hints at an awareness on Jobey's part that this previously "blank canvas" had the potential to shape Europeans' perceptions of their own culture.[72]

In Jobey's novels, then, operatic performance and its physical locations become mutually influencing, as opera shapes its surroundings and in turn finds itself shaped by the environments in which it is performed, in both literal and more broadly metaphorical ways. Both texts, in a way, are examples of what Syrine Hout calls "the cultural dialogue" in travel writing, where the voice of the Other is not simply bypassed as the European writer soliloquizes, but is actively engaged (if ventriloquized) in the formation of the text.[73] These texts have, to borrow Jennifer Yee's formulation, the "potential to disturb a culture's monologue with itself, to remind it that it is not absolute."[74] In his stories (as in his career), the opera house becomes a site for the simultaneous affirmation of Eurocentric ideas of cultural consumption and, at the same time, the undermining of those ideas. Opera becomes a means through which aspects of the European self are both centered and decentered, repeatedly destabilized in more or less unfamiliar settings, to the point where, in "Le lac Cathahoula," the opera house itself, with its veneer of civilization, disappears altogether. Ultimately, Jobey's stories show that international operatic production, like travel writing, can expose the European subject to alternative and sometimes troubling perceptions of even the most apparently incontrovertible features of their "civilized" cultural identity.

OPERA AND THE TRAVEL EXPERIENCE: EDWARD DURELL'S *NEW ORLEANS AS I FOUND IT*

If scenes featuring opera were Jobey's invitation to his Parisian readers to reflect back upon their own society, while at the same time providing them with a kind of exotic titillation, opera facilitates a different kind of travel experience in Durell's *New Orleans as I Found It*. Over the course of 125 pages, each composed of two closely typed columns, Durell recalls his earliest impressions of everything from the local geography (urban and rural) to politics and administration: the city, he says, is a "world in miniature," and he sets out to explore as much of it as he can.[75] The fifteenth chapter of the book, the close of Durell's second day in New Orleans, recalls an evening at the Théâtre d'Orléans. Durell goes to the theater in the company of the doctor and the lawyer, the two most frequently invoked of the book's dramatis personae. While neither the doctor nor the lawyer are Creole ("of that portion of the population of New Orleans whose distinctive character has colored that of all the rest," as Durell puts it), the doctor professes himself to be a lover of the opera, and keeps a box at the theater. Sunday, he says, is the most fashionable night to be in attendance at the opera.[76]

As a visitor from the North with its Puritan legacies, Durell professes to his reader his amazement and discomfort at going to the theater on the Sabbath. He cannot resist noting that the theaters in the American sector of the city are patronized mainly by foreign visitors on a Sunday evening: the Anglo-Americans, he says, although they have adapted to Creole customs in certain respects, "retain many of the scruples of an early [northern] education," and do not generally frequent their own theater on a Sunday night.[77] Nonetheless, he decides that accompanying the doctor and the lawyer to the theater is part of the experience of this "most remarkable city in our country," so he puts his conscience aside and goes along.[78]

The experience of theatergoing described by Durell initially bears many of the features common to almost all travel literature about New Orleans in this period. He provides, as do so many other authors, a brief description of the theater and the patrons gathered there. Unlike Jobey and many other European visitors, however, he makes no mention of the theater's black patrons, dwelling instead on the "pit and boxes already filled with the elite and beauty of the French quarter, interspersed, here and there, with a representative from the American."[79] He seems interested only in presenting the theater as a place of gathering for the city's elites (be they Creole or Anglo-American).

Given Durell's northern background and education—he hailed from New Hampshire, where legislation toward the (very) gradual abolition of slavery had been introduced in 1783—this avoidance of the subject of slavery is surprising. Indeed, the whole book barely makes mention of the topic, in comparison with many European accounts of the American South from the time that focused at length (and, in the case of such works as James Silk Buckingham's *The Slave States of America*, exclusively) on the conditions of slavery.[80] Whatever the reasons for Durell's avoidance of the subject as a whole, there are perhaps specific literary reasons for his presentation of the theater as a space occupied only by white, and predominantly Creole, elites.

While Jobey saw the Théâtre d'Orléans as a microcosm of society at large, Durell's interpretation is very different. In the opening paragraphs of *New Orleans as I Found It,* he described the city as a "world in miniature," but his presentation of the Théâtre d'Orléans deliberately contains only a small part of that world: the Germans, the Jewish people, the Spaniards, the Irish, the sailors, and the Native Americans, among others, all of whom populate the rest of Durell's book, are not to be found in his description of the theater at all, and instead are featured separately in other chapters. Durell's presentation of the theater audience might be reductive, then, but his presentation of New Orleans society as a whole in the book is far broader than Jobey's, even if he is unashamedly biased toward Anglo-American achievements.

In this formulation, the Théâtre d'Orléans functions not as a microcosm of the world, but as one piece of an ever-expanding mosaic of city life. Nonetheless, Durell preserved the idea that the world might be understood through the theater, as on the very first page of his account, he goes on to talk of his "world in miniature" as "the theatre that I am about to describe."[81] He was far from alone in doing so, as countless other visitors to the city remarked on its theatrical qualities, creating a sense of its being unusually spectacular and unlike any other city in the United States. The opening of a poem by an Anglophone visitor from the North in the late 1820s, Colonel James R. Creecy, captures this perfectly: "Have you ever been to New Orleans? If not, you'd better go. / It's a nation of queer places; day and night a show!"[82] Durell, then, was able to build on existing literary tropes when characterizing New Orleans.

But where does this theatricalization of the city leave the actual experience of theatergoing and operagoing? After all, it could be seen as stripping the theater of its privileged position as social microcosm. Durell's visit to the opera, it turns out, initially appears to have very little to do with opera itself: he explains that his companion, the lawyer, was not a lover of music and "could not distinguish one note from another," and freely admits that he himself was "more attracted to the novelty of the show than to the music of the opera."[83] They occupy themselves by watching the other members of the audience, and Durell does not even tell us the name of the opera they attend, let alone describe anything of the performance.

But the evening at the opera plays an important role within Durell's travel account. He has the following to say about his experience:

> I felt transported to a European city—the language sung was foreign to my ear, and the features and dress of those about me equally foreign to my eye. The mustached lips of the men, the richness of their toilet—which had neither the

> plainness nor that nice keeping in colors which mark the American or English gentleman—the dark hair, dark eyes, and somewhat dark complexion of the women, with the exquisite taste and set of the French millinery, carried me to Paris; everything was Parisian about me, and I was, in spirit, three thousand miles distant from American soil.[84]

It is not the music that he finds important, but the atmosphere: being surrounded by the city's elites in all their exotic finery transports Durell in his mind to Paris. There is a point of contact here, then, between Roger's visit to the opera in Jobey's *L'Amour d'un nègre* and Durell's own account. The connection between the two cities was, after all, an obvious enough one for Durell to make, as an American attending the French opera for the first time.

The nature of the experience that leads to the drawing of such a connection, however, is perceived very differently by the two writers. It was the performance itself (the behavior of the performers and audience) that made the connection for Jobey's protagonist, Roger, setting in motion a complex process of recognizing oneself in the exotic, but for Durell the initial points of connection with Paris are language and dress, rather than anything specifically related to the performance. What is more, for Jobey, the experience is a shared one, belonging to both New Orleans and Paris, as distinctively local features color the protagonist's reminiscences of Paris; for Durell, on the other hand, the experience is exclusively Parisian. In his figuration, the distance between the two cities is not reduced, but instead he feels himself directly transported away from New Orleans and American soil.

Indeed, operagoing in *New Orleans as I Found It* facilitates a travel experience of its own, during which the reader is transported to Paris by way of New Orleans, without ever leaving their seat. While it is impossible to know who exactly read Durell's book, it was published in New York, and it would likely have been read by New Yorkers, for whom Paris and New Orleans would doubtless both have seemed distant and potentially exotic locations. Imagined travel—to places that are unfamiliar or Other in some way, in particular—is fundamental to Durell's account: throughout the book, Durell's own observations are interspersed with travel stories narrated by people whom he meets during his time in the city, and these stories involve places far from New Orleans. The doctor, for example, introduces the reader to nineteenth-century Hamburg through the (highly antisemitic) tale of a Jewish patient he treats;[85] an elderly sailor Durell meets on the levee recounts a tale of being robbed on the road to Natchez, Mississippi;[86] the lawyer tells the story of a boy named Oceanus who voyages upon the seas, to mention but three.[87] Each of these stories, and Durell's own story of his evening at the opera, position New Orleans not simply as a "world in miniature," but rather as the gateway to the world: through Durell's experiences in the city, the reader is able to travel further afield than they could ever have anticipated.

MUSIC AND INTERIORIZED TRAVEL

In this light, the scene at the theater might initially appear to be simply a device on Durell's part to create one more exciting trip on the imaginary world tour in which he invites his readers to partake, with opera itself serving as nothing more than a convenient backdrop. Nonetheless, it becomes clear that opera has a particular significance for Durell. As he looks around the theater, he sees that "the whole audience seemed composed of amateurs, so profound was its attention, and so much enjoyment was depicted upon the faces of all."[88] The doctor is one of these amateurs, and while Durell tells us nothing at all of the performance itself, he describes the doctor's response to it in precise detail:

> He never missed the leader's first note, and sat, during the whole performance, with his eyes closed, and his head reclining upon the cushioned rail, wrapped in elysium. The pantomime of an opera was nothing to him.[89]

This could not be further from the description of the audience or its listening practices in *L'Amour d'un nègre*. The evocation of silent listening is more reminiscent of the important changes in operatic reception in the city that were explored in chapter 2 than the noisy engagement of Jobey's audience and what we know of historical audience behavior (as discussed in chapter 3). Although Durell himself claims that he is unable to comment on the experience of listening in this manner, the doctor speaks eloquently about it:

> He said "that the gestures and grimaces of the actors interfered with and lessened the effect of the music; that it was impossible to gratify, to their utmost capacity for pleasure, any two of the senses at one and the same time; that the words of an opera, however admirable as a poetical composition, added nothing to its effect, and were of use only as being the model upon which sounds are constructed." He made the poet subservient to the composer, and esteemed his verse merely as the setting which held together and exhibited to the best advantage the diamonds of his collaborator.[90]

The doctor's words, then, are no longer about the theatrical experience at all, but rather an elevated discourse of music as the highest of all the arts. As the doctor claims that the only way to listen is with one's eyes closed, opera is actively stripped of its dramatic power: the performers who had been so central in Jobey's account are moved to the very fringes of this experience, and the visual spectacle for which the Théâtre d'Orléans was so well known is dismissed as "interfering" with and "lessening" the impact of the music.

This arresting excerpt is in actual fact only the beginning of a more extended discourse about music in Durell's book, as at the end of the performance, Durell encounters a man whom he has been observing throughout the evening and accepts an invitation to his house in the French Quarter.[91] Once there, Durell mentions the opera, prompting a lengthy and enthusiastic reply from his host:

> "The opera," said the strange gentleman, "combining, as it does, two arts proceeding from the loftiest qualities of the mind, is at once the most artificial and most perfect of man's intellectual creations. Music, like poetry, is incapable of being defined. The difficulty consists partly in the barrenness of language, its inability to give expression to many of our highest thoughts and feelings, and partly in ourselves. . . . Language is not subtle enough nor flexible enough to comprehend it; nor does the resemblance end here. Poetry is one and the same to all, as the sun is one and the same to all; seen with a clear or more obscure vision. It is confined to no class of objects, and dwells equally with life, decay, and death; music walks hand in hand at her side."[92]

Even by the standards of nineteenth-century writing, this little monologue is striking in both its abstraction and the way it comes across as preprepared rather than spontaneous: the strange gentleman pours forth a well-formed disquisition at a moment's notice on the subject of music's position within the arts and on the nature of musicality, but without reference to a particular composer or work.[93] The passage would not have been out of place in a philosophical treatise on the arts, so influenced does it seem to have been by German Romanticism. Certainly, as chapter 2 explored, with the introduction of *grand opéra* to New Orleans in the 1830s, a newly elevated style of critical discourse emerged—surprisingly early, given that a similar style was only just beginning to crystallize in Europe at the same time—arguing for the primacy of music in the operatic experience. The old man's words, however, go much further than that, not using contemporary philosophy to comment on opera, but using opera as a way into talking about the arts as a whole. The evening's performance at the theater, in all its imperfect reality, is quickly left aside, and it is replaced with a more idealized, abstract conception of opera.

Tempting as it is to pause longer over the intricacies of these passages, the pressing question for my purposes here is what such statements might be doing in a travelogue and, moreover, this particular travelogue, which has up to this point shown few artistic inclinations. Indeed, as recently as in the previous chapter, Durell was recounting a trivial story of a coffin salesman, and it takes a large registral shift to reach the old man's reflections. It is the only place in the book where the arts are discussed at length, even if the epigrams with which Durell begins each chapter suggest certain pretensions to philosophical grandeur, taken as they are from the likes of Schiller and Sophocles. The sudden emphasis on such modern cultural discourse and musical listening practices might simply have been a way of suggesting the uncommon sophistication he perceived among the elite theatergoing "amateurs" of New Orleans, further sketching out the nuances of the society he observed.

Durell's apparent desire to create an imagined travel experience for his reader, however, offers another interpretation of the presence of these unexpected artistic and philosophical interludes. As the evening unfolds, the strange gentlemen speaks at even greater length about opera, moving on to discuss ideas of the beautiful and the sublime in music, the "sister arts" of music and poetry, and the positions of all the arts, including sculpture, painting, and dance, exploring their relationship to language and philosophy.[94] The gentleman's wife performs for them, exemplifying his ideas as they pour forth. First she sings a Scottish song, then gives an impassioned rendition of the *Marseillaise* on the organ, followed by a dance, accompanied by a slave sitting cross-legged upon the floor playing the lute.[95] With features described as "approaching the Grecian nearer than any other model," the strange gentleman's wife appears to be a personification of the Muses: with all the classical overtones, the sensuality of the dance, and the strangeness of the situation in which Durell finds himself, the scene is as exotic as any description of a foreign locale.[96]

In a way, then, the scene, with all its extended philosophical discussions of the arts, affords a kind of travel experience of its own. It is an internal one, beginning with the doctor's serene and attentive listening at the opera and ending with the burning passions of the woman's final performance, which leaves both the strange gentleman and Durell feeling that "every nerve trembled with emotion."[97] The emphasis on listening (and, in the doctor's case, *closing one's eyes* and listening) in this passage is, once again, highly significant: while Durell, unlike the doctor, does not close his eyes at the theater, the primacy of the visual in his account is temporarily challenged at the strange old gentleman's house as he seeks to capture the sounds he hears around him.[98] The very foundations of the travel experience are altered in this scene.

The opera, although it is seemingly forgotten by the end of the chapter, serves here as a catalyst: while Durell found himself fascinated but not much moved emotionally by his experience at the opera house, once the strange gentleman and his wife begin to explain and illustrate the arts to him, he finds himself on an inner journey that leaves him feeling breathless. If New Orleans is the gateway to the world in Durell's formulation, the theater becomes the gateway to a unique personal experience. This inner journey, of course, has an imagined physical counterpart: from Paris, Durell finds himself transported to Scotland, back to Paris, to Greece, to eastern lands, all in the course of an evening. But at the end of it he finds his head spinning, unsure that he has actually been anywhere at all, but deeply moved all the same. It is not so much the places visited that matter as the experience of traveling.

Unlike Jobey's precise presentation of Anglophone-Francophone and interracial relations, as well as opera's relationships to them, it is the breadth and variety of New Orleans that concerns Durell. For him, a northerner from a small town, New Orleans was most astonishing in its diversity. The local particulars that Durell would gradually get to know so well during his time in the city appear in *New Orleans as I Found It* to be less important than the possibilities for travel, both literal and imaginary, afforded by the city. And the opera plays its role within that: having pointed out early on in the chapter that New Orleans's operatic life was unusual within the United States, he goes on to show the new worlds that have been opened up to him by experiences in and encounters at the opera house. Opera is not granted a special status in itself (in fact, it is valued only for its music), but it holds a special place in this narrative by virtue of the fact that it sets in motion such an intense inner journey: its significance is located in its ability to facilitate emotional travel and development and philosophical growth, rather than in the specificities of its local entanglements.

In the story, then, opera becomes a facilitator of mobility (albeit an imagined mobility) both for Durell as the protagonist and for his readers. Once again, we can read this as complicating the underlying imperial agendas that many scholars have argued to be inherent in travel writing. Here, opera serves not as a tool through which a mobile observing subject controls a static "rest of the world," but as something that enables movement. In Durell's account, New Orleans is not merely a place to be surveyed and "collected," but rather a place that is changing constantly and at a great pace, due to its "rapid growth in population, in business, and in wealth."[99] Durell, as the observer, is all too aware that his subject is evolving at a pace he cannot equal in his writing, as he explains in the preface that the speed of change "render[s] it impossible to draw a portrait which will be equally recognized from every point of time."[100] Opera's role as a facilitator of movement in both a literal sense (i.e., the production of opera in New Orleans leading to the movement of people and materials across the Atlantic) and an imaginative one, then, is vital when it comes to understanding the nineteenth-century New Orleans that Durell sought to capture: it is only through a mobile lens that we are able to gain a sense of the constantly evolving city.

Jobey and Durell give two very different perspectives on New Orleans and of the potential of opera to facilitate travel experiences. It is unsurprising that their takes are different: Durell professes his own indifference to opera in performance, although he was clearly taken with its imaginative possibilities, whereas Jobey participated in the practical networks of transatlantic operatic production explored in the earlier chapters of this book. The experiences of listening to opera from the auditorium of a theater and the experience of hearing one's own performance echoed back or seeing the ways that performance apparently affects the immediate environment produce quite different results. For Durell, opera creates the beginning of a fantasy that allows travel across time and space; for Jobey, the local responses to opera unsettle fundamental ideas about his own culture.

As Jennifer Yee has suggested, it is often at the margins, the peripheries, that we can begin "to find traces of other stances and echoes of discourses that are not given centre stage."[101] There are not many texts more marginal than those considered in this chapter: as examples of travel writing, they already sit at the fringes of the nineteenth-century canon; their little-known authors make them more peripheral still. And we do begin to see within these texts, as Yee suggests, hints of subversion, or at least different possibilities for reading dominant narratives of both opera and travel writing itself. Indeed, we find good examples in all three of what James Duncan and Derek Gregory call the "ambivalence" of travel writing, whereby the self-reflexivity of the genre gives a "sense of its own authorities and assumptions being called into question."[102] If readings of travel writing through the lens of imperialism have typically looked for strategies of control on the part of the observing subject over the people and places observed, the evocation of opera in these texts becomes a means of expressing the subject's perception of a certain lack of control in their travel experience: the European performers at the Théâtre d'Orléans in *L'Amour d'un nègre* may serve as the catalyst for the riot, but they have no control over the breakdown of order that ensues.

Meanwhile, Durell finds himself transported in spite of his professed lack of interest in opera as he sits first in the Théâtre d'Orléans and later in the strange gentleman's house.

Opera serves in these accounts both as a real object—the bread and butter of Jobey's employment and an evening's entertainment in the theater for a slightly bewildered Durell—and also as an imaginative ideal. In both, albeit in different ways, opera creates the opportunity for the real and the imagined to blur. In doing so, it serves as an invitation to understand the city of New Orleans in a way that is neither wholly factual nor wholly fictional, neither wholly local nor wholly global, but which is nonetheless a potent, imaginative combination of the two. The city, in other words, creates opera, but opera in turn creates the nineteenth-century city.

Epilogue

From the Transatlantic to the Global

Beyond the Théâtre d'Orléans

In 1859, a local disagreement led to a profound shift in both the theater's position in city life and, ultimately, the nature of New Orleans's operatic connections. That year, a dispute arose between Charles Boudousquié, the then manager of the theater (Pierre Davis having retired in 1853), and the owner of the theater building, Henry Parlange.[1] The pair could not reach an agreement over the lease and Boudousquié, enraged, decided to channel his efforts into setting up and incorporating a French Opera House Association, with the intention of building a dedicated opera house in the city to replace the Théâtre d'Orléans as home to the French opera company (fig. E.1).

On March 4, 1859, the stock company of the French Opera House was registered. It had $100,000, held in 200 shares of $500 each, and Boudousquié made a substantial personal investment in the project.[2] The following month, construction of the new theater, which was to seat 1,800 people, began on a site at the corner of Bourbon and Toulouse Streets, and it opened on December 1 that year.[3] Boudousquié took with him to the new opera house the troupe from the Théâtre d'Orléans, leaving that once-proud theater to limp on until it was claimed by fire in December 1866.[4]

The move to the new French Opera House brought significant, albeit initially subtle changes to the system of operatic production and reception developed between 1819 and 1859. In December 1860, Boudousquié engaged the seventeen-year-old Adelina Patti for three months of performances at the French Opera House. The tour had been negotiated by Patti's brother-in-law, the theatrical impresario Maurice Strakosch, as a means of preparing for and filling the time before her London debut, which was arranged for the spring

FIGURE E.1 The French Opera House, as pictured in *Godey's Lady's Book* (Philadelphia), June 1, 1897. Available in the public domain through Wikimedia Commons.

of 1861. Patti's engagement was something of a break with tradition. While New Orleans had played host to visiting vocal stars long before 1860—Jenny Lind and Henriette Sontag, among others—it was highly unusual for these singers to perform in the Théâtre d'Orléans's productions.[5] Instead, they often gave separate concerts, or sometimes short recitals between the acts of an opera. As Jack Belsom has pointed out, this is what the local press initially assumed would happen during Patti's visit.[6]

Boudousquié, however, had other ideas, and alongside a series of concert engagements, he contracted Patti to make six appearances in works at the French Opera House over a three-week period. She made her debut in the title role of Donizetti's *Lucie de Lammermoor* (to give the work the French title under which it was billed) on December 19, 1860, to rapturous critical acclaim. So well was Patti received that Boudousquié and Strakosch quickly added new dates to her engagement: she performed at the French Opera House on twenty-seven occasions over the next three months, appearing in a wide range of repertoire from *Lucie* to Meyerbeer's *Les Huguenots* and

Le Pardon de Ploërmel, via *Le Barbier de Séville, Le Trouvère, Rigoletto,* and *Martha.* She gave a final gala performance on March 22, 1861, and departed soon after for Havana and then London.

Patti's guest appearances, much loved as they were by the people of New Orleans, signaled the first real departure from the tight, company-oriented ethos developed by the Davises at the Théâtre d'Orléans, by introducing a guest star into their already well-known productions. The Théâtre d'Orléans had been different from most theater troupes in the nineteenth-century United States in relying on a stable company, recruited for the whole season, rather than on visiting stars.[7] Furthermore, while the French theater had prided itself on staying close to the Parisian originals, Patti freely interpolated her own favorite arias, and indeed some of the audience's favorite songs (such as "Home, Sweet Home") into her performances.[8] Her engagement in the early years of the French Opera House, then, signaled a break with the Théâtre d'Orléans's long-established practices, on which the transatlantic identity of the city's Francophone operatic life had relied.

Patti's visit brought about a further, possibly even more fundamental rupture in the French operatic tradition in the city, by departing from the French language.[9] As Belsom has pointed out, Patti herself sang her roles in Italian (with the exception of the part of Valentine in *Les Huguenots,* which the local press noted she sang in French in order to pay homage to her local friends and their devotion to this particular Meyerbeer opera).[10] Meanwhile, the rest of the cast sang in French, as was their usual practice and as had, of course, been the tradition at the Théâtre d'Orléans. In order to complement Patti's Italian performances, members of the French Opera House company were on occasion persuaded to relearn particular roles (or parts thereof) in Italian. It appears, for example, that the tenor Mathieu sang the role of Manrico (to Patti's Leonora) in *Le Trouvère* mainly in Italian on January 2, 1861, and the usual baritone, Melchisedec, was replaced in the role of the Count di Luna by Patti's half-brother Ettore Barili.

Although this model of visiting stars performing with the resident company and mixed-language performances was not ultimately sustained at the French Opera House, the new theater shifted away from the practices on which the Théâtre d'Orléans had thrived. Following the four-year period of closure during the Civil War and the shocking loss of the entire French opera troupe heading for New Orleans in the shipwreck of the *Evening Star* in 1866, the opera house reopened with a new set of connections.[11] From that point on, it was managed by a series of different impresarios, often changing from one season to the next. Some years it had its own resident troupe (the most sustained period was from 1869 to 1874, when it was managed in turn by a local French Opera Association and then by Louis Placide Canonge), while at other times it played host to visiting touring troupes for just a few months a year.

These changes pointed to a different kind of internationalized operatic future from the earlier connections the Théâtre d'Orléans had established: one that involved a global system of operatic performance, rather than the more geographically contained, but no less intricate, transatlantic one discussed in the preceding five chapters. The theater came to rely increasingly on visiting Italian- and German-language troupes—run by such important figures on the American operatic scene as Max Maretzek, Maurice Strakosch, James Mapleson, and Eugenie Pappenheim—which tended to have been set up in the northeastern United States (principally in New York and Boston); the loss of a resident troupe not only marked a definitive departure from French theatrical systems, but also meant that the French Opera House's connections with the wider world were now mediated by these cities, even as the troupes themselves circulated over larger and larger areas, as technological advances made travel and advertising easier and quicker. As the theater came to participate more closely with national systems of performance—including the rising ticket prices for foreign-language opera and increasingly white, wealthy audiences—it lost its distinctive transatlantic identity, both in practical terms and in terms of its imaginative significance.

The forty years for which the Théâtre d'Orléans sat at the heart of New Orleans, culturally and geographically, offer a glimpse into the ways in which opera can help us understand the nineteenth-century world. The transatlantic connections—practical and imaginative—that opera created reveal much about France and the United States in the first half of the nineteenth century, from how the theater industries in both places relied on a mixture of local, national, and transnational systems to how each nation was perceived in the popular imagination of the other.

Far from providing a utopian or idealized vision of interconnection, however, foregrounding these same transatlantic networks casts into sharp relief what Nancy L. Green has called "the limits of transnationalism," both then and now: as lived experience for the people of the nineteenth century and as historiographical paradigm for scholars rethinking the ways in which we make sense of and narrate that period.[12] For every network that enabled the Théâtre d'Orléans's transatlantic recruitment to thrive, there was a network that failed its participants: transnational connection brought performers to New Orleans, but it also meant that in some cases they could feel unrooted, caught between France and the United States, and unprotected by both.

A focus on the transnational provides a tantalizing opportunity to break free from methodological nationalism in opera studies, meanwhile, but the risk remains of simply replacing national frameworks with an idealized vision of unfettered, unchallenged global movement, of smoothing out the kinks and frictions of connection.

In this light, applying the microhistorical lens and exploring how opera became embedded in nineteenth-century New Orleans and adapted to suit its environment—social, cultural, and even geographical—proves a valuable way of grounding that transnationalism. It is by looking at the transnational as it plays out within the local that we can, to quote Green once again, read "modes of circulation, connected histories, and other forms of entanglement . . . in conjunction with the power relations in which they are embedded and the frictions that can occur."[13] New Orleans, simultaneously a "small space" (to follow David Bell)[14] and Durell's "world in miniature,"[15] invites us to do just that. Only in the process of drawing out the specific, but nonetheless enormously varied, textures of local operatic life—opera's entanglements inside and outside the theater, the people who engaged with it in various spaces, and the media that enabled them to do so—do broader ideas of the transnationalism or globalization of opera come to mean something. In both its real and imagined forms, therefore, the city of New Orleans creates a window onto the ways in which the nineteenth-century world shaped opera and opera shaped the nineteenth-century world.

Acknowledgments

During the seven years over which this book has taken shape, I have been extremely fortunate to have had the support of a great many individuals and institutions, and I wish to express my thanks to them here. This research would not have been possible without generous financial assistance from the Arts and Humanities Research Council, UK, the University of Cambridge Faculty of Music, the Royal Musical Association, the Music and Letters Trust, and Emmanuel College, Cambridge.

The process of archival research can be tricky to navigate, and I gratefully acknowledge the assistance of the following people, who smoothed the path in various ways: Alfred E. Lemmon and the staff of the Historic New Orleans Collection; Melissa Smith, David Kunian, and Erin Kinchen of the Louisiana State Museums; Sally Reeves and Erin Alderton at the Research Centre of the New Orleans Notarial Archives; Christina Bryant of the New Orleans Public Library; Leon Miller and the staff of the Louisiana Research Collection and Hogan Jazz Archive at Tulane University; and Germain Bienvenu and the staff of the Hill Memorial Library, Louisiana State University.

John Baron and Jack Belsom have both been very generous in sharing their vast knowledge of musical life in nineteenth-century New Orleans, while Candace Bailey, Juliane Braun, Warren Kimball, and Jennifer C. H. J. Wilson all kindly allowed me to read unpublished work. Laura Protano-Biggs and Suzanne Aspden gave insightful feedback on parts of chapters 2 and 5, respectively, and Oliver Mayeux assisted me with the translation of the Louisiana Creole text in appendix 2. Katharine Ellis, Axel Körner, Marina Frolova-Walker, Julia Guarneri, Gavin Williams, Sarah Hibberd, Susan Rutherford, and Katherine K. Preston offered valuable advice at various times.

The Fellows of Emmanuel College, Cambridge, and my colleagues at Newcastle University offered support at various stages of this project. Thanks must also go to Mary Ann Smart and David Levin, editors of the Opera Lab series, and my anonymous readers for providing such stimulating comments and helping shape the project with care. At Chicago, Marta Tonegutti, Dylan Joseph Montanari, and Kristin Rawlings have led me expertly through the development of this monograph.

This book would never have been finished without the support of many other colleagues and friends. Rachel Becker, Alessandra Jones, José Manuel Izquierdo König, Marco Ladd, Danielle Padley, Ditlev Rindom, Francesca Vella, and Vera Wolkowicz discussed ideas with me and read early drafts, but they also helped me forget about it all at the right moments. David Whittle, meanwhile, has shaped my love of music in innumerable, lasting ways, and I am thankful for his continued friendship. I have had the most supportive and inspiring mentor I could ever have hoped for in Benjamin Walton. His encouragement and attention to detail have made this an immeasurably better book.

I could not have done any of this without my wonderful family, especially my parents, Adrian and Katherine Bentley; my brother, Alexander; and my grandparents, Alan and Mary Bentley. Their unwavering love and belief that I would manage to get this manuscript finished mean the world to me. My gran, Joan Hume, regrettably did not get to see this project begin, but she was always my biggest musical cheerleader and chief source of "ditties." Finally, Alex Kolassa deserves my deepest thanks. He has accompanied me on this journey with enormous enthusiasm, and he has undoubtedly spent more time over the last seven years thinking about and discussing nineteenth-century New Orleans than he ever intended. For his insights, boundless curiosity and, above all, love, I am forever grateful.

Author's Note

An earlier version of the material relating to the reception of Meyerbeer's *Robert le diable* and *Les Huguenots* in chapter 2 appeared in print as "The Race for *Robert* and Other Rivalries: Negotiating the Local and (Inter)national in Nineteenth-Century New Orleans," in *Cambridge Opera Journal* 29/1 (March 2017): 94–112. Some of the material relating to Charles Jobey that appears in chapter 5 was published as "Between the Frontier and the French Quarter: Operatic Travel Writing and Nineteenth-Century New Orleans," in *Operatic Geographies: The Place of Opera and the Opera House*, ed. Suzanne Aspden (Chicago: University of Chicago Press, 2018), 105–18.

Appendix 1

Théâtre d'Orléans Pro Forma Contract

ENTRE M. PIERRE DAVIS, D'UNE PART, ET M. [BLANK], Artiste Dramatique et lyrique, libre de tout engagement qui pourrait contrarier le présent, d'autre part;

Il est convenu et réciproquement accepté ce qui suit, savoir:

MOI [BLANK] M'engage pour jouer dans la troupe de la Nouvelle-Orléans, sur le Théâtre français de cette ville, ou tout autre, les emplois dits de [LARGE BLANK SPACE]

Le tout en chef, ou partage du tout, ou de partie, à la volonté de l'administration.

Je m'engage, en outre, à consacrer mes talents au bien de l'entreprise, à apprendre et chanter les chœurs dans tous les opéras et vaudevilles, à paraître dans les pièces à spectacle, pantomimes, mélodrames et ballets, à jouer au moins douze rôles dits de complaisance, dans le courant de mon engagement;

A suivre la troupe, en tout ou partie, partout où il plaira au Directeur de l'envoyer, sans exiger d'autre dédommagement que les frais de transport;

A me fournir tous les costumes nécessaires aux rôles que je jouerai, sans restriction.

Dans toutes les pièces où mon emploi ne me donnera pas un rôle, je m'engage à jouer celui qui me sera distribué, de quelque genre qu'il soit, jeune ou vieux, sérieux ou comique, et lors même qu'il serait réputé accessoire.

Dans le cas où, pour le bien d'un ouvrage, le Directeur du Théâtre, ou son régisseur, jugerait à propos que je jouasse un autre rôle que le mien, je m'engage à me déplacer, l'administration se réservant le droit de distribuer les pièces nouvelles à sa volonté, sans que l'artiste puisse faire aucune réclamation.

Je partirai pour joindre mon engagement dans le courant de [BLANK] ou [BLANK] à la volonté du Directeur.

Je ne jouerai sur aucun Théâtre, ne jouerai et ne chanterai à aucun concert payant ou particulier, ni ne me livrerai à aucun travail étranger à ma profession, sans l'autorisation expresse et par écrit du Directeur.

Dans les ouvrages nouveaux, je m'engage à apprendre trente-cinq lignes par jour, indépendamment des études occasionnées par les remises de pièces.

Je me conformerai strictement au règlement dont la teneur suit, et de tout autre qu'il plairait au Directeur de faire pour le meilleur service de l'entreprise.

REGLEMENT DU THÉÂTRE D'ORLÉANS

1. Aucun artiste ne pourra s'absenter de la Ville de la Nouvelle-Orléans, sans en prévenir l'administration et désigner l'endroit où l'on pourra le trouver en cas d'accident ou de changement de spectacle.
2. L'artiste qui, à la représentation, se fera attendre à l'heure précise du lever du rideau, paiera une amende de 10 pour 100 sur ses appointements du mois; si cette attente durait plus d'un quart-d'heure, l'amende doublerait pour chaque quart-d'heure en sus.
3. L'artiste qui manquera une entrée à la représentation, paiera 10 pour 100 de ses appointements du mois; s'il manque une scène entière, 30 pour 100; s'il manque la représentation, la recette entière, évaluée à la plus forte possible. L'artiste qui arrivera aux répétitions générales d'un ouvrage sans savoir son rôle, sera sujet à une amende de cinq piastres. L'amende sera doublée à la représentation.
4. L'artiste qui, par sa faute, fera retarder la représentation d'une des pièces affichées pour un jour fixé, paiera 36 pour 100 sur ses appointements du mois.
5. L'artiste qui, par sa faute, fera retarder la représentation d'une pièce jouée depuis 4, 5 et 6 mois, et annoncée depuis 48 heures à l'avance, paiera un mois de ses appointements; la raison qu'il faut remettre un rôle n'étant point admissible. Le refus d'un rôle, exigible d'après les clauses de l'engagement, entraînera une amende de deux mois d'appointements, si toutefois l'administration ne juge pas à propos d'exiger de plus forts dédommagements. Chaque artiste devant paraître et chanter les chœurs, celui qui manquera à cette partie du devoir sera pointé comme s'il manquait un rôle. L'artiste qui, en scène, se dispenserait de chanter les chœurs, paiera dix piastres d'amende.
6. Toute pièce qui aura été jouée, ne pourra être refusée sur le répertoire de la semaine; et toutes celles jouées depuis 3 mois seront exigibles du matin au soir,

sous peine d'une amende de 20 pour cent des appointements de l'artiste en défaut.

7. Les cas d'indisposition qui feront suspendre le service et changer la représentation affichée, entraîneront l'obligation d'en prévenir de suite la Régie, qui fera constater la maladie (s'il est nécessaire), et de rester surtout chez soi, sans se montrer au spectacle, ni ailleurs, le jour où on aura ainsi changé la représentation, sous peine de l'amende qu'il plaira à l'administration de fixer.
8. Tout artiste qui aura suspendu son service pour cause d'indisposition, et qui néanmoins chantera chez lui ou s'absentera indiscrètement, soit pour des parties de campagne, de souper, ou pour faire des écoliers en ville, subira une retenue égale au quintuple de ses appointements du nombre de jours qu'il aura passé sans service.
9. Toute indisposition dont la feinte sera prouvée par des médecins, autorisera la rupture de l'engagement, et tous dommages et intérêts qu'il plaira à l'administration de demander.
10. Les répétitions commenceront précisément à l'heure indiquée. L'artiste qui manquera sa réplique paiera 4 escalins; pour un quart-d'heure une piastre, et en doublent ainsi de quart-d'heure en quart-d'heure, jusqu'à la concurrence de dix piastres. L'artiste qui quittera la répétition avant qu'elle soit tout à fait terminée, paiera la même amende que s'il l'avait manquée entièrement. Si l'artiste est absent au moment de sa réplique, quoiqu'ayant déjà paru, il sera soumis à l'amende d'une piastre, et ainsi de suite, en doublant de quart-d'heure en quart-d'heure, jusqu'à la concurrence de six piastres. L'acteur qui se fera appeler à sa réplique, paiera, au troisième appel du souffleur, 2 escalins d'amende. L'amende sera la même pour les leçons de rôle et des chœurs, dont personne ne peut se dispenser à moins d'être en état d'étudier seul.
11. Les répétitions générales se feront avec le même soin que les représentations. Dans le moment où l'on répétera, les personnes qui parleront sur la scène, ou s'y tiendront sans y avoir affaire, paieront 4 escalins, et 4 de plus chaque fois que le régisseur les priera de faire silence ou de s'éloigner. En outre, on ne pourra coudre ni faire aucun ouvrage d'aiguille, ou autre, lorsque l'on répétera en scène, sous peine de cinq piastres d'amende.
12. L'artiste qui manquant l'heure de la répétition, refusera de venir au Théâtre lorsqu'on l'enverra chercher, paiera dix piastres d'amende, s'il n'a pas fait part à l'administration, dès le matin, à 8 heures, de l'indisposition qui le force à rester chez lui; les dix piastres ne détruisant pas l'amende de la répétition.
13. L'artiste qui, ayant chez lui une partition ou une brochure, négligera de l'envoyer au Théâtre, au concierge, une heure avant la répétition, paiera dix piastres d'amende. Pour la représentation l'amende sera doublée.
14. Le plus profond silence doit être observé au Théâtre, lorsque le spectacle est

commencé. L'artiste qui, dans les coulisses, parlerait assez haut pour être entendu sur la scène, paiera 10 piastres d'amende, et l'amende doublera à chaque injonction faite par le régisseur pour engager au silence. L'artiste qui, lorsqu'il est sur la scène, soit dans les chœurs, soit dans une simple comparution, causera ou rira dans une scène sérieuse paiera dix piastres d'amende.

15. Chaque artiste peut avoir au Théâtre un ou une domestique, mais ces domestiques ne peuvent rester dans les coulisses pendant la représentation; leur place est dans la loge de leurs maitres; et ils ne peuvent la quitter, ni se montrer sans exposer leurs maitres à une amende d'une piastre chaque fois qu'il seront en défaut.
16. Les artistes danseurs sont soumis au même mode de règlement que les autres artistes.
17. Messieurs les musiciens se trouveront à l'orchestre un quart-d'heure avant le lever du rideau, sous peine de deux piastres d'amende, et en doublant pour chaque quart-d'heure que durera leur absence pendant la représentation jusqu'à la concurrence de dix piastres; et pour les répétitions, il sera payé une piastre par celui qui manquera au premier coup d'archet qui sera donné par le chef d'orchestre à l'heure indiquée. Cette amende doublera pour chaque quart-d'heure que durera la répétition, jusqu'à la concurrence de cinq piastres. Le musicien qui quittera la répétition avant qu'elle soit entièrement terminée, paiera la même amende que s'il avait manquée tout entière. En outre, ces Messieurs sont priés de ne point franchir la cloison qui sépare l'orchestre des fauteuils, et aller dans la salle par ce chemin; l'infraction à cet article entraînerait 25 piastres d'amende et, lorsque le coup de cloche annoncera la fin de l'entracte, tout musicien absent paiera une piastre d'amende.
18. Il sera placé dans le foyer du Théâtre un tableau qui annoncera le travail du jour.
19. Toute discussion étrangère au travail du Théâtre est interdite. Celui qui contreviendrait à cet article serait amendé de vingt piastres, et pour un sujet étranger au Théâtre, de cinquante.
20. Le magasin n'étant établi que pour les choristes et figurants, n'est point à la disposition des artistes qui ne pourront réclamer un costume pour un rôle quelconque, l'administration ne reconnaissant point d'habits de magasin en aucune circonstance, même pour les rôles de complaisance.
21. Dans le cas où la répétition, pour un motif quelconque, ne commencerait pas à l'heure indiquée, les artistes doivent attendre; celui qui quitterait le Théâtre paierait une piastre pour un quart-d'heure, et en doublant ainsi de quart-d'heure en quart-d'heure, jusqu'à la concurrence de dix piastres. La pendule du Théâtre sera le seul régulateur du service.
22. Les artistes ne pourront prétendre à aucun rôle de début, l'administration se réservant le droit de les fixer à sa volonté.

23. Il est expressément convenu entre les soussignés, que le Directeur a le droit d'annuler, de sa seule volonté, l'engagement de tout artiste qui nuirait à l'activité du service et du répertoire, par défaut de conduite, ou qui troublerait l'ordre et la tranquillité par des tracasseries, injures ou provocations envers ses camarades. Il en sera de même pour toute maladie chronique, ou provenant d'inconduite, et sans que le pensionnaire puisse prétendre à aucune indemnité.

Et M. Pierre Davis, s'oblige, les clauses du présent engagement strictement remplies par M. [BLANK] à lui payer la somme de [LARGE BLANK] mois, en piastres (évaluées à Fr. 5 25 chacune), laquelle somme sera répartie en portions égales payées de mois en mois.

Il fera, en temps utile, à M. [BLANK] et à titre de prêt, une avance de la somme de [BLANK] qui lui sera retenue en portions égales d [*sic*] [BLANK] jusqu'à concurrence du parfait remboursement.

Il paiera le voyage de M. [BLANK]; savoir: sa personne par voiture publique, et ses effets par voie de roulage ordinaire, de [BLANK] au port de départ, et du port à la ville de jonction. Il en sera de même du voyage de retour, jusqu'au premier port de France.

Le présent engagement sera de [BLANK] mois, à compter du jour du début à la ville de jonction.

Il est convenu entre les soussignés que dans le cas de fermeture du Théâtre par suite d'incendie, ou pour cause de quelqu'événement majeur, interdiction, calamité publique, ou par ordre du gouvernement ou des autorités locales, les appointements cesseront de courir, pour ne recommencer que du jour de la réouverture.

Le présent engagement, une fois signé, ne pourra être annulé que du consentement des deux parties: celle qui voudra le rompre, paiera à l'autre un délit de la somme de [BLANK] exigible par corps, comme affaire de commerce, par devant les tribunaux, en tout pays et sous toute sorte de juridiction; et, dans ce cas, le premier réclamant s'oblige de le faire timbrer à ses frais.

FAIT DOUBLE ENTRE NOUS, et de bonne foi, pour servir et valoir ce que de raison, et comme passé par devant notaire.

Appendix 2

Harris's Song from "Le lac Cathahoula"

This is an approximate translation, as Jobey's transcription of the Louisiana Creole is at times somewhat inconsistent, and tends toward French orthography, which sometimes confuses the meaning. For the sake of space, I have only included the text from "Le lac Cathahoula": the text from the other published versions of the story differs occasionally in orthography, and the two stanzas marked * appear only in the 1861 Parisian version. I am extremely grateful to Oliver Mayeux for his assistance in translating the trickier passages, and all remaining errors are my own.

Mouché Préval, Li donné grand bal, Li fait nègues payé Pou sauté un pé.	Mister Préval gave a grand ball. He made slaves pay To dance a little.
Li donné soupé, Pou nègues régalé. So vié la musique, Té baye la colique.	He gave dinner So the slaves feasted. His old music Gave them stomach ache.
Mouché Préval, Té capitaine bal, So cocher Louis, Té maîte crémoni.	Mister Préval Was captain of the ball, His coachman Louis Was master of ceremonies.

Ala ain bourrique,
Tendé la musique,
Li vini valsé,
Com quand li cabré.

Then a donkey
Heard the music,
He came to waltz,
Like when he rears up on his hind legs.

Yavé des néguesses,
Belles com yé maîtresses
Yé té volé bel bel,
Dans l'ormoir mamzel.

There were slaves
Dressed up like their mistresses
They stole beautiful things
From Mademoiselle's wardrobe.

Blanc et pi noir,
Yé dansé bamboula,
Vous pas jamais voir,
Un plus grand gala.

White and black alike
They danced the bamboula,
You've never seen
Such a big gala.

Ala le gardien la geôle,
Li trouvé ça ben drôle;
Li dit: Mo aussi,
Ma fé bal ici

Then the guardian of the jail
Found it very funny.
He said: "I too
Will have a ball here!"

Et pi lé wacheman,
Yé tombé làdan,
Yé fé branleba,
Dans licherie la.

And then the watchmen
Went on down
And made a commotion
In the debauchery.

Yé méné yé tous,
Dans la calabous;
Lendemain matin,
Yé fouetté yé bien.

They led them all
To the jail.
The next morning
They whipped them well.

Yé té volé bel chaîne,
Yé té volé Romaine,
Yé té volé nécrin,
Et pi jouyé fin.

They stole beautiful chains,
They stole dresses,
They stole jewelry boxes
And fine shoes.

*Yé té volé faussé qué
So maîtresse n'a plus chevé!
Yé té volé polisson là
Qui té fé madame gra!

They stole the wig so that
His mistress no longer had hair!
They stole the bustle
Which made Madame fat.

Un mari godiche,
Vini mandé postiche,
Qui té servi so femme,
Pou fai la bel dame.

A simple-minded husband
Came to ask for a wig
Which his wife had used
To make herself beautiful.

Comment, sapajou!
To pran, ma Kilotte? –
Non, mo maite, mo di vou,
Mo j'ai pris vos botte.

"What's all this, Sapajou,
Have you taken my trousers?"
"No, master, I tell you,
I've only taken your boots!"

Peti maîtresse,
Li t'apré crié,
To voir néguesse
C'est mo robe to volé.

The little mistress
was shouting,
"Look here, slave,
It's my dress you've taken."

Chez mouché Préval,
Dans la rue n'opital,
Yé fé nègue payé,
Pou sauté un pé.

At Mister Préval's
In Hospital Street
They made slaves pay
For dancing a little.

*Ché mo pou sorti.
Va payé bien pli.
Cinq piasse, m'en va cappe,
Ma f . . . fouet pou la *niappe*.

"At my place, for going out
[you] will pay more dearly
Five dollars, [SENSE NOT CLEAR]
I'll [f . . .] whip [you] for good measure."

Pové mouché Préval,
Mo cré li bien mal,
Ya pli encor bal,
Dans la rue n'opital.

Poor Mister Préval,
I think he's sick,
There's no more balls
In Hospital Road.

Li payé cent piasse,
Li couri à la chasse,
Li dit: C'est fini,
Ya pli bal sans permi.

He paid 100 dollars,
He went hunting,
He said: "It's finished,
No more balls without a permit!"

Notes

INTRODUCTION

1. This myth is recounted by John Smith Kendall in *History of New Orleans*, vol. 2 (Chicago: Lewis Publishing Co., 1922), 727; see also André Lafargue, "Opera in New Orleans in Days of Yore," *Publications of the Louisiana Historical Society* 29 (1946): 662. Many others recount a similar tale, and details of these can be found in Réné J. Le Gardeur Jr., "Les Premières Années du Théâtre à la Nouvelle-Orléans," *Comptes-rendues de l'Athénée louisianais* (1954): 70–72.
2. As Henry Kmen points out, Tabary would only have been a teenager in 1791, and it is unlikely he would have been managing his own theater troupe. Kmen, *Music in New Orleans: The Formative Years, 1791–1841* (Baton Rouge: Louisiana State University Press, 1966), 57.
3. Kmen, *Music in New Orleans*, 58–59.
4. This apparent hedonism scandalized many northern visitors of more puritan tastes, and complaints that "the Sabbath in New Orleans exists only in its Almanacs" can be found throughout the first half of the nineteenth century. This specific complaint was made by a James Davidson in 1836, quoted in Kmen, *Music in New Orleans*, 202.
5. The next theater to have anything approaching a permanent opera company was the Academy of Music, New York, founded in 1854: while not actually an in-house company, Max Maretzek's Italian Opera Company performed a season at the theater every year from 1854 to 1878. It was not until after the Civil War that theaters maintained in-house, "stock" companies. Katherine K. Preston discusses this throughout *Opera on the Road: Traveling Opera Troupes in the United States, 1835–60* (Urbana: University of Illinois Press, 1993) and *Opera for the People: English-Language Opera and Women Managers in Late 19th-Century America* (New York: Oxford University Press, 2017).
6. For more on the tours, see Mary Grace Swift, "The Northern Tours of the Théâtre d'Orléans, 1843 and 1845," *Louisiana History: The Journal of the Louisiana Historical Association* 26/2 (1985): 155–93; Jennifer C. H. J. Wilson, "The Impact of French Opera in Nineteenth-Century New York: The New Orleans French Opera Company from 1827–1845" (PhD diss., City University of New York, 2015); and Sylvie Chevalley, "Le Théâtre d'Orléans en Tournée dans les Villes du Nord 1827–1833," *Comptes-rendues de L'Athénée louisianais* (March 1955): 27–71.

7. Caldwell's other theaters were in St. Louis, Mobile, Cincinnati, and Nashville. See Felicia Hardison Londré and Daniel J. Watermeier, *History of the North American Theater: The United States, Canada and Mexico—From Pre-Columbian Times to the Present* (New York: Continuum, 1998), 114.
8. The St. Charles Theatre cost an estimated $352,000. Londré and Watermeier, *History of the North American Theater*, 114. This sum would be equivalent to roughly $8,943,903 today (calculated using the inflation calculator at www.in2013dollars.com).
9. Kmen, *Music in New Orleans*; John Baron, *Concert Life in Nineteenth-Century New Orleans: A Comprehensive Reference* (Baton Rouge: Louisiana State University Press, 2013); Jack Belsom, "Reception of Major Operatic Premieres in New Orleans during the Nineteenth Century" (MA diss., Louisiana State University, 1972). Belsom has also published a short, twenty-page history entitled *Opera in New Orleans* (New Orleans: New Orleans Opera Association, 1993), and he is a regular contributor to *Opera Magazine*.
10. José Manuel Izquierdo König has recently written about the importance of imaginative engagements with opera in Chile in the first half of the nineteenth century, in "Rossini's Reception in Latin America: Scarcity and Imagination in Two Early Chilean Sources," in *Gioachino Rossini 1868–2018: La musica e il mondo*, ed. Ilaria Narici, Emilio Sala, Emanuele Senici, and Benjamin Walton (Pesaro: Fondazione Rossini Pesaro, 2018), 413–35, esp. 427.
11. The period of Spanish rule in New Orleans is explored in José Montero de Pedro, *The Spanish in New Orleans and Louisiana*, trans. Richard E. Chandler (Gretna, LA: Pelican Publishing, 2000).
12. The term "Creole" has become problematic to define, as Carl Brasseaux has demonstrated: its meanings have changed enormously over time and have been intended as both complimentary and derogatory at various points. The term was originally used by French settlers to denote anyone who was born in Louisiana, regardless of their skin color. It later came to mean specifically the descendants of white settlers, with the term "Creoles of color" denoting their black counterparts. More recently, certain writers have used the term to suggest people of mixed racial background, although this is not in keeping with its original meaning. Carl A. Brasseaux, *French, Cajun, Creole, Houma: A Primer on Francophone Louisiana* (Baton Rouge: Louisiana State University Press, 2005), 88–98. I use the term to mean anyone born in the Americas, but I will clarify their racial background wherever it is relevant to my argument.
13. For detailed information on the circumstances of the Louisiana Purchase and its effects, see *The Louisiana Purchase and Its Aftermath, 1800–1830*, ed. Dolores Egger Labbé (Lafayette: Center for Louisiana Studies, University of Southwestern Louisiana, 1998).
14. Brasseaux, *French, Cajun, Creole, Houma*, 22.
15. Brasseaux, *French, Cajun, Creole, Houma*, 22. While the first wave of refugees consisted almost entirely of white French-Caribbean Creoles, the second contained around 3,000 black, Francophone slaves who also fled the violence.
16. Carl Brasseaux explores French immigration to Louisiana in *The Foreign French: Nineteenth-Century French Immigration into Louisiana, Volume 1: 1820–1839, Volume 2: 1840–1848*, and *Volume 3: 1849–1852* (Lafayette: Center for Louisiana Studies, University of Southwestern Louisiana, 1990). For more of an overview of the city's demographics in the nineteenth century, see the essays by Joseph G. Tregle Jr., Paul F. Lachance, and Joseph Logsdon and Caryn Cossé Bell in *Creole New Orleans: Race and Americanization*, ed. Arnold R. Hirsch and Joseph Logsdon (Baton Rouge: Louisiana State University Press, 1992).
17. See Joseph G. Tregle Jr., "Creoles and Americans," in *Creole New Orleans*, 153–60.

18. For the history of German immigration to New Orleans, see Ellen C. Merrill, *The Germans of Louisiana* (Gretna, LA: Pelican, 2005); and John Frederick Nau, *The German People of New Orleans: 1850–1900* (Leiden: E. J. Brill, 1958). For the history of Irish immigration, see Laura D. Kelley, *The Irish in New Orleans* (Lafayette: University of Louisiana at Lafayette Press, 2014).
19. For population figures, see "Population of the 46 Urban Places: 1810," US Bureau of the Census, 1810, accessed March 12, 2021, https://www2.census.gov/library/working-papers/1998/demo/pop-twps0027/tab04.txt; and "Population of the 100 Largest Urban Places: 1860," US Bureau of the Census, 1860, accessed March 12, 2021, https://www2.census.gov/library/working-papers/1998/demo/pop-twps0027/tab09.txt.
20. While there were many white Creoles in the area and, of course, large numbers of enslaved people, an apparently disproportionate number of properties in the Marigny were owned by free women of color, who had often been enabled to buy the houses and land by wealthy, white Creole men. See Emily Clark, *The Strange History of the American Quadroon: Free Women of Color in the Revolutionary Atlantic World* (Chapel Hill: University of North Carolina Press, 2013). The Marigny also became home to many of the city's later immigrants, particularly Germans. Rashauna Johnson writes of the Marigny's mixed demographics in "'Laissez les bons temps rouler!' and Other Concealments: Households, Taverns and Irregular Intimacies in Antebellum New Orleans," in *Interconnections: Gender and Race in American History*, ed. Carol Faulkner and Alison M. Parker (Rochester, NY: University of Rochester Press, 2012), 51–74.
21. Rashauna Johnson, *Slavery's Metropolis: Unfree Labor in New Orleans during the Age of Revolutions* (Cambridge: Cambridge University Press, 2016), 2.
22. Paul F. Lachance provides a useful graph showing the city's racial and linguistic composition in "The Foreign French," in *Creole New Orleans*, 118. See also his even more detailed table in Paul F. Lachance, "The Limits of Privilege: Where Free People of Colour Stood in the Hierarchy of Wealth in Antebellum New Orleans," in *Against the Odds: Free Blacks in the Slave Societies of the Americas*, ed. Jane G. Landers (London: Frank Cass, 1996), 68.
23. For more on the position of free people of color within New Orleans society as a whole, see Lachance, "The Limits of Privilege," 65–84. Others have argued more recently that free people of color in New Orleans had a relatively privileged position in society compared with free people of color elsewhere; see Kenneth R. Aslakson, *Making Race in the Courtroom: The Legal Construction of Three Races in Early New Orleans* (New York: New York University Press, 2014), 1–16. Nonetheless, Lachance demonstrates that they were still not able in general to achieve the levels of prosperity gained by wealthy white people. Lachance, "The Limits of Privilege," 67.
24. For a discussion of perceived divisions between Francophone and Anglophone people of color, see Joseph Logsdon and Caryn Cossé Bell, "The Americanization of Black New Orleans, 1850–1900," *Creole New Orleans*, 202–4. The Act Prohibiting Importation of Slaves, ratified in 1807, came into effect on January 1, 1808, after which it was illegal to import new slaves into the United States. The domestic slave trade, however, continued.
25. For more on the history of Louisiana Creole and its relationship with French, see *French and Creole in Louisiana*, ed. Albert Valdman (New York: Plenum, 1997). On the early history of African American English, see Donald Winford, "The Origins of African American Vernacular English: Beginnings," in *The Oxford Handbook of African American Language*, ed. Jennifer Bloomquist, Lisa J. Green, and Sonja L. Lanehort (Oxford: Oxford University Press, 2015), 85–104.

26. Quadroons, to use Clark's words, were "technically, people whose racial makeup was one-quarter African." Clark, *The Strange History of the American Quadroon*, 2.
27. Clark highlights this in *The Strange History of the American Quadroon*, 2–5.
28. In reality, neither the label "quadroon" nor the people it was used to describe were unique to New Orleans, as Clark stresses throughout *The Strange History of the American Quadroon*, but in particular on 11–37.
29. Cécile Vidal, *Caribbean New Orleans: Empire, Race, and the Making of a Slave Society* (Chapel Hill: University of North Carolina Press, 2019).
30. Amy R. Sumpter, "Segregation of the Free People of Color and the Construction of Race in Antebellum New Orleans," *Southeastern Geographer* 48/1 (2008): 19–37.
31. Clark, *The Strange History of the American Quadroon*, especially 120.
32. Kmen, *Music in New Orleans*; Baron, *Concert Life in Nineteenth-Century New Orleans*; Belsom, "Reception of Major Operatic Premieres in New Orleans during the Nineteenth Century"; Belsom, "En Route to Stardom"; Juliane Braun, *Creole Drama: Theatre and Society in Antebellum New Orleans* (Charlottesville: University of Virginia Press, 2019).
33. Kmen, *Music in New Orleans*; and Baron, *Concert Life in Nineteenth-Century New Orleans*.
34. Belsom, "Reception of Major Operatic Premieres in New Orleans during the Nineteenth Century"; and Belsom, "En Route to Stardom: Adelina Patti at the French Opera House, New Orleans, 1860–1861." *Opera Quarterly* 10/3 (1994): 113–30.
35. Braun, *Creole Drama*.
36. Joseph Roach, *Cities of the Dead: Circum-Atlantic Performance* (New York: Columbia University Press, 1996). For more on the field of Atlantic history more broadly, see Horst Pietschmann, "Introduction: Atlantic History—History between European History and Global History," in *Atlantic History: History of the Atlantic System, 1580–1830*, ed. Horst Pietschmann (Göttingen: Vandenhoeck & Ruprecht, 2002), 8–54.
37. See Braun, *Creole New Orleans*, 11–41.
38. For more on the long process of abolition after 1807, see *Liberated Africans and the Abolition of the Slave Trade, 1807–1896*, ed. Richard Anderson and Henry B. Lovejoy (Rochester, NY: University of Rochester Press, 2020).
39. Before Haitian independence, however, there had been important connections, as Julia Prest has explored in "Parisian Palimpsests and Creole Creations: Mme. Marsan and Dlle Minette play Nina on the Caribbean Stage," *Early Modern French Studies* 41/2 (2019): 170–88.
40. Mary Grace Swift discusses their visit to Montréal briefly in "The Northern Tours of the Théâtre d'Orléans, 1843 and 45," 164–65. As Elizabeth Forbes suggests in her *Grove* article, most of the city's operatic life in the nineteenth century was provided by touring troupes coming up from the United States. Forbes, "Montreal (opera)," *Grove Music Online, Oxford Music Online*, accessed March 13, 2021, https://www.oxfordmusiconline.com/grovemusic/view/10.1093/gmo/9781561592630.001.0001/omo-9781561592630-e-5000007373.
41. Axel Körner and Paulo Kühl, "Opera and Italianità in Transnational and Global Perspective: An Introduction," in *Italian Opera in Global and Transnational Perspective: Reimagining Italianità in the Long Nineteenth Century* ed. Axel Körner and Paulo Kühl (Cambridge: Cambridge University Press, 2021), 8. Körner also advocates for a similar approach in "Dalla storia transnazionale all'opera transnazionale. Per una critica delle categorie nazionali," *Saggiatore Musicale* 24 (2017/1): 81–98; and "Beyond Nationaloper. For a Critique of Methodological Nationalism in Reading Nineteenth-Century Italian and German Opera," *Journal of Modern Italian Studies* 25/4 (2020): 402–19.
42. Prasenjit Duara, *Rescuing History from the Nation: Questioning Narratives of Modern China*

(Chicago: University of Chicago Press, 1995). Even large-scale world histories, such as Jürgen Osterhammel's *The Transformation of the World* and Christopher Bayly's *The Birth of the Modern World,* which focus on globalization and on the ways in which political and social changes across the globe during the period were both interconnected and interdependent, still acknowledge the importance of nationalism to nineteenth-century intellectual thought, although they ultimately seek to write a history that moves beyond the borders of the nation-state. Jürgen Osterhammel, *The Transformation of the World: A Global History of the Nineteenth Century,* trans. Patrick Camiller (Princeton, NJ: Princeton University Press, 2014), first published as *Die Verwandlung der Welt* (Munich: C. H. Beck, 2009); and Christopher Bayly, *The Birth of the Modern World: Global Connections and Comparisons, 1780–1914* (Malden, MA: Blackwell, 2004).

43. Preston, *Opera on the Road* and *Opera for the People.*
44. Francesca Vella, *Networking Operatic Italy* (Chicago: University of Chicago Press, 2021).
45. See Vella, *Networking Operatic Italy*; and Vella, "(De)railing Mobility: Opera, Stasis, and Locomotion on Late-Nineteenth-Century Italian Tracks," *Opera Quarterly* 34/1 (2018): 6.
46. For more on global microhistory, see John-Paul Ghobrial, "Seeing the World like a Microhistorian," in *Global History and Microhistory: A Supplement Volume of Past and Present,* ed. John-Paul Ghobrial, *Past & Present Supplement* 14 (2019): 1–22.
47. Jürgen Osterhammel, *The Transformation of the World,* 5.
48. Benjamin Walton, "Italian Operatic Fantasies in Latin America," *Journal of Modern Italian Studies* 17/4 (2012): 460. See also Benjamin Walton, "*L'italiana* in Calcutta," in *Operatic Geographies: The Place of the Opera House,* ed. Suzanne Aspden (Chicago: University of Chicago Press, 2019), 119–32; and Benjamin Walton, "Escasez y abundancia en la historiografía operística del Río de la Plata," trans. Vera Wolkowicz, *Revista Argentina de Musicología* 21/1 (2020): 33–49.
49. The challenges of writing a global history of music more generally have recently been explored by Martin Stokes in "Notes and Queries on 'Global Music History,'" in *Studies on a Global History of Music: A Balzan Musicology Project,* ed. Reinhard Strohm (Abingdon: Routledge, 2018), 3–18. The rest of this volume, too, explores case studies and issues in writing such a history.
50. David A. Bell, "Replies to Richard Drayton and David Motadel," in Richard Drayton and David Motadel, "Discussion: The Futures of Global History," *Journal of Global History* 13 (2018): 17.
51. Baron, *Concert Life in Nineteenth-Century New Orleans.*
52. Kmen, *Music in New Orleans.*
53. Mark Everist, *Music Drama at the Paris Odéon, 1824–1828* (Berkeley: University of California Press, 2002); Frederic William John Hemmings, *The Theatre Industry in Nineteenth-Century France* (Cambridge: Cambridge University Press, 2009).
54. In this sense, my work resonates with the concept of "institutional entrepreneurship" that has been explored in the fields of organization studies and sociology, often to look at large companies in the present day. I do not engage with the details of this concept here, but I take the idea of exploring the agencies of individuals embedded within a larger institutional structure as an important point of departure. For an example of work on institutional entrepreneurship, see Raghu Garud, Cynthia Hardy, and Steve Maguire, "Institutional Entrepreneurship as Embedded Agency: An Introduction to the Special Issue," *Organization Studies* 28/7 (2007): 957–69.
55. Jean Fouchard, *Artistes et répertoire des scènes de Saint-Domingue* (Port-au-Prince, Haiti:

H. Deschamps, 1988); and *Le Théâtre à Saint-Domingue* (Port-au-Prince, Haiti: H. Deschamps, 1988). Many other studies of operatic life in America also make heavy use of the press. For two of the most successful, see Karen Ahlquist and George Martin's respective city studies of New York and San Francisco. Ahlquist, *Democracy at the Opera: Music, Theater and Culture in New York City, 1815–60* (Urbana: University of Illinois Press, 1997); and Martin, *Verdi at the Golden Gate: Opera and San Francisco in the Gold Rush Years* (Berkeley: University of California Press, 1993).

56. *L'Abeille* can be accessed at http://nobee.jplibrary.net/. The website contains image files only, and so the paper is not text searchable. *The Daily Picayune* is available via subscription through www.newsbank.com.
57. For an example of work on the European press that explores the relationship between opera criticism and wider city life, see Emanuele Senici, "Delirious Hopes: Napoleonic Milan and the Rise of Modern Italian Operatic Criticism," *Cambridge Opera Journal* 27/2 (2015): 97–127.
58. The specific archives I used were the Archives départementales de la Seine-Maritime in Rouen, and the Archives municipales de la Ville du Havre.
59. Benjamin Walton, "Quirk Shame," *Representations* 132 (2015): 121–29.
60. Ted Underwood has discussed the problems of OCR and text searching in "Theorizing Research Practices We Forgot to Theorize Twenty Years Ago," *Representations* 127 (2014): 66.
61. Miles Fairburn, *Social History: Problems, Strategies, and Methods* (Basingstoke: Macmillan, 1999), 41.
62. Lara Putnam, "To Study the Fragments/Whole: Microhistory and the Atlantic World," *Journal of Social History* 39/3 (2006): 615–30.
63. For one discussion of the "exceptional normal," see John-Paul Ghobrial, "Moving Stories and What They Tell Us: Early Modern Mobility Between Microhistory and Global History," *Global History and Microhistory: A Supplement Volume of Past and Present*, ed. John-Paul Ghobrial, *Past & Present Supplement* 14 (2019): 249.
64. Glenda Goodman, "Transatlantic Music Studies," in *Oxford Handbooks Online*, Oxford University Press (2015), accessed March 12, 2021, 10.1093/oxfordhb/9780199935321.013.79.
65. Ann Laura Stoler, *Along the Archival Grain: Epistemic Anxieties and Colonial Common Sense* (Princeton, NJ: Princeton University Press, 2009). Antoinette Burton's edited volume *Archive Stories: Facts, Fictions, and the Writing of History* (Durham, NC: Duke University Press, 2005) similarly focuses on the way archives construct and reconstruct different kinds of knowledge in a variety of colonial and postcolonial settings.
66. Juliane Braun, "On the Verge of Fame: The Free People of Color and the French Theatre in Antebellum New Orleans," in *Liminale Anthropologien: Zwischenzeiten, Schwellenphänomene, Zwischenräume in Literatur und Philosophie*, ed. Jochen Achilles, Roland Borgards, and Brigitte Burrichter (Würzburg: Königshausen & Neumann, 2012), 165–66.
67. For information on these composers, see Lester Sullivan, "Composers of Color of Nineteenth-Century New Orleans: The History behind the Music," *Black Research Journal* 9/1 (1988): 51–82. Sally McKee's book on Dédé explores his early life in New Orleans and his move to Europe. See Sally McKee, *The Exile's Song: Edmond Dédé and the Unfinished Revolutions of the Atlantic World* (New Haven, CT: Yale University Press, 2017).
68. Braun, *Creole Drama*, 72–109.
69. As Braun has remarked, "it is more often than not by understanding what has been omitted that a coherent picture emerges." Braun, "On the Verge of Fame," 164.

70. Clark uses letters written by Thomas Jefferson to illustrate this in *The Strange History of the American Quadroon*, 2–5.

CHAPTER ONE

1. "Un théâtre est une machine difficile à mouvoir et dont les rouages sont bien nombreux." "De la résiliation de l'engagement théâtrale: premier article," *La Lorgnette*, February 19, 1843.
2. Tracy C. Davis, *The Economics of the British Stage, 1800–1914* (Cambridge: Cambridge University Press, 2000), 12.
3. Tracy Davis and David Hemmings have both expressed the difficulties of writing a "complete" economic history of theatrical life in any given period in their respective work on London and Paris in the nineteenth century. The evidential lacunae and methodological issues they face multiply in the case of nineteenth-century New Orleans. See Davis, *The Economics of the British Stage*; and Frederic William John Hemmings, *The Theatre Industry in Nineteenth-Century France* (Cambridge: Cambridge University Press, 2009).
4. Henry Kmen discusses elements of the financing and running of the theater in its early years in *Music in New Orleans*, but the picture I paint here is somewhat different: Kmen traces all the minor local ups and downs as reported in the press, whereas I have endeavored to provide an impression, created from a larger selection of sources, of particular administrative and financial decisions that best help place the theater in the context of other institutions on both sides of the Atlantic at the time.
5. This information can be found on the death certificate for John Davis, "Court of Probates, Davis, John, Estate of, 1839," City Archives, *NOPL*.
6. For more on the impact of the Saint-Domingue revolution on New Orleans, see *The Road to Louisiana: The Saint-Domingue Refugees, 1792–1809*, ed. Carl A. Brasseaux and Glenn R. Conrad (Lafayette: Center for Louisiana Studies, University of Southwestern Louisiana, 1992).
7. Henri (Henrico) Davis is listed as being buried in St. Louis Cemetery no. 1, according to the cemetery index held at the Historical Centre of the Louisiana State Museums at the Old US Mint. Henri's gravestone lists that he was a native of Santiago de Cuba.
8. Whether Davis was a planter in Saint-Domingue or worked in some other profession, I have been unable to find out, but he must have had a reasonably lucrative occupation. I have found no evidence to suggest his work had anything to do with the island's theaters. There is no mention of him in either Jean Fouchard's *Artistes et répertoire des scènes de Saint-Domingue* (Port-au-Prince, Haiti: H. Deschamps, 1988) or *Le Théâtre à Saint-Domingue* (Port-au-Prince, Haiti: H. Deschamps, 1988).
9. Juliane Braun even suggests that Davis's business interests extended to cigar manufacture and furniture retail, although I have not found anything to confirm that. Juliane Braun, "Petit Paris en Amérique? French Theatrical Culture in Nineteenth-Century Louisiana" (PhD diss., Julius-Maximilians-Universität Würzburg, 2013), 29–30.
10. For Davis's gambling monopoly, see William Norman Thompson, *Gambling in America: An Encyclopedia of History, Issues, and Society* (Santa Barbara, CA: ABC-CLIO, 2001), 86.
11. Stanley Arthur, *Old New Orleans: A History of the Vieux Carré, Its Ancient and Historical Buildings* [1936] (Reprinted Westminster, MD: Heritage Books, 2007), 121–22.
12. For the plans to do with St. Louis Cathedral, see Jean Boze to Baron de Sainte-Gême, March 28, 1836, Ste-Gême Family Papers, MSS 100, Folder 267, 2–3, *HNOC*. In 1819, Davis wrote a letter to the mayor and aldermen of New Orleans, proposing that if they paid him $400 each year he would undertake the upkeep of the road leading from the city to the

Bayou St. John. Public-spirited as this gesture might have seemed, Davis owned a hotel on the Bayou, and maintaining the road was in his own financial interests. Letter from John Davis to the Mayor of New Orleans, July 9, 1819. Rosemonde E. and Emile Kuntz Collection, Series 4: Municipal Papers, A. New Orleans, 1817–1824, Box 17, *LARC*.

13. "Le soussigné a l'honneur d'annoncer au public qu'il vient d'acheter des actionnaires du Théâtre d'Orléans les débris de cet édifice et le local sur lequel il était situé." John Davis, "Prospectus pour la reconstruction du Théâtre d'Orléans," *L'Ami des lois*, November 14, 1816.
14. "Un édifice qui aurait fait honneur en Europe à une ville de seconde ordre." John Davis, "Prospectus pour la reconstruction du Théâtre d'Orléans."
15. Davis, "Prospectus pour la reconstruction du Théâtre d'Orléans."
16. Davis, "Prospectus pour la reconstruction du Théâtre d'Orléans." For all the calculations about equivalencies between the dollar in the past and the present, I have used https://www.officialdata.org/ (accessed May 21, 2021). This online inflation calculator uses data supplied by the US Department of Labor and allows the conversion of a sum between any two years specified by the user.
17. Davis, "Prospectus pour la reconstruction du Théâtre d'Orléans."
18. See Henry Kmen, *Music in New Orleans: The Formative Years, 1791–1841* (Baton Rouge: Louisiana State University Press, 1966), 85 and 88–89.
19. Indeed, he likely even had financial assistance to buy the land on which the former Théâtre d'Orléans had stood in the autumn of 1816: Davis's name never appeared on the chain of title for the lot of land on which he built the theater, but that land was indeed sold in the autumn of 1816, to a man named Edward Hollander, who went on to own it for the next twenty years, selling it in 1836, the year in which John Davis eventually retired. The Chain of Title information for the plot of land can be viewed online: "717–737 Orleans Street," "Collins C. Diboll Vieux Carré Survey: Property Info," Historic New Orleans Collection, accessed May 24, 2021, https://www.hnoc.org/vcs/property_info.php?lot=18627-01.
20. For the loan from the city, see Kmen, *Music in New Orleans*, 89. For the smaller loans, see "Davis Jean to A. Carraby, David Olivier and others (mortgage)," Philippe Pedesclaux, vol. 7, Act 337, April 29, 1819, *NONA*.
21. "Davis Jean to A. Carraby, David Olivier and others (mortgage)," and "Mortgage to Gaspard Debuys, Labranche and others," Philippe Pedesclaux, vol. 8, Act 429, 1819, *NONA*.
22. "Davis Jean to A. Carraby, David Olivier and others (mortgage)," Philippe Pedesclaux, vol. 7, Act 337, April 29, 1819, *NONA*.
23. Lauren Clay, "Patronage, Profits, and Public Theaters: Re-Thinking Cultural Unification in Ancien-Régime France," *Journal of Modern History* 79/4 (2007): 766.
24. Jean Boze, the business manager appointed by an old Saint-Domingue friend of Davis's who had returned to France, regularly mentioned Davis's dealings in his letters to his employer full of local news. He mentions that Davis has just bounced back from the brink of bankruptcy in Jean Boze to Baron de Sainte-Gême, July 20, 1829, Ste-Gême Family Papers, MSS 100, Folder 143, 7, *HNOC*.
25. "On fait riche ce directeur incomparable de plus d'une somme de 200 mille Gourdes qui lui assure annuellement une rente de 20 mille Gourdes dit-on!" Jean Boze to Baron de Sainte-Gême, November 6–December 4, 1829, *HNOC*, Ste-Gême Family Papers, MSS 100, Folder 150, 2.
26. *Courrier de la Louisiane*, April 18, 1835.
27. "Examination in chief," *Davis, John vs. Caldwell, James* (1822), docket 4622 of the First Judicial Court, *NOPL*.

28. See Jutta Toelle, "Opera as Business? From Impresari to the Publishing Industry," *Journal of Modern Italian Studies* 17/4 (2012): 448–59, especially 452.
29. John Smith Kendall, *History of New Orleans* (Chicago: Lewis Publishing Co., 1922), 530.
30. Lease from John Davis to Jackson Oliver, Carlile Pollock, vol. 18, January 4, 1826, *NONA*.
31. *L'Ami des Lois*, July 18, 1823 (quoted in Kmen, *Music in New Orleans*, 98); and *L'Ami des Lois*, April 6, 1824 (quoted in Kmen, *Music in New Orleans*, 102).
32. *L'Ami des Lois*, July 18, 1823. Quoted in Kmen, *Music in New Orleans*, 98.
33. Girls, in contrast, tended to be educated closer to home at local private schools, often convent schools. See Eliza Ripley, *Social Life in Old New Orleans: Being Recollections of My Girlhood* (New York: D. Appleton and Company, 1912), 7.
34. William H. Coleman, *Historical Sketch Book and Guide to New Orleans and Environs* (New York: W. H. Coleman, 1885), 203–4.
35. Coleman, *Historical Sketchbook and Guide to New Orleans and Environs*, 203–4.
36. "Société entre Jean Davis et Pierre Davis," Theodore Seghers, vol. 8, Act 162, March 27, 1834, *NONA*.
37. See his obituary in *L'Abeille*, June 15, 1839. His body was returned to New Orleans and buried in St. Louis Cemetery no. 2. For Davis's will, see "Court of Probates, Davis, John, Estate of, 1839," City Archives, *NOPL*.
38. The documents detailing the handover are preserved in the New Orleans Notarial Archives. See Félix de Armas, vol. 48, Act 333, May 11, 1836, *NONA*.
39. Félix de Armas, vol. 48, Act 333, May 11, 1836, *NONA*.
40. "De la résiliation de l'engagement théâtrale: premier article," *La Lorgnette*, February 19, 1843.
41. "De la résiliation de l'engagement théâtrale: premier article."
42. "De la résiliation de l'engagement théâtrale: premier article."
43. Mary Grace Swift mentions the period of financial troubles before the tour of 1843 in "The Northern Tours of the Théâtre d'Orléans, 1843 and 1845," *Louisiana History: The Journal of the Louisiana Historical Association* 26/2 (1985): 157.
44. "De la résiliation de l'engagement théâtrale: premier article."
45. "De la résiliation de l'engagement théâtrale: premier article."
46. "De la résiliation de l'engagement théâtrale: deuxième article," *La Lorgnette*, February 23, 1843.
47. I discuss the municipalities further in chapter 2. See also Virginia R. Domínguez, *White by Definition: Social Classification in Creole Louisiana* (New Brunswick, NJ: Rutgers University Press, 1986), 110–32. For more on the money printed by each municipality, see "Municipal Currency in New Orleans," "US Mint in New Orleans," and "Money, Money, Money," Historic New Orleans Collection, accessed May 21, 2021, https://www.hnoc.org/virtual/money-money-money/municipal-currency-new-orleans.
48. "De la résiliation de l'engagement théâtrale: deuxième article."
49. The local press carried adverts for these positions, along the lines of the following: "Musicians desirous to enter the orchestra of the Théâtre d'Orléans are requested to call immediately at [*sic*] Messrs Auguste Douce and St. Estève [the *régisseurs*]," which appeared in the *Louisiana Courier* on June 20, 1823.
50. Contract letter written by L. Fiot, Cohen vs Davis (1846), docket 00349 of the Third District Court, *NOPL*.
51. Kmen, *Music in New Orleans*, 103–4.
52. In some years, however, the season closed as early as the end of April. Henry Kmen discusses

how unpredictable weather (including not just extreme heat but also heavy rain showers) and disease affected the length of the theater season in Kmen, *Music in New Orleans*, 167–69.

53. Davis posted a notice in a local newspaper early in the month, asking his friends and clients to see him as soon as possible to settle all their accounts before his departure. *Courrier de la Louisiane*, April 8, 1822.

54. "Le navire Américain, *Cecilia*, capitaine A. Liberal, parti du Havre le 16 Septembre, est entré à la Balize mardi matin, et était arrivé mercredi à 2 heures après-midi devant l'habitation Caselar, où il s'est arrêté pour mettre à terre ses passagers, qu'on a craint de faire monter en ville dans ce moment. Mr. J. Davis, le directeur du Théâtre d'Orléans, qui avait entrepris, à grands frais, le voyage de France afin de se procurer des acteurs pour compléter sa troupe, est le fréteur de ce navire, et amène avec lui vingt-cinq personnes attachées à son théâtre. Nous avons appris avec plaisir que Mr. Davis s'est procuré des charmans [*sic*] sujets pour l'opéra, la comédie et le vaudeville, ainsi qu'une jolie troupe de danseurs pour monter des ballets." *Courrier de la Louisiane*, November 8, 1822.

55. "Procuration from John Davis to Pierre Davis," Theodore Seghers, vol. 5, Act 129, March 29, 1832, *NONA*.

56. Plantation manager Jean Boze mentioned Pierre's trip in 1834 in one of the regular letters of local news that he sent to his employer in France. "M. Davis a été reconnaissant à votre souvenir et à celui pour son fils, qui se trouve depuis quelques mois à Paris pour y recruter sans doute des comédiens pour les spectacles de cet hiver." Jean Boze to Baron de Sainte-Gême, July 18, 1834, Ste-Gême Family Papers, MSS 100, Folder 243, 4, *HNOC*.

57. An anecdote published in the Parisian press appears to confirm that Pierre Davis was recruiting for the Théâtre d'Orléans in Paris as late as 1859: A. Denis, "Chronique," *Le Nouvelliste*, August 12, 1851. The entries in Meyerbeer's daybooks and diaries discussed later in this chapter also confirm that Davis was in Paris in August 1854, the year after he handed over control of the theater to Boudousquié.

58. "Chronique étrangère," *Revue et Gazette musicale de Paris*, January 31, 1841.

59. For an account of Bernard's directorship of the Odéon, see Mark Everist, *Music Drama at the Paris Odéon, 1824–1828* (Berkeley: University of California Press, 2002), 46–59.

60. Prévost won first prize in the Prix de Rome in 1831. John Baron, *Concert Life in Nineteenth-Century New Orleans: A Comprehensive Reference* (Baton Rouge: Louisiana State University Press, 2013), 179.

61. See S. Frederick Starr, *Louis Moreau Gottschalk* (Urbana: University of Illinois Press, 1995), 34. Elie also owned a thriving music shop in New Orleans in the late 1840s and 1850s, located at 12 Royal Street: his advertisements declared him to be an "importer of musical instruments, Pleyel pianos, Italian and French strings, sheet music, and music paper." These advertisements were printed in the programs/libretti sold to accompany the Théâtre d'Orléans performances and can be found in many archives in New Orleans. Concert and opera programs were no exceptions to the American desire to advertise on every available surface (a fact which is revealed by even a cursory glance at any of the newspapers published in New Orleans during the period: the front page of every broadsheet newspaper was filled almost entirely with adverts).

62. See "Procuration from John Davis to J. B. Sel," Félix de Armas, vol. 2, Act 271, June 7, 1824, *NONA*.

63. The document states that Sel should act as follows: "sur son prochain départ pour [la] France de, pour le dit sieur Davis et en son nom, faire choix de tous acteurs, danseurs, et chanteurs ou autres que le sieur Sel croira capable de remplir le but [du théâtre], prendre avec eux

tels arrangements, leur abonner pour leurs gages tels prix et somme, faire tels avances et de bourses qu'il croira à propos, s'obliger en tout et partout de la même manière que le dit sieur Sel la jugera convenable." "Procuration from John Davis to J. B. Sel," Félix de Armas, vol. 2, Act 271, June 7, 1824, *NONA*.

64. "Et de rembourser le dit Sieur Sel de tous frais avances et de bourse que le dit Sieur Sel fera au nom du dit [Davis]." "Procuration from John Davis to J. B. Sel," Félix de Armas, vol. 2, Act 271, June 7, 1824, *NONA*.
65. The visit was dated July 7, 1849. See *The Diaries of Giacomo Meyerbeer: 1840–49*, ed. Robert Letellier, vol. 2 (London: Associated University Presses, 2001), 357. Mme. Moisson was likely Joséphine Moisson, who sang at the Paris Opéra from 1846 to 1847, but who had her contract canceled by the directors. See Kimberly White, *Female Singers on the French Stage, 1830–1848* (Cambridge: Cambridge University Press, 2018), 156.
66. Bertini played the role of Marguerite d'Anjou in the New Orleans premiere of Meyerbeer's opera of that name in April 1854, for example. The audition organized by Meyerbeer in 1853 was a reaudition, as Bertini had already sung with the New Orleans troupe, performing the role of Berthe in the Théâtre d'Orléans premiere of *Le Prophète* in 1850.
67. The New Orleans press suggested that Davis had remarked to Meyerbeer that "if he could not find a good [prima donna], the great maestro's operas would of course be butchered here. Such a hint was enough, and Madame Bertini was recommended." *New Orleans Daily Delta*, November 6, 1853.
68. A biography of Collignon can be found in *The Crescent City Illustrated: The Commercial, Social, Political, and General History of New Orleans*, ed. Edwin L. Jewell (New Orleans, 1873). This volume does not contain page numbers, but it is fully accessible and text searchable through Google Books.
69. "De l'Administration du Théâtre d'Orléans," *La Lorgnette*, July 17, 1842. This suggests that he might have been related to the owners of the Collignon Agence Théâtrale that operated in Paris during the 1830s and 1840s, although it is unlikely that Gustave Collignon himself was the proprietor of this business, since it was operating at least as early as 1835, when he would have been only seventeen years old. The Collignon Agence Théâtrale was listed at 9 Rue de Cléry by *Le Monde dramatique: revue de spectacles anciens et modernes* in 1835 (142). By 1845, Collignon himself was listed at that address as a piano teacher. See *Annuaire musical: contenant les noms et adresses des amateurs, artistes et commerçants en musique de Paris, des départemens et de l'étranger, par une société de musiciens* (Paris, 1845), 245. The Théâtre d'Orléans may well have had a longer association with the Collignons even before their theatrical agency began to operate formally, as another M. Collignon accompanied Pierre Davis and his recruits to Le Havre at the end of the young Pierre's first recruiting trip in 1832. See "Nouvelles diverses," *Gazette des théâtres*, September 13, 1832.
70. Hemmings, *The Theater Industry in Nineteenth-Century France*, 194–95.
71. Hemmings also points out how frequently performers were exploited by such "bureaux de placements" (*The Theater Industry in Nineteenth-Century France*, 193–95). See also Lauren R. Clay, "Theater and the Commercialization of Culture in Eighteenth-Century France" (PhD diss., University of Pennsylvania, 2003), 167 and 285.
72. John Rosselli, *The Opera Industry in Italy from Cimarosa to Verdi: The Role of the Impresario* (Cambridge: Cambridge University Press, 1984), 149. Rosselli points out that agents began to ask for 8 to 10 percent commission for arranging troupes for the Americas by the second half of the nineteenth century. Rosselli, *The Opera Industry in Italy from Cimarosa to Verdi*, 143.

73. To give but one example, he was thanked as follows in *La France théâtrale*: "Tout porte à croire qu'il en sera ainsi, car jamais notre ville n'a vu une troupe aussi belle que celle qu'a pris soin de composer M. Collignon, ce correspondant si habile de Paris. Les efforts de ce dernier ont été couronnés du plus beau succès, merci et reconnaissance à M. Collignon." *La France théâtrale*, December 26, 1844, n.p. Gustave Collignon and his wife and baby are listed in the immigration records as arriving in New Orleans on the *Espirance* from Le Havre on November 7, 1848, along with the new recruits for the Théâtre d'Orléans troupe. See Carl Brasseaux, *The Foreign French: Nineteenth-Century French Immigration into Louisiana, Volume 2: 1840–48* (Lafayette: Center for Louisiana Studies, University of Southwestern Louisiana, 1990), 74.
74. This was the long-established period in which provincial theatrical recruitment took place in Paris, until the use of "bureaux de correspondance dramatique" became widespread. See Hemmings, *The Theatre Industry in Nineteenth-Century France*, 194.
75. "Pour pouvoir atteindre pareil but, il est indispensable que la Direction ait envoyé traiter à Paris huit ou dix jours avant Pâques." "De l'Administration du Théâtre d'Orléans," *La Lorgnette*, July 17, 1842.
76. Of Collignon, Canonge has the following to say: "M. Collignon, le courtier des théâtres et l'homme de confiance de l'Administration d'Orléans, à force de Robert-Macairisme, lui fait avaler des ténors enroués, des dramaturges d'un échevelé désespérant, des basses-tailles Bernardet [this is a reference to Bernadet, a singer discussed later in this chapter who had a very difficult relationship with the theater administration], et des premières cantatrices sans dents." "De l'Administration du Théâtre d'Orléans," *La Lorgnette*, July 17, 1842.
77. Georges Bell, "Etudes contemporaines: Mademoiselle Béatrix Person," *La Sylphide*, March 30, 1855.
78. See Hemmings, *The Theatre Industry in Nineteenth-Century France*, 194.
79. Hemmings points out, for example, that many French provincial theater seasons only ran in the winter months, while the season in Toulouse ran for many years from January to September, with a hiatus from March to June. Hemmings, *The Theatre Industry in Nineteenth-Century France*, 62–63.
80. Agreement between J. Davis and Allen P. Holdridge, Carlile Pollock, vol. 19, May 12, 1826, 113–15, *NONA*. I take as my basis for all conversions between dollars and francs in this book the equivalency of $1 and 5.25 francs.
81. For the currency conversion, see https://www.officialdata.org/ (accessed May 21, 2021).
82. "Mr Toto, le fils de Mr Jean Davis, a fait route pour France sur un bâtiment allant au Havre . . . On pense que son voyage a pour but le recrutement de quelques bons acteurs qui manquaient, dit-on, ici à cette troupe." Jean Boze to Baron de Ste-Gême, March 2, 1836, Ste-Gême Family Papers, MSS 100, Folder 267, 3, *HNOC*.
83. I use the slightly unusual term "lampist" throughout this book to signify a role that was partly what we would think of today as a stage lighting technician and partly in charge of maintaining candles and, later, gaslights elsewhere in the theater building.
84. For a more detailed look at this, see Charlotte Bentley, "Resituating Transatlantic Opera: The Case of the Théâtre d'Orléans, New Orleans, 1819–1859" (PhD diss., University of Cambridge, 2017), 63–104.
85. The ship's "Rôles de bord" document can be accessed via the Archives départementales de Loire-Atlantique at (accessed March 22, 2019) https://www.archinoe.fr/v2/ad44/visualiseur/navires_nominatif.html?id=440585809.
86. "Nouvelles," *Revue et gazette musicale de Paris*, August 15, 1839.

87. See "Chronique départementale," *Revue et gazette musicale de Paris*, September 18, 1842; and "Tableaux de troupes," *Journal des théâtres*, October 22, 1843.
88. "Théâtres des départemens," *La France théâtrale*, February 13, 1845.
89. Charles Jobey mentions this in "Le lac Cathahoula," in *L'Amour d'une blanche* (Paris, 1861), 199.
90. Jobey describes the family in his short story "Le lac Cathahoula," which is discussed in chapter 5. See "Le lac Cathahoula," 200–202.
91. One of the difficulties of tracing many female singers of the period is that they are frequently referred to in the press by their title and surname, rather than by their first name and surname. This leads to difficulties in identifying the movements of specific individuals, particularly if they belonged to a theatrical family where several performers shared the same surname.
92. Baron talks of Prévost and his daughter in *Concert Life in Nineteenth-Century New Orleans*, 179. Prévost's wife, Eléonore Colon, was also a singer, and she was part of the troupe at Le Havre with Prévost, but she does not appear ever to have sung in New Orleans, even though she accompanied her husband there.
93. The opera in which they performed was Gregorio Curto's *Le Lepreux*. Curto was a Spanish-born bass who joined the Théâtre d'Orléans troupe in 1830. After spending two years in the troupe, he remained in New Orleans, devoting himself to church music in the city. For more biographical information on Gregorio Curto, see Baron, *Concert Life in Nineteenth-Century New Orleans*, 146–63. For an earlier account of Curto's life, see *The Crescent City Illustrated*, ed. Jewell.
94. Pierre Constant, *Le Conservatoire national de musique et de déclamation: documents historiques et administratifs recueillis ou rencontrés par l'auteur* (Paris: Imprimerie nationale, 1900), 863.
95. Jobey describes in a footnote to one of his stories Cherubini's assessment—in his role as director of the Conservatoire—of Vallière's talents at the first competition he took part in, in 1828: "The jury has decided that Joseph Vallière merited the first prize; but, on account of his considerable youth, he will have to make do with the second, in order to compel him to stay here for another year." Jobey makes fun of Cherubini's heavily accented and somewhat imperfect French in his transcription of the words: "Le zury il a décidé que Zoseph Vallière il avait mérité le premier prix; ma, attendu sa trop grande zeunesse, il aura gué lé second, pour le forcer à rester ici encore oune année de plous." Charles Jobey, "Le lac Cathahoula," 270. For his first prize, see Constant, *Le Conservatoire national de musique*, 630.
96. The *Courrier de la Louisiane* mentions the sorry losses on October 21, 1839.
97. For more on Jobey's activities as an editor and journalist, see chapter 5.
98. Among the cast for the premiere of Adam's *Si j'étais roi* at the Théâtre-Lyrique was the bass François-Marcel Junca (playing the role of Prince Kadoor), who became a member of the New Orleans troupe in 1855. Charles H. Parsons, *Opera Premieres: An Index of Casts A–J*, vol. 13 of the Mellen Opera Reference Index (New York: Edwin Mellen Press, 1992), 5.
99. See *L'Argus*, March 22, 1851, for Lecourt's appointment as director of the Théâtre du Vaudeville.
100. Many of Chéret's pieces can be found in the catalog of the Bibliothèque nationale de France.
101. "Correspondance," *Revue et Gazette musicale*, October 10, 1852, discussed Cambier's performances in Brussels. The same newspaper discussed her performances in Liège on December 5, 1852, for example.
102. Geismar had a particularly mobile career, as she also worked at theaters in Nantes, Lyon,

Bordeaux, Marseille, Toulouse, Rouen, and Angers, as well as at the Paris Opéra. For a biography of Geismar (who became Mme. Écarlat-Geismar), see T. Faucon, *Le nouvel Opéra: monument, artistes* (Paris: Michel Lévy Frères, 1875), 295–96.

103. Blès sang at Bordeaux, Lille, and Lyon in the French provinces. Information about his career can be found in *Almanach des Spectacles de 1831 à 1834* (Paris, 1834) and in Arnaud Detcheverry's *Histoire des Théâtres de Bordeaux* (Bordeaux: Imprimerie typographique de J. Delmas, 1860). See also the lists of singers seeking work in Paris in *La France théâtrale* from September 12, 1844, to the end of that year.

104. "Theatricals," *Calcutta Monthly Journal and General Register*, November 1836, 630.

105. For the story about Person, see Georges Bell, "Etudes contemporaines: Mademoiselle Béatrix Person," *La Sylphide*, March 30, 1855. For the story about Chéret, see "Théâtre du Havre," *Journal du Havre. Commercial, Maritime et Littéraire, annonces légales et avis divers*, July 27, 1827 (accessed May 21, 2021), https://dezede.org/sources/id/4682/.

106. All of this information can be found in Auguste Laget's *Le Monde Artiste* (Paris: Heugel, 1883), the sixth chapter of which focuses entirely on Lagrave and his career.

107. "Le passage de de Lagrave à l'Opéra ne laissa point de trace dans le firmament lumineux du monde artistique, ou, s'il y fut remarqué, ce fut à l'état d'étoile filante." Laget, *Le Monde Artiste*, 202.

108. "Plusieurs journaux ont annoncé la mort du ténor Lagrave. Ce bruit est complétement faux. Nous apprenons que cet artiste est en route pour Paris venant de la Nouvelle-Orléans, où il a chanté pendant trois ans. Il se propose de donner quelques représentations au Havre et à Rouen avant de se rendre à Paris, où nous le reverrons vers la fin d'octobre." *Le Ménestrel*, September 26, 1858.

109. "Sa santé n'a pu résister au climat de la Nouvelle-Orléans et sa famille vient d'acquérir la certitude de sa mort." *Le Ménestrel*, January 13, 1861.

110. Karl-Josef Kutsch and Leo Riemens, "Rousseau-Lagrave, Théophile," *Großes Sängerlexikon*, ed. Karl-Josef Kutsch and Leo Riemens, vol. 4 (Bern: Francke, 1987), 4038. Adolphe Orain, *Au pays de Rennes* (Rennes: Hyacinthe Caillière, 1892), 161.

111. Martin Foucault, *Les Seigneurs de Laval* (Paris: E. Jamin, 1875), 131.

112. "Il se mit courageusement à l'étude de la langue et du chant italiens." Laget, *Le Monde Artiste*, 205.

113. Laget, *Le Monde Artiste*, 208.

114. The ten singers who in 1840 wrote a long letter about their experiences in New Orleans to the Parisian newspaper, the *Gazette des théâtres*, stated that they had all been contracted to the theater for that length of time, too. "Encore quelques renseignements utiles aux artistes qui voudraient venir à la Nouvelle-Orléans," *Gazette des théâtres*, July 5, 1840. From the contracts I have located and reports in the local press, it is clear that eighteen months was the most common length of engagement.

115. "Mlle Cordier, une des brillantes élèves de M. Laget, l'excellent professeur du Conservatoire de Musique, vient de contracter un engagement de trois ans à l'Opéra-Comique. M. Roqueplan a accordé à sa nouvelle pensionnaire un congé de six mois, qui lui permet d'aller tenir l'emploi de chanteuse à roulades à la Nouvelle-Orléans." *Le Ménestrel*, September 26, 1858.

116. "Vous vous engagez en qualité de danseuse au théâtre d'Orléans, danser dans tous les ouvrages qu'il plaire à l'administration de faire représenter, dans les entr'actes, ballets, pantomimes, paraitre dans les ouvrages à spectacle, jouer les rôles mimes qui vous seront distribués, etc." Contract letter written by L. Fiot, *Cohen vs. Davis* (1846), docket 00349 of the Third District Court, *NOPL*.

117. I have found very few surviving complete contracts personalized to individual performers, but one such contract does exist in "Contract between Pierre Davis and M. and Mme Richer," Charles Boudousquié, vol. 16, Act 239, December 16, 1844, *NONA*.
118. These assistants may have been paid servants rather than enslaved people, as a group of singers listed payments of $12 (FF 67) a month for a "domestic servant" among their expenses in an open letter I discuss later in this chapter. I cannot categorically say that no performer at the Théâtre d'Orléans ever owned a slave, however.
119. White discusses retirement benefits at the Paris Opéra, and their eventual removal, in *Female Singers on the French Stage*, 61–64.
120. See clauses 7–9 in the contract pro forma in appendix 1.
121. For a history of child labor in the United States, see Chaim M. Rosenberg, *Child Labor in America: A History* (Jefferson, NC: McFarland and Company Inc., 2013).
122. Her father took Pierre Davis to court in 1846, as I discuss later in this chapter. *Cohen vs. Davis* (1846), docket 00349 of the Third District Court, *NOPL*.
123. Lee S. Weissbach, "Child Labor Legislation in Nineteenth-Century France," *Journal of Economic History* 37/1 (1977): 268–71.
124. The difference in how the management valued them became clear when both broke the terms of their contract in 1825 and John Davis took them to court in New Orleans. In the official case brought against them, Warnet was described as "one of the best performers," while Clozel was simply listed as "a performer." In fact, the clerk who prepared the documents had initially described Clozel in the same terms as Warnet, but somewhat damningly, someone later repeatedly crossed through the words "one of the best performers." *Davis, John vs. Warnet, Boniface Henri* (1825), docket 6699 of the First Judicial Court, *NOPL*; and *Davis, John vs. Clozel* (1825), docket 6719 of the First Judicial Court, *NOPL*.
125. G.A.M., "Affaire théâtrales: Réponse," *L'Abeille*, September 16, 1840.
126. *Journal des beaux-arts et de la littérature*, July 10, 1840.
127. White, *Female Singers on the French Stage*, 68.
128. White mentions the "feux" throughout *Female Singers on the French Stage*, but especially in chapter 3, 60–88.
129. See White, *Female Singers on the French Stage*, 118.
130. Contract letter written by L. Fiot, *Cohen vs. Davis* (1846), docket 00349 of the Third District Court, *NOPL*.
131. This salary information is given in David Pinkney, *Decisive Years in France: 1840–7* (Princeton, NJ: Princeton University Press, 1986), 84.
132. The information is based on the salary of a professor of pharmacy at a Parisian College of Pharmacy as given by Robley Dunglison in *The American Medical Intelligencer*, vol. 4 (Philadelphia: A. Waldie, 1841), 170. Orlando Figes, however, suggests that by 1851, a professor at the Sorbonne earned about 12,000 francs a year. See Figes, *The Europeans: Three Lives and the Making of a Cosmopolitan Culture* (London: Penguin, 2019), xi.
133. For salaries in nineteenth-century Paris, see A. and W. Galignani, *New Paris Guide* (Paris: A. and W. Galignani and Company, 1841), 119.
134. The salary of the attorney general is given in Merritt M. Robinson, *A Digest of the Penal Law of the State of Louisiana: Analytically Arranged* (New Orleans, 1841), 225. The salary of a plantation overseer was reported in a court case in which an overseer took his employer to court, arguing that he ought to be paid $500 a year, not $425. See Merritt M. Robinson, *Reports of Cases Argued and Determined in the Supreme Court of Louisiana, Volume 1: October 1841–March 1842* (New Orleans: 1842), 27.

135. "Encore quelques renseignements utiles aux artistes qui voudraient venir à la Nouvelle-Orléans," *Gazette des théâtres*, July 5, 1840. Kmen mentions this letter in "Singing and Dancing in New Orleans: A Social History of the Birth and Growth of Balls and Opera, 1791–1841" (PhD diss., Tulane University, 1961), 220–21; and Juliane Braun mentions it in *Creole Drama: Theatre and Society in Antebellum New Orleans* (Charlottesville: University of Virginia Press, 2019), 33.
136. "Lors des engagements à Paris, les artistes sont entourés d'égards, de prévenance et de soins, on leur fait les plus belles promesses du monde; mais une fois à la Nouvelle Orléans, tout change de face, la direction se montre à visage découvert, les plaintes deviennent ridiculés et les réclamations risibles. On est à 2000 lieues de France !!! . . . Nous avons beaucoup trop de nos camarades qui sont, à la Nouvelle Orléans, dans la plus affreuse position, pour n'avoir pas assez réfléchi et pris assez de précautions lorsqu'ils ont signé leur engagement en France; eux la sont les parias de l'administration qui exploite leur misère . . . [A] moins d'un miracle, ne reverront jamais le sol de leur patrie!" "Encore quelques renseignements utiles aux artistes qui voudraient venir à la Nouvelle-Orléans," *Gazette des théâtres*, July 5, 1840.
137. "Il y a un artiste qui pour compléter un costume de voltigeur, a dépensé $16 ou FF 84. Les dames sont obligées de payer à leur frais leur habilleuse et coiffeur, le moins est encore de 40 francs par mois. Hors les costumes de figurations tout est à vos frais, même les costumes de travestissements. Il y a quatre ans, lorsque l'on a monté l'Eclair, la personne qui remplissait le rôle de Georges (par complaisances vu le vide de ténors qu'il y avait à cette époque) a été forcée de payer les costumes de sa poche." "Encore quelques renseignements utiles aux artistes qui voudraient venir à la Nouvelle-Orléans," *Gazette des théâtres*, July 5, 1840.
138. See clauses 20 and 21 of the contract pro forma in appendix 1.
139. Bernadet to Nonnon, April 1, 1842, *F-Po*, NLAS-392. Jean-Louis Nonnon (1786–1852) was first employed at the Opéra as an assistant in the costume department on August 1, 1828. He was promoted to the role of "maître tailleur" on July 1, 1829, and remained in that position until his death in 1852. His wife and daughter also worked in the costume department of the Opéra. See *Les Cancans de l'Opéra: chroniques de l'Académie royale de musique et du théâtre à Paris sous les deux Restaurations*, ed. Jean-Louis Tamvaco, vol. 1 (Paris: CNRS Editions, 2000), 129.
140. Parisian fashion magazines were available to buy in New Orleans during this period, as can be seen from copies of *L'Élégant: Journal des tailleurs*, which was stocked (according to the lists of business subscribers on the back cover) in New Orleans by "Ferdinand Fanis, coiffeur," throughout the 1830s.
141. "Le luxe des costumes faits par Nonon de l'Opéra," "Théâtres des Départements," *Tribune dramatique: revue théâtrale, artistique, littéraire et des modes*, September 6, 1846, 264.
142. For more on the importance of Parisian fashion in the nineteenth century, see Agnès Rocamora, *Fashioning the City: Paris, Fashion and the Media* (London: I. B. Tauris, 2009).
143. "Je suis encore ici, mon bon M. Nonnon, pour un mois 1/2. Si-tôt sorté de ce misérable pays, je me rends à Paris. . . . J'ai été trompé par la direction, j'ai éprouvé une perte de huit pourcent, ce qui me fait mille huit cent francs de moins que l'engagement [illeg.] m'aurait dû rapporter, et sans compter plusieurs autres filibustres que j'ai éprouvé de la part de la direction." Bernadet to Nonnon, April 1, 1842, *F-Po*, NLAS-392.
144. For more on the financial crisis of 1837, see Jessica M. Lepler, *The Many Panics of 1837: People, Politics, and the Creation of a Transatlantic Financial Crisis* (Cambridge: Cambridge University Press, 2013); and Alasdair Roberts, *America's First Great Depression: Economic Crisis and Political Disorder after the Panic of 1837* (Ithaca, NY: Cornell University Press, 2012).

145. "Encore quelques renseignements utiles aux artistes qui voudraient venir à la Nouvelle-Orléans," *Gazette des théâtres*, July 5, 1840.

146. Victor Bulmer-Thomas shows that the exchange rate between the US dollar and the French franc was essentially stable throughout the period covered by my study. See Bulmer-Thomas, *The Economic History of the Caribbean Since the Napoleonic Wars* (Cambridge: Cambridge University Press, 2012), 496.

147. "Il y avait à bord une vache, 550 volailles, 2,000 œufs, 24 porcs et moutons, 6 veaux, 300 caisses de conserves, petits pois, pâtés de foies, 150 fromages, 6 pièces de bon vin, 40 caisses de vin de Bordeaux et de Champagne, 20 caisses de liqueurs, 500 livres de sucre, café, chocolat, etc." "Nouvelles diverses," *Gazette des théâtres*, February 8, 1835. A similar article appeared in the journal two and a half years earlier, suggesting that such lavish provisions were a regular feature of the voyages. "Nouvelles diverses," *Gazette des théâtres*, September 13, 1832.

148. "Nouvelle-Orléans," *Revue et Gazette musicale*, July 1, 1855.

149. For more on rivalries between singers and the ways in which the press sometimes blew such rivalries up to grander proportions than they had in real life, see Suzanne Aspden, *The Rival Sirens: Performance and Identity on Handel's Operatic Stage* (Cambridge: Cambridge University Press, 2013), especially 138–77.

150. *Daily Picayune*, March 30, 1841.

151. "[N]ous demanderons à Mr C[oeuriot], le second ténor, qui n'était pourtant pas en première position sur notre théâtre, puisque son chef d'emploi gagnait $80 de plus, si les $190 ou 950fr qu'il recevait par mois, ne suffisaient pas à ses dépenses et s'il n'a pas trouvé le moyen, lui, comme tant d'autres, de s'en retourner en France avec d'assez belles économies." G.A.M., "Affaire théâtrales: Réponse," *L'Abeille*, September 16, 1840. G.A.M. was likely Guillaume Montmain, who wrote theatrical criticism in New Orleans throughout the 1830s. He regularly wrote for the *Courrier de la Louisiane*, but in this case his response appeared in *L'Abeille*. Kmen mentions him in *Music in New Orleans*, 123–36.

152. "Mais lorsque la plupart de ces messieurs voudront, en pays étranger, faire plus de dépenses qu'ils ne le peuvent, singer les premiers sujets, aller au bal, jouer, passer les trois quarts de leur existence dans les restaurants et les cafés; lorsque ce dames à leur tour, voudront rivaliser d'élégance avec les premières dames de la ville, dans leurs robes et leurs bijoux . . . ." G.A.M., "Affaire théâtrales: Réponse," *L'Abeille*, September 16, 1840.

153. Coeuriot unfortunately became ill and died during the company's tour to New York in the summer of 1845. See Swift, "The Northern Tours of the Théâtre d'Orléans, 1843 and 1845," 176–77.

154. *Davis, John vs. Warnet, Boniface Henri* (1825), docket 6699 of the First Judicial Court, *NOPL*; and *Davis, John vs. Clozel* (1825), docket 6719 of the First Judicial Court, *NOPL*.

155. *Cohen vs. Davis* (1846), docket 00349 of the Third District Court, *NOPL*.

156. The *Daily Picayune* reported that the case was eventually brought to court and decided on May 1, 1848, after two years' delay. See *Daily Picayune*, May 2, 1848.

CHAPTER TWO

1. "J'ai demandé à Messieurs les directeurs de l'Opéra que vous puissiez venir sur la scène de l'Opéra à la représentation d'aujourd'hui & à celle de Vendredi (que [*sic*] sera la dernière du *Prophète*) pour pouvoir examiner de près les décors, la machinerie etc." In *Giacomo Meyerbeer: Briefwechsel und Tagebücher*, ed. Sabine Henze-Döhring, 8 vols., vol. 5 (Berlin: de Gruyter, 1998), 24.

2. An earlier version of this chapter was published as "The Race for *Robert* and Other Rivalries: Negotiating the Local and (Inter)national in Nineteenth-Century New Orleans," in *Cambridge Opera Journal* 29/1 (March 2017): 94–112. Here, I have augmented the previously published material with a detailed discussion of the differences between the twin productions of *Robert,* in order to give an insight into what performances of *grand opéra* consisted of in New Orleans.
3. One example of this is when Meyerbeer wrote to Brandus with instructions that he could sell the score of *Le Prophète* to people in most places, other than Germany and Italy. "A propos Veuillez dire à Monsieur Brandus que je l'autorise à vendre la partition pour Odessa & la Nouvelle Orléans ainsi qu'il me le demande, mais pas pour Trieste. En général qu'il la vende partout excepté en Allemagne & en Italie." [Autograph (La): SBB, PK, Musikabteilung, N. Mus. Nachl. 97, M/14.] September 1849. Letter from Meyerbeer to Louis Gouin in Paris, *Giacomo Meyerbeer,* ed. Henze-Döhring, vol. 5, 76.
4. For a report on the importing of materials, see "Chronique étrangère," *Revue et Gazette musicale de Paris,* February 20, 1840.
5. Jens Hesselager, *Grand Opera Outside Paris: Opera on the Move in Nineteenth-Century Europe* (London: Routledge, 2018); and see also the essays by many of the contributors to the aforementioned collection; Cormac Newark, "'In Italy We Don't Have the Means for Illusion': Grand Opéra in Nineteenth-Century Bologna," *Cambridge Opera Journal* 19/3 (2007): 199–222.
6. Henry Kmen, *Music in New Orleans: The Formative Years, 1791–1841* (Baton Rouge: Louisiana State University Press, 1966), 63 and 74. Other French composers well represented in the early nineteenth century were Pierre-Alexandre Monsigny, Nicolo Isouard, Henri Berton, Pierre Gaveaux, and Luigi Cherubini. See Kmen, *Music in New Orleans,* 82 and 92. Grétry's *Richard, Cœur du Lion* was also extremely popular, and was said to have been the favorite opera of President John Quincy Adams. Kmen, *Music in New Orleans,* 63.
7. Both Henry Kmen and Jack Belsom provide detailed information on the Théâtre d'Orléans's repertoire at various points in its history. See Kmen, *Music in New Orleans*; and Belsom, "Reception of Major Operatic Premieres in New Orleans during the Nineteenth Century" (MA diss., Louisiana State University, 1972).
8. Prévost's *La Esmeralda* was a *grand opéra* in four acts and seven scenes, which was performed on various occasions in the 1840s. It is unclear, however, whether Prévost wrote the work in New Orleans or whether he brought it with him from France when he moved from Le Havre to take up the position of *chef d'orchestre* in New Orleans in 1838. Nonetheless, the work was never part of the *grand opéra* repertoire in Paris.
9. Robert Ignatius Letellier, *Meyerbeer's* Les Huguenots*: An Evangel of Religion and Love* (Newcastle: Cambridge Scholars Publishing, 2014), 122. The fire that destroyed the French Opera House was not the end of opera in New Orleans: since 1943, the New Orleans Opera Association has brought performances to the New Orleans public most years. Scholarly accounts focusing specifically on the performance and reception of *grand opéra* in the city, however, are few and far between. Belsom, "Reception of Major Operatic Premieres"; and Sarah Hibberd, "Grand Opera in Britain and the Americas," in *The Cambridge Companion to Grand Opera,* ed. David Charlton (Cambridge: Cambridge University Press, 2003), 417–18, are the two most detailed, but they are both relatively brief.
10. Hesselager, *Grand Opera Outside Paris.*
11. In the very early years of the nineteenth century, the English-language sections of these news-

papers were often direct translations of the French sections; by the 1830s, however, they contained different material to suit the interests of the city's divided linguistic communities.

12. For more on the history of New Orleans's newspapers in this period, see Samuel J. Marino, "Early French-Language Newspapers in New Orleans," *Louisiana History: The Journal of the Louisiana Historical Association* 7/4 (1966): 309–21.
13. See *L'Abeille*, May 3, 1831, and May 24, 1831.
14. "Cette grande conception musicale"; "L'un des mérites de cette pièce est dans la pompe théâtral [*sic*] et le décor"; "En somme, la *Muette de Portici* est l'un de ces spectacles qu'il faut voir." *L'Abeille*, May 3, 1831.
15. These papers were most often founded by either a sole editor or at most a pair. For more on the emergence and disappearance of newspapers during this period, see Edward Larocque Tinker, *Bibliography of the French Newspapers and Periodicals of Louisiana* (Worcester, MA: American Antiquarian Society, 1933).
16. New York, by contrast, had 123,706 inhabitants according to the 1820 census, while Paris had some 714,000 according to the census of 1817. See "Population of the 61 Urban Places: 1820," US Census Bureau, accessed June 16, 2020, https://www.census.gov/population/www/documentation/twps0027/tab05.txt; and, for the Paris figure, see Daniel Roche, *The People of Paris: An Essay in Popular Culture in the 18th Century*, trans. Marie Evans in association with Gwynne Lewis (Berkeley: University of California Press, 1987), 20.
17. *Le Courrier* and *L'Abeille* were both exceptional in their longevity, surviving until 1860 and 1923, respectively.
18. Carl Brasseaux, *The Foreign French: Nineteenth-Century French Immigration into Louisiana, Volume 1: 1820–1839* (Lafayette: Center for Louisiana Studies, University of Southwestern Louisiana, 1990), xi; and "Population of the 100 Largest Urban Places: 1840," accessed June 16, 2020, http://www.census.gov/population/www/documentation/twps0027/tab07.txt.
19. See Nancy McKenzie Dupont, "'Lawless Louisiana': New Orleans Newspapers, Race, and the Battle of Liberty Place," in *Sensationalism: Murder, Mayhem, Mudslinging, Scandals, and Disasters in 19th-Century Reporting*, ed. David B. Sachsman and David W. Bulla (New Brunswick, NJ: Transaction Publishers, 2013), 340.
20. See, for example, *L'Ami des Lois*, May 31, 1823, and June 7, 1823.
21. The *Louisiana Gazette* (1804–1826), however, while it did not employ a full-time music critic, did employ a regular feuilletonist, Alexis Daudet, from 1819 until 1825. Daudet initially wrote his column on local poetry and arts, but by the end of his term had simply begun to reprint articles from Parisian newspapers. See Marino, "Early French-Language Newspapers in New Orleans," 309–21.
22. See, for example, the article on this subject published in *L'Argus*, January 7, 1826.
23. Kmen, *Music in New Orleans*, 133–37; Hibberd, "Grand Opera in Britain and the Americas," 417; Catherine Jones, *Literature and Music in the Atlantic World, 1767–1867* (Edinburgh: Edinburgh University Press, 2014), 89–90. Jennifer C. H. J. Wilson discusses the reception of the Théâtre d'Orléans's production of *Robert le diable* in New York as part of the 1845 summer tour in "Meyerbeer and the New Orleans French Opera Company in New York City, 1845: 'How, Therefore, Could New York Have Remained Behind?'" in *Meyerbeer and Grand Opéra from the July Monarchy to the Present*, ed. Mark Everist (Turnhout: Brepols, 2016), 361–82.
24. For more on the city's demographic changes during this period, see Joseph G. Tregle Jr., "Creoles and Americans," in *Creole New Orleans: Race and Americanization*, ed. Arnold R.

Hirsch and Joseph Logsdon (Baton Rouge: Louisiana State University Press, 1992), 153–60. See also Carl Brasseaux, *The Foreign French, Volume 1: 1820–1839*, xi.

25. See Katherine K. Preston, *Opera for the People: English-Language Opera and Women Managers in Late 19th-Century America* (New York: Oxford University Press, 2017), especially 100–112 (on Caroline Richings) and 268–78 (on Emma Abbot).
26. *The Bee*, April 2, 1835.
27. *The Bee*, March 14, 1835. John Martin produced a serialized illustrated edition of Milton's *Paradise Lost* in 1823–1824, which were released monthly to the public between 1825 and 1827. In 1841, he produced an oil painting of Pandemonium, which brings out many of his earlier ideas in full color.
28. "Quant aux décors, c'est la partie qui semble avoir été le plus soignée; et à cet égard, on n'a que des éloges à faire à l'artiste chargé de ce soin." "Théâtre de la Rue du Camp: *Robert-le-diable*," *Le Courrier de la Louisiane*, April 1, 1835.
29. *The Bee*, April 2, 1835.
30. "Il est fâcheux pourtant que les accessoires ne répondent point aux objets principaux; les tombeaux, par exemple, sont trop étroits, et la statue de Sainte Rosalie pourrait être mieux dessinée et mieux peinte." "Théâtre de la Rue du Camp: *Robert-le-diable*," *Le Courrier de la Louisiane*, April 1, 1835.
31. Advertisement for *Robert le diable*, *L'Abeille*, May 11, 1835. Develle had trained in the late 1810s and early 1820s with Pierre-Luc-Charles Cicéri, scene painter of the Paris Opéra. Cicéri had sole responsibility for designing the sets for the earliest *grands opéras*, including *La Muette de Portici*, *Guillaume Tell*, and *Robert le diable*, and he was involved in the teams of designers who produced the scenery for later productions. For information on Cicéri, see Simon Williams, "The Spectacle of the Past in Grand Opéra," in *The Cambridge Companion to Grand Opéra*, ed. David Charlton (Cambridge: Cambridge University Press, 2003), 63–64.
32. See *The Bee*, May 13, 1835, and May 16, 1835.
33. See, for example, *The Bee*, April 3, 1835. For more on Rice and his Jim Crow act, see W. T. Lhamon Jr., *Jump Jim Crow: Lost Plays, Lyrics, and Street Prose of the First Atlantic Popular Culture* (Cambridge, MA: Harvard University Press, 2003).
34. *The Bee*, May 14, 1835.
35. For more on practices of inserting popular songs into operas at the American Theatre, see Kmen, *Music in New Orleans*, 177.
36. Mrs. Wood was born Mary Ann Paton in Edinburgh in 1802 and had a successful career as a soprano at London's Covent Garden, Haymarket, Drury Lane, and King's theaters, before she and her husband, the tenor Joseph Wood, embarked on tours of the United States in 1833–1836 and the early 1840s.
37. *The Bee*, May 14, 1835.
38. *The Bee*, May 14, 1835. Presumably the text for this moment was rewritten, in order to avoid the incongruity of Alice singing Bertram's devilish thoughts: "Ah, L'honnête homme! / Ah, le pauvre homme! / Mais voyez comme / En mes filets / Je me prendrais / Si je voulais! / Faiblesse humaine / Que l'or entraîne, / Que l'on enchaîne / Par des bienfaits." *Robert le diable*, act 3, scene 1.
39. *The Bee*, May 16, 1835. While it might seem surprising that the critic was able to quote at length from other productions, he may well have been able to find this information from the London newspapers that found their way to New Orleans. He might also have been able to obtain the information directly from Thomas Reynoldson, the director of the American Theatre's production, as Reynoldson had previously performed the role of Bertram in the opera

at Covent Garden and the King's Theatre in London (see "Robert le diable," *The Bee*, April 1, 1835; and "For the *Courrier:* Opera of *Robert le diable*," *The Louisiana Courier*, March 30, 1835, for more information). Reynoldson had also translated the libretto afresh for the American Theatre's production. Supplying information about the various translations would have been in Reynoldson's own interest, since the critic used them in order to stress the originality of his production.

40. "Nous demanderons d'abord aux véritables connaisseurs s'ils croient qu'un orchestre de quinze ou seize musiciens suffit pour exécuter un opéra qui, pour le moins, en exige un quarantaine, et qui en outre d'une exécution habile, ne doit montrer aucun vide dans l'instrumentation." "Théâtre de la Rue du Camp: *Robert-le-diable*," *Le Courrier de la Louisiane*, April 1, 1835. The American Theatre's orchestra had generally been thought of in all sections of the New Orleans press as inferior to the one at the Théâtre d'Orléans, but by the early 1830s even French critics conceded that the American Theatre was capable of presenting operas in a reasonably good style, with an orchestra "only a little inferior to the Orleans orchestra." *L'Abeille*, February 28, 1834, quoted in Kmen, *Music in New Orleans*, 129.
41. *The Bee*, May 13, 1835.
42. *The Bee*, May 16, 1835.
43. Kaye DeMetz, "Dancing Families in New Orleans' Nineteenth-Century English-Language Theatres," *Louisiana History: The Journal of the Louisiana Historical Association* 33/4 (1992): 381–97. Henry Kmen discusses the irregularity with which dance troupes were employed at the Théâtre d'Orléans in Kmen, *Music in New Orleans*, 188–89.
44. DeMetz, "Dancing Families in New Orleans' Nineteenth-Century English-Language Theatres," 286.
45. "Que signifient ensuite ces espèces de tabourets à un pied sur lesquels sont perchées les personnes qui figurent les nonnes? Ne valait-il pas mieux placer celles-ci dans des niches, ou bien entourer ces bâtons à perroquet d'une toile peinte imitant un tronçon de colonne? On rirait bien à Paris, où cette pièce a pris naissance, si l'on voyait ainsi perchées les cinquante danseuses qui représentent de si saintes personnes." "Théâtre de la Rue du Camp: *Robert-le-diable*," *Le Courrier de la Louisiane*, April 1, 1835.
46. *The Bee*, May 16, 1835.
47. Kmen's examination of the opera, the most detailed to date, draws almost entirely on the two reviews written by the French critic for the *Courrier*, making only passing mention of *L'Abeille*'s French- and English-language reviews. Kmen, *Music in New Orleans*, 133–37.
48. For an exploration of a similar shift in the periodical press of Milan at the beginning of the century, see Emanuele Senici, "Delirious Hopes: Napoleonic Milan and the Rise of Modern Italian Operatic Criticism," *Cambridge Opera Journal* 27/2 (2015): 97–127.
49. *The Bee*, March 27, 1835, and March 28, 1835.
50. It was (and remained) highly unusual for theatrical news to be reported on the first page of the paper, which normally carried mainly news on legislature and notices about auctions (among other advertisements). Daily news of all sorts usually appeared on the second page.
51. *The Bee*, May 21, 1831.
52. *The Bee*, May 21, 1831.
53. See Carl Dahlhaus, *Nineteenth-Century Music*, trans. J. Bradford Robinson (Berkeley: University of California Press, 1989), in particular 8–15.
54. *The Bee*, May 15, 1835. As John Baron shows, there had been references to "Philharmonic Societies" in New Orleans since 1825, but these early examples seem to have been informal groups that did not last beyond a concert or two. In December 1835, there was a drive for the

creation of a society with formalized bylaws and officers. The society began to meet in 1836, but it was not until 1837 that it gave its first concert. H. E. Lehmann, whose piano arrangements of operas will be discussed in chapter 4, was a leading member of this society. For an account of the foundation of philharmonic societies in the city, see Baron, *Concert Life in Nineteenth-Century New Orleans: A Comprehensive Reference* (Baton Rouge: Louisiana State University Press, 2013), 68–76.

55. Regular examples of operatic criticism from London and Paris would have been available to both Francophone and Anglophone critics in New Orleans during the 1830s: reviews and theatrical articles from the foreign press were often reprinted in New Orleans's own newspapers.

56. Christina Fuhrmann, *Foreign Opera at the London Playhouses: From Mozart to Bellini* (Cambridge: Cambridge University Press, 2015), 146–69.

57. "For the *Courrier*: Opera of *Robert le diable*," *Louisiana Courier*, March 30, 1835. Butler was the husband of British actress and diarist Fanny Kemble.

58. For a brief insight into Reynoldson's adaptation of the score for the melodrama version in New York in 1834, see Wilson, "Meyerbeer and the New Orleans French Opera Company in New York City," 366–67.

59. "For the *Courrier*: Opera of *Robert le diable*," *The Louisiana Courier*, March 30, 1835.

60. "For the *Courrier*: Opera of *Robert le diable*," *The Louisiana Courier*, March 30, 1835.

61. "*Robert le diable*," *The Bee*, April 1, 1835; and "For the *Courrier*: Opera of *Robert le diable*," *The Louisiana Courier*, March 30, 1835.

62. See *The Bee*, April 3, 1835; and *The Louisiana Courier*, March 30, 1835.

63. See *The Bee*, April 1, 1835.

64. "Théâtre de la Rue du Camp: *Robert-le-diable*," *Le Courrier de la Louisiane*, April 1, 1835. So venomous were his comments that even the critic for *L'Abeille* felt compelled to defend the American Theatre, saying it had "made great progress." "Le théâtre de la Rue du Camp, on ne peut le nier, a fait de très-grand progrès." *L'Abeille*, April 3, 1835.

65. The *Courrier* printed one review and a biographical article about Meyerbeer copied from the Parisian press, while *L'Abeille* managed just a single review. "Théâtre d'Orléans: *Robert le diable*," *Le Courrier de la Louisiane*, May 14, 1835; "Théâtre d'Orléans: *Robert le diable* (2)," *Le Courrier de la Louisiane*, May 18, 1835; "Théâtre d'Orléans," *L'Abeille*, May 14, 1835.

66. "Jamais pompe théâtrale n'avait été poussée à un aussi haut degré à ce théâtre." "Théâtre d'Orléans: *Robert le diable*," *Le Courrier de la Louisiane*, May 14, 1835.

67. The English-language critics, however, were quick to point out that the French theater's production, though good, had not been quite as luxurious or polished as they had expected. That they had the confidence in their own theater's production to feel justified in criticizing the French theater's is particularly remarkable, given that in the months preceding the *Robert* affair the same critics had advised audiences to go to the French theater's production of *The Barber of Seville* rather than the American Theatre's heavily rearranged version, since there they would "see and hear it properly done." *The Bee*, March 5, 1835.

68. A call for subscribers for this new theater appeared in *L'Abeille*, April 2, 1835.

69. The authors claimed that the Francophone citizens of New Orleans had a need for such a Théâtre Louisianais to help young artists foster their genius and to ensure that they were given the place they deserved in history. "D'un nouveau théâtre français," *L'Abeille*, April 2, 1835. John Davis felt compelled to respond to this challenge, publishing an article in which he stated that the city would not be able to sustain two French theaters and pleaded with

the Francophone citizens to devote their patronage to his theater. See "Théâtre d'Orléans," *L'Abeille*, April 17, 1835; and *Le Courrier de la Louisiane*, April 18, 1835.

70. For more on the municipalities and Creole/Anglo-American tensions at this time, see Virginia R. Domínguez, *White by Definition: Social Classification in Creole Louisiana* (New Brunswick, NJ: Rutgers University Press, 1993), 110–32. For more on the financial implications of the division into municipalities, see my discussions in chapter 1, pp. 28–29.

71. For more on the history of the St. Charles, see Lucile Gafford, "A History of the St. Charles Theatre in New Orleans, 1835–43" (PhD diss., University of Chicago, 1930). This theater also played host to a number of visiting English-language companies, some of which attempted versions of *grands opéras* (*Masaniello*, *Gustave III*, and *The Jewess*). These performances by visiting companies do not seem to have provoked the same level of critical engagement as the "home-grown" challenge made by Caldwell's *Robert*. See Kmen, *Music in New Orleans*, 163. For information about the reception of these visiting companies, see Charlotte Bentley, "Southern Exchanges: Italian Opera in New Orleans, 1836–1842," in *Italian Opera in Global and Transnational Perspective: Reimagining Italianità in the Long Nineteenth Century*, ed. Axel Körner and Paulo Kühl (Cambridge: Cambridge University Press, 2022), 113–32.

72. Information on theatrical repertoires in the city in the first half of the century can be found in Kmen, *Music in New Orleans*. For a full list of all opera performances in New Orleans between 1796 and 1841, see Henry Kmen, "Singing and Dancing: A Social History of Music in New Orleans" (PhD diss., Tulane University, 1961), appendix III.

73. "Fireside Talk—No. IX," *The Daily Picayune*, December 9. 1838.

74. "Fireside Talk—No. IX," *The Daily Picayune*, December 9, 1838.

75. While space does not permit me to do so here, in chapter 5 I focus more on literary presentations of opera. For more on the creation of literary spheres of operatic experience, see Cormac Newark, *Opera in the Novel from Balzac to Proust* (Cambridge: Cambridge University Press, 2011).

76. For an account of the formation of distinct elite and popular artistic spheres in America later in the nineteenth century, see Lawrence W. Levine, *Highbrow/Lowbrow: The Emergence of a Cultural Hierarchy in America* (Cambridge, MA: Harvard University Press, 1988); and Joseph A. Mussulman, *Music in the Cultured Generation: A Social History of Music in America, 1870–1900* (Evanston, IL: Northwestern University Press, 1971).

77. "*Les Huguenots*," *The Bee*, April 30, 1839.

78. The Anglo-American Eliza Ripley, writing at the start of the twentieth century of her childhood in the 1830s and 1840s, noted that "French was the fashion then" among high society in the city, and that people looked down on those who were seen as being "horribly English" (69). She also wrote of Anglo-American girls going to French-speaking schools in the city, and of the French teacher who went from house to house giving lessons in the American sector of the city (7–10). Eliza Ripley, *Social Life in Old New Orleans: Being Recollections of My Girlhood* (New York: D. Appleton and Company, 1912).

79. See for example, "Feuilleton. Théâtre: *Les Huguenots*," *L'Abeille*, May 7, 1839.

80. Baron, *Concert Life in Nineteenth-Century New Orleans*, 303.

81. Juliane Braun discusses this work in detail in *Creole Drama: Theatre and Society in Antebellum New Orleans* (Charlottesville: University of Virginia Press, 2019), 58–64. See also Juliane Braun, "Petit Paris en Amérique? French Theatrical Culture in Nineteenth-Century Louisiana" (PhD diss., Julius-Maximilians-Universität Würzburg, 2013), 87–97.

82. See *L'Abeille*, May 4, 1839, and May 7, 1839, for example.

83. *The Daily Picayune*, April 30, 1839.
84. "Théâtre d'Orléans: *Les Huguenots*," *L'Abeille*, June 8, 1839.
85. "(Communiqué) Théâtre d'Orléans: Bénéfice de Mr Develle," *L'Abeille*, May 28, 1839. See also "Feuilleton. Théâtre: *Les Huguenots*," *L'Abeille*, May 7, 1839.
86. See Cormac Newark, "'In Italy We Don't Have the Means for Illusion,'" 199–222.
87. "Théâtre: *Les Huguenots*, Opéra en cinq actes de Meyerbeer," *L'Abeille*, May 3, 1839.
88. See "Feuilleton. Théâtre: *Les Huguenots*," *L'Abeille*, May 7, 1839.
89. "C'était pour nous un bonheur indicible de voir ce public sérieux, attentive . . . s'associer par l'intelligence aux créations du génie." "Théâtre d'Orléans: *Les Huguenots*," *L'Abeille*, June 8, 1839.
90. Quoted in Thomas Forrest Kelly, *First Nights at the Opera* (New Haven, CT: Yale University Press, 2004), 193. For an exploration of Parisian responses to Meyerbeer's works, see Cormac Newark, "Metaphors for Meyerbeer," *Journal of the Royal Musical Association* 127/1 (2002): 23–43.
91. Jennifer C. H. J. Wilson reveals that similar comments featured in the New York reception of *Les Huguenots* following its premiere there in 1845 by the Théâtre d'Orléans troupe, but they belong within a very different local context. See "Meyerbeer and the New Orleans French Opera Company in New York City," 371–73.
92. Newark explores this in "Metaphors for Meyerbeer," 42.
93. For the review, see *L'Abeille*, May 18, 1839; and for the reader's letter, see *L'Abeille*, May 27, 1839.
94. "Les français n'auront jamais de musique." J.-J. Rousseau, quoted in "Théâtre d'Orléans: 3ème représentation des *Huguenots*," *L'Abeille*, May 18, 1839.
95. "C'est-à-dire de musique indigène, nationale, absolument à elle"; "En effet, la France à toutes les époques, depuis Lulli jusqu'à Meyerbeer, a toujours marché à la remorque des grands compositeurs de l'Italie ou de l'Allemagne." See "Théâtre d'Orléans: 3ème représentation des *Huguenots*," *L'Abeille*, May 18, 1839.
96. "L'arbre est exotique, mais le fruit est indigne." See "Au M. le rédacteur de *l'Abeille*: de la musique en France," *L'Abeille*, May 27, 1839.
97. "Madame de Staël dit quelque part: 'Le génie n'a pas le sexe'; ajoutons aussi qu'il n'a pas de patrie." See "Au M. le rédacteur de *l'Abeille*: de la musique en France," *L'Abeille*, May 27, 1839.
98. A comprehensive account of the emergence of specialist periodicals and journals can be found in Tinker, *Bibliography of the French Newspapers and Periodicals of Louisiana*. Surviving examples of all these periodicals I mention can be found at the Louisiana Research Collection and the Howard-Tilton Memorial library at Tulane University.
99. There were, however, some music periodicals founded in the northern United States as early as 1838 (such as the *Boston Musical Gazette*), but it is unlikely they ever had a wide enough circulation to be available in New Orleans. Even the renowned *Dwight's Journal of Music*, published in Boston for some thirty years from 1852, only ever had a circulation of about 1,500 copies. See Katherine K. Preston, "Art Music from 1800 to 1860," in *The Cambridge History of American Music*, ed. David Nicholls (Cambridge: Cambridge University Press, 1998), 207.
100. For more on the role types, see Olivier Bara, "The Company at the Heart of the Operatic Institution: Chollet and the Changing Nature of Comic-Opera Roles Types during the July Monarchy," in *Music, Theater and Cultural Transfer, Paris, 1830–1814*, ed. Annegret Fauser and Mark Everist (Chicago: University of Chicago Press, 2009), 11–28.
101. In the early 1840s, the new role designations provoked debate in *La Lorgnette*, one of the city's newly founded theatrical periodicals, when Julia Calvé, a soprano who had been beloved of

local audiences since her arrival in New Orleans in 1837, wished to move from singing the lead roles in *opéra-comique* to those in *grand opéra*. Although the critic for *La Lorgnette* doubted whether her vocal power and sweet tone would allow her to perform *grand opéra* successfully, by 1845 she had become a firm favorite with local audiences in *grands opéras*. See *La Lorgnette*, December 1841 and January 1842.

CHAPTER THREE

1. "Quelque goût que puisse avoir pour les jeux de la scène, la portion de la population qui soutient le Théâtre d'Orléans, elle est à peine assez nombreuse pour couvrir les dépenses extraordinaires qu'occasionnent les voyages et l'éloignement où nous nous trouvons au lieu de recrutement. On le comprendra sans peine quand on songera que le public est toujours le même; et quiconque a observé d'un œil attentif ceux qui l'entouraient à une représentation, est à peu près sûr de retrouver les mêmes voisins à la suivante." "Théâtre d'Orléans," *L'Abeille*, April 17, 1835.
2. Steven Huebner, "Opera Audiences in Paris, 1830–1870," *Music & Letters* 70/2 (1989): 206–25; James H. Johnson, *Listening in Paris: A Cultural History* (Berkeley: University of California Press, 1996); Eleanor Cloutier, "Repetitive Novelty: Italian Opera in Paris and London in the 1830s and 1840s" (PhD diss., University of California, Berkeley, 2016), 9–35.
3. See, for example, the Carl Kohn Letterbook (1832–33), MSS 269, *HNOC*; and the Diary of Clarissa Peirce Cenas (1859–65), MSS 649, *HNOC*. The novels and travel accounts I discuss in chapter 5 are exceptions to this, but they are not private, personal accounts in the same way that diaries and letters are.
4. Carlotta Sorba, "To Please the Public: Composers and Audiences in Nineteenth-Century Italy," *Journal of Interdisciplinary History* 36/4 (2006): 595–614.
5. Sorba, "To Please the Public," 599.
6. Robert Wakefield and Devin Knighton, "Distinguishing among Publics, Audiences, and Stakeholders in the Social Media Era of Unanticipated Publics," *Public Relations Review* 45/5 (2019): 1–7, https://doi.org/10.1016/j.pubrev.2019.101821. For more on the relationship between audiences and publics, see Sonia Livingstone, "On the Relation between Audiences and Publics," in *Audiences and Publics: When Cultural Engagement Matters for the Public Sphere*, ed. Sonia Livingstone (Bristol: Intellect Books, 2005), 17–41.
7. Wakefield and Knighton, "Distinguishing among Publics, Audiences, and Stakeholders in the Social Media Era of Unanticipated Publics," 2.
8. John Dewey, *The Public and Its Problems: An Essay in Political Inquiry* (New York: Holt, 1927).
9. See Jürgen Habermas, *The Structural Transformation of the Public Sphere*, trans. Thomas Burger, with the assistance of Frederick Lawrence (Cambridge: Polity Press, 1989).
10. Michael Warner discusses the importance of attention to formulations of a public in "Publics and Counterpublics," *Public Culture* 14/1 (2002): 60–61.
11. Over thirty French-language publications were founded in the 1840s. Rien Fertel, *Imagining the Creole City: The Rise of Literary Culture in Nineteenth-Century New Orleans* (Baton Rouge: Louisiana State University Press, 2014), 21. Nearly all of the arts periodicals were solely Francophone: with the exception of the short-lived bilingual *La Loge de l'opéra/The Opera Box*, which was produced in 1856 and 1857, I have found no evidence of any English-language music periodicals produced in New Orleans before the Civil War.
12. Juliane Braun, "On the Verge of Fame: The Free People of Color and the French Theatre in Antebellum New Orleans," in *Liminale Anthropologien: Zwischenzeiten, Schwellenphänomene,*

Zwischenräume in Literatur und Philosophie, ed. Jochen Achilles, Roland Borgards, and Brigitte Burrichter (Würzburg: Königshausen & Neumann, 2012), 166.

13. See, for example, the advertisement for the Théâtre d'Orléans in the *Daily Picayune*, January 19, 1853, which states that children would be admitted at half price.
14. See Braun, "On the Verge of Fame," 166.
15. *Davis, John vs. The Mayor, Aldermen and Inhabitants of New Orleans*, December 30, 1820, docket 3615 of the First Judicial Court, *NOPL*.
16. *Davis, John vs. The Mayor et al.*, December 30, 1820.
17. See Braun, "Petit Paris en Amérique? French Theatrical Culture in Nineteenth-Century Louisiana," (PhD diss., Julius-Maximilians-Universität Würzburg, 2013), 122; and Braun, *Creole Drama: Theatre and Society in Antebellum New Orleans* (Charlottesville: University of Virginia Press, 2019), 78–79.
18. By the very end of the decade, however, they had once again been displaced from the second tier and were permitted to sit in the third-tier gallery only. Adverts from 1853 still made a distinction between boxes and seats for them (in the second tier) and admission for slaves (to the third-tier gallery alone), but similar advertisements for tickets in 1859 stated simply that people of color were permitted to sit in the gallery (the third tier) and nowhere else, suggesting that by that year free people of color had been displaced from their usual second tier. The advertisement made no separate mention of enslaved people: whether free and enslaved people of color were expected to share the third tier, or whether enslaved people were no longer welcome in the theater by 1859, I have not been able to discover. See, for example, "Orleans Theatre," *Daily Picayune*, October 22, 1859.
19. Braun, *Creole Drama*, 72–109.
20. For the St. Charles, see Lucile Gafford, "A History of the St. Charles Theatre in New Orleans, 1835–43," (PhD diss., University of Chicago, 1930), 28.
21. Braun, *Creole Drama*, 83.
22. "Grande Loge de l'état de la Louisiane/procès Mque du F. Henry Beebe" (1824), HS717.L6 F74 1824, *HNOC*.
23. Patricia Brady, "Free Black Artists in Antebellum New Orleans," in *KnowLA Encyclopedia of Louisiana*, ed. David Johnson. Louisiana Endowment for the Humanities, April 28, 2011, accessed October 8, 2021, http://www.knowlouisiana.org/entry/free-black-artists-in-antebellum-new-orleans.
24. "Grande Loge de l'état de la Louisiane/procès Mque du F. Henry Beebe," 17.
25. "Grande Loge de l'état de la Louisiane/procès Mque du F. Henry Beebe," 17–18.
26. Marisa J. Fuentes, *Dispossessed Lives: Enslaved Women, Violence, and the Archive* (Philadelphia: University of Pennsylvania Press, 2016), 138.
27. Henry Kmen, *Music in New Orleans: The Formative Years, 1791–1841* (Baton Rouge: Louisiana State University Press, 1966), 89.
28. Kmen, *Music in New Orleans*, 89.
29. *Davis, John vs. The Mayor, Aldermen and Inhabitants of New Orleans*, December 30, 1820, docket 3615 of the First Judicial Court, *NOPL*.
30. Katherine K. Preston has pointed out that lowering the prices was a fairly common tactic employed in theaters across the United States to retain audiences during the summer months. Katherine K. Preston, *Opera on the Road: Traveling Opera Troupe in the United States, 1835–60* (Urbana: University of Illinois Press), 155.
31. For more on this, see chapter 1 of this book, p. 28.
32. In addition, there was to be a ticket lottery, for which the artists planned to sell 1,500 tickets

at $1 each and award fifty "prizes": those whose numbers were selected would win either a seat anywhere in the auditorium or even a whole box, which would be theirs for twelve performances. "La Société des Artistes," *La Lorgnette*, March 2, 1843.

33. *Daily Picayune*, October 27, 1859.
34. Preston says that Martí y Torrens's visiting troupe from Havana charged fifty cents a ticket for large-scale performances at New York's Castle Garden, and that they performed there "before audiences of thousands of working- and middle-class individuals," suggesting that paying fifty cents for an evening's entertainment was not beyond the reach of these individuals. Preston, *Opera on the Road*, 155–56.
35. Gafford, "A History of the St. Charles Theatre in New Orleans, 1835–43," 28.
36. Gafford, "A History of the St. Charles Theatre in New Orleans, 1835–43," 28.
37. *L'Abeille*, November 20, 1834.
38. Advertisement in *Daily Picayune*, May 21, 1839.
39. Letter by James Emile Armour, March 18, 1841, *NOPL*.
40. Advertisement in *New Orleans Crescent*, February 19, 1851.
41. Advertisement in *Daily Picayune*, April 15, 1852.
42. See advertisements in *Daily Picayune*, April 21, 1839, and May 21, 1839.
43. Advertisement in the *Daily Picayune*, May 7, 1847.
44. Advertisement in the *Daily Picayune*, April 4, 1849.
45. Advertisement in the *Daily Picayune*, April 15, 1852.
46. Preston, *Opera on the Road*, 103.
47. Preston, *Opera on the Road*, 110.
48. Lyle Saxon, *Old Louisiana* (Reprint, Gretna, LA: Pelican Publishing Company, Inc., 1998), 122; and Herman de Bachelle Seebold, *Old Louisiana Plantation Homes and Family Trees*, vol. 1 (Reprint, Gretna, LA: Pelican Publishing Company, Inc., 2004), 7.
49. "Théâtre d'Orléans," *La Lorgnette*, December 11, 1842.
50. "Une seule dame était aux premières, et regardait avec un sentiment de terreur les bancs inoccupés." "Théâtre d'Orléans," *La Lorgnette*, December 11, 1842.
51. "Théâtre d'Orléans, *Guillaume Tell*, Première représentation," *La Lorgnette*, December 15, 1842.
52. Johnson, *Listening in Paris*; and Katharine Ellis, "Researching Audience Behaviors in Nineteenth-Century Paris: Who Cares if You Listen?," in *The Oxford Handbook of Music Listening in the 19th and 20th Centuries*, ed. Christian Thorau and Hansjakob Ziemer (Oxford: Oxford University Press, 2019), 37–50. Where Johnson presents a teleological progression from noisy audience behavior to silent listening, however, Ellis presents a more complex picture where silent or attentive listening remained rare in practice in the final third of the nineteenth century in Paris, even though it had become an aesthetic ideal.
53. Lawrence W. Levine discusses the fact that this behavior was widespread in nineteenth-century America in *Highbrow/Lowbrow: The Emergence of a Cultural Hierarchy in America* (Cambridge, MA: Harvard University Press, 1988), 179–80.
54. "Théâtre d'Orléans," *La Lorgnette*, December 11, 1842.
55. See Levine, *Highbrow/Lowbrow*.
56. I discuss this in chapter 1, p. 50.
57. When the St. Charles Theatre opened in 1835, its advertisements made a point of banning peanuts from all areas of the theater. See Gafford, "A History of the St. Charles Theatre in New Orleans, 1835–43," 28. Canonge noted the throwing of pistachios at the Théâtre d'Orléans in "Théâtre d'Orléans," *La Lorgnette*, April 9, 1843.

58. Kmen, *Music in New Orleans*, 196.
59. As with most theaters during this period, the Théâtre d'Orléans always had an associated policeman to help keep order during performances. In 1823, the theater had two dedicated police officers, a man named Thomas Raffo and another named Alexandre Bonneval. Their names and information about their roles can be found in "Grande Loge de l'état de la Louisiane/procès Mque du F. Henry Beebe."
60. Charles Testut, "Au Public," *HNOC*.
61. "Grande Loge de l'état de la Louisiane/procès Mque du F. Henry Beebe." Beebe's attack on Oddo is recorded in detail in documents compiled for his murder trial, not in a criminal court, but as part of the internal disciplinary proceedings of the masonic lodge to which Beebe belonged. I have not found any evidence that Beebe ever underwent a criminal trial for his attack. Instead, he was tried in June 1824 in the presence of twenty-nine voting members of the Grande Loge de l'état de la Louisiane, of which he was a member. A number of witness statements were read at Beebe's masonic trial, all of which are recorded in the lodge's proceedings. Among them are accounts by Davis and Caldwell, their stage managers, a variety of other theater personnel (including two orchestral musicians and a lampist), the doctor who treated Oddo, and the policeman appointed to the theater. While Lyle Saxon mentions the murder of Oddo in his *The Golden Age of the New Orleans Theater*, suggesting that Beebe was acquitted of the charge of murder because the American masons felt he acted reasonably in self-defense, court documents show that quite the opposite was the case: Beebe was found guilty, stripped of his membership of the lodge, and banned from all other lodges in the area.
62. "Grande Loge de l'état de la Louisiane/procès Mque du F. Henry Beebe," 8–9.
63. "Grande Loge de l'état de la Louisiane/procès Mque du F. Henry Beebe," 13.
64. Kmen, *Music in New Orleans*, 154–55 and 196–97.
65. "Mesdames et Messieurs, Vous êtes priés d'assister au convoi, service et enterrement de feu Théâtre d'Orleans, décédé le 12, à 10 heures moins cinq minutes du soir, après une maladie de courte durée. Le cortège partira de la maison mortuaire où le corps est exposé, rue d'Orléans, entre Bourbon et Royale. La marche en est ainsi réglée: La tête du convoi sera conduite par l'ex-orchestre du pauvre défunt, et des marches funèbres seront exécutées. Suivront les figurants et les comparses, etc. Le tam-tam et le chapeau chinois seront les grands pleureurs. L'ex-régisseur est chargé d'attacher les crêpes et l'ex-lampiste de la distribution des petits cierges. L'autopsie du cadavre a prouvé à la foule assemblée que le ci-devant était mort de consomption. Cœurs sensibles, priez Dieu pour le repos de son âme!!! Requiescat in pace! Amen. N. B. Les rédacteurs des journaux de cette ville doivent prononcer sur la tombe du trépassé des oraisons funèbres, et notre sténographe est en mesure de les transmettre au public. Dans nos prochains numéros, nous ferons en sorte de faire connaitre les vices et les vertus, s'il y a lieu, du trépassé, ainsi que les causes et les symptômes qui ont fait naitre et accompagné cette cruelle mais inévitable catastrophe. Le maitre des cérémonies, Grisbourdon." Grisbourdon, "Théâtre d'Orléans: Relâche," *L'Impartial*, November 14, 1839.
66. "Hier, en rentrant chez moi, je trouvai sur ma table une lettre à mon adresse. Je rompis le cachet. Hélas! quelle fut ma douleur! c'ét ait un billet d'enterrement, et de quel enterrement: de l'illustre et économe théâtre d'Orléans! L'infortuné. Il avait succombé la veille au soir, à dix heures moins cinq à une attaque de *pénurie foudroyante*.

"Après s'être débattu pendant trois jours contre la mort, après avoir vainement imploré le secours de médecins auxquels il défendait pourtant son abord, et sentant sa fin approcher, il réunit toutes ses forces, et fit appeler ses héritiers. Ceux-ci arrivèrent silencieusement, et quand ils furent assez près pour entendre: 'Mes enfans, leur souffla le théâtre d'Orléans, . . . j'ai deux ou trois petits conseils à vous adresser, et que ma mort prochaine vous engagera sans doute à suivre, si vous voulez prospérer! Et d'abord: vous ne devrez jamais vous charger de la représentation d'aucune pièce locale, vu que pour huit sous pièce, on peut se procurer à Paris, et par milliers, des drames, vaudevilles . . . et autres. Et puis (et ceci est surtout important), n'ayez jamais aucun commerce ni aucune liaison avec les feuilletonistes! Le feuilletoniste est un vampire; il m'a sucé jusqu'à la dernière goutte de mon sang! Hélas! Hélas! Il est un journal que vous devrez poursuivre de votre haine, et de votre interdiction d'entrée, jusqu'à extinction de chaleur naturelle et de vos lampions; car celui-là m'a tué, et il nous tuera tous!'

"Il allait en dire davantage, quand la mort vint lui couper le sifflet! Il s'endormit du sommeil éternel, après en avoir endormi tant d'autres sur cette terre! Il laisse une famille inconsolable, et de nombreuses bévues à réparer!

"Et nous, pauvre feuilletoniste, nous, contre qui il a vomi toute sa colère, nous le plaignons cependant, et le regrettons! Mais nous prenons courage, et nous nous écrions avec l'Evangile: 'Le Seigneur avait donné le théâtre d'Orléans! Le Seigneur a repris le théâtre d'Orléans! Béni soit le nom du Seigneur!'" Un Hibou de ses Amis, "Article Nécrologique," *L'Impartial*, November 14, 1839.

67. *L'Impartial* reported their deaths in its first issue on October 24, 1839. Vallière and his colleagues are discussed further in chapters 1 and 5 of this book.

68. Canonge reported this on January 2, 1842, and he further reported on January 13, 1842, that *La Lorgnette* had additionally been banned from outside the theater.

69. See *La Lorgnette*, January 2, 1842.

70. *La Lorgnette*, January 8, 1843. Canonge reported improvements in *La Lorgnette*, January 12, 1843.

71. See *La Lorgnette*, February 3, 1842, and February 17, 1842.

72. See, for instance, *La Lorgnette*, February 3, 1842, and May 1, 1842.

73. *La Lorgnette*, January 20, 1842.

74. "Théâtre d'Orléans," *L'Impartial*, November 19, 1839.

75. "Le théâtre d'Orléans est maintenant le palladium de la langue française: là encore, Créoles et Français, nous pouvon s voir avec orgueil dominer notre langue maternelle: le tuer serait donc nous tuer nous-mêmes, ce serait presqu'un crime." "Théâtre d'Orléans," *L'Impartial*, November 19, 1839.

76. "Théâtre d'Orléans: Les cancans—explications," *L'Impartial*, November 17, 1839.

77. *La Lorgnette*, January 2, 1842.

78. In Britain, the issue of journalistic anonymity was much debated, as can be seen clearly in entries throughout E. M. Palmegiano's *Perceptions of the Press in Nineteenth-Century British Periodicals: A Bibliography* (London: Anthem Press, 2012).

79. "Si c'était M. T. . . . , a-t-on dit. —Mais non, a répondu quelqu'un, ce n'est pas M. T . . . , il ne va pas au théâtre. —C'est vrai. —Peut-être est-ce M. M. . . . , a pensé un troisième. —Cela pourrait être, a-t-on répliqué. —Était-il au théâtre tel jour? —Non. —Décidément ce n'est pas M. M . . .—Ha! j'y suis, a fait un malin; pourquoi ne serait-ce pas M. G.? on lui a l'autre jour attribué un article sur la *Physiologie de la Toilette*, signe X. Y. Z., et le damnable factum sur le théâtre porte les mêmes initiales. —Irréfragable! point d'objection à cela. Aux voix! Et sur cette forte preuve, il a été décidé à l'unanimité que c'était M. G. . . . Néanmoins, quelqu'un se ravisant a fait observer que les initiales pourraient bien être un moyen employé par les éditeurs pour dépayser les curieux." "Théâtre d'Orléans: Les cancans—explications," *L'Impartial*, November 17, 1839.

80. For more on these troupes, see Charlotte Bentley, "Southern Exchanges: Italian Opera in New Orleans, 1836–1842," in *Italian Opera in Global and Transnational Perspective: Reimagining Italianità in the Long Nineteenth Century*, ed. Axel Körner and Paulo Kühl (Cambridge: Cambridge University Press, 2022), 113–32.
81. "Italian Opera Company," *Daily Picayune*, December 11, 1838.
82. Benjamin Walton has argued that the scarcity of operatic performances in Buenos Aires and Montevideo drove the development of thriving discursive engagements with opera. Benjamin Walton, "Canons of Real and Imagined Opera: Buenos Aires and Montevideo, 1810–1860," in *The Oxford Handbook of the Operatic Canon*, ed. Cormac Newark and William Weber (Oxford: Oxford University Press, 2020), 271–89.
83. "Italian Opera Company," *Daily Picayune*, December 11, 1838.
84. It was not necessarily confined to only those of a particular national background, however. Indeed, the anonymous author of the article, writing in English, may not have belonged to any of those national groups that he mentioned, and yet he still included himself when he wrote "*we* are a southern people," perhaps suggesting that he had absorbed some of the musicality of his fellow residents of New Orleans.
85. "D'un nouveau théâtre français," *L'Abeille*, April 2, 1835.
86. "En facilitant à notre jeunesse les moyens de faire des œuvres conformés à ses goûts, nous verrons jaillir une foule de génies qui, sans cela seraient restes ensevelis dans la poussière des magasins ou dans les paperasses poudreuses d'un notaire ou d'un avocat." "D'un nouveau théâtre français," *L'Abeille*, April 2, 1835.
87. Such were the concerns about a lack of distinctively American culture that the composer William Henry Fry was moved to declare in the mid-1850s that the United States was in dire need of "a Declaration of Independence in Art." Richard Crawford et al., "United States of America," *Grove Music Online, Oxford Music Online*, Oxford University Press, accessed August 4, 2017, http://www.oxfordmusiconline.com/subscriber/article/grove/music/28794pg1.
88. New works are frequently mentioned in passing throughout Kmen, *Music in New Orleans*; and John Baron, *Concert Life in Nineteenth-Century New Orleans: A Comprehensive Reference* (Baton Rouge: Louisiana State University Press, 2013).
89. Katherine Preston, *Opera for the People: English-Language Opera and Women Managers in Late 19th-Century America* (New York: Oxford University Press, 2017), 410–94.
90. *La Lorgnette*, January 19, 1843.
91. Katharine Ellis, "Gautier, Théophile," *Grove Music Online, Oxford Music Online*, accessed June 12, 2020, https://www.oxfordmusiconline.com/grovemusic/view/10.1093/gmo/9781561592630.001.0001/omo-9781561592630-e-0000010760.
92. Ellis, "Gautier, Théophile." It is easy to see why Canonge might have been drawn to a figure like Gautier: like Canonge, Gautier also wrote poetry and plays, and his music criticism avoided complex terminology or in-depth, technical analysis, while making perceptive comments about works, performers, and the social and cultural contexts in which he heard them.
93. *La Lorgnette*, January 19, 1843.

CHAPTER FOUR

1. Eliza Ripley, *Social Life in Old New Orleans: Being Recollections of My Girlhood* (New York: D. Appleton and Company, 1912), 146.
2. For biographical information on Ripley, see Melissa Daggett, "Eliza Ripley," *64 Parishes*, accessed March 30, 2021, https://64parishes.org/entry/eliza-ripley.

3. Ripley, *Social Life in Old New Orleans*, 20.
4. Peter Mondelli, "The Sociability of History in French Grand Opera: A Historical Materialist Perspective," *19th-Century Music* 37/1 (2013): 39.
5. Michael Twyman, *A History of Chromolithography: Printed Colour for All* (London: British Library Publishing Division, 2013).
6. Over thirty French-language publications were founded in the 1840s. Rien Fertel, *Imagining the Creole City: The Rise of Literary Culture in Nineteenth-Century New Orleans* (Baton Rouge: Louisiana State University Press, 2014), 21.
7. For more on the emergence of a sheet music trade in New Orleans and its links with national (and, later, confederate identity), see Warren K. Kimball, "Northern Music Culture in Antebellum New Orleans" (PhD diss., Louisiana State University, 2017).
8. There were occasional exceptions to this pattern. E. Johns et Cie., the book publishing company founded by Paul Emile Johns (a pianist and composer based in the city, to whom Chopin dedicated his Op. 7 Mazurkas), published a few pieces of sheet music as early as the 1830s. Peggy C. Boudreaux discusses Johns's publishing activities in "Music Publishing in New Orleans in the Nineteenth Century" (MA diss., Louisiana State University, 1977), 6–11.
9. Steam crossings of the Atlantic reduced the journey time from Bristol to New York from an average of 30.5 days on sail ships to 16.5 days under steam power, thereby nearly halving the traveling time for troupes undertaking transatlantic tours. Peter J. Hugill, *World Trade Since 1431: Geography, Technology, and Capitalism* (Baltimore: Johns Hopkins University Press, 1993), 127.
10. The basics of Lehmann's biography can be gleaned from his gravestone, in Saint Louis Cemetery No. 3 in New Orleans: "Hermann Edward Lehmann. Born in Berlin, Prussia. Died 20 October 1866, aged 61 years." Lehmann arrived in New Orleans a few years before the major waves of German immigration that would later significantly expand the city. He moved with the rest of the Théâtre d'Orléans company to the new French Opera House in 1859.
11. A full list of the opera-based pieces is provided in the bibliography.
12. I have been able to uncover very little biographical information about Fiot, including whether he was born in France or in New Orleans. His name appears fairly regularly in the New Orleans press between the mid-1840s and the mid-1850s, but disappears after that time.
13. James Q. Davies, "Julia's Gift: The Social Life of Scores, c. 1830," *Journal of the Royal Musical Association* 131/2 (2006): 291.
14. Candace Bailey, "Binder's Volumes as Musical Commonplace Books: The Transmission of Cultural Codes in the Antebellum South," *Journal of the Society for American Music* 10/4 (2016): 446–69.
15. Alexander Rehding, *Music and Monumentality: Commemoration and Wonderment in Nineteenth-Century Germany* (Oxford: Oxford University Press, 2009), 78.
16. "Possess" is a term Eleanor Cloutier uses in her article on emerging celebrity culture. See "Ways to Possess a Singer in 1830s London," *Cambridge Opera Journal* 29/2 (2018): 189–214.
17. He also made an arrangement of Jean Baptiste Édouard Montaubry's music for Théodore Barrière and Lambert Thiboust's "drame mêlé de chant," *Les Filles de marbre*, which inspired the publication of a glut of solo piano arrangements on both sides of the Atlantic. Searching for "*Les Filles de marbre*" brings up twenty sheet music arrangement results in the Bibliothèque nationale de France catalog alone.
18. Derek B. Scott, *Sounds of the Metropolis: The 19th-Century Popular Music Revolution in London, New York, Paris and Vienna* (Oxford: Oxford University Press, 2008), esp. 43–57 and 131–43.

19. Mark Everist, "The Commendatore and the Clavier (Quadrille)," in *Mozart's Ghosts: Haunting the Halls of Musical Culture* (New York: Oxford University Press, 2012), 75–125; Maribeth Clark, "The Quadrille as Embodied Musical Experience in 19th-Century Paris," *Journal of Musicology* 19/3 (2002): 503–26.
20. For the pieces published in New York, see Lehmann, "Filles de Marbre Polka de Pieces d'or" (New York: J. L. Peters, 1854), cover title: *Favorite Compositions of H. E. Lehmann.* This item is part of the Natchez Trace Sheet Music Collection at the Dolph Briscoe Center for American History at the University of Texas at Austin. Only a couple of his pieces appeared with publishing companies in New Orleans, including one of his arrangements of Grisar's *Les Amours du diable,* which appeared with T. E. Benoit (a music importer who turned to publishing in the 1840s).
21. In fact, the only exception to this rule seems to be the arrangements of *Il trovatore,* which were published the year after the work's Théâtre d'Orléans premiere. This pair of arrangements is also a little different from Lehmann's other works in that he preserved Verdi's Italian title for the work, when it had been performed at the Théâtre d'Orléans in 1857 under the French title *Le trouvère.* On the whole, though, Lehmann's arrangements appeared in the wake of their introduction at the French theater.
22. For information on the work's New Orleans premiere, see Jack Belsom, "Reception of Major Operatic Premieres in New Orleans during the Nineteenth Century" (MA diss., Louisiana State University, 1972), 147–48.
23. *The Bee,* April 17, 1855.
24. The Pelican Club was an exclusive social club, which "made a special appeal to bankers, lawyers, physicians, and to the British representatives of Liverpool cotton houses." Robert C. Reinders, *End of an Era: New Orleans, 1850–1860* (Gretna, LA: Pelican Publishing Company, 1964), 159.
25. See H. E. Lehmann, "The Pelican Polka" (New Orleans, 1855), M31.L4 P4 1855, *HNOC.*
26. "Orleans Theatre Grand Concert," *Daily Picayune,* November 5, 1844.
27. Ripley, *Social Life in Old New Orleans,* 149–50.
28. Matthew Head, "'If the Pretty Little Hand Won't Stretch': Music for the Fair Sex in Eighteenth-Century Germany," *Journal of the American Musicological Society* 52/2 (1999): 208.
29. Denise Gallo has highlighted, through the case of Rossini's military marches, that dedications to renowned individuals improved the salability of popular sheet music in the first half of the nineteenth century. Gallo, "Selling 'Celebrity': The Role of the Dedication in Marketing Piano Arrangements of Rossini's Military Marches," in *The Idea of Art Music in a Commercial World, 1800–1930,* ed. Christina Bashford and Roberta Montemorra Marvin (Woodbridge: Boydell Press, 2016), 18–38.
30. Heloise Cenas was the sister of Clarissa Pierce Cenas, whose diary is held at the Historic New Orleans Collection (MSS 649). They were the daughters of Hilary Breton Cenas, a notary public in the city from 1834 to 1859 (Clarissa's diary begins in the aftermath of her father's death that year, recording the family's grief at that time). The US Census for 1870 lists Heloise and "Clarisse" Cenas as living with their mother (Margaret Cenas) and siblings in New Orleans. This information can be found by searching for "Heloise Cenas" and a date range from 1800 to 1890 in www.familysearch.org.
31. Ripley, *Social Life in Old New Orleans,* 149.
32. Gottschalk's concerts were advertised in the local press between March 1855 and May 7, 1855, when he gave his farewell concert.

33. Sarah Fuchs, "The Castrato as Creator: Velluti's Voice in the London Sheet-Music Market," in *London Voices, 1820–1840: Vocal Performers, Practices, Histories*, ed. Roger Parker and Susan Rutherford (Chicago: University of Chicago Press, 2019), 71–92.
34. Other copies, however, do not, suggesting that customers could request to have their lithographs hand-colored or that two versions were available. Color lithography had been introduced in the United States by William Sharp in 1840 and quickly became popular. See Philip B. Meggs, *A History of Graphic Design* (New York: John Wiley & Sons, Inc., 1998), 147.
35. The opera was an immediate success, with *L'Abeille* printing a full two-column review of the work three days after its premiere. "Feuilleton," *L'Abeille*, March 27, 1856. In November the following year, the *Daily Picayune* heralded the work's performance at the start of the 1857–1858 season, saying that "last season, and the season previous [it] was always the most popular piece the management of the Théâtre d'Orléans could announce for representation." *Daily Picayune*, November 18, 1857.
36. Of the other two pieces, one was an illustration by P. Arendt, while the other was a collaboration between Arendt and an artist named Mey.
37. Colson's name is listed in the premiere cast in the copy of the Parisian libretto held in the Bibliothèque nationale de France, département littérature et art, 4-YTH-152. Available on Gallica, accessed July 4, 2019, https://gallica.bnf.fr/ark:/12148/bpt6k5626533z.
38. As discussed in chapter 1, principal singers at the Théâtre d'Orléans were required to provide their own costumes. Kimberly White has discussed how this practice also took place at Parisian theaters like the Opéra-Comique, and it might, therefore, have been the case at the Théâtre Lyrique, where the premiere of *Les Amours du diable* took place. Kimberly White, *Female Singers on the French Stage, 1830–1848* (Cambridge: Cambridge University Press, 2018), 74.
39. "*La Lorgnette* publiera désormais des Lithographies qui seront, pour la plupart des temps, l'exacte reproduction de celles du *Charivari* et du *Corsaire*." *La Lorgnette*, January 15, 1843. The *Charivari* was founded in 1832 by Charles Philipon, joining the older *Corsaire*, which had been published since 1823. The artist in New Orleans signed himself on a number of the lithographs as "R. G. d'apres H. D." (with H. D. presumably referring to the caricaturist Honoré Daumier, whose drawings of Robert Macaire in the Charivari from 1836 made his name).
40. "Souvent, cependant, elle offrira aussi à ses lecteurs des dessins d'un intérêt local, surtout si nos grands hommes politiques prêtent le flanc à la caricature: ce qui n'arrive a malheureusement que trop communément. L'exécution en est due à un jeune homme de notre ville, dont le mérite est incontestable, et dont la touche vigoureuse et hardie doit compter plus d'un succès." *La Lorgnette*, January 15, 1843.
41. Unsigned, "Vue du Bayou St-Jean," *La Lorgnette*, February 12, 1843.
42. Ripley, *Social Life in Old New Orleans*, 151.
43. Thomas Christensen, "Four-Hand Piano Transcription and Geographies of Nineteenth-Century Musical Reception," *Journal of the American Musicological Society* 52/2 (1999): 256.
44. Lehmann's opera arrangements were considerably longer than his other compositions, which rarely exceeded two or three pages. There are hints, then, that Lehmann viewed the process of producing opera arrangements as a more artistically elevated task—or at least one that offered opportunities for greater musical ambition—than producing his non-opera-based parlor music.
45. Mark Everist discusses the relationship between opera-based quadrilles and their source op-

eras (via piano transcriptions of the full works) in *Mozart's Ghosts*, 75–125. Rachel Becker has recently explored the narrative elements of virtuosic woodwind fantasias. See Becker, "'Trash Music': Valuing Nineteenth-Century Italian Opera Fantasias for Woodwinds" (PhD diss., University of Cambridge, 2018).

46. Christensen, "Four-Hand Piano Transcription and Geographies of Nineteenth-Century Musical Reception," 255–98.
47. H. E. Lehmann, "La Couronne impériale de *L'Etoile du nord*: grande valse" (New Orleans: H. E. Lehmann, 1855).
48. H. E. Lehmann, "Azucena du Trovatore" (New Orleans: H. E. Lehmann, 1858).
49. Everist points out that labeling of this kind was also not uncommon in Parisian arrangements. Everist, *Mozart's Ghosts*, 99–101.
50. Mephistopheles, "Chronique des bals," *Loge de l'Opéra*, February 7, 1857.
51. Kmen, *Music in New Orleans*, 8. Kmen does not mention Lehmann by name, but he does observe that the pit was floored over.
52. *Daily Picayune*, February 22, 1852. On another occasion, fourteen years earlier, the St. Charles Theatre in the American sector pulled off a theatrical coup when it followed each of its eight performances of an English version of *Gustavus III: A Masked Ball* with an actual ball for the audience in the theater building, deliberately blurring the lines between theatrical fiction and reality. Auber was not mentioned anywhere in the advertisement, leaving the possibility that the music was something of a potpourri of compositions, and not strictly the opera *Gustave III*. *Daily Picayune*, April 8, 1838. That event is mentioned in Kmen, *Music in New Orleans*, 21.
53. H. E. Lehmann, "La Couronne impériale de *L'Etoile du nord*: grande valse."
54. Emily Clark explores some of these accounts and interrogates their more outlandish claims in *The Strange History of the American Quadroon: Free Women of Color in the Revolutionary Atlantic World* (Chapel Hill: University of North Carolina Press, 2013), 162–87.
55. See Kmen, *Music in New Orleans*, 15–16.
56. See, for instance, Mephistopheles, "Chronique des bals," *Loge de l'Opéra*, February 7, 1857, and February 14, 1857.
57. See Kmen, *Music in New Orleans*, 15.
58. See *The New ball-room guide; or, Dancing made easy, comprising the etiquette of dancing, with the latest and most fashionable figures of cotillions, quadrilles, gallopades, mazourkas, polonaises, etc. etc.* (New York: Burgess and Stringer, 1844), 11.
59. *The New ball-room guide*, 11.
60. Grace King's *Creole Families of New Orleans* (New York: Macmillan, 1921) shows just how important lineage and "breeding" were to the most elite Creole families in the city.
61. Home visiting was an important part of social life (and of interaction between the sexes) in nineteenth-century New Orleans, whether or not there were any underlying romantic intentions. Eliza Ripley describes the importance of gentlemen callers at the New Year, for instance, in *Social Life in Old New Orleans*, 50–57.
62. For information on the role of music (and the piano in particular) in female education in the Old South, see Candace Bailey, *Music and the Southern Belle: From Accomplished Lady to Confederate Composer* (Carbondale: Southern Illinois University Press, 2010); and Candace Bailey, "The Antebellum 'Piano Girl' in the American South," *Performance Practice Review* 13/1 (2008), Article 1: 1–44, https://doi.org/10.5642/perfpr.200813.01.01. See also Julia Eklund Koza, "Music Instruction in the Nineteenth Century: Views from 'Godey's Lady's Book,' 1830–77," *Journal of Research in Music Education* 38/4 (Winter 1990): 245–57.

63. See also Candace Bailey, *Unbinding Gentility: Women Making Music in the Nineteenth-Century South* (Urbana-Champaign: University of Illinois Press, 2021). This issue was certainly not limited to New Orleans, and Katharine Ellis discusses the issue of female pianists and virtuosity in "Female Pianists and Their Male Critics in Nineteenth-Century Paris," *Journal of the American Musicological Society* 50/2–3 (1997): 353–85.
64. The availability of works by these composers is confirmed by their presence in binders' volumes in New Orleans. See, for instance, the volumes belonging to Emilia Carrière now held at the Hogan Jazz Archive, Tulane University. One volume alone contains pieces by Chopin, Hummel, Thalberg, Henri Herz, and Joseph Ascher. Vol. 29, Maxwell Sheet Music Collection, *HJA*.
65. *Daily Picayune*, January 18, 1839.
66. Clark, "The Quadrille as Embodied Musical Experience in 19th-Century Paris," 525.
67. Clark, "The Quadrille as Embodied Musical Experience in 19th-Century Paris," 525.
68. James H. Johnson, *Listening in Paris: A Cultural History* (Berkeley: University of California Press, 1995).
69. See Katherine K. Preston, *Opera on the Road: Traveling Opera Troupes in the United States, 1835–60* (Urbana: University of Illinois Press, 1993); and Katherine K. Preston, *Opera for the People: English-Language Opera and Women Managers in Late 19th-Century America* (New York: Oxford University Press, 2017). For an account of the emergence of ideas of "high" and "low" art in the United States, see Lawrence W. Levine, *Highbrow/Lowbrow: The Emergence of a Cultural Hierarchy in America* (Cambridge, MA: Harvard University Press, 1988).
70. Lisa Lowe, *The Intimacies of Four Continents* (Durham, NC: Duke University Press, 2015), 21.
71. Cloutier, "Ways to Possess a Singer in 1830s London."
72. Lowe, *The Intimacies of Four Continents*, 1–41.
73. Examples of these libretti can be found in the Special Collections at Louisiana State University, the Louisiana Research Collection at Tulane University, and the Historic New Orleans Collection.
74. The size of the libretti is similar to modern A5 paper.
75. Catherine Jones mentions the libretti, suggesting that "the series reinvigorated the tradition of bilingual publication in New Orleans that had its origins in law-making and the need to disseminate information to French and English speakers in the territorial area." Jones, *Literature and Music in the Atlantic World, 1767–1867* (Edinburgh: Edinburgh University Press, 2014), 89–90.
76. These essentials usually amounted to the date, time, information for obtaining tickets, a cast list, and a few words proclaiming the merits of the work (usually through reference to the very great success it had obtained in Paris). A number of playbills can be found in archives around New Orleans. See, for one example, a playbill for *Les Diamans de la Couronne*, January 24, 1843, ML1850.075 1843, *HNOC*.
77. These programs were doubtless created at the instigation of publicity master P. T. Barnum, who was the impresario behind Lind's American tours. They were printed in New Orleans at the print shop of the *Daily Picayune*, the English-language local newspaper.
78. Some of them, it seems, were not simply kept on a shelf, but were used: a number of them contain pencil markings, and a copy of the libretto for *Robert le diable* held at the Historic New Orleans Collection contains numerous doodles and illustrations of devilish characters. "Couret French Opera Collection," vol. 1, *HNOC*.
79. Mozart, *Don Juan*, Fiot's Edition. ML50. M939 D523 1854 LARA, *SCLSU*.
80. This is evidenced by a volume of eight of the libretti held at the Historic New Orleans Col-

lection. "Librettos of operas performed in New Orleans," ML48. A2, *HNOC*. A substantial number of loose libretti still survive in archival collections around Louisiana: I have been able to locate copies of nineteen of Fiot's thirty published libretti, and there are duplicates to be found of many. The fact that a relatively large number have survived is particularly remarkable considering how fragmentary most of the material traces of French opera in New Orleans are, and suggests that Fiot's customers did indeed collect and care for them.

81. Junca was part of the troupe from 1855 to 1859.
82. Verdi, *Jerusalem*, Fiot's Edition. ML50.V4 J4 1850, *HNOC*.
83. The contents of table 4.1 are exactly as printed in Fiot's libretti, spelling mistakes and unusual translations included, as well as the acknowledgment only of the French translator rather than the original librettist in cases where the libretto was translated from Italian or German. Numbers 1–23 reflect the order of publication as listed on the back cover of the booklet for *Le Caïd*. The order of the final seven libretti in the set is not certain, as these libretti contain the date of the year of publication, but do not specify whether this was the date of the first edition or a later reprint.
84. This preface is printed in a large number of the publications; the italics are mine.
85. Vera Wolkowicz, "Opera as a Moral Vehicle: Situating Bellini's Norma in the Political Complexities of Mid-Nineteenth-Century Buenos Aires," *Nineteenth-Century Music Review*, First View (2021): 1–23, https://doi.org/10.1017/S1479409820000506.
86. It should be pointed out, however, that it was still seen as acceptable for acts of operas to be performed individually at the Théâtre d'Orléans on occasion, particularly for singers' or theater personnel's benefits. See, for example, the advertisement for the theater in *L'Abeille*, May 12, 1845, which lists the second act of *Robert le diable* and the second act of *Lucie de Lammermoor* as part of a benefit concert for M. Colin. The event was reviewed in *L'Abeille* on May 13, 1845.
87. Similarly, his emphasis on the completeness and conformity between libretto and score in the works he selected overlooks the numerous benefit performances taken by singers and other members of theater personnel that involved favorite arias and scenes excerpted from a wide variety of works.
88. As the theater's *régisseur*, Fiot likely had a degree of control in a very literal sense over the relationship between performances and the sales of his libretti, hence my comment above that the libretti both reflected and drove processes of canon formation. For more on the varied nature of operatic canon formation and its cross-historical manifestations, see James Parakilas, "The Operatic Canon," in *The Oxford Handbook of Opera*, ed. Helen M. Greenwald (Oxford: Oxford University Press, 2014), 862–81. For an exploration of the complexities and problems of operatic canon formation in the nineteenth century with a focus on France, see William Gibbons, *Building the Operatic Museum: Eighteenth-Century Opera in Fin-de-Siècle Paris* (Rochester, NY: Rochester University Press, 2013); and Flora Willson, "Operatic Futures in Second Empire Paris" (PhD diss., King's College London, 2013).
89. For more on the fervor for Italian opera in the early 1840s, see Charlotte Bentley, "Southern Exchanges: Italian Opera in New Orleans, 1836–1842," in *Italian Opera in Global and Transnational Perspective: Reimagining Italianità in the Long Nineteenth Century*, ed. Axel Körner and Paulo Kühl (Cambridge: Cambridge University Press, 2022), 113–32.
90. Indeed, Henry Kmen points out that *Les Noces de Figaro* was withdrawn as a failure after only a single performance at the French theater c. 1830, but fared better at Caldwell's American Theatre. See Kmen, *Music in New Orleans*, 125–27. Mozart's operas seem to have been

popular at the St. Charles Theatre, where they were performed from the mid-1830s in Italian. Kmen, *Music in New Orleans*, 139 and 163. Concert excerpts from Mozart's operas seem to have found favor much earlier on, and the Overture to *The Magic Flute* was listed on a concert program in the city as early as 1806. See Kmen, *Music in New Orleans*, 219.

91. For more on the issue of changing Mozart reception in Paris and the idea of making his operas canonical, see Gibbons, *Building the Operatic Museum*; Rachel Cowgill, "Mozart Productions and the Emergence of Werktreue at London's Italian Opera House, 1780–1830," in *Operatic Migrations: Transforming Works and Crossing Boundaries*, ed. Roberta Montemorra Marvin and Downing A. Thomas (Aldershot: Ashgate, 2006), 145–86; and Christina Fuhrmann, *Foreign Opera at the London Playhouses: From Mozart to Bellini* (Cambridge: Cambridge University Press, 2015).
92. Karen Ahlquist, "International Opera in Nineteenth-Century New York: Core Repertories and Canonic Values," in *The Oxford Handbook of the Operatic Canon*, ed. Cormac Newark and William Weber (Oxford: Oxford University Press, 2020), 244–67; and Benjamin Walton, "Canons of Real and Imagined Opera: Buenos Aires and Montevideo, 1810–1860," in *The Oxford Handbook of the Operatic Canon*, ed. Cormac Newark and William Weber (Oxford: Oxford University Press, 2020), 271–89.
93. Mozart, *Don Juan*, Fiot's Edition. ML50. M939 D523 1854 LARA, *SCLSU*.
94. See "Population of 100 Largest Urban Places: 1850," US Bureau of the Census, accessed October 30, 2021, https://www2.census.gov/library/working-papers/1998/demo/pop-twps0027/tab08.txt.
95. See, for example, Bellini, *La Somnambule*, Fiot's Edition. Albert Voss Collection, Manuscripts Collection 856, Series 1, Box 1 Folder 1, *LARC*; and Thomas, *Le Caïd*, Fiot's Edition. Albert Voss Collection, Manuscripts Collection 856, Series 1, Box 1 Folder 1, *LARC*.
96. Bellini, *La Somnambule*, Fiot's Edition. For the names of the performers who went on the 1843 and 1845 tours, see Mary Grace Swift, "The Northern Tours of the Théâtre d'Orléans, 1843 and 1845," *Louisiana History: The Journal of the Louisiana Historical Association* 26/2 (1985): 192–93.
97. Preston, *Opera on the Road* and *Opera for the People*; Levine, *Highbrow/Lowbrow*; and Joseph A. Mussulman, *Music in the Cultured Generation: A Social History of Music in America, 1870–1900* (Evanston, IL: Northwestern University Press, 1971).
98. For more on this process, see the first half of Preston, *Opera for the People*.
99. As with Fiot's libretti, many of Schweitzer's libretti survive in the Special Collections of the Hill Memorial Library, Louisiana State University, the Louisiana Research Collection, Jones Hall, Tulane University, and the Historic New Orleans Collection.
100. For an annotated copy with comments on the English translations, see the libretto for *Robert le diable* in "Couret French Opera Collection," vol. 1, *HNOC*.

CHAPTER FIVE

1. Didimus [pseudonym of Edward Henry Durell], *New Orleans as I Found It* (New York: Harper & Brothers, 1845), 51–52.
2. Bernhard, Duke of Saxe-Weimar-Eisenach, *Travels Through America in the Years 1825–6* (Philadelphia, 1828); Eliza Potter, *A Hairdresser's Experience in High Life* (Cincinnati, 1859). Biographical information on Eliza Potter can be found in Quincy T. Mills, *Cutting Along the Color Line: Black Barbers and Barber Shops in America* (Philadelphia: University of Penn-

sylvania Press, 2013), 57–58. While Potter wrote of the "enchanting music" she heard at the theater in the 1850s (292), the Duke was less pleased by the performance of spoken drama he attended in 1825, proclaiming that the "dramatic corps was merely tolerable, such as those of the small French provincial towns" (57).

3. The idea of "scripting" is explored by Derek Gregory in "Scripting Egypt: Orientalism and the Cultures of Travel," in *Writes of Passage: Reading Travel Writing*, ed. James Duncan and Derek Gregory (London and New York: Routledge, 2002), 114–50. For more on the places and activities sought out by visitors to New Orleans, see Florence Roos Brink, "Literary Travellers in Louisiana Between 1803 and 1860," *Louisiana Historical Quarterly* 31/2 (1949): 399.
4. Didimus, *New Orleans as I Found It*; Charles Jobey, *L'Amour d'un nègre* (Paris: Michel Lèvy Frères, 1860); Charles Jobey, "Le lac Cathahoula," in *L'Amour d'une blanche* (Paris: E. Jung-Treuttel, 1861), 194–272. For details of other published versions, see note 39 in this chapter.
5. He was listed as *rédacteur* of *La Constitution* of Cognac, *rédacteur* of *L'Interêt publique* of Rochefort, former *rédacteur* of the *Républicain de Tarn-et-Garonne*, and "many other organs of democratic opinion in the départements," including *La Liberté* in his native Rouen. "Plusieurs autres organes de l'opinion démocratique dans les départements." "Nécrologie," *Le Temps*, March 15, 1877; and "Nécrologie," *La Presse*, March 16, 1877. He was listed as the *rédacteur* of *La Liberté* in Henri-Michel Saint-Denis, *Histoire d'Elbeuf, Tome XI (1866 à 1879)* (Elbeuf: Imprimerie Saint-Denis, 1898), 503. All these journalistic activities featured in the obituary notices published in the Parisian press on his death in March 1877, but none made mention of his earlier, far from illustrious musical career.
6. Having practiced law in the city for a number of years, Durell went on to hold the position of mayor for a period in 1863, and he served as district judge from 1864 to 1874. "Biographical Directory of Federal Judges: Durell, Edward Henry," History of Federal Judiciary, Federal Judicial Center, n.d., accessed August 2, 2021, https://www.fjc.gov/history/judges/durell-edward-henry. For more information on Durell and his career, see Charles Lane, "Edward Henry Durell: A Study in Reputation," *The Green Bag* 13/2 (2010): 153–68.
7. Virginia E. Whealton, "Travel, Ideology and the Geographical Imagination: Parisian Musical Travelogues, 1830–1870" (PhD diss., Indiana University, 2018).
8. Benjamin Walton, "*L'italiana* in Calcutta," in *Operatic Geographies: The Place of Opera and the Opera House*, ed. Suzanne Aspden (Chicago: University of Chicago Press, 2018), 119–32.
9. Jan Borm has argued against seeing travel writing as a genre in itself, instead suggesting that it is a "collective term for a variety of texts both predominantly fictional and nonfictional whose main theme is travel" (13). Nonetheless, she concedes that "travel memoir," "travel story," and "travelogue" are all valid terms when talking about particular kinds of travel accounts. Borm, "Defining Travel: On the Travel Book, Travel Writing and Terminology," in *Perspectives on Travel Writing*, ed. Glenn Hooper and Tim Youngs (London: Routledge, 2004), 13–26.
10. While Chateaubriand's novels were supposedly based on his experiences in the United States in the 1790s (which he later detailed in *Voyage en Amérique* [1821]), scholars have long questioned not only the veracity of some of his descriptions, but also whether he even traveled to all the places he claimed to have. See, for example, Raymond Lebègue, "Le Problème du voyage de Chateaubriand en Amérique," *Journal des Savants* 1/1 (1965): 456–65.
11. Jobey, *L'Amour d'un nègre*, 3.
12. "Nous avions toujours pensé qu'il était indispensable d'avoir voyagé pour parler des pays lointains, pour écrire sur les mœurs et les usages des peuples qui les habitent. Nous nous étions trompé, nous le reconnaissons, car nous voyons tous les jours des gens n'ayant jamais

franchi le mur d'enceinte de Paris écrire des histoires très amusantes, dont les scènes se passent à quatre mille lieues de là." Jobey, *L'Amour d'une blanche*, iii–iv.

13. Tim Youngs, *Travellers in Africa: British Travelogues 1815–1900* (Manchester: Manchester University Press, 1994), 8.
14. The term "transculturation," meaning the merging and converging of cultures, was coined by Fernando Ortiz in his *Cuban Counterpoint: Tobacco and Sugar*, trans. Harriet de Onís (Durham, NC: Duke University Press, 1947), but it has since been taken up by many other scholars.
15. Homi Bhabha, *The Location of Culture* (London: Routledge, 1994).
16. Mary Louise Pratt, *Imperial Eyes: Travel Writing and Transculturation*, 2nd ed. (London: Routledge, 2008). Barbara Korte has gone so far as to argue that the principal mission of nineteenth-century travel writing was the promotion of the values of empire. Korte, *English Travel Writing from Pilgrimages to Postcolonial Explorations* (London: Palgrave Macmillan, 2000). James Duncan and Derek Gregory, meanwhile, have more cautiously discussed it in terms of the "translation of one place into the cultural idiom of another," thereby taking the sole focus off imperialism and foregrounding a wider negotiation of cultural similarity and difference, and the power dynamics that result. James Duncan and Derek Gregory, "Introduction," *Writes of Passage: Reading Travel Writing*, ed. James Duncan and Derek Gregory (London: Routledge, 2002), 5. As Tim Youngs rightly points out, "Travel writing is not a literal and objective record of journeys undertaken. It carries preconceptions that, even if challenged, provide a reference point. It is influenced, if not determined, by its authors' gender, class, age, nationality, cultural background and education. It is ideological." Youngs, "Introduction: Filling the Blank Spaces," in *Travel Writing in the Nineteenth Century: Filling the Blank Spaces*, ed. Tim Youngs (London: Anthem Press, 2006), 2–3.
17. Rogério Budasz, "Music, Authority, and Civilisation in Rio de Janeiro, 1763–1790," in *Music and Urban Society in Colonial Latin America*, ed. Geoffrey Baker and Tess Knighton (Cambridge: Cambridge University Press, 2011), 151–70; Rogério Budasz, *Opera in the Tropics: Music and Theater in Early Modern Brazil* (Oxford: Oxford University Press, 2019); and Benjamin Walton, "Italian Operatic Fantasies in Latin America," *Journal of Modern Italian Studies* 17:4 (2012): 460–71. For another instance of an exploration of opera's relationship with empire, see Esmeralda Monique Antonia Rocha, "Imperial Opera: The Nexus Between Opera and Imperialism in Victorian Calcutta and Melbourne, 1833–1901" (PhD diss., University of Western Australia, 2012).
18. Vanessa Agnew, *Enlightenment Orpheus: The Power of Music in Other Worlds* (New York: Oxford University Press, 2008); and Ruth E. Rosenberg, *Music, Travel, and Imperial Encounter in 19th-Century France: Musical Apprehensions* (New York: Routledge, 2015).
19. For more on the Collection Michel Lévy, see Jean-Yves Mollier, *Michel & Calmann Lévy, ou la naissance de l'édition moderne, 1836–1891* (Paris: Calmann-Lévy, 1984).
20. Orlando Figes, *The Europeans: Three Lives and the Making of a Cosmopolitan Culture* (London: Penguin, 2019), xi.
21. I have previously published some of this material on *L'Amour d'un nègre* and "Le lac Cathahoula" as "Between the Frontier and the French Quarter: Operatic Travel Writing and Nineteenth-Century New Orleans," in *Operatic Geographies: The Place of Opera and the Opera House*, ed. Suzanne Aspden (Chicago: Chicago University Press, 2018), 105–18.
22. The scene can be found in Jobey, *L'Amour d'un nègre*, 146–61.
23. "—Mademoiselle Dupuis! le rôle d'Adèle ne vous appartient pas, nous ne vous le laisserons pas jouer." Jobey, *L'Amour d'un nègre*, 151. It is, of course, highly appropriate that this par-

ticular opera should serve as the backdrop for the climax of the diva war: Auber's *Le Concert à la cour* tells the story of a young soprano's struggles to find favor at court in Stuttgart, as a jealous superintendent of the Prince's music tries to thwart her efforts.

24. "A ces mots, la tempête éclate de plus belle, tout le monde est debout, à l'orchestre, au parterre, dans les loges; on s'injurie, on se menace. L'actrice, cause de tout ce bruit, prend le parti de se trouver mal sur la scène. Le désordre est à son comble, les provocations personnelles s'échangent, les bourrades, les soufflets, les coups de poings pleuvent de tous côtés. Un poignard est tiré, et, à l'instant même, vingt, cinquante, cent, deux cents poignards, couteaux, cannes à dard, pistolets, brillent dans la salle." Jobey, *L'Amour d'un nègre*, 151.
25. As I discussed in chapter 1, one particularly notable conflict took place between New Orleans's most-loved prima donna, Julia Calvé, and her rival Mme. Bamberger in March 1841. See *Daily Picayune*, March 30, 1841.
26. Cormac Newark, *Opera in the Novel from Balzac to Proust* (Cambridge: Cambridge University Press, 2011), 3.
27. Newark, *Opera in the Novel*, 3.
28. The tradition's roots can be traced all the way back to Lucian's *Vera Historia* of the second century or, more conservatively, Thomas More's *Utopia* from 1516.
29. See, for example, Auguste Robert, "Souvenirs atlantiques: Nouvelle Orléans," *La France littéraire*, 1832, 79–82; and L. Xavier Eyma, "Les Femmes du Nouveau-Monde, IV," *La Sylphide*, July 1848, 59. The vogue for periodicals containing articles about travel and foreign lands was by no means exclusively a French one in the nineteenth century. Axel Körner comments on the space devoted to such articles in Italian periodicals in *America in Italy: The United States in the Political Thought and Imagination of the Risorgimento, 1763–1865* (Princeton, NJ: Princeton University Press, 2017), 16.
30. On race in New Orleans's theaters, see Juliane Braun, "On the Verge of Fame: The Free People of Color and the French Theatre in Antebellum New Orleans," in *Liminale Anthropologien: Zwischenzeiten, Schwellenphänomene, Zwischenräume in Literatur und Philosophie*, ed. Jochen Achilles, Roland Borgards, and Brigitte Burrichter (Würzburg: Königshausen & Neumann, 2012), 166.
31. Jobey, *L'Amour d'un nègre*, 150. It is interesting to note Jobey's wording here: the "titi parisien" was associated specifically with Parisian boulevard theaters and their perceived lack of artistic and moral refinement, but here they are watching an *opéra-comique* in a theater that also produced *grand opéra*. It is not clear, however, whether Jobey's link here was meant to cast aspersions on the quality of productions at the Théâtre d'Orléans, or whether the comparison between lower-class French people and slaves was part of a wider agenda concerning the representation of race in the novel.
32. "Les secondes loges, réservées aux gens de couleur, n'avaient pu donner place qu'à la moitié de ceux qui s'étaient présentés au contrôle. Les troisièmes, enfin, contenaient toute une population de nègres et de négresses . . . le tout tassé comme des harengs." Jobey, *L'Amour d'un nègre*, 149–50.
33. ". . . Les conversations se firent à haute voix sur tous les points de la salle." Jobey, *L'Amour d'un nègre*, 150.
34. Jobey, *L'Amour d'un nègre*, 42.
35. This is not to suggest that there was any causative link between the opera and the Belgian Revolution of 1830 (much scholarship has demonstrated the complexities and coincidences involved in the relationship between grand opera and politics), but the imaginative potential of the incident remains important here. See Sonia Slatin, "Opera and Revolution: *La Muette*

de Portici and the Belgian Revolution of 1830 Revisited," *Journal of Musicological Research* 3 (1979): 45–62.

36. It was by no means uncommon for white men to have children with free women of color or enslaved women in nineteenth-century New Orleans, but the gender reversal of the couple here was seen at the time to be far less acceptable. For more on relationships between white men and free women of color, see Emily Clark, *The Strange World of the American Quadroon: Free Women of Color in the Revolutionary Atlantic World* (Chapel Hill: University of North Carolina Press, 2013).
37. Jobey, *L'Amour d'un nègre*, 246.
38. Philippe Roger, *The American Enemy: The History of French Anti-Americanism*, trans. Sharon Bowman (Chicago: University of Chicago Press, 2005), especially 157–202.
39. "Souvenirs de la Louisiane," *Journal pour tous*, March 15, 1856, and March 22, 1856. "Souvenirs de la Louisiane," *La Loge de L'Opéra*, November 15, 22, 29, 1856; December 6, 13, 20, 27, 1856; January 3, 1857. "Souvenirs de la Louisiane," *Le Villageois*, November 7, 14, 21, 1857; December 2, 9, 18, 1857; January 2, 9, 16, 1858.
40. "Catahoula" is the modern spelling; the story consistently uses "Cathahoula."
41. While "Le lac Cathahoula" has the first-person narrator more common to the personal travelogue style, *L'Amour d'un nègre* has a more novelistic third-person narrator.
42. "Un seul d'entre nous osa d'abord mêler sa voix à cette grande symphonie de la nature." Jobey, "Le lac Cathahoula," 270.
43. "Et les voûtes de la forêt vierge retentirent, pour la première et sans doute pour la dernière fois, de cette belle prière de la *Muette*, dont le chant si simple, si large, commence par un pianissimo, ressemblant au souffle de la brise, et se terminant par un énergique point d'orgue, que l'écho nous renvoya comme un tonnerre lointain." Jobey, "Le lac Cathahoula," 272.
44. Vallière and Bailly did indeed die in St. Martinville in the summer of 1839, and their deaths were reported in *L'Impartial*, October 24, 1839.
45. Bernard McGrane, *Beyond Anthropology: Society and the Other* (New York: Columbia University Press, 1989), 116. For more on travel writing's visual focus, see Giorgia Alù and Sarah Patricia Hill, "The Travelling Eye: Reading the Visual in Travel Narratives," *Studies in Travel Writing* 22/1 (2018): 1–15.
46. Alessandra Jones, "Noise and Silence in *Rigoletto*'s Venice," *Cambridge Opera Journal* 31/2–3 (2019): 188–210.
47. On musical encounters with the non-European Other, see Ruth E. Rosenberg, *Music, Travel, and Imperial Encounter in 19th-Century France*. Vanessa Agnew also explores musical encounters with other cultures (and the limits of music's potential within those encounters) in the eighteenth century in her *Enlightenment Orpheus*.
48. Roy Bridges, "Exploration and Travel outside Europe (1720–1914)," in *The Cambridge Companion to Travel Writing*, ed. Peter Hulme and Tim Youngs (Cambridge: Cambridge University Press, 2002), 53.
49. "'Voyons, mon nègre, continua Zénon, avale ce coup de tafia, et montre à l'honorable compagnie tes talents d'improvisateur.'" Jobey, "Le lac Cathahoula," 261.
50. He is in this sense a version of what Jennifer Yee calls the "elite Other," but his elite status lies in his cultural prowess rather than in noble birth. Yee, *Exotic Subversions in Nineteenth-Century French Fiction* (London: Legenda, 2008), 8.
51. Ruth E. Rosenberg examines these encounters more fully in *Music, Travel, and Imperial Encounter in 19th-Century France*, 81–83 and 94–96, respectively. It is particularly interesting to note that in both encounters, there is not just a cultural meeting with an Other, but also

an encounter with the legacy of an earlier European "*mission civilisatrice*." The comparison with Pradel evokes a similar situation in Jobey's novel.

52. Jennifer Yee uses the term "bon nègre" to signify the figure of the cultivated black (often enslaved) male, in her discussions of Victor Hugo's *Bug-Jargal* (1826); see Yee, *Exotic Subversions*, 46.

53. Slavery was finally fully abolished in the French colonies in 1848, but persisted in the United States until the end of the Civil War. For more on French literary works supporting abolition, see Tanya Lee Margaret Campbell, "Representations of Slavery in French Writing: From Revolution to Abolition" (PhD diss., Queen's University Belfast, 2009). See also *Translating Slavery: Gender and Race in French Women's Writing, 1783–1823*, ed. Doris Y. Kadish and Françoise Massardier-Kenney (Kent, OH: Kent State University Press, 1994).

54. George Washington Cable, "The Dance in Place Congo," *The Century Magazine* (February 1886): 527–28; and "An Old Creole Song," *Daily Picayune*, March 4, 1900. The song was also referenced in passing in an English-language novel from the first half of the twentieth century, *Toucoutou* (1928), by the Creole author Edward Laroque Tinker. Edward Laroque Tinker, *Toucoutou* (New York: Dodd, Mead & Co., 1928), 102.

55. George Washington Cable, "The Dance in Place Congo"; "An Old Creole Song," *Daily Picayune*, March 4, 1900.

56. For information about the history and grammar of Louisiana Creole, see *French and Creole in Louisiana*, ed. Albert Valdman (New York: Plenum, 1997).

57. In the novel by Jobey considered earlier in this chapter, *L'Amour d'un nègre*, a white Creole woman speaks Louisiana Creole with her slaves, and they at times speak with her in French.

58. *Anthologie de poésie louisianaise du XIX siècle*, ed. D. A. Kress, Margaret E. Mahoney, and Rebecca Skelton (Shreveport, LA: Éditions Tintamarre, 2010), 242.

59. This is strikingly different from the literary use of comically broken English to convey the speech of black characters—and especially enslaved black characters—in other novels from the time.

60. Cable suggests that it was adapted in various ways as "a vehicle for the white Creole's satire; for generations the man of municipal politics was fortunate who escaped entirely a lampooning set to its air." George Washington Cable, "The Dance in Place Congo," 527.

61. The bamboula is a type of dance (named after the drum that accompanies it) of African origin. It came to New Orleans via Saint-Domingue (modern-day Haiti), and enslaved people could often be seen dancing it on Sundays at the city's Congo Square in the first half of the nineteenth century.

62. For more on Europeans travelers' views of slavery in the United States, see chapter 8, "The Issue of Slavery," in Thomas K. Murphy, *A Land without Castles: The Changing Image of America in Europe, 1780–1830* (New York: Lexington Books, 2001), 185–214.

63. "Que la honte de cette monstruosité retombe sur les chrétiens du dix-neuvième siècle, qui ont l'infamie de maintenir l'esclavage!" Jobey, "Le lac Cathahoula," 215; and "Souvenirs de le Louisiane," *Journal pour tous*, March 15, 1856.

64. Jobey, "Le lac Cathahoula," 203. In referencing the Civil War and making abolitionist comments in the Parisian versions of the story, Jobey perhaps sought to capitalize on the fervent European reactions to the publication of Harriet Beecher Stowe's *Uncle Tom's Cabin* in 1852. As Axel Körner has suggested, Beecher Stowe's novel had "a more important impact on images of the United States than Tocqueville's writings . . . or even those of James Fenimore Cooper," and the details of American life expressed in her book went on to frame European discussions of the Civil War in the 1860s. Körner, *America in Italy*, 207.

65. Paul Smethurst, *Travel Writing and the Natural World, 1768–1840* (Basingstoke: Palgrave Macmillan, 2013), 2.
66. Smethurst, *Travel Writing and the Natural World,* 5.
67. "Vallière avait bien choisi son heure pour faire éprouver à la plupart d'entre nous, qui l'entendions pourtant tous les jours au théâtre, des émotions qui nous étaient inconnues jusqu'alors.—Ce n'est pas dans les salles de concert, dans les théâtres, à la lumière des lustres, ni devant des femmes parées de dentelles et des diamants qu'il faut entendre le hautbois; c'est à l'heure calme et rouge du crépuscule, au bord d'un lac, à l'ombre des bois, au milieu des retraites paisibles de la nature." Jobey, "Le lac Cathahoula," 270–71.
68. "Nous écoutions le frémissement du feuillage . . . la note plaintive du moqueur . . . la voix adoucie du chat-tigre . . . ; les plaintes sonores des caïmans, tourmentées d'ardeurs amoureuses." Jobey, "Le lac Cathahoula," 269.
69. The evocation of the diversity of the natural world and its power here is in complete contrast to disparaging French Enlightenment views of the New World and its flora and fauna as "a continuum where likeness won out over contrast, uniformity over difference," as Philippe Roger puts it. See Roger, *The American Enemy,* 4. Nonetheless, Jobey's descriptions do preserve something of the eighteenth-century characterizations Roger discusses of "poisonous America," in which the land and its creatures are portrayed as inherently dangerous. See Roger, *The American Enemy,* 14–19.
70. Ban Wang, "Inscribed Wilderness in Chateaubriand's 'Atala,'" *Romance Notes* 33/3 (1993): 279–87.
71. John W. Lowe, "Not-So-Still Waters: Travellers to Florida and the Tropical Sublime," in *The Oxford Handbook of the Literature of the U.S. South,* ed. Fred Hobson and Barbara Ladd (Oxford: Oxford University Press, 2016), 180–95.
72. Axel Körner has discussed the ways in which European views of the United States as a "blank canvas" persisted from its initial colonization into the nineteenth century. See Körner, *America in Italy,* 1–7.
73. Syrine Hout, "Viewing Europe From the Outside: Cultural Encounters and European Culture Critiques in the Eighteenth-Century Pseudo-Oriental Travelogue and the Nineteenth-Century 'Voyage en Orient'" (PhD diss., Columbia University, 1994).
74. Yee, *Exotic Subversions,* 7.
75. Didimus, *New Orleans as I Found It,* 5.
76. Didimus, *New Orleans as I Found It,* 52.
77. It is interesting to note here that Durell considers the Anglo-Americans of New Orleans to have adapted to Creole customs, in light of the stories discussed in chapter 2 surrounding the production and reception of *grand opéra* in the city, which seem to imply that the process operated exclusively in reverse: that the Creoles adopted to Anglo-American customs rather than vice versa. Didimus, *New Orleans as I Found It,* 52.
78. Didimus, *New Orleans as I Found It,* 52. He describes it as such in Didimus, "Dedication," *New Orleans as I Found It,* [no page number].
79. Didimus, *New Orleans as I Found It,* 52.
80. James Silk Buckingham, *The Slave States of America* (2 vols.; London and Paris: Fisher, Son and Co., 1842). For more on European travelers' views of slavery in America, see Murphy, *A Land without Castles,* 185–214.
81. Didimus, *New Orleans as I Found It,* 5.
82. Colonel James R. Creecy, "A Duel in New Orleans" (1829), published in *Scenes in the South and Other Miscellaneous Pieces* (Washington, DC: T. McGill, 1860), 275.

83. Didimus, *New Orleans as I Found It*, 52 and 53.
84. Didimus, *New Orleans as I Found It*, 52. Durell underestimates the distance between New Orleans and Paris here by nearly 1,800 miles.
85. Didimus, *New Orleans as I Found It*, 45–51.
86. Didimus, *New Orleans as I Found It*, 9–14.
87. Didimus, *New Orleans as I Found It*, 69–125.
88. Didimus, *New Orleans as I Found It*, 52.
89. Didimus, *New Orleans as I Found It*, 52.
90. Didimus, *New Orleans as I Found It*, 52.
91. This particular passage accounts for ten densely typed pages in the book (each page contains two columns). Although this might not seem like much, it is the longest chapter of the book, save for the multipart tale of Oceanus, the boy who travels the world, that concludes the book, and to which all the other stories lead.
92. Didimus, *New Orleans as I Found It*, 54.
93. In this, it sits a little apart from similar passages in other literature of the first half of the nineteenth century that reach aesthetic issues through the ostensible discussion of particular operatic works, such as the discussion of Rossini's *Mosè* in Balzac's short story *Massimilla Doni* (1837–1839). Here, in response to Durell's question, the old gentleman reaches straight for "opera" in its most general sense.
94. Didimus, *New Orleans as I Found It*, 54–60.
95. Here we have another portrayal of musicality in an enslaved person. In contrast to Jobey's portrayal, however, in Durell's account, the enslaved woman's performance serves only to support the creativity of the white woman that takes place in the foreground.
96. Didimus, *New Orleans as I Found It*, 54.
97. Didimus, *New Orleans as I Found It*, 60.
98. Pratt's *Imperial Eyes* is, of course, the most obvious source to mention for a discussion of travel writing's focus on the visual, but there are many other examples. See, for instance, Marguerite Helmers and Tilar Mazzeo, "Unraveling the Traveling Self," in *The Traveling and Writing Self*, ed. Marguerite Helmers and Tilar Mazzeo (Newcastle: Cambridge Scholars Publishing, 2007), 9–11.
99. Didimus, "Dedication," *New Orleans as I Found It*, [no page number].
100. Didimus, "Dedication," *New Orleans as I Found It*, [no page number].
101. Yee, *Exotic Subversions*, 18.
102. Duncan and Gregory, "Introduction," *Writes of Passage*, 5.

EPILOGUE

1. Back in September 1848, the Orleans Theatre Company had sold the building of the Théâtre d'Orléans to the Union Bank of Louisiana, following a significant financial loss in a court case. Details of the Chain of Title are recorded in the Historic New Orleans Collection's Vieux Carré Survey, accessible online at http://www.hnoc.org/vcs/property_info.php?lot=18627-01 (accessed August 23, 2021). See also John Smith Kendall, *History of New Orleans* (Chicago and New York: Lewis Publishing Co., 1922), 730.
2. For more on the history of the French Opera House, see Lyle Saxon, *Fabulous New Orleans* (New York and London: D. Appleton-Century Company, 1939), 280–83.
3. It was, therefore, substantially larger and more comfortable than the Théâtre d'Orléans, which had only three tiers, rather than four. All of this is according to Thierry Beauvert,

Opera Houses of the World (London: Thames and Hudson, 1998), 198. The information provided by Beauvert conflicts with that given by Harry Brunswick Loeb, who suggests the house had an even larger capacity, seating 2,078 people. See Loeb, "The Opera in New Orleans," *Publications of the Louisiana Historical Society* 9 (1916): 34.

4. The Théâtre d'Orléans burned to the ground on December 7, 1866. See "The Orleans Theatre Burned," *Daily Picayune*, December 7, 1866. For more on the history of the French Opera House, see Joseph Gabriel de Baroncelli, *Le Théâtre-français à la Nouvelle Orleans: essai historique* (New Orleans: Imprimerie G. Muller, 1906), 75–83.
5. The only exception to this seems to have been Laure Cinti-Damoreau, who made guest appearances in several opera performances at the Théâtre d'Orléans during her concert tour of 1844. The roles she performed in New Orleans were ones she had sung at the works' Paris premieres: La Comtesse Adèle in Rossini's *Le Comte Ory*, and Henriette and Angèle in Auber's *L'Ambassadrice* and *Le Domino noir*, respectively. These performances were billed as "représentations extraordinaires," and they appear to have been entirely exceptional in the history of the Théâtre d'Orléans; they are distinct from the performances later given by Patti at the French Opera House, in the sense that Cinti-Damoreau was not simply engaged for her star vocal qualities, but for her close links with the operas' creation in Paris.
6. Jack Belsom, "En Route to Stardom: Adelina Patti at the French Opera House, New Orleans, 1860–1861," *Opera Quarterly* 10/3 (1994): 116. Patti's stay in New Orleans has also been explored by John S. Kendall in "Patti in New Orleans," *Southwest Review* 16/4 (1931): 460–68.
7. For more on the company and star systems, see Katherine K. Preston, *Opera on the Road: Traveling Opera Troupes in the United States, 1835–60* (Urbana: University of Illinois Press, 1993). Preston signals the Théâtre d'Orléans's uniqueness in this respect in *Opera on the Road*, 32.
8. Belsom, "En Route to Stardom," 122.
9. What is more, *Il trovatore* and various other works had already been performed in the 1860–1861 season before Patti's arrival and would, therefore, still have been fresh in audiences' minds, thus making the impact of introducing a visiting star even greater.
10. Belsom, "En Route to Stardom," 123.
11. Saxon, *Fabulous New Orleans*, 282. Baroncelli also discusses the closure of the Opera House during the Civil War and the shipwreck of the *Evening Star*. See Baroncelli, *Le Théâtre-français à la Nouvelle Orleans*, 81–87.
12. Nancy L. Green, *The Limits of Transnationalism* (Chicago: University of Chicago Press, 2019).
13. Green, *The Limits of Transnationalism*, 140.
14. I discussed Bell's idea of "small spaces" in the introduction to this book. David A. Bell, "Replies to Richard Drayton and David Motadel," in Richard Drayton and David Motadel, "Discussion: The Futures of Global History," *Journal of Global History* 13 (2018): 17.
15. Didimus [pseudonym of Edward Henry Durell], *New Orleans as I Found It* (New York: Harper & Brothers, 1845), 5.

Bibliography

ARCHIVES

Archives nationales de France, Paris
Bibliothèque de l'Arsenal, Bibliothèque nationale de France, Paris
Bibliothèque musée de l'Opéra, Bibliothèque nationale de France, Paris
Hogan Jazz Archive, Tulane University, New Orleans
Louisiana Historical Center, Louisiana State Museums, New Orleans
Louisiana Research Collection, Tulane University, New Orleans
New Orleans Notarial Archives
New Orleans Public Library
Special Collections, Louisiana State University, Baton Rouge, Louisiana
Special Collections, Xavier University of Louisiana
Williams Research Center, Historic New Orleans Collection

NEWSPAPERS AND PERIODICALS CITED

New Orleans and Louisiana

L'Abeille de la Nouvelle-Orléans/The New Orleans Bee
Le Courrier de la Louisiane/The Louisiana Courier
The Daily Picayune
L'Impartial
La Loge de l'opéra/The Opera Box
La Lorgnette
The New Orleans Daily Delta
Le Villageois (Marksville)

Rest of the United States

The American Almanac and Repository of Useful Knowledge (Boston)
The Century Magazine

Paris

L'Annuaire musical: contenant les noms et adresses des amateurs, artistes et commerçants en musique de Paris, des départemens et de l'étranger, par une société de musiciens (1845)
L'Argus des théâtres
L'Élégant: journal des tailleurs
La France musicale
La France théâtrale
La Gazette des théâtres
Le Journal des beaux-arts et de la littérature
Le Ménestrel
Le Monde dramatique: revue de spectacles anciens et modernes
Le Nouvelliste
La Revue et gazette musicale
La Sylphide
La Tribune dramatique: revue théâtrale, artistique, littéraire et des modes

French Provinces

Le Journal du Havre. Commercial, Maritime et Littéraire, annonces légales et avis divers (Le Havre)

OPERA-BASED SHEET MUSIC (CALL NUMBERS LISTED WHERE AVAILABLE)

Lehmann, H. E. "Filles de Marbre Polka de Pieces d'or." New York: J. L. Peters, 1854.
———. "*Les Amours du diable*, polka." New Orleans: H. E. Lehmann, 1857. LC: M31.L4/A45 1857, *HNOC*.
———. "*Les Amours du diable*, polka mazurka." New Orleans: H. E. Lehmann, 1856. LC: M39.L45/A56 1856, *HNOC*.
———. "*Les Amours du diable*, schottische." New Orleans: H. E. Lehmann, 1857. LC: M31.L4/A4 1857, *HNOC*.
———. "Azucena du *Trovatore*." New Orleans: H. E. Lehmann, 1858. LC: M39.L45/A9 1858, *HNOC*.
———. "Le Campe Russe de *L'Etoile du Nord*, grande schottische." New Orleans: H. E. Lehmann, 1856. M31.L4 C3 1856, *HNOC*.
———. "La Couronne impériale de *L'Etoile du nord*: grande valse." New Orleans: H. E. Lehmann, 1855. 1855 "Music Collection of New Orleans Imprints," LLMVC M1 .M86 LARA, Box 5, Item 15, *SCLSU*.
———. "Les Enclumes du *Trovatore*." New Orleans: H. E. Lehmann, 1858. *LSM*.
———. "*L'Etoile du nord*, grande polka." New Orleans: H. E. Lehmann, 1855. Blackmar Sheet Music Collection, HJA/MS 017, Box 4, *HJA*.
———. "*Les Filles de marbre*, polka." New Orleans: H. E. Lehmann, 1854. LC: M31.M65/P6 1854, *HNOC*.
———. "Grande valse sur un motif favori de *La Sirène*." New Orleans: H. E. Lehmann, n.d. Lillie Gray Collection. Instrumental Selections. LLMVC M20.L55 LARA, vol. 1, *SCLSU*.
———. "Polka mazurka sur un motif favori de *Gastibelza*." New Orleans: H. E. Lehmann, n.d. M32.L45 G37 1850z, *HNOC*.

———. "*Si j'étais roi*, grande polka." New Orleans: H. E. Lehmann, 1856. LLMVC M1.M86 LARA. Box 1, Item 16, *SCLSU*.

PUBLISHED LITERATURE

Agnew, Vanessa. *Enlightenment Orpheus: The Power of Music in Other Worlds*. New York: Oxford University Press, 2008.

Ahlquist, Karen. *Democracy at the Opera: Music, Theater and Culture in New York City, 1815–60*. Urbana: University of Illinois Press, 1997.

———. "International Opera in Nineteenth-Century New York: Core Repertories and Canonic Values." In *The Oxford Handbook of the Operatic Canon*, ed. Cormac Newark and William Weber, 244–67. Oxford: Oxford University Press, 2020.

Alù, Giorgia, and Sarah Patricia Hill. "The Travelling Eye: Reading the Visual in Travel Narratives." *Studies in Travel Writing* 22/1 (2018): 1–15.

Anderson, Richard, and Henry B. Lovejoy, eds. *Liberated Africans and the Abolition of the Slave Trade, 1807–1896*. Rochester, NY: University of Rochester Press, 2020.

[Anon.] *Les Épaves par un Louisianais*. New Orleans, 1847.

[Anon.] *Eugène de Pradel dans cette ville*. Châlons, 1837.

[Anon.] *The New ball-room guide; or, Dancing made easy, comprising the etiquette of dancing, with the latest and most fashionable figures of cotillions, quadrilles, gallopades, mazourkas, polonaises, etc.* New York: Burgess and Stringer, 1844.

Arthur, Stanley. *Old New Orleans: A History of the Vieux Carré, Its Ancient and Historical Buildings* [1936]. Reprinted Westminster, MD: Heritage Books, 2007.

Aslakson, Kenneth R. *Making Race in the Courtroom: The Legal Construction of Three Races in Early New Orleans*. New York: New York University Press, 2014.

Aspden, Suzanne. *The Rival Sirens: Performance and Identity on Handel's Operatic Stage*. Cambridge: Cambridge University Press, 2013.

Bailey, Candace. "The Antebellum 'Piano Girl' in the American South." *Performance Practice Review* 13/1 (2008). Article 1: 1–44. https://doi.org/10.5642/perfpr.200813.01.01.

———. "Binder's Volumes as Musical Commonplace Books: The Transmission of Cultural Codes in the Antebellum South." *Journal of the Society for American Music* 10/4 (2016): 446–69.

———. *Music and the Southern Belle: From Accomplished Lady to Confederate Composer*. Carbondale: Southern Illinois University Press, 2010.

———. *Unbinding Gentility: Women Making Music in the Nineteenth-Century South*. Urbana-Champaign: University of Illinois Press, 2021.

Bailyn, Bernard. *Atlantic History: Concept and Contours*. Cambridge, MA: Harvard University Press, 2005.

Bara, Olivier. "The Company at the Heart of the Operatic Institution: Chollet and the Changing Nature of Comic-Opera Roles Types during the July Monarchy." In *Music, Theater and Cultural Transfer, Paris, 1830–1814*, ed. Annegret Fauser and Mark Everist, 11–28. Chicago: University of Chicago Press, 2009.

Baron, John. *Concert Life in Nineteenth-Century New Orleans: A Comprehensive Reference*. Baton Rouge: Louisiana State University Press, 2013.

———. "Vieuxtemps (and Ole Bull) in New Orleans." *American Music* 8 (1990): 210–26.

Baroncelli, Joseph Gabriel de. *Le Théâtre-français à la Nouvelle Orleans: essai historique*. New Orleans: Imprimerie G. Muller, 1906.

Bayly, Christopher. *The Birth of the Modern World: Global Connections and Comparisons, 1780–1914*. Malden, MA: Blackwell, 2004.

Beauvert, Thierry. *Opera Houses of the World*. London: Thames and Hudson, 1998.

Becker, Rachel N. "'Trash Music': Valuing Nineteenth-Century Italian Opera Fantasias for Woodwinds." PhD diss., University of Cambridge, 2018.

Belsom, Jack. "En Route to Stardom: Adelina Patti at the French Opera House, New Orleans, 1860–1861." *Opera Quarterly* 10/3 (1994): 113–30.

———. *Opera in New Orleans*. New Orleans: New Orleans Opera Association, 1993.

———. "Reception of Major Operatic Premieres in New Orleans during the Nineteenth Century." MA diss., Louisiana State University, 1972.

Bentley, Charlotte. "Between the Frontier and the French Quarter: Operatic Travel Writing and Nineteenth-Century New Orleans." In *Operatic Geographies: The Place of Opera and the Opera House*, ed. Suzanne Aspden, 105–18. Chicago: Chicago University Press, 2018.

———. "The Race for *Robert* and Other Rivalries: Negotiating the Local and (Inter)national in Nineteenth-Century New Orleans." *Cambridge Opera Journal* 29/1 (March 2017): 94–112.

———. "Resituating Transatlantic Opera: The Case of the Théâtre d'Orléans, New Orleans, 1819–1859." PhD diss., University of Cambridge, 2017.

———. "Southern Exchanges: Italian Opera in New Orleans, 1836–1842." In *Italian Opera in Global and Transnational Perspective: Reimagining Italianità in the Long Nineteenth Century*, ed. Axel Körner and Paulo Kühl, 113–32. Cambridge: Cambridge University Press, 2022.

Bérard, Stéphanie. *Théâtres des Antilles: traditions et scènes contemporaines*. Paris: Harmattan, 2009.

Bhabha, Homi. *The Location of Culture*. London: Routledge, 1994.

Binder, Wolfgang, ed. *Creoles and Cajuns: French Louisiana (La Louisiane française)*. Frankfurt am Main and New York: Peter Lang, 1998.

"Biographical Directory of Federal Judges: Durell, Edward Henry." History of Federal Judiciary, Federal Judicial Center, n.d. Accessed August 2, 2021, https://www.fjc.gov/history/judges/durell-edward-henry.

Bishop, John. "'They Manage Things Better in France': French Plays and English Critics, 1850–1855." *Nineteenth-Century Theatre* 22/1 (1994): 5–29.

Blumenthal, Henry. *American and French Culture, 1800–1900: Interchanges in Art, Science, Literature, and Society*. Baton Rouge: Louisiana State University Press, 1975.

Boelhower, William, ed. *New Orleans in the Atlantic World: Between Land and Sea*. London and New York: Routledge, 2010.

Borm, Jan. "Defining Travel: On the Travel Book, Travel Writing and Terminology." In *Perspectives on Travel Writing*, ed. Glenn Hooper and Tim Youngs, 13–26. London: Routledge, 2004.

Boudreaux, Peggy C. "Music Publishing in New Orleans in the Nineteenth Century." MA diss., Louisiana State University, 1977.

Brady, Patricia. "Free Black Artists in Antebellum New Orleans." In *KnowLA Encyclopedia of Louisiana*, ed. David Johnson. Louisiana Endowment for the Humanities, April 28, 2011. Accessed October 8, 2021, http://www.knowlouisiana.org/entry/free-black-artists-in-antebellum-new-orleans.

Brasseaux, Carl A. *The Foreign French: Nineteenth-Century French Immigration into Louisiana, Volume 1: 1820–1839, Volume 2: 1840–1848, and Volume 3: 1849–1852*. Lafayette: Center for Louisiana Studies, University of Southwestern Louisiana, 1990.

———. *French, Cajun, Creole, Houma: A Primer on Francophone Louisiana*. Baton Rouge: Louisiana State University Press, 2005.

Brasseaux, Carl A., and Glenn R. Conrad, eds. *The Road to Louisiana: The Saint-Domingue Ref-*

ugees, 1792–1809. Lafayette: Center for Louisiana Studies, University of Southwestern Louisiana, 1992.

Braun, Juliane. *Creole Drama: Theater and Society in Antebellum New Orleans*. Charlottesville: University of Virginia Press, 2019.

———. "On the Verge of Fame: The Free People of Color and the French Theatre in Antebellum New Orleans." In *Liminale Anthropologien: Zwischenzeiten, Schwellenphänomene, Zwischenräume in Literatur und Philosophie*, ed. Jochen Achilles, Roland Borgards, and Brigitte Burrichter, 161–82. Würzburg: Königshausen & Neumann, 2012.

———. "Petit Paris en Amérique? French Theatrical Culture in Nineteenth-Century Louisiana." PhD diss., Julius-Maximilians-Universität Würzburg, 2013.

Bridges, Roy. "Exploration and Travel outside Europe (1720–1914)." In *The Cambridge Companion to Travel Writing*, ed. Peter Hulme and Tim Youngs, 53–69. Cambridge: Cambridge University Press, 2002.

Brink, Florence Roos. "Literary Travellers in Louisiana Between 1803 and 1860." *Louisiana Historical Quarterly* 31/2 (1949): 394–424.

Buckingham, James Silk. *The Slave States of America*. 2 vols. London and Paris: Fisher, Son and Co., 1842.

Budasz, Rogério. "Music, Authority, and Civilisation in Rio de Janeiro, 1763–1790." In *Music and Urban Society in Colonial Latin America*, ed. Geoffrey Baker and Tess Knighton, 151–70. Cambridge: Cambridge University Press, 2011.

———. *Opera in the Tropics: Music and Theater in Early Modern Brazil*. Oxford: Oxford University Press, 2019.

Bulmer-Thomas, Victor. *The Economic History of the Caribbean Since the Napoleonic Wars*. Cambridge: Cambridge University Press, 2012.

Burton, Antoinette. *Archive Stories: Facts, Fictions, and the Writing of History*. Durham, NC: Duke University Press, 2005.

Campanella, Richard. *Time and Place in New Orleans: Past Geographies in the Present Day*. Gretna, LA: Pelican Publishing, 2002.

Campbell, Tanya Lee Margaret. "Representations of Slavery in French Writing: From Revolution to Abolition." PhD diss., Queen's University Belfast, 2009.

Carriere, Marius M. Jr. *The Know Nothings in Louisiana*. Jackson: University Press of Mississippi, 2018.

Chaudenson, Robert. *Creolization of Language and Culture*. London: Routledge, 2001.

Chevalley, Sylvie. "Le Théâtre d'Orléans en Tournée dans les Villes du Nord 1827–1833." *Comptes-rendues de L'Athénée louisianais* (March 1955): 27–71.

Chew, William L. III, ed. *National Stereotypes in Perspective: Americans in France, Frenchmen in America*. Amsterdam: Rodopi, 2001.

Chmaj, Betty E. "Fry versus Dwight: American Music's Debate over Nationality." *American Music* 3/1 (1985): 63–84.

Christensen, Thomas. "Four-Hand Piano Transcription and Geographies of Nineteenth-Century Musical Reception." *Journal of the American Musicological Society* 52/2 (1999): 255–98.

———. "Public Music in Private Spaces: Piano Vocal Scores and the Domestication of Opera." In *Music and the Cultures of Print*, ed. Kate van Orden, 67–95. New York and London: Garland Publishing Inc., 2000.

Clark, Emily. *Masterless Mistresses: The New Orleans Ursulines and the Development of a New World Society, 1727 to 1834*. Chapel Hill: University of North Carolina Press, 2007.

———. *The Strange History of the American Quadroon: Free Women of Color in the Revolutionary Atlantic World*. Chapel Hill: University of North Carolina Press, 2013.

Clark, Maribeth. "The Quadrille as Embodied Musical Experience in 19th-Century Paris." *Journal of Musicology* 19/3 (2002): 503–26.

———. "Understanding French Grand Opera through Dance." PhD diss., University of Pennsylvania, 1998.

Clay, Lauren R. "Patronage, Profits, and Public Theaters: Re-Thinking Cultural Unification in Ancien-Régime France." *Journal of Modern History* 79/4 (2007): 729–71.

———. "Provincial Actors, the Comédie-Française, and the Business of Performing in Eighteenth-Century France." *Eighteenth-Century Studies* 33/4 (2005): 651–79.

———. *Stagestruck: The Business of Theater in Eighteenth-Century France and Its Colonies*. Ithaca, NY: Cornell University Press, 2013.

———. "Theater and the Commercialization of Culture in Eighteenth-Century France." PhD diss., University of Pennsylvania, 2003.

Cloutier, Eleanor. "Repetitive Novelty: Italian Opera in Paris and London in the 1830s and 1840s." PhD diss., University of California, Berkeley, 2016.

———. "Ways to Possess a Singer in 1830s London." *Cambridge Opera Journal* 29/2 (2018): 189–214.

Coleman, William H. *Historical Sketch Book and Guide to New Orleans and Environs*. New York, 1885.

Cowgill, Rachel. "Mozart Productions and the Emergence of Werktreue at London's Italian Opera House, 1780–1830." In *Operatic Migrations: Transforming Works and Crossing Boundaries*, ed. Roberta Montemorra Marvin and Downing A. Thomas, 145–86. Aldershot: Ashgate, 2006.

Craiutu, Aurelian, and Jeffrey C. Isaac. *America through European Eyes: British and French Reflections on the New World from the Eighteenth Century to the Present*. University Park: Pennsylvania State University Press, 2009.

Cramer, Lloyd S. *Nationalism in Europe and America: Politics, Cultures and Identities since 1775*. Chapel Hill: University of North Carolina Press, 2011.

Crawford, Richard, et al. "United States of America." *Grove Music Online. Oxford Music Online*. Oxford University Press. Accessed August 4, 2017, http://www.oxfordmusiconline.com/subscriber/article/grove/music/28794pg1.

Creecy, Colonel James R. *Scenes in the South and Other Miscellaneous Pieces*. Washington, DC: T. McGill, 1860.

Daggett, Melissa. "Eliza Ripley." *64 Parishes*. Accessed March 30, 2021, https://64parishes.org/entry/eliza-ripley.

Dahlhaus, Carl. *Nineteenth-Century Music*, trans. J. Bradford Robinson. Berkeley: University of California Press, 1989.

Davies, James Q. "Julia's Gift: The Social Life of Scores, c. 1830." *Journal of the Royal Musical Association* 131/2 (2006): 287–309.

Davis, Ronald L. *A History of Music in American Life, Volume 1: The Formative Years, 1620–1865*. Malabar, FL: Robert Krieger Publishing Company, 1982.

———. *A History of Opera in the American West*. Upper Saddle River, NJ: Prentice-Hall, 1965.

Davis, Tracy C. *The Economics of the British Stage, 1800–1914*. Cambridge: Cambridge University Press, 2000.

Delanty, Gerard. "Introduction." In *Routledge Companion to Cosmopolitanism Studies*, ed. Gerard Delanty, 1–8. London: Routledge, 2012.

DeMetz, Kaye. "Theatrical Dancing in Nineteenth-Century New Orleans." *Louisiana History: The Journal of the Louisiana Historical Association* 21/1 (1980): 23–42.

Detcheverry, Arnaud. *Histoire des Théâtres de Bordeaux*. Bordeaux: Imprimerie typographique de J. Delmas, 1860.

Dewey, John. *The Public and Its Problems: An Essay in Political Inquiry*. New York: Holt, 1927.

Didimus [pseudonym of Edward Henry Durell]. *New Orleans as I Found It*. New York: Harper & Brothers, 1845.

Dizikes, John. *Opera in America: A Cultural History*. New Haven, CT: Yale University Press, 1993.

Domínguez, Virginia R. *White by Definition: Social Classification in Creole Louisiana*. New Brunswick, NJ: Rutgers University Press, 1986.

Drayton, Richard, and David Motadel. "Discussion: The Futures of Global History." *Journal of Global History* 13 (2018): 1–21.

Duara, Prasenjit. *Rescuing History from the Nation: Questioning Narratives of Modern China*. Chicago: University of Chicago Press, 1995.

Duncan, James, and Derek Gregory, eds. *Writes of Passage: Reading Travel Writing*. London and New York: Routledge, 2002.

Dunglison, Robley. *The American Medical Intelligencer*. Vol. 4. Philadelphia: A. Waldie, 1841.

Duplantier, Jean-Marc Allard. "'Nos frères d'outre-golfe': Spiritualism, Vodou and the Mimetic Literatures of Haiti and Louisiana." PhD diss., Louisiana State University, 2006.

Dupont, Nancy McKenzie. "'Lawless Louisiana': New Orleans Newspapers, Race, and the Battle of Liberty Place." In *Sensationalism: Murder, Mayhem, Mudslinging, Scandals, and Disasters in 19th-Century Reporting*, ed. David B. Sachsman and David W. Bulla, 339–56. New Brunswick, NJ: Transaction Publishers, 2013.

Ellis, Katharine. "Female Pianists and Their Male Critics in Nineteenth-Century Paris," *Journal of the American Musicological Society* 50/2–3 (1997): 353–85.

———. "Funding Opera in Regional France: Ideologies of the Mid-Nineteenth Century." In *Art and Ideology in European Opera: Essays in Honour of Julian Rushton*, ed. Rachel Cowgill, David Cooper, and Clive Brown, 67–84. Woodbridge: Boydell and Brewer, 2010.

———. "Gautier, Théophile." *Grove Music Online, Oxford Music Online*. Accessed June 12, 2020, https://www.oxfordmusiconline.com/grovemusic/view/10.1093/gmo/9781561592630.001.0001/omo-9781561592630-e-0000010760.

———. *Music Criticism in Nineteenth-Century France: La Revue et gazette musicale de Paris, 1834–1880*. Cambridge: Cambridge University Press, 1995.

———. "Opera Criticism and the Paris Periodical Press." *Revue Belge de Musicologie* 66 (2012): 127–31.

———. "Researching Audience Behaviors in Nineteenth-Century Paris: Who Cares if You Listen?" In *The Oxford Handbook of Music Listening in the 19th and 20th Centuries*, ed. Christian Thorau and Hansjakob Ziemer, 37–50. Oxford: Oxford University Press, 2019.

Everist, Mark. *Mozart's Ghosts: Haunting the Halls of Musical Culture*. Oxford: Oxford University Press, 2012.

———. *Music Drama at the Paris Odéon, 1824–1828*. Berkeley: University of California Press, 2002.

Fairburn, Miles. *Social History: Problems, Strategies, and Methods*. Basingstoke: Macmillan, 1999.

Faucon, T. *Le nouvel Opéra: monument, artistes*. Paris: Michel Lévy Frères, 1875.

Faul, Michel. *Louis Jullien: musique, spectacle et folie au XIXe siècle*. Biarritz: Atlantica, 2006.

Fauser, Annegret, and Mark Everist, eds. *Music, Theater, and Cultural Transfer: Paris, 1830–1914*. Chicago: University of Chicago Press, 2009.

Faust, Drew Gilpin. *A Sacred Circle: The Dilemma of the Intellectual in the Old South, 1840–60*. Baltimore: Johns Hopkins University Press, 1977.

Fernandez, Mark F. *From Chaos to Continuity: The Evolution of Louisiana's Judicial System, 1712–1862*. Baton Rouge: Louisiana State University Press, 2001.

Fertel, Rien. *Imagining the Creole City: The Rise of Literary Culture in Nineteenth-Century New Orleans*. Baton Rouge: Louisiana State University Press, 2014.

Fick, Carolyn E. *The Making of Haiti: The Saint Domingue Revolution from Below*. Knoxville: University of Tennessee Press, 1990.

Figes, Orlando. *The Europeans: Three Lives and the Making of a Cosmopolitan Culture*. London: Penguin, 2019.

Forbes, Elizabeth. "Lind, Jenny." *Grove Music Online. Oxford Music Online*. Oxford University Press. Accessed January 5, 2015, http://www.oxfordmusiconline.com/subscriber/article/grove/music/16676.

———. "Montreal (opera)." *Grove Music Online, Oxford Music Online*, Oxford University Press. Accessed March 13, 2021, https://www.oxfordmusiconline.com/grovemusic/view/10.1093/gmo/9781561592630.001.0001/omo-9781561592630-e-5000007373.

Fossier, A. E. *New Orleans: The Glamour Period, 1800–1840*. New Orleans: Pelican Publishing, 1957.

Foster, Daniel H. "Sheet Music Iconography and Music in the History of Transatlantic Minstrelsy." *Modern Language Quarterly* 70/1 (2009): 147–61.

Foucault, Martin. *Les Seigneurs de Laval*. Paris: E. Jamin, 1875.

Fouchard, Jean. *Artistes et répertoire des scènes de Saint-Domingue*. Port-au-Prince, Haiti: H. Deschamps, 1988.

———. *Le Théâtre à Saint-Domingue*. Port-au-Prince, Haiti: H. Deschamps, 1988.

Fuchs, Sarah. "The Castrato as Creator: Velluti's Voice in the London Sheet-Music Market." In *London Voices, 1820–1840: Vocal Performers, Practices, Histories*, ed. Roger Parker and Susan Rutherford, 71–92. Chicago: University of Chicago Press, 2019.

Fuentes, Marisa J. *Dispossessed Lives: Enslaved Women, Violence, and the Archive*. Philadelphia: University of Pennsylvania Press, 2016.

Fuhrmann, Christina. *Foreign Opera at the London Playhouses: From Mozart to Bellini*. Cambridge: Cambridge University Press, 2015.

Fyfe, Aileen. *Steam-Powered Knowledge: William Chambers and the Business of Publishing, 1820–1860*. Chicago and London: University of Chicago Press, 2012.

Gafford, Lucile. "A History of the St. Charles Theatre in New Orleans, 1835–43." PhD diss., University of Chicago, 1930.

Galignani, A. and W. *New Paris Guide*. Paris: A. and W. Galignani and Company, 1841.

Gallo, Denise. "Selling 'Celebrity': The Role of the Dedication in Marketing Piano Arrangements of Rossini's Military Marches." In *The Idea of Art Music in a Commercial World, 1800–1930*, ed. Christina Bashford and Roberta Montemorra Marvin, 18–38. Woodbridge: Boydell Press, 2016.

Garud, Raghu, Cynthia Hardy, and Steve Maguire. "Institutional Entrepreneurship as Embedded Agency: An Introduction to the Special Issue." *Organization Studies* 28/7 (2007): 957–69.

Gayarré, Charles. *Histoire de la Louisiane*. New Orleans, 1846.

Ghobrial, John-Paul. "Moving Stories and What They Tell Us: Early Modern Mobility Between Microhistory and Global History." *Global History and Microhistory: A Supplement Volume of Past and Present*, ed. John-Paul Ghobrial, *Past & Present Supplement* 14 (2019): 243–80.

———. "Seeing the World like a Microhistorian." In *Global History and Microhistory: A Supplement Volume of Past and Present*, ed. John-Paul Ghobrial, *Past & Present Supplement* 14 (2019): 1–22.

Gibbons, William. *Building the Operatic Museum: Eighteenth-Century Opera in Fin-de-Siècle Paris*. Rochester, NY: Rochester University Press, 2013.

Gienow-Hecht, Jessica C. E. *Sound Diplomacy: Music and Emotions in Transatlantic Relations, 1850–1920*. Chicago and London: University of Chicago Press, 2009.

Gitlin, Jay. *The Bourgeois Frontier: French Towns, French Traders, and American Expansion*. New Haven, CT: Yale University Press, 2010.

Glixon, Beth L., and Jonathan E. Glixon. *Inventing the Business of Opera: The Impresario and His World in Seventeenth-Century Venice*. Oxford: Oxford University Press, 2006.

Goldstein, Robert Justin, ed. *The Frightful Stage: Political Censorship of the Theatre in Nineteenth-Century Europe*. New York and Oxford: Berghahn Books, 2009.

Goodman, Glenda. "Transatlantic Music Studies." In *Oxford Handbooks Online*, Oxford University Press (2015). Accessed March 12, 2021, https://doi.org/10.1093/oxfordhb/9780199935321.013.79.

Gooley, Dana, et al. "Cosmopolitanism in the Age of Nationalism, 1848–1918." *Journal of the American Musicological Society* 66/2 (2013): 523–49.

Gottschalk, Louis Moreau. *Notes of a Pianist*, ed. Jeanne Behrend. New York: A. A. Knopf, 1964.

Goubault, Christian. "La Décentralisation de l'art lyrique à Rouen (1830–1900)." In *Regards sur l'opéra: du* Ballet comique de la reine *à l'opéra de Pékin*, [no editor listed], 47–88. Paris: Presses universitaires de France, 1976.

Gramit, David. "The Transnational History of Settler Colonialism and the Music of the Urban West: Resituating a Local Music History." *American Music* 32/3 (2014): 272–91.

Green, Nancy L. *The Limits of Transnationalism*. Chicago: University of Chicago Press, 2019.

Griffith, Connie G. "Collections in the Manuscript Sections of Howard-Tilton Memorial Library, Tulane University." *Louisiana History: The Journal of the Louisiana Historical Association* 1/4 (1960): 320–27.

Grima, Edgar. "Municipal Support of Theatres and Operas in New Orleans." *Publications of the Louisiana Historical Society* 9 (1916): 43–45.

Habermas, Jürgen. *The Structural Transformation of the Public Sphere*, trans. Thomas Burger, with the assistance of Frederick Lawrence. Cambridge: Polity Press, 1989.

Hambrick, Keith S. "The Swedish Nightingale in New Orleans: Jenny Lind's Visit of 1851." *Louisiana History: The Journal of the Louisiana Historical Association* 22/4 (1981): 387–417.

Hanger, Kimberley S. "Patronage, Property, and Persistence: The Emergence of a Free Black Elite in Spanish New Orleans." In *Against the Odds: Free Blacks in the Slave Societies of the Americas*, ed. Jane G. Landers, 44–64. London: Frank Cass, 1996.

Head, Matthew. "'If the Pretty Little Hand Won't Stretch': Music for the Fair Sex in Eighteenth-Century Germany." *Journal of the American Musicological Society* 52/2 (1999): 203–54.

Helmers, Marguerite, and Tilar Mazzeo, eds. *The Traveling and Writing Self*. Newcastle: Cambridge Scholars Publishing, 2007.

Hemmings, Frederic William John. "Child Actors on the Paris Stage in the Eighteenth and Nineteenth Centuries." *Theatre Research International* 12/1 (1987): 9–22.

———. *The Theatre Industry in Nineteenth-Century France*. Cambridge: Cambridge University Press, 1993.

Henze-Döhring, Sabine, ed. *Giacomo Meyerbeer: Briefwechsel und Tagebücher*, 8 vols. (vols. 1–4 ed. Heinz Becker, vols. 5–8 ed. Sabine Henze-Döhring), vol. 5 and vol. 6. Berlin: De Gruyter, 1998 and 2002.

Hesselager, Jens. *Grand Opera Outside Paris: Opera on the Move in Nineteenth-Century Europe*. London: Routledge, 2018.

Hibberd, Sarah. *French Grand Opera and the Historical Imagination*. Cambridge: Cambridge University Press, 2009.

———. "Grand Opera in Britain and the Americas." In *The Cambridge Companion to Grand Opera*, ed. David Charlton, 403–22. Cambridge: Cambridge University Press, 2003.

Hickey, Maclyn le Bourgeois. "Louis Develle." In *KnowLA Encyclopedia of Louisiana*, ed. David Johnson. Louisiana Endowment for the Humanities, December 10, 2013. Accessed October 8, 2016, http://www.knowlouisiana.org/entry/louis-develle.

Hirsch, Arnold R., and Joseph Logsdon, eds. *Creole New Orleans: Race and Americanization*. Baton Rouge: Louisiana State University Press, 1992.

Holland, Patrick, and Graham Huggan. *Tourists with Typewriters: Critical Reflections on Contemporary Travel Writing*. Ann Arbor: University of Michigan Press, 1998.

Hopkins, Antony G., ed. *Globalisation in World History*. London: Pimlico, 2002.

Hostetler, Paul S. "'Elsslermania' in New Orleans." *Theatre Survey* 10/2 (1969): 121–35.

———. "James Caldwell: Theatre Manager." PhD diss., Louisiana State University, 1964.

Hout, Syrine. "Viewing Europe from the Outside: Cultural Encounters and European Culture Critiques in the Eighteenth-Century Pseudo-Oriental Travelogue and the Nineteenth-Century 'Voyage en Orient.'" PhD diss., Columbia University, 1994.

Huebner, Steven. "L'Etoile du Nord," *The New Grove Dictionary of Opera, Grove Music Online, Oxford Music Online*, Oxford University Press. Accessed September 18, 2017, http://www.oxfordmusiconline.com/subscriber/article/grove/music/O002263.

———. "Opera Audiences in Paris, 1830–1870." *Music & Letters* 70/2 (1989): 206–25.

Hugill, Peter J. *World Trade Since 1431: Geography, Technology, and Capitalism*. Baltimore and London: Johns Hopkins University Press, 1993.

Hulme, Peter, and Tim Youngs, eds. *Cambridge Companion to Travel Writing*. Cambridge: Cambridge University Press, 2002.

Izquierdo König, José Manuel. "Rossini's Reception in Latin America: Scarcity and Imagination in Two Early Chilean Sources." In *Gioachino Rossini 1868–2018: La musica e il mondo*, ed. Ilaria Narici, Emilio Sala, Emanuele Senici, and Benjamin Walton, 413–35. Pesaro: Fondazione Rossini Pesaro, 2018.

Jewell, Edwin L., ed. *The Crescent City Illustrated: The Commercial, Social, Political, and General History of New Orleans*. New Orleans: [no publisher information listed], 1873.

Jobey, Charles. *L'Amour d'une blanche: conte américain*. Paris: E. Jung-Treuttel, 1861.

———. *L'Amour d'un nègre*. Paris: Michel Lèvy Frères, 1860.

Johnson, James H. *Listening in Paris: A Cultural History*. Berkeley: University of California Press, 1995.

Johnson, Jerah. "La Coutume de Paris: Louisiana's First Law." *Louisiana History: The Journal of the Louisiana Historical Association* 30/2 (1989): 145–55.

Johnson, Rashauna. "'Laissez les bons temps rouler!' and Other Concealments: Households, Taverns and Irregular Intimacies in Antebellum New Orleans." In *Interconnections: Gender and Race in American History*, ed. Carol Faulkner and Alison M. Parker, 51–74. Rochester, NY: University of Rochester Press, 2012.

———. *Slavery's Metropolis: Unfree Labor in New Orleans During the Age of Revolutions*. Cambridge: Cambridge University Press, 2016.

Jones, Alessandra. "Noise and Silence in *Rigoletto*'s Venice." *Cambridge Opera Journal* 31/2–3 (2019): 188–210.

Jones, Catherine. *Literature and Music in the Atlantic World, 1767–1867*. Edinburgh: Edinburgh University Press, 2014.

Jones, Howard Mumford. *America and French Culture, 1750–1848*. Chapel Hill: University of North Carolina Press, 1927.

Joyce, John. "Boudousquié, Charles." *The New Grove Dictionary of Opera. Grove Music On-*

line. Oxford Music Online, Oxford University Press. Accessed January 5, 2015, http://www.oxfordmusiconline.com/subscriber/article/grove/music/O900809.

Joyce, John, and Katherine K. Preston. "Davis, John." *The New Grove Dictionary of Opera. Grove Music Online. Oxford Music Online*, Oxford University Press. Accessed January 13, 2015, http://www.oxfordmusiconline.com/subscriber/article/grove/music/O002516.

Joyce, John, et al. "New Orleans." *Grove Music Online. Oxford Music Online*, Oxford University Press. Accessed October 15, 2014, http://www.oxfordmusiconline.com/subscriber/article/grove/music/42080.

Jumonville, Florence M. *Bibliography of New Orleans Imprints, 1764–1864*. New Orleans: Historic New Orleans Collection, 1989.

———. "Set to Music: The Engravers, Artists, and Lithographers of New Orleans Sheet Music." *Proceedings of the American Antiquarian Society* (1995): 127–44.

Kadish, Doris Y., and Françoise Massardier-Kenney, eds. *Translating Slavery: Gender and Race in French Women's Writing, 1783–1823*. Kent, OH, and London: Kent State University Press, 1994.

Kelley, Laura D. *The Irish in New Orleans*. Lafayette: University of Louisiana at Lafayette Press, 2014.

Kelly, Thomas Forrest. *First Nights at the Opera*. New Haven, CT: Yale University Press, 2004.

Kendall, John Smith. *The Golden Age of the New Orleans Theater*. Baton Rouge: Louisiana State University Press, 1952.

———. *History of New Orleans*. 3 vols. Chicago and New York: Lewis Publishing Co., 1922.

———. "New Orleans' Musicians of Long Ago." *Louisiana Historical Quarterly* 31/1 (1948): 130–49.

———. "Patti in New Orleans." *Southwest Review* 16/4 (1931): 460–68.

Kimball, Warren K. "Northern Music Culture in Antebellum New Orleans." PhD diss., Louisiana State University, 2017.

King, Grace. *Creole Families of New Orleans*. New York: Macmillan, 1921.

———. *Memories of a Southern Woman of Letters*. New York: Macmillan Co., 1932.

Kmen, Henry. *Music in New Orleans: The Formative Years, 1791–1841*. Baton Rouge: Louisiana State University Press, 1966.

———. "Singing and Dancing: A Social History of Music in New Orleans, 1791–1841." PhD diss., Tulane University, 1961.

Körner, Axel. *America in Italy: The United States in the Political Thought and Imagination of the Risorgimento, 1763–1865*. Princeton, NJ: Princeton University Press, 2017.

———. "Beyond Nationaloper. For a Critique of Methodological Nationalism in Reading Nineteenth-Century Italian and German Opera." *Journal of Modern Italian Studies* 25/4 (2020): 402–19.

———. "Dalla storia transnazionale all'opera transnazionale. Per una critica delle categorie nazionali." *Saggiatore Musicale* 24/1 (2017): 81–98.

Körner, Axel, and Paulo Kühl. "Opera and Italianità in Transnational and Global Perspective: An Introduction." In *Italian Opera in Global and Transnational Perspective: Reimagining Italianità in the Long Nineteenth Century*, ed. Axel Körner and Paulo Kühl, 1–40. Cambridge: Cambridge University Press, 2021.

Körner, Axel, Nicola Miller, and Adam I. P. Smith, eds. *America Imagined: Explaining the United States in Nineteenth-Century Europe and Latin America*. New York: Palgrave Macmillan, 2012.

Korte, Barbara. *English Travel Writing from Pilgrimages to Postcolonial Explorations*. London: Palgrave Macmillan, 2000.

Koza, Julia Ecklund. "Music and the Feminine Sphere: Images of Women as Musicians in 'Godey's Lady's Book,' 1830–1877." *Musical Quarterly* 75/2 (1991): 103–29.

———. "Music Instruction in the Nineteenth Century: Views from 'Godey's Lady's Book,' 1830–77," *Journal of Research in Music Education* 38/4 (Winter 1990): 245–57.

Kramer, Lloyd S. *Nationalism in Europe and America: Politics, Cultures and Identities since 1775*. Chapel Hill: University of North Carolina Press, 2011.

Kress, D. A., Margaret E. Mahoney, and Rebecca Skelton. *Anthologie de poésie louisianaise du XIX siècle*. Shreveport, LA: Éditions Tintamarre, 2010.

Kutsch, Karl-Josef, and Leo Riemens. *Großes Sängerlexikon*, vol. 4. Bern: Francke, 1987.

Labbé, Dolores Egger, ed. *The Louisiana Purchase and its Aftermath, 1800–1830*. Lafayette: Center for Louisiana Studies, University of Southwestern Louisiana, 1998.

Lachance, Paul F. "The Foreign French." In *Creole New Orleans: Race and Americanization*, ed. Arnold R. Hirsch and Joseph Logsdon, 101–30. Baton Rouge: Louisiana State University Press, 1992.

———. "The Limits of Privilege: Where Free People of Colour Stood in the Hierarchy of Wealth in Antebellum New Orleans." In *Against the Odds: Free Blacks in the Slave Societies of the Americas*, ed. Jane G. Landers, 65–85. London: Frank Cass, 1996.

Lacombe, Hervé. *The Keys to French Opera in the Nineteenth-Century*, trans. Edward Schneider. Berkeley: University of California Press, 2001.

Lafargue, André. "Opera in New Orleans in Days of Yore." *Louisiana Historical Quarterly* 29 (1946): 660–78.

Laget, Auguste. *Le Chant et les Chanteurs*. Paris, 1874.

———. *Le Monde Artiste*. Paris: Heugel, 1883.

Lahee, Henry. *Grand Opera in America*. Boston: L. C. Page, 1902.

Lane, Charles. "Edward Henry Durell: A Study in Reputation." *The Green Bag* 13/2 (2010): 153–68.

Lawrence, Vera Brodsky. *Strong on Music: The New York Music Scene in the Days of George Templeton Strong*. 3 vols. Chicago and London: University of Chicago Press, 1988, 1995, 1999.

Leary-Warsaw, Jacqueline J. "Nineteenth-Century French Art Song of New Orleans: A Repertoire Study." PhD diss., Peabody Institute of the Johns Hopkins University, 2000.

Lebègue, Raymond. "Le Problème du voyage de Chateaubriand en Amérique." *Journal des Savants* 1/1 (1965): 456–65.

Le Gardeur, Réné Jr. "Les Premières Années du Théâtre à la Nouvelle-Orléans." *Comptes-rendues de L'Athénée louisianais* (1954): 33–73.

LeMay, Michael C. *Transforming America: Perspectives on U.S. Immigration, Volume 1—The Making of a Nation of Nations: The Founding to 1865*. Santa Barbara, CA: Praeger, 2013.

Lemmon, Alfred E. "Introduction to Part V." In *Cross, Crozier, and Crucible: A Volume Celebrating the Bicentennial of a Catholic Diocese in Louisiana*, ed. Glenn R. Conrad, 458–63. New Orleans: Archdiocese of New Orleans in cooperation with the Center for Louisiana Studies, 1993.

Lepler, Jessica M. *The Many Panics of 1837: People, Politics, and the Creation of a Transatlantic Financial Crisis*. Cambridge: Cambridge University Press, 2013.

Letellier, Robert Ignatius, ed. *The Diaries of Giacomo Meyerbeer, Volume 2: 1840–49*. London: Associated University Presses, 2001.

———. *Meyerbeer's* Les Huguenots*: An Evangel of Religion and Love*. Newcastle: Cambridge Scholars Publishing, 2014.

Levine, Lawrence W. *Highbrow/Lowbrow: The Emergence of a Cultural Hierarchy in America*. Cambridge, MA: Harvard University Press, 1988.

Levy, Lester S. *Grace Notes in American History: Popular Sheet Music from 1820 to 1900*. Norman: University of Oklahoma Press, 1967.

Lewis, Peirce F. *New Orleans: The Making of an Urban Landscape.* 2nd ed. Santa Fe, NM, and Harrisonburg, VA: Center for American Places Inc., 2003.

Lhamon, W. T. Jr. *Jump Jim Crow: Lost Plays, Lyrics, and Street Prose of the First Atlantic Popular Culture.* Cambridge, MA: Harvard University Press, 2003.

Livingstone, Sonia. "On the Relation between Audiences and Publics." In *Audiences and Publics: When Cultural Engagement Matters for the Public Sphere*, ed. Sonia Livingstone, 17–41. Bristol: Intellect Books, 2005.

Loeb, Harry Brunswick. "The Opera in New Orleans." *Publications of the Louisiana Historical Society* 9 (1916): 29–41.

Loesser, Alfred. *Men, Women and Pianos: A Social History.* London: Victor Gollancz, 1955.

Loewenberg, Alfred. *Annals of Opera, 1597–1940.* 3rd ed. London: John Calder, 1978.

Loggins, Vernon. *Where the World Ends: The Life of Louis Moreau Gottschalk.* Baton Rouge: Louisiana State University Press, 1958.

Logsdon, Joseph, and Caryn Cossé Bell. "The Americanization of Black New Orleans, 1850–1900." In *Creole New Orleans: Race and Americanization*, ed. Arnold R. Hirsch and Joseph Logsdon, 201–61. Baton Rouge: Louisiana State University Press, 1992.

Londré, Felicia Hardison, and Daniel J. Watermeier. *History of the North American Theater: The United States, Canada and Mexico—From Pre-Columbian Times to the Present.* New York: Continuum, 1998.

Lowe, John W. "Not-So-Still Waters: Travellers to Florida and the Tropical Sublime." In *The Oxford Handbook of the Literature of the U.S. South*, ed. Fred Hobson and Barbara Ladd, 180–95. Oxford and New York: Oxford University Press, 2016.

Lowe, Lisa. *The Intimacies of Four Continents.* Durham, NC: Duke University Press, 2015.

Mahar, William J. *Behind the Burnt Cork Mask: Early Blackface Minstrelsy and Antebellum American Popular Culture.* Champaign: University of Illinois Press, 1998.

Maretzek, Max. *Crotchets and Quavers: Or Revelations of an Opera Manager in America.* New York, 1855.

Marigny, Bernard. *Mémoire de Bernard Marigny, habitant de la Louisiane: addréssée à ses concitoyens.* Paris, 1822.

Marino, Samuel J. "Early French-Language Newspapers in New Orleans." *Louisiana History: The Journal of the Louisiana Historical Association* 7/4 (1966): 309–21.

Marsh, Kate, and Nicola Frith, eds. *France's Lost Empires: Fragmentation, Nostalgia and* La Fracture Coloniale. Lanham, MD, and Plymouth: Lexington Books, 2011.

Martin, George. *Verdi at the Golden Gate: Opera and San Francisco in the Gold Rush Years.* Berkeley: University of California Press, 1993.

Martin-Fugier, Anne. *Comédienne: de Mlle Mars à Sarah Bernhardt.* Paris: Seuil, 2001.

McGrane, Bernard. *Beyond Anthropology: Society and the Other.* New York: Columbia University Press, 1989.

McKee, Sally. *The Exile's Song: Edmond Dédé and the Unfinished Revolutions of the Atlantic World.* New Haven, CT: Yale University Press, 2017.

McKinney, Louise. *New Orleans: A Cultural History.* Oxford: Oxford University Press, 2006.

McMurtrie, Douglas C. "The French Press of Louisiana." *Louisiana Historical Quarterly* 18/4 (1935): 947–65.

McNeill, John Robert, and William McNeill. *The Human Web: A Bird's-Eye View of World History.* New York and London: Norton, 2003.

Meggs, Philip B. *A History of Graphic Design.* New York: John Wiley & Sons, Inc., 1998.

Mehrländer, Andrea. *The Germans of Charleston, Richmond and New Orleans During the Civil War Period, 1850–1870: A Study and Research Compendium*. Berlin: De Gruyter, 2011.

Merrill, Ellen C. *Germans of Louisiana*. Gretna, LA: Pelican Publishing, 2005.

Miller, Joseph C., ed. *The Princeton Companion to Atlantic History*. Princeton, NJ: Princeton University Press, 2015.

Mills, Quincy T. *Cutting Along the Color Line: Black Barbers and Barber Shops in America*. Philadelphia: University of Pennsylvania Press, 2013.

Mills, Sara. *Discourses of Difference: An Analysis of Women's Travel Writing and Colonialism*. London and New York: Routledge, 1993.

Mollier, Jean-Yves. *Michel & Calmann Lévy, ou la naissance de l'édition moderne, 1836–1891*. Paris: Calmann-Lévy, 1984.

Monaghan, Frank. *French Travellers in the United States, 1765–1932*. New York: Antiquarian Press Ltd., 1961.

Mondelli, Peter. "The Sociability of History in French Grand Opera: A Historical Materialist Perspective." *19th-Century Music* 37/1 (2013): 37–55.

Mott, Frank Luther. *American Journalism: A History of Newspapers in the United States through 250 Years, 1690 to 1940*. New York: Macmillan Company, 1947.

Murphy, Thomas K. *A Land without Castles: The Changing Image of America in Europe, 1780–1830*. New York: Lexington Books, 2001.

Mussulman, Joseph A. *Music in the Cultured Generation: A Social History of Music in America, 1870–1900*. Evanston, IL: Northwestern University Press, 1971.

Nau, John Frederick. *The German People of New Orleans: 1850–1900*. Leiden: E. J. Brill, 1958.

Newark, Cormac. "'In Italy We Don't Have the Means for Illusion': Grand Opéra in Nineteenth-Century Bologna." *Cambridge Opera Journal* 19/3 (2007): 199–222.

———. "Metaphors for Meyerbeer." *Journal of the Royal Musical Association* 127/1 (2002): 23–43.

———. *Opera in the Novel from Balzac to Proust*. Cambridge: Cambridge University Press, 2011.

Norman, Benjamin M. *Norman's New Orleans and Environs: Containing a Brief Historical Sketch of the Territory and State of Louisiana and the City of New Orleans*. New Orleans, 1845.

Nugent, Walter T. K. *Crossings: The Great Transatlantic Migrations, 1870–1914*. Bloomington: Indiana University Press, 1992.

O'Connor, Brendon, and Martin Griffith, eds. *The Rise of Anti-Americanism*. London: Routledge, 2006.

Orain, Adolphe. *Au pays de Rennes*. Rennes: Hyacinthe Caillière, 1892.

Ortiz, Fernando. *Cuban Counterpoint: Tobacco and Sugar*. Translated by Harriet de Onís. Durham, NC: Duke University Press, 1947.

Ostendorf, Ann. *Sounds American: National Identity and the Music Cultures of the Lower Mississippi River Valley, 1800–1860*. Athens and London: University of Georgia Press, 2011.

Osterhammel, Jürgen. *The Transformation of the World: A Global History of the Nineteenth Century*, trans. Patrick Camiller. Princeton, NJ: Princeton University Press, 2014. First published as *Die Verwandlung der Welt*. Munich: C. H. Beck, 2009.

Osterhammel, Jürgen, and Niels P. Petersson. *Globalisation: A Short History*, trans. Dona Geyer. Princeton, NJ: Princeton University Press, 2003.

Ottenberg, June. *Opera Odyssey: Toward a History of Opera in Nineteenth-Century America*. Westport, CT, and London: Greenwood Press, 1994.

Oursel, N. N. "Jobey (Charles)." *Nouvelle biographie normande*. Paris, 1886.

Palmegiano, E. M. *Perceptions of the Press in Nineteenth-Century British Periodicals: A Bibliography*. London: Anthem Press, 2012.

Panzeri, Louis. *Louisiana Composers*. New Orleans: Dinstuhl Printing and Publishing, 1972.

Parakilas, James. "The Operatic Canon." In *The Oxford Handbook of Opera*, ed. Helen M. Greenwald, 862–81. Oxford and New York: Oxford University Press, 2014.

Parsons, Charles H. *Opera Premieres: An Index of Casts A–J*. Vol. 13 of the Mellen Opera Reference Index. New York: Edwin Mellen Press, 1992.

Pedro, José Montero de. *The Spanish in New Orleans and Louisiana*, trans. Richard E. Chandler. Gretna, LA: Pelican Publishing, 2000.

Phillips, Faye. "Writing Louisiana Colonial History in the Mid-Nineteenth Century: Charles Gayarré, Benjamin Franklin French, and the Louisiana Historical Society." *Louisiana History: The Journal of the Louisiana Historical Association* 49/2 (2008): 163–90.

The Picayune's Guide to New Orleans. New Orleans, 1897.

Pierre, Constant. *Le Conservatoire national de musique et de déclamation: documents historiques et administratifs recueillis ou rencontrés par l'auteur*. Paris: Imprimerie nationale, 1900.

Pietschmann, Horst, ed. *Atlantic History: History of the Atlantic System, 1580–1830*. Göttingen: Vandenhoeck & Ruprecht, 2002.

Pinkney, David. *Decisive Years in France: 1840–7*. Princeton, NJ: Princeton University Press, 1986.

Popkin, Jeremy D. *Press, Revolution, and Social Identities in France, 1830–35*. University Park: Pennsylvania State University Press, 2002.

Portes, Jacques. *Fascination and Misgivings: The United States in French Opinion, 1870–1914*, trans. Elborg Forster. Cambridge: Cambridge University Press, 2000.

Potter, Eliza. *A Hairdresser's Experience in High Life*. Cincinnati, 1859.

Powell, Lawrence N. *The Accidental City: Improvising New Orleans*. Cambridge, MA: Harvard University Press, 2012.

Prado, Fabrício. *Edge of Empire: Atlantic Networks and Revolution in Bourbon Río de la Plata*. Berkeley: University of California Press, 2015.

Pratt, Mary Louise. *Imperial Eyes: Travel Writing and Transculturation*. 2nd ed. London: Routledge, 2008.

Prest, Julia. "Parisian Palimpsests and Creole Creations: Mme Marsan and Dlle Minette play Nina on the Caribbean Stage." *Early Modern French Studies* 41/2 (2019): 170–88.

Preston, Katherine K. "A Rarefied Art? Opera and Operatic Music as Popular Entertainment in Late Nineteenth-Century Washington City." In *Music, American Made: Essays in Honor of John Graziano*, ed. John Koegel, 3–46. Sterling Heights, MI: Harmonie Park Press, 2011.

———. "Art Music from 1800 to 1860." In *The Cambridge History of American Music*, ed. David Nicholls, 186–213. Cambridge: Cambridge University Press, 1998.

———. *Opera for the People: English-Language Opera and Women Managers in Late 19th-Century America*. New York: Oxford University Press, 2017.

———. *Opera on the Road: Traveling Opera Troupes in the United States, 1835–60*. Urbana: University of Illinois Press, 1993.

———. "To the Opera House? The Trials and Tribulations of Operatic Production in Nineteenth-Century America." *Opera Quarterly* 23/1 (2007): 39–65.

Price, Curtis, Judith Milhous, and Robert D. Hume. *The Impresario's Ten Commandments: Continental Recruitment for Italian Opera in London 1763–64*. London: Royal Musical Association, 1992.

Putnam, Lara. "To Study the Fragments/Whole: Microhistory and the Atlantic World." *Journal of Social History* 39/3 (2006): 615–30.

Rehding, Alexander. *Music and Monumentality: Commemoration and Wonderment in Nineteenth-Century Germany*. Oxford: Oxford University Press, 2009.

Reinders, Robert Clemens. *End of an Era: New Orleans, 1850–1860*. New Orleans: Pelican Publishing Company,1964.

Rémond, René. *Les États-Unis devant l'opinion française, 1815–1852*. Paris: A. Colin, 1962.

Ripley, Eliza. *Social Life in Old New Orleans: Being Recollections of My Girlhood*. New York: D. Appleton and Company, 1912.

Roach, Joseph. *Cities of the Dead: Circum-Atlantic Performance*. New York: Columbia University Press, 1996.

Roberts, Alasdair. *America's First Great Depression: Economic Crisis and Political Disorder after the Panic of 1837*. Ithaca, NY: Cornell University Press, 2012.

Robinson, Merritt M. *A Digest of the Penal Law of the State of Louisiana: Analytically Arranged*. New Orleans, 1841.

———. *Reports of Cases Argued and Determined in the Supreme Court of Louisiana. Volume 1: October 1841–March 1842*. New Orleans: [no publisher information listed], 1842.

Rocamora, Agnès. *Fashioning the City: Paris, Fashion and the Media*. London: I. B. Tauris, 2009.

Rocha, Esmeralda Monique Antonia. "Imperial Opera: The Nexus Between Opera and Imperialism in Victorian Calcutta and Melbourne, 1833–1901." PhD diss., University of Western Australia, 2012.

Roche, Daniel. *The People of Paris: An Essay in Popular Culture in the 18th Century*, trans. Marie Evans in association with Gwynne Lewis. Berkeley and Los Angeles: University of California Press, 1987.

Roger, Philippe. *The American Enemy: The History of French Anti-Americanism*, trans. Sharon Bowman. Chicago and London: University of Chicago Press, 2005.

Rosenberg, Chaim M. *Child Labor in America: A History*. Jefferson, NC, and London: McFarland and Company Inc., 2013.

Rosenberg, Ruth E. *Music, Travel, and Imperial Encounter in 19th-Century France: Musical Apprehensions*. New York: Routledge, 2015.

Rosselli, John. *The Opera Industry in Italy from Cimarosa to Verdi: The Role of the Impresario*. Cambridge: Cambridge University Press, 1984.

Rosselli, John, et al. "Travelling Troupes." *The New Grove Dictionary of Opera. Grove Music Online. Oxford Music Online*, Oxford University Press. Accessed January 13, 2015, http://www.oxfordmusiconline.com/subscriber/article/grove/music/O004387.

Rutherford, Susan. *The Prima Donna and Opera, 1815–1930*. Cambridge: Cambridge University Press, 2006.

Saint-Denis, Henri-Michel. *Histoire d'Elbeuf, Tome XI (1866 à 1879)*. Elbeuf: Imprimerie Saint-Denis, 1898.

Saxe-Weimar-Eisenach, Bernhard, Duke of. *Travels Through America in the Years 1825–6*. Philadelphia, 1828.

Saxon, Lyle. *Fabulous New Orleans*. New York and London: D. Appleton-Century Company, 1939.

———. *Old Louisiana*. Reprint, Gretna, LA: Pelican Publishing Company, Inc., 1998.

Schweninger, Loren. "Free People of Color." In *KnowLA Encyclopedia of Louisiana*, ed. David Johnson. Louisiana Endowment for the Humanities, April 28, 2011. Accessed October 14, 2017, http://www.knowlouisiana.org/entry/free-people-of-color.

Scott, Derek B. *Sounds of the Metropolis: The 19th-Century Popular Music Revolution in London, New York, Paris and Vienna*. Oxford: Oxford University Press, 2008.

Seebold, Herman de Bachelle. *Old Louisiana Plantation Homes and Family Trees*, vol. 1. Reprint, Gretna, LA: Pelican Publishing Company, Inc., 2004.

Seed, David. "Nineteenth-Century Travel Writing: An Introduction." In *The Yearbook of English Studies* 34 (2004): 1–5.

Senici, Emanuele. "Delirious Hopes: Napoleonic Milan and the Rise of Modern Italian Operatic Criticism." *Cambridge Opera Journal* 27/2 (2015): 97–127.

Shea, Dan, and James Karst, eds. *Our Times: New Orleans through the Pages of the* Times-Picayune. New Orleans: Times-Picayune, 2011.

Shepherd, Samuel C. Jr., *New Orleans and Urban Louisiana: Settlement to 1860*. Lafayette: Center for Louisiana Studies, University of Louisiana at Lafayette, 2005.

Slatin, Sonia. "Opera and Revolution: *La Muette de Portici* and the Belgian Revolution of 1830 Revisited." *Journal of Musicological Research* 3 (1979): 45–62.

Smethurst, Paul. *Travel Writing and the Natural World, 1768–1840*. Basingstoke: Palgrave Macmillan, 2013.

Smith, Thomas Ruys. *Southern Queen: New Orleans in the Nineteenth Century*. London and New York: Continuum, 2011.

Smither, Nellie. "A History of the English Theatre at New Orleans, 1806–42." *Louisiana Historical Quarterly* 28/1 (1945): 85–276.

———. *A History of the English Theatre in New Orleans*. New York: B. Blom, 1967.

Sorba, Carlotta. "To Please the Public: Composers and Audiences in Nineteenth-Century Italy." *Journal of Interdisciplinary History* 36/4 (2006): 595–614.

Starr, S. Frederick. *Louis Moreau Gottschalk*. Urbana: University of Illinois Press, 1995.

Stokes, Martin. "Music, Travel and Tourism: An Afterword." *The World of Music* 41/3 (1999): 141–55.

———. "Notes and Queries on 'Global Music History.'" *Studies on a Global History of Music: A Balzan Musicology Project*, ed. Reinhard Strohm, 3–18. Abingdon: Routledge, 2018.

Stoler, Ann Laura. *Along the Archival Grain: Epistemic Anxieties and Colonial Common Sense*. Princeton, NJ: Princeton University Press, 2009.

Sullivan, Lester. "Composers of Color of Nineteenth-Century New Orleans: The History behind the Music." *Black Research Journal* 9/1 (1988): 51–82.

Sumpter, Amy R. "Segregation of the Free People of Color and the Construction of Race in Antebellum New Orleans." *Southeastern Geographer* 48/1 (2008): 19–37.

Swift, Mary Grace. "The Northern Tours of the Théâtre d'Orléans, 1843 and 1845." *Louisiana History: The Journal of the Louisiana Historical Association* 26/2 (1985): 155–93.

Tamvaco, Jean-Louis, ed. *Les Cancans de l'Opéra: chroniques de l'Académie royale de musique et du théâtre à Paris sous les deux Restaurations*. Paris: CNRS Editions, 2000.

Tatham, David. *The Lure of the Striped Pig: The Illustration of Popular Music in America, 1820–1870*. Barre, MA: Imprint Society, 1973.

Taylor, Troy. *Wicked New Orleans: The Dark Side of the Big Easy*. Charleston: History Press, 2010.

Thelen, David. "Of Audiences, Borderlands, and Comparisons: Toward the Internationalization of American History." *Journal of American History* 79/2 (1992): 432–62.

Thompson, Carl. *Travel Writing*. London and New York: Routledge, 2010.

Thompson, Christopher W. *French Romantic Travel Writing: From Chateaubriand to Nerval*. Oxford: Oxford University Press, 2012.

Thompson, William Norman. *Gambling in America: An Encyclopedia of History, Issues, and Society*. Santa Barbara, CA: ABC-CLIO, 2001.

Tinker, Edward Larocque. *Bibliography of the French Newspapers and Periodicals of Louisiana*. Worcester, MA: American Antiquarian Society, 1933.

———. *Les Écrits de langue française en Louisiane au XIX siècle*. Paris: Librairie Ancienne Honoré Champion, 1932.

———. *Toucoutou*. New York: Dodd, Mead & Co., 1928.

Tocqueville, Alexis de. *Democracy in America*, vol. 1, trans. Henry Reeve, ed. Francis Bowen. 3rd ed. Cambridge, MA: Sever and Francis, 1863.

Toelle, Jutta. "Opera as Business? From Impresari to the Publishing Industry." *Journal of Modern Italian Studies* 17/4 (2012): 448–59.

Tregle, Joseph G. Jr. "Creoles and Americans." In *Creole New Orleans: Race and Americanization*, ed. Arnold R. Hirsch and Joseph Logsdon, 153–60. Baton Rouge: Louisiana State University Press, 1992.

Tsing, Anna L. *Friction: An Ethnography of Global Connection*. Princeton, NJ: Princeton University Press, 2005.

Turner, Kristen. "Opera in English: Class and Culture in America, 1878–1910." PhD diss., University of North Carolina at Chapel Hill, 2015.

Twyman, Michael. *A History of Chromolithography: Printed Colour for All*. London: British Library Publishing Division, 2013.

Underwood, Ted. "Theorizing Research Practices We Forgot to Theorize Twenty Years Ago." *Representations* 127 (2014): 64–72.

Valdman, Albert, ed. *French and Creole in Louisiana*. New York: Plenum, 1997.

Vella, Francesca. "(De)railing Mobility: Opera, Stasis, and Locomotion on Late-Nineteenth-Century Italian Tracks." *Opera Quarterly* 34/1 (2018): 3–28.

———. *Networking Operatic Italy*. Chicago: University of Chicago Press, 2021.

Vidal, Cécile. *Caribbean New Orleans: Empire, Race, and the Making of a Slave Society*. Chapel Hill: University of North Carolina Press, 2019.

Vogeley, Nancy. "Italian Opera in Early National Mexico." *Modern Language Quarterly* 57/2 (1996): 279–88.

Wade, Richard C. *Slavery in the Cities: The South, 1820–1860*. Oxford and New York: Oxford University Press, 1964.

Wakefield, Robert, and Devin Knighton. "Distinguishing among Publics, Audiences, and Stakeholders in the Social Media Era of Unanticipated Publics." *Public Relations Review* 45/5 (2019): 1–7.

Walton, Benjamin. "Canons of Real and Imagined Opera: Buenos Aires and Montevideo, 1810–1860." *The Oxford Handbook of the Operatic Canon*, ed. Cormac Newark and William Weber, 271–89. Oxford: Oxford University Press, 2020.

———. "Escasez y abundancia en la historiografía operística del Río de la Plata." Translated by Vera Wolkowicz. *Revista Argentina de Musicología* 21/1 (2020): 33–49.

———. "Italian Operatic Fantasies in Latin America." *Journal of Modern Italian Studies* 17/4 (2012): 460–71.

———. "*L'italiana* in Calcutta." In *Operatic Geographies: The Place of the Opera House*, ed. Suzanne Aspden, 119–32. Chicago: University of Chicago Press, 2019.

———. "Quirk Shame." *Representations* 132 (2015): 121–29.

Wang, Ban. "Inscribed Wilderness in Chateaubriand's 'Atala.'" *Romance Notes* 33/3 (1993): 279–87.

Warmouth, C. V. *A Louisiana Purchase*. Bloomington: Trafford, 2012.

Warner, Michael. "Publics and Counterpublics." *Public Culture* 14/1 (2002): 49–90.

Weber, William. "Cosmopolitan, Regional and National Identities in 18th-Century European Musical Life." In *The Oxford Handbook of the New Cultural History of Music*, ed. Jane Fulcher, 208–27. New York: Oxford University Press, 2011.

Weissbach, Lee S. "Child Labor Legislation in Nineteenth-Century France." *Journal of Economic History* 37/1 (1977): 268–271.

Whealton, Virginia E. "Travel, Ideology and the Geographical Imagination: Parisian Musical Travelogues, 1830–1870." PhD diss., Indiana University, 2018.

White, Kimberly. *Female Singers on the French Stage, 1830–1848*. Cambridge: Cambridge University Press, 2018.

Whitfield, Peter. *Travel: A Literary History*. Oxford: Bodleian Library Publishing, 2011.

Williams, Simon. "The Spectacle of the Past in Grand Opéra." In *The Cambridge Companion to Grand Opéra*, ed. David Charlton, 58–75. Cambridge: Cambridge University Press, 2003.

Willson, Flora. "Operatic Futures in Second Empire Paris." PhD diss., King's College London, 2013.

Wilmer, S. E. *Theatre, Society and the Nation: Staging American Identities*. Cambridge and New York: Cambridge University Press, 2002.

Wilmeth, Don B., and Christopher Bigsby, eds. *The Cambridge History of American Theatre, Volume 1: Beginnings to 1870*. Cambridge: Cambridge University Press, 1998.

Wilson, Jennifer C. H. J. "The Impact of French Opera in Nineteenth-Century New York: The New Orleans French Opera Company from 1827–1845." PhD diss., City University of New York, 2015.

———. "Meyerbeer and the New Orleans French Opera Company in New York City, 1845: 'How, Therefore, Could New York Have Remained Behind?'" In *Meyerbeer and Grand Opéra from the July Monarchy to the Present*, ed. Mark Everist, 361–82. Turnhout: Brepols, 2016.

Winford, Donald. "The Origins of African American Vernacular English: Beginnings." In The Oxford Handbook of African American Language, ed. Jennifer Bloomquist, Lisa J. Green, and Sonja L. Lanehort, 85–104. Oxford: Oxford University Press, 2015.

Withey, Lynne. *Grand Tours and Cook's Tours: A History of Leisure Travel, 1750–1914*. London: Aurum Press, 1997.

Wolf, Alvin Duain. "Nineteenth-Century Louisiana Composers." MA diss., North Texas State University, 1968.

Wolkowicz, Vera. "Opera as a Moral Vehicle: Situating Bellini's Norma in the Political Complexities of Mid-Nineteenth-Century Buenos Aires." *Nineteenth-Century Music Review*, First View (2021): 1–23. https://doi.org/10.1017/S1479409820000506

Yee, Jennifer. *Exotic Subversions in Nineteenth-Century French Fiction*. London: Legenda, 2008.

Youngman, Charles F., ed. *Historic Sketch of* L'Abeille *or* The New Orleans Bee, *From September 1827 to December 1923*. New Orleans: City Archives, 1938.

———. *Historic Sketch of* Le Courrier de La Louisiane *or* the Courrier, *From October 14, 1807 to November 24, 1860*. New Orleans: City Archives, 1938.

Youngs, Tim. "Introduction: Filling the Blank Spaces." In *Travel Writing in the Nineteenth Century: Filling the Blank Spaces*, ed. Tim Youngs, 1–18. London: Anthem Press, 2006.

———. *Travellers in Africa: British Travelogues 1815–1900*. Manchester: Manchester University Press, 1994.

Zietz, Karyl Lynn. *Opera Companies and Houses of the United States: A Comprehensive, Illustrated Reference*. Jefferson, NC, and London: McFarland, 1995.

Index

The letter f *following a page number denotes a figure*